D0913204

◆ BUY NOW, PAY LATER ◆

MARTHA L. OLNEY

◆BUY NOW◆ ◆PAY LATER

ADVERTISING, CREDIT, AND CONSUMER
◆ ◆ ◆ DURABLES IN THE 1920s ◆ ◆ ◆

THE UNIVERSITY OF NORTH CAROLINA PRESS ◆ CHAPEL HILL AND LONDON

© 1991 The University of North Carolina Press

The paper in this book meets the guidelines for
permanence and durability of the Committee
on Production Guidelines for Book Longevity of
the Council on Library Resources.

Printed in the United States of America

95   94   93   92   91   5   4   3   2   1

Library of Congress Cataloging-in-Publication
Data

Olney, Martha L.
    Buy now, pay later : advertising, credit,
and consumer durables in the 1920s /
Martha L. Olney.
        p.   cm.
    Includes bibliographical references and
index.
    ISBN 0-8078-1958-1 (cloth : alk. paper)
    1. Durable goods, Consumer—United
States—Purchasing—History.
    2. Advertising—United States—History.
    3. Consumer credit—United States—
History.   I. Title.
HC110.C6045   1991
381′.45′000973—dc20   90-49565
                                          CIP

♦ TO ESTHER ♦

◆ CONTENTS ◆

◆ ◆ ◆ CONTENTS ◆ ◆ ◆

♦ TABLES AND FIGURES ♦

TABLES

FIGURES

♦ ACKNOWLEDGMENTS ♦

To continue the metaphor repeated throughout *Working It Out: 23 Women Writers, Artists, Scientists, and Scholars Talk about Their Lives and Work* (New York, 1977), this book has had a most troubled birthing. The preliminaries were completed as we struggled through the prolonged and tortured dying of my partner's father. The writing began within days of returning home from his funeral. It was thrown off track by news in late August of a swimming accident of a dear friend in California that resulted in a broken neck and chest-down paralysis. And as the conclusions were being penned, the 7.1 earthquake that was not The Big One struck the San Francisco Bay Area, home to all of my relatives and hundreds of friends. But although the birthing has been troubled, I remain convinced that the child thus created—this book—has been worth it all.

The debts I have amassed in the six years since this project first began are beyond what can be reasonably recounted. Friends, colleagues, family members, patient librarians, institutions, lenders, and others have all contributed. I now more fully understand why many authors apologetically thank the multitudes without naming each and every person. Lest I leave out someone, I must follow suit.

The working and published papers that formed the basis for much of what I have written here were widely circulated among my professional colleagues. Their generosity in responding, offering comments and suggestions, asking questions, probing, and challenging often left me overwhelmed (in more ways than one!). I can never directly repay them for their time and effort. But I can pass it on. The time they gave to me I can in turn give to someone else. As my way of thanking each of you, I have tried and will continue to try to be generous with my comments and suggestions on others' work.

This said, there are a few people who deserve special mention. Richard Sutch guided this project in its early stages. Paul Betz of the University of North Carolina Press courted me tirelessly in his efforts to see this book come into being. Bob Gallman and Sam Williamson generously agreed to read and comment on the entire draft of the manuscript. Lee Alston, Jeremy Atack, Michael Bernstein, Lou Cain, Susan Carter, Jim Crotty, Michael Edelstein, Price Fishback, Nancy Folbre, Jerry Friedman, Claudia Goldin, Joan Underhill Hannon, Carol Heim, Dorene Isenberg, Jim Kindahl, the late Simon Kuznets, Larry Neal, Roger Ransom, Elyce Rotella, Harry Scheiber, Steve Tolliday, John Wallis, Tom Weiss, and Jeffrey Williamson all deserve thanks for their varied contributions over the past several years. Participants in seminars at the University of California at Berkeley, University of Michigan at Ann Arbor, University of Western Ontario, Columbia University, Harvard University, Indiana University, Barnard College, University of Massachusetts at Amherst, the Washington, D.C., Area, as well as participants in meetings of the Cliometric Society, the Economic History Association, and the Social Science History Association offered many valued comments.

Research assistance was provided over the years by Paul Lockard, Joanna Piccirillo, Lynn Duggan, David Doyle, Tobi Elkins, and Jason Asuncion. Thanks to each of them. Those in particular who were involved in measuring or tabulating advertisements from *Ladies Home Journal* surely wondered what was to come of all their efforts. I trust each will be pleased to see the result.

Financial assistance in a variety of forms was provided by the All–University of California Group in Economic History, the Department of Economics of the University of Massachusetts at Amherst, a faculty research grant of the Graduate Faculty of the University of Massachusetts at Amherst, the Lilly Endowment Teaching Fellows Program of the University of Massachusetts at Amherst, and an Arthur H. Cole Grant-in-Aid of the Economic History Association. I am grateful to each of these organizations for their support.

Recently I ran across an old family photo taken in Oakland, California, in about 1931 of my then-teenaged father and his two brothers standing with beaming faces but grease-stained pants in front of my uncle's Ford. My mother has a photo taken in Los Angeles in the early 1920s of her father's fleet of taxi cabs (each owned by its driver). She recounts the many times she drifted off to sleep to the sounds of the drivers playing cribbage in the kitchen while they awaited calls from customers. Her sister tells stories of how their father would go to the record store Saturday afternoon, buy a new record, play it on their Victrola over and over and over Saturday evening and Sunday, and then after enjoying it for the weekend return it

Monday morning saying, "I don't really like this one." By the time they entered high school in 1928, both of my parents were living in what we now call female-headed homes. My mother's mother worked throughout the Great Depression as a chambermaid in Berkeley; my father's mother was a private caterer for upper-crust families in Oakland and Piedmont. My parents grew up in families that owned the so-called "luxury" durable goods, but these were hard-working families that were far from anything even pretending to "upper-middle-class" status. These are the families that inspire my look into why and how the typical family bought so many more durable goods in the 1920s. In many ways, the family stories I have heard over the years influenced me much more than I usually realize. For their unsuspecting role in the conception of this book, I lovingly thank my family.

An extra thank you goes to my brother Donald. Unbeknownst to him, he was my internal audience as I wrote. It was the sound of his voice in my head that continually guided me as I strove to write a book accessible to the "general reader" as well as to my professional colleagues. If I have succeeded, it is due in no small part to his influence.

Finally, special thanks, gratitude, and love to Esther. I shirked most of my household duties from June to November 1989 while I was glued to my desk chair. I was oblivious to conversations, simple requests, and the weather. I lost perspective only a few times, but those few times were rather extraordinary. And through it all, you never wavered. "Thanks" does not begin to cover my debt, nor does dedicating this book to you. Consider them a down payment. The remaining installments are yet to come.

April 1990
Shutesbury, Massachusetts

◆ BUY NOW, PAY LATER ◆

INTRODUCTION

A s we near the end of the twentieth century, many American households own a variety of durable goods—automobiles, furniture, appliances, televisions, VCRs—many of which are judged "luxury" items,
many of which are advertised daily in a variety of mediums, and many of
which are purchased with credit. At the end of the nineteenth century,
most American households owned just a few durable goods—a horse car-
riage, furniture, a laundry tub, a piano—all of which were judged "necessity" items, few of which were advertised in any medium, and few of which
were purchased with credit. This book is about the economic forces behind the transition between two such different worlds.

Some of the most pronounced change occurred during the interwar
years when, simultaneous with the growth of the installment credit industry, not only saving rates and consumption patterns but also the mix of
assets owned by households suddenly shifted. Households bought more
durable goods, substituting these goods for perishable goods to some degree but substituting them for saving especially. Indeed the growth in
expenditure for durable goods was so strong in the 1920s that the episode
is often termed a Consumer Durables Revolution.

Not all durable goods enjoyed the same growth, however. Using a new
data set, we will see in chapter 2 that although American households did
purchase many more autos, appliances, radios, and other major durable
goods in the 1920s, they purchased proportionately fewer minor durable
goods—items such as china, house furnishings, books, and jewelry. And

although the relative price of durable goods did fall in most years during the 1920s, the overall average for the 1920s nevertheless remained above that for previous decades. In fact, until the 1970s the price of durable goods relative to the prices of other consumer goods and services remained above pre–World War I levels. We will also see in chapter 2 that although 1920s households were shifting their disposable income toward consumption in general and away from saving, in a more fundamental sense they were actually saving no less but simply saving differently. Because buying a durable good provides the household with that good's services for several years, the purchase is essentially an act of saving, a use of economic resources that allows future consumption of goods or services.

Whether or not the episode constituted a "revolution" is to some degree a matter of interpretation. Economists and historians will no doubt continue to debate the proper set of standards by which to assess the issue. For some, whether an event is "revolutionary" depends upon the nature of the event's effects on the society, economy, culture, and so on. For others (and in particular for economists), whether an event is "revolutionary" depends upon the nature of its causes. Each set of standards is designed to address a different underlying question, to explore a different "grand theme of the discipline." One set of standards is by no means better than another. But given one agreed-upon set of standards, the question can be resolved.

In chapter 3, following economists who studied the episode some years ago, I define the existence of a Consumer Durables Revolution as the existence of shifts in demand for durable goods (strictly, the absence of stability of demand). If the *causes* of the rise in household expenditure for durable goods are something "out of the ordinary"—in this case, something other than responses to changes in those usual demand-determining factors, relative price and income—a revolution in the consumer durables sector can be said to have occurred. In this sense, a Consumer Durables Revolution did indeed occur in the United States after World War I. Changes in relative price and income cannot alone explain interwar patterns of household expenditure for durable goods. Demand shifted. Households responded more vigorously to changes in relative prices and income. In more technical jargon, the own-price and income elasticities of demand increased after World War I.

In chapters 4 and 5 we explore two possible reasons for these demand changes: changes in the availability of consumer credit and changes in the volume of advertising. Marketing enthusiasts would no doubt have us believe that the Consumer Durables Revolution is the ultimate testimony to the power of marketing. Was not GMAC, the financing arm of General Motors, established in 1919 to market cars through easy credit financing? Was not the absolute explosion in print advertising after World War I the outgrowth of manufacturers' final recognition of advertising's ability to build demand? In both cases the perhaps surprising answer is: apparently not.

Yes, there was a vast expansion of consumer debt in the 1920s. Yes, by the end of the 1920s, up to 90 percent of durable goods were purchased with credit. Yes, sales finance companies such as GMAC provided most of that credit. But *no*, GMAC and like companies were *not* established to market cars. Rather, auto manufacturers established or contracted with such companies in order to solve a production problem: the need to finance finished goods inventory so they could smooth seasonal production fluctuations. The initial establishment of installment credit facilities was not an effort to market durable goods. Yet the result of their establishment was nevertheless increased availability of credit, which in turn made possible increased demand for durable goods. Credit availability mattered, but the marketing tale does not account for its initial expansion. The argument is presented in chapter 4.

Also in chapter 4 we will look at how consumer credit worked in the interwar years. What was the extent of credit financing? How much did financing cost consumers? Records of the National Association of Sales Finance Companies are used to answer these questions, as well as to see what finance charges typically were in the 1920s and 1930s. The records also reveal the geographic distribution of sales finance companies in the United States during that period and the apparent effectiveness of these financing arrangements (especially wholesale financing of dealer inventory) in smoothing seasonal fluctuations in the production of General Motors cars.

Others have ably demonstrated the expansion in business expenditure for advertising in the 1910s and 1920s. In chapter 5 a new annual series of the quantity of print advertising drawn from a survey of October issues of

Ladies Home Journal, 1901–41, is examined. The series confirms the estimates of business expenditure. There was much, much more advertising in the 1920s than previously—more pages of advertisements and larger advertisements. But while a shift toward more advertising of major durable goods did take place, it was less pronounced than we might expect, given the boom in sales of such goods. Further damaging the notion that credit facilities were established to market durable goods, it is also noted that advertisements for major durable goods other than pianos hardly mention the availability of time-payment schemes until the early 1930s, nearly fifteen years after the boom in the use of such schemes began.

Was this expansion of advertising a testament by manufacturers to the efficacy of advertising? Having observed the tremendous success of the World War I Liberty Bond campaign that the government mounted through private advertisers, did manufacturers flock to advertising agencies clamoring for their own campaigns? The argument in chapter 5 suggests such a spirited tale is at best incomplete. The federal government instituted an excess profits tax in 1917 to help cover its war-related expenses. Advertising was fully deductible. A dollar spent on advertising lowered profit by one dollar and thus lowered a firm's excess profits tax by as much as sixty-five cents. From the manufacturer's perspective, advertising became much, much cheaper! Perhaps manufacturers were won over to the power of advertising by the Liberty Bond campaign, but they were most definitely further enticed into advertising agencies by this precipitous drop in the effective price of advertising. Had the boom in advertising simply been the result of new belief in its efficacy, we would not expect much change in the clientele of advertising agencies. But agencies reported that as their total volume of business grew remarkably in the 1920s, their list of clients shrunk. Small accounts left the agencies; large accounts grew larger.

Quite frankly, this is not the story I set out to write. Six years ago when I began studying consumer durables, I presumed I would wind up telling a tale the marketing enthusiasts would embrace. Received wisdom is a powerful thing. Mine was that credit was created to market cars and other durable goods and that manufacturers used more advertising because the Liberty Bond campaign illustrated how it could market their products. I thought I would tell a tale that economists would at best dismiss, one that showed that manufacturers had successfully and independently employed marketing tactics that shifted demand. Instead I find myself convinced that using credit to market cars (a practice we saw so often in the late 1980s) was an afterthought and that the astounding changes in advertising were inspired more by efforts to lower tax bills than by any newfound belief in the practice.

The methodological approach I have taken in this study is largely "clio-metrics"—the use of economic theory and statistical techniques to understand and analyze data—combined with more traditional approaches to the task. Chapter 3 is especially cliometric in approach. The economist's question of a Consumer Durables Revolution, of the existence of shifts in demand, cannot be answered any other way. But this book is not just for cliometricians. Every effort has been made to keep even chapter 3 as accessible as possible. Much of the technical and theoretical material of that chapter and the remainder of the book is confined to one of the four appendixes. The general reader who begins to get bogged down in chapter 3 is encouraged to skim ahead; the gist of the tale will not be lost by skimming over the minutiae.

**CONTOURS OF THE
CONSUMER DURABLES
REVOLUTION**

A merican households bought many more durable goods in the 1920s than in previous decades. Their new spending habits altered not only the typical bundle of goods and services they bought but also the level and form of household saving. Durable goods were more expensive in the 1920s than previously, both absolutely and relative to other consumer goods and services; increased purchases of durable goods occurred despite these discouraging price movements. The extent of the changes in purchases of durable goods has led many to characterize the episode as a Consumer Durables Revolution.

WHAT IS A DURABLE GOOD?

Estimates of aggregate household spending are regularly compiled by the Department of Commerce for the national income and product accounts. They currently distinguish between three categories of products that households buy: durable goods, nondurable goods, and consumer services. By definition, a durable good is a product whose services can be consumed for three years or more.[1] The three-year benchmark is an average; clearly there can be no guarantee that any particular durable good will yield services for a minimum of three years. Accidental damage or destruction can occur, or technological change can render the good obsolete.

Within the general category "durable goods" lies a variety of commodities: books, china, jewelry, sewing machines, lamps, automobiles, yachts, eyeglasses, and so on. While all these products have expected service lives of three years or more, they have widely ranging price tags. Because the purchase of high-priced items requires most households to draw down their savings and perhaps borrow part of the purchase price, a distinction is made between "major durable goods"—big-ticket, relatively expensive durable goods—and "minor durable goods"—those with relatively low prices.

Several economists have distinguished between major and minor durable goods, but no uniform set of commodity groups is associated with each category. Harry Oshima emphasized exclusively the role of credit financing in defining major durables. His theoretical concern was use of the economy's "excess savings" to finance consumer asset formation—purchases of housing and major durable goods. For Oshima, major durables were only goods normally purchased with credit, specifically furniture, refrigerators, stoves, dishwashers, washing machines and dryers, air conditioners, sewing machines, vacuum cleaners, television sets, and automobiles.[2] F. Thomas Juster defined major durables consistently but more broadly as goods "characterized by relatively long service lives, by the existence of commercial markets in which the services of similar assets [can] be purchased, and by unit costs high enough so that purchase with borrowed funds [is] a common method of acquisition." He defined minor durables as all other durable goods. Juster designated only automobiles (but not automobile parts), furniture, household appliances, and musical instruments as major durable goods.[3]

The commodity groups Juster used were from then-current Department of Commerce publications. Conceptual changes have since been introduced to the national expenditure accounts; the Department of Commerce has added "other motor vehicles" as a separate category and now combines expenditures for automobile parts and automobiles. The definitions of major and minor durable goods used here take these changes into account. Throughout this book, the commodity groups included in each category and their abbreviations are:

Major durable goods

Automobiles and parts (AUT)
Other motor vehicles (OMV)
Horse-drawn vehicles (HDV)
Furniture (FUR)
Household appliances (APP)
Radios, televisions, phono-
   graphs, pianos and other
   musical instruments
   (MUS)

Minor durable goods

China and tableware (CHI)
House furnishings (HSF)
Jewelry and watches (JWL)
Orthopedic and ophthalmic
   products (MED)
Books and maps (BKS)
Miscellaneous other durable
   goods—includes wheel
   goods, durable toys and
   sports equipment, pleasure aircraft, and non-
   commercial boats (MIS)

A few comments on these commodity groups are in order. Furniture includes mattresses and box springs as well as other furniture items. House furnishings includes floor coverings, comforters, quilts, blankets, pillows, picture frames, mirrors, art products, portable lamps, clocks, writing equipment, hand tools, power tools, and garden tools. Pleasure aircraft and boats are included with minor durable goods because expenditure for these rather expensive goods is only a small part of total expenditure for "miscellaneous other durable goods," which consists primarily of the much less expensive bicycles, toys, and sports equipment. Finally, household expenditure for horse-drawn vehicles is included with expenditure for other motor vehicles in a composite category, "Other Vehicles," not shown above. Reflecting modern habits, in the estimates published by the Department of Commerce, horse-drawn vehicles are not included with consumer expenditure but are instead included in the producer durable category "Agricultural Machinery, except Tractors."[4] While designation of horse-drawn vehicles as a producer rather than consumer durable good is of little statistical consequence after 1929, that is not the case for earlier years. In the late nineteenth century, for example, over 6 percent of household expenditure for durable goods was for horse-drawn vehicles. Therefore it is important to have estimates of this expenditure.

HOUSEHOLD PURCHASES OF DURABLE GOODS

Growth in household purchases of durable goods can be assessed in any number of ways. We look first at growth over time in spending per household on each type of durable good.[5] Spending for all types of durable goods except horse-drawn vehicles rose throughout the late nineteenth and into the early twentieth centuries, as seen in table 2.1. Spending fell during the Great Depression and World War II, then resumed its nearly uninterrupted climb into the present. Between 1899 and 1908, households annually spent an average of $79 each to purchase durable goods, spending $34 for various major durables (mostly furniture) and $45 for various minor durables (mostly china and tableware, house furnishings, and jewelry and watches). Between 1919 and 1928, they spent annually an average of $267 each on durable goods—$172 for major durables (now mostly automobiles and parts rather than furniture) and only $96 for minor durables (still mostly china and tableware, house furnishings, and jewelry and watches). By 1979–86 (1986 being the last year for which we have estimates), households annually spent an average of $3,271 each for durable goods, with $2,230 for major durables (still predominantly automobiles and parts) and $1,041 for minor durable goods (now house furnishings, miscellaneous other durable goods, and jewelry and watches).

Such growth in spending—nearly tripling in the first two decades of this century and then increasing over twelve times in the next six decades—reflects both increases in the quantity of durable goods purchased by households and increases in prices of durable goods. To see the growth in how many durable goods were purchased, we look at changes over time in annual spending per household, where each annual estimate is theoretically computed using a constant set of prices; here, prices from 1982. The estimates are in table 2.2.

The picture changes somewhat. Over time, annual purchases of durable goods per household still rose. Evaluated in constant prices, households annually purchased, on average, $784 of durable goods between 1899 and 1908, $955 between 1919 and 1928, and $3,353 between 1979 and 1986. Rather than the tripling in spending we saw earlier, household purchases of durable goods only increased by about 20 percent in the first two decades of this century. Rather than increase twelvefold in the next six de-

Table 2.1A. Spending for Major Durable Goods per Household, Current Price Estimates, 1880-1986 (Dollars per Household)

Years	Autos and Parts	Horse-Drawn Vehicles	Other Motor Vehicles	Subtotal: Transp'n Vehicles	Furniture	Household Appliances	TVs, Radios, and Phono's	Pianos and Musical Instrum'ts	Subtotal: TVs and Musical Instrum'ts	Total: Major Consumer Durables
1880-1897	0.11	4.03	0.00	4.14	13.16	3.22	0.04	3.52	3.56	24.08
1898-1916	9.00	2.75	0.16	11.91	17.41	6.50	1.45	5.95	7.40	43.22
1922-1929	89.23	0.30	1.76	91.29	43.51	22.93	19.24	7.51	26.75	184.49
1930-1940	58.44	0.03	2.46	60.94	23.95	18.13	10.68	1.68	12.36	115.38
1948-1986	559.46	0.00	101.64	661.10	155.33	130.16	n.a.	n.a.	148.75	1,095.34
1880-1916	4.67	3.37	0.08	8.13	15.35	4.90	0.76	4.77	5.53	33.91
1922-1940	71.40	0.14	2.17	73.72	32.19	20.15	14.28	4.14	18.42	144.48
Averages by Overlapping Decades:										
1884-1893	0.00	4.33	0.00	4.33	13.58	3.25	0.02	3.86	3.88	25.03
1889-1898	0.29	3.73	0.00	4.02	12.32	3.19	0.08	3.47	3.55	23.07
1894-1903	0.67	3.24	0.00	3.92	12.37	4.17	0.33	4.04	4.37	24.83

Table 2.1A, continued

Years	Autos and Parts	Horse-Drawn Vehicles	Other Motor Vehicles	Subtotal: Transp'n Vehicles	Furniture	Household Appliances	TVs, Radios, and Phono's	Pianos and Musical Instrum'ts	Subtotal: TVs and Musical Instrum'ts	Total: Major Consumer Durables
1899-1908	2.28	3.37	0.04	5.68	15.60	5.69	0.81	5.87	6.68	33.65
1904-1913	8.23	2.75	0.15	11.13	18.81	6.89	1.45	6.65	8.10	44.94
1909-1918	22.53	1.89	0.39	24.81	21.83	9.19	3.19	6.36	9.55	65.39
1914-1923	50.83	1.03	0.84	52.71	32.98	15.08	7.83	7.39	15.22	115.98
1919-1928	80.15	0.43	1.30	81.88	43.90	21.86	15.82	8.29	24.11	171.76
1924-1933	80.59	0.21	1.93	82.73	35.67	20.55	18.89	4.92	23.82	162.76
1929-1938	61.63	0.06	2.53	64.21	24.63	17.97	12.59	1.81	14.40	121.21
1934-1943	49.95	0.00	2.40	52.35	28.00	19.65	10.15	1.90	11.95	111.94
1939-1948	57.63	0.00	4.55	62.18	43.41	30.76	n.a.	n.a.	19.11	155.46
1944-1953	160.17	0.00	10.20	170.37	63.70	59.22	n.a.	n.a.	37.44	330.74
1949-1958	281.71	0.00	14.28	295.99	81.82	80.90	n.a.	n.a.	55.13	513.83
1954-1963	329.59	0.00	16.00	345.59	91.94	83.35	n.a.	n.a.	60.37	581.25

Table 2.1A, continued

Years	Autos and Parts	Horse-Drawn Vehicles	Other Motor Vehicles	Subtotal: Transp'n Vehicles	Furniture	Household Appliances	TVs, Radios, and Phono's	Pianos and Musical Instrum'ts	Subtotal: TVs and Musical Instrum'ts	Total: Major Consumer Durables
1959-1968	400.22	0.00	24.41	424.64	106.83	87.12	n.a.	n.a.	82.86	701.45
1964-1973	501.29	0.00	53.34	554.63	134.97	109.10	n.a.	n.a.	124.28	922.98
1969-1978	615.68	0.00	127.59	743.27	177.01	144.34	n.a.	n.a.	173.14	1,237.76
1974-1983	795.02	0.00	198.45	993.46	236.45	188.10	n.a.	n.a.	240.64	1,658.66
1979-1986	1,086.16	0.00	286.05	1,372.21	291.53	234.36	n.a.	n.a.	331.73	2,229.83

Table 2.1B. Spending for Minor Durable Goods per Household, Current Price Estimates, 1880-1986 (Dollars per Household)

Years	China and Tableware	House Furnishings	Jewelry and Watches	Medical Products	Books and Maps	Miscellaneous Other Durables	Subtotal: Minor Consumer Durables	Total: All Consumer Durables
1880-1897	7.63	11.68	7.38	0.59	3.37	3.07	33.72	57.80
1898-1916	11.57	15.08	10.92	1.61	4.41	4.26	47.85	91.07
1922-1929	19.17	37.25	19.15	4.50	9.02	6.94	96.03	280.52
1930-1940	13.79	23.55	9.65	4.24	6.55	5.24	63.02	178.40
1948-1986	65.62	145.02	92.24	32.09	41.16	106.78	482.91	1,578.25
1880-1916	9.65	13.43	9.20	1.12	3.91	3.68	40.98	74.89
1922-1940	16.05	29.32	13.65	4.35	7.59	5.96	76.92	221.40

Averages by Overlapping Decades:

Years	China and Tableware	House Furnishings	Jewelry and Watches	Medical Products	Books and Maps	Miscellaneous Other Durables	Subtotal: Minor Consumer Durables	Total: All Consumer Durables
1884-1893	7.77	12.26	7.99	0.59	3.49	2.77	34.88	59.91
1889-1898	7.35	11.54	7.18	0.77	3.35	3.68	33.87	56.94
1894-1903	8.36	12.02	7.61	0.95	3.63	4.13	36.69	61.52

13

Table 2.1B, continued

Years	China and Tableware	House Furnishings	Jewelry and Watches	Medical Products	Books and Maps	Miscellaneous Other Durables	Subtotal: Minor Consumer Durables	Total: All Consumer Durables
1899-1908	11.19	14.42	10.39	1.22	4.16	3.86	45.25	78.90
1904-1913	12.40	15.85	12.19	1.58	4.49	4.09	50.60	95.54
1909-1918	13.91	18.36	12.22	3.25	5.12	5.17	58.03	123.42
1914-1923	17.35	27.28	15.71	5.16	6.85	6.52	78.87	194.86
1919-1928	19.31	36.06	19.61	4.95	8.73	7.05	95.70	267.46
1924-1933	17.30	31.83	15.81	4.04	8.41	6.04	83.42	246.19
1929-1938	14.46	24.33	10.31	4.08	6.92	5.12	65.22	186.43
1934-1943	14.96	27.39	12.50	5.41	6.99	6.45	73.70	185.64
1939-1948	22.16	42.55	25.01	8.15	10.80	12.71	121.38	276.84
1944-1953	31.33	61.44	32.89	10.94	15.28	19.46	171.34	502.08
1949-1958	34.78	70.46	34.84	12.50	17.84	26.56	196.98	710.82
1954-1963	34.37	76.86	37.45	14.39	21.00	35.09	219.15	800.41
1959-1968	39.72	99.48	45.70	18.36	26.91	49.88	280.04	981.49
1964-1973	52.21	124.65	62.91	25.65	37.31	79.90	382.64	1,305.62

Table 2.1B, continued

Years	China and Tableware	House Furnishings	Jewelry and Watches	Medical Products	Books and Maps	Miscellaneous Other Durables	Subtotal: Minor Consumer Durables	Total: All Consumer Durables
1969-1978	73.11	161.10	102.69	36.30	48.25	133.20	554.64	1,792.40
1974-1983	104.40	223.73	165.41	52.23	64.00	198.44	808.21	2,466.87
1979-1986	130.96	284.75	216.37	71.14	82.59	255.50	1,041.31	3,271.14

Sources: Current price estimates of expenditure from table A.6. Estimates of number of households, 1900-1969, from U.S. Bureau of the Census, *Historical Statistics*, Ser. A350, p. 43; extended to 1880 using estimates of population in U.S. Bureau of the Census, *Historical Statistics*, Ser. A7, p. 8. Estimates of households for more recent years from U.S. Bureau of the Census, *Current Population Reports* (and updates), table 6.

Table 2.2A. Spending for Major Durable Goods per Household, Constant Price Estimates, 1880-1986 (1982 Dollars per Household)

Years	Autos and Parts	Horse-Drawn Vehicles	Other Motor Vehicles	Subtotal: Transp'n Vehicles	Furniture	Household Appliances	TVs, Radios, and Phono's	Pianos and Musical Instrum'ts	Subtotal: TVs and Musical Instrum'ts	Total: Major Consumer Durables
1880-1897	0.03	61.95	0.00	61.98	225.37	16.60	0.05	4.79	4.85	308.80
1898-1916	21.22	37.25	0.58	59.06	223.56	26.47	1.62	6.89	8.51	317.60
1922-1929	314.63	2.39	6.97	323.99	213.32	40.03	10.73	4.35	15.07	592.41
1930-1940	233.90	0.25	10.90	245.05	151.44	42.83	13.35	2.23	15.59	454.91
1948-1986	848.64	0.00	131.19	979.82	248.80	178.07	n.a.	n.a.	163.20	1,569.90
1880-1916	10.91	49.27	0.30	60.48	224.44	21.67	0.86	5.87	6.73	313.32
1922-1940	267.89	1.15	9.24	278.29	177.50	41.65	12.25	3.12	15.37	512.81
Averages by Overlapping Decades:										
1884-1893	0.00	66.55	0.00	66.55	228.71	16.58	0.03	5.26	5.28	317.11
1889-1898	0.08	59.94	0.00	60.02	230.64	17.36	0.12	5.06	5.19	313.22

Table 2.2A, continued

Years	Autos and Parts	Horse-Drawn Vehicles	Other Motor Vehicles	Subtotal: Transp'n Vehicles	Furniture	Household Appliances	TVs, Radios, and Phono's	Pianos and Musical Instrum'ts	Subtotal: TVs and Musical Instrum'ts	Total: Major Consumer Durables
1894-1903	0.53	53.08	0.01	53.62	231.29	22.06	0.43	5.62	6.06	313.03
1899-1908	2.56	47.70	0.07	50.33	241.71	25.99	0.94	6.97	7.91	325.94
1904-1913	14.88	33.95	0.41	49.24	233.39	27.47	1.59	7.28	8.87	318.97
1909-1918	60.63	21.03	1.58	83.24	200.31	29.55	3.37	6.83	10.20	323.30
1914-1923	148.94	10.03	3.38	162.35	192.63	33.64	6.32	6.30	12.61	401.24
1919-1928	265.39	3.15	5.05	273.59	213.70	39.33	9.44	5.21	14.65	541.28
1924-1933	293.80	1.64	7.74	303.19	189.98	38.20	12.66	3.00	15.66	547.02
1929-1938	239.57	0.45	10.89	250.92	151.86	40.66	12.95	2.03	14.98	458.42
1934-1943	201.52	0.00	10.65	212.17	161.09	46.88	13.26	2.48	17.11	437.24
1939-1948	191.49	0.00	14.78	206.27	164.91	54.92	n.a.	n.a.	21.91	448.01
1944-1953	379.80	0.00	26.21	406.01	171.03	86.75	n.a.	n.a.	33.79	697.58
1949-1958	605.98	0.00	32.13	638.11	200.30	119.82	n.a.	n.a.	51.86	1,010.09
1954-1963	652.56	0.00	32.58	685.14	215.51	133.15	n.a.	n.a.	62.28	1,096.08

17

Table 2.2A, continued

Years	Autos and Parts	Horse-Drawn Vehicles	Other Motor Vehicles	Subtotal: Transp'n Vehicles	Furniture	Household Appliances	TVs, Radios, and Phono's	Pianos and Musical Instrum'ts	Subtotal: TVs and Musical Instrum'ts	Total: Major Consumer Durables
1959-1968	766.86	0.00	47.69	814.55	238.89	151.81	n.a.	n.a.	93.36	1,298.61
1964-1973	939.11	0.00	98.88	1,037.99	265.45	189.93	n.a.	n.a.	146.87	1,640.25
1969-1978	1,009.14	0.00	198.03	1,207.17	277.58	218.49	n.a.	n.a.	197.24	1,900.48
1974-1983	1,004.57	0.00	248.21	1,252.79	286.03	225.36	n.a.	n.a.	253.94	2,018.12
1979-1986	1,107.07	0.00	288.03	1,395.10	294.02	241.51	n.a.	n.a.	363.67	2,294.30

Table 2.2B. Spending for Minor Durable Goods per Household, Constant Price Estimates, 1880-1986 (1982 Dollars per Household)

Years	China and Tableware	House Furnishings	Jewelry and Watches	Medical Products	Books and Maps	Miscellaneous Other Durables	Subtotal: Minor Consumer Durables	Total: All Consumer Durables
1880-1897	96.06	133.09	36.51	4.39	55.72	13.49	339.25	648.05
1898-1916	167.44	160.43	59.71	9.55	59.17	16.21	472.51	790.11
1922-1929	131.05	146.33	52.25	15.85	53.66	19.22	418.36	1,010.77
1930-1940	110.10	113.45	31.50	16.27	43.86	17.20	332.38	787.29
1948-1986	132.91	218.51	130.95	51.41	80.57	147.86	762.21	2,332.11
1880-1916	132.71	147.13	48.42	7.04	57.49	14.89	407.68	721.00
1922-1940	118.92	127.29	40.24	16.09	47.99	18.05	368.58	881.39
Averages by Overlapping Decades:								
1884-1893	98.66	140.93	39.15	4.24	57.37	11.88	352.23	669.35
1889-1898	100.88	146.13	38.10	5.89	58.25	17.13	366.37	679.58
1894-1903	116.38	156.01	42.09	7.18	62.73	19.11	403.50	716.53

19

Table 2.2B, continued

Years	China and Tableware	House Furnishings	Jewelry and Watches	Medical Products	Books and Maps	Miscellaneous Other Durables	Subtotal: Minor Consumer Durables	Total: All Consumer Durables
1899-1908	153.99	165.11	54.22	7.90	61.73	15.25	458.21	784.15
1904-1913	183.95	162.61	68.17	9.21	57.96	14.45	496.34	815.31
1909-1918	186.20	149.37	63.11	15.24	53.38	17.48	484.78	808.08
1914-1923	157.00	133.44	49.26	19.83	50.02	18.16	427.72	828.96
1919-1928	133.35	140.26	51.84	17.34	52.61	18.07	413.47	954.75
1924-1933	127.01	136.15	46.05	14.57	50.89	17.17	391.85	938.88
1929-1938	114.27	116.78	32.91	15.51	45.46	16.25	341.17	799.59
1934-1943	111.68	116.48	36.69	20.76	46.91	21.38	353.91	791.15
1939-1948	129.89	131.37	55.58	29.07	62.84	34.41	443.17	891.18
1944-1953	147.38	149.71	64.80	34.88	72.35	45.74	514.86	1,212.44
1949-1958	139.04	155.47	69.55	36.63	68.42	58.62	527.73	1,537.83
1954-1963	117.04	156.09	76.89	39.20	68.57	74.87	532.65	1,628.73
1959-1968	117.66	191.29	93.64	45.12	77.01	100.27	625.00	1,923.61

Table 2.2B, continued

Years	China and Tableware	House Furnishings	Jewelry and Watches	Medical Products	Books and Maps	Miscellaneous Other Durables	Subtotal: Minor Consumer Durables	Total: All Consumer Durables
1964-1973	132.46	229.28	120.26	53.41	92.38	147.52	775.31	2,415.55
1969-1978	135.54	256.36	164.59	58.99	96.01	204.10	915.59	2,816.07
1974-1983	133.23	277.43	201.93	63.18	87.87	238.86	1,002.50	3,020.62
1979-1986	135.52	290.37	220.21	70.39	82.43	260.24	1,059.17	3,353.47

Sources: Constant price estimates of expenditure from table A.7. Estimates of households as for table 2.1.

21

cades, household purchases increased just three-and-one-half times between 1919–28 and 1979–86. The differences in growth between the current price (table 2.1) and constant price (table 2.2) estimates are due to price increases.

In addition to this tempering of overall growth, with the constant price estimates, some products now show only very small growth over time in purchases. Moreover, for some types of durable goods the quantity purchased each year has actually fallen over the twentieth century. Strong growth in purchases of automobiles and parts remains evident: average annual purchases for 1919–28 were four times greater than the average for 1909–18, and growth continued through the post–World War II years. Purchases of household appliances and the "entertainment complex"—radios, televisions, pianos, and other musical instruments—showed a similar pattern (though pre–World War I growth was much more gradual for both groups than for autos and parts), as did purchases of miscellaneous other durable goods. But only gradual increases in annual purchases per household are evident for furniture and for house furnishings (where purchases were below late nineteenth- and early twentieth-century levels until the 1960s), for jewelry and watches (with a peak in the early 1910s that was not surpassed until the 1950s), and for books and maps (with a peak at about 1900 that was not surpassed until the 1960s). And purchases of china and tableware have declined throughout the twentieth century, never regaining the peak hit in the early 1910s.

TOTAL SPENDING BY HOUSEHOLDS

We gain additional insight into the place of durable goods in household spending when we look at all spending by households. First we compare spending for all minor and all major durable goods with the remainder of total household expenditure. Here we use the Department of Commerce estimates from the national expenditure accounts, breaking their category "total consumption expenditure" into five subgroups: expenditures for perishable goods, semidurable goods, major durable goods, minor durable goods, and services. This breakdown is slightly more detailed than the one now used by the Department of Commerce; as noted above, they only distinguish between nondurable goods, durable goods, and services. The definitions of perishable and semidurable goods are from early work by Simon Kuznets. Perishable goods (food, toiletries, fuel oil, gasoline, cleaning supplies, etc.) are goods with an expected service life of less than six months; semidurable goods (clothing, shoes, linens, etc.) are expected to yield services for six months to three years.[6] Services include items such as doctors' fees, domestic servants' wages, electricity costs, public transportation fares, theater tickets, and housing rent (including the imputed value of space rent of owner-occupied housing).

Department of Commerce estimates of household expenditure date back to 1929 and are published in *The National Income and Product Accounts of the United States, 1929–82.* Their estimates for the 1930s are from the pioneering work of Simon Kuznets and his associates at the National Bureau of Economic Research. Kuznets published estimates of consumer expenditure by subgroup for 1869 to 1928 in *Capital in the American Economy,* but these figures are five-year moving averages, not annual estimates. (The figure for 1873, for example, is the average value of unpublished annual estimates for 1871 to 1875.)[7] John Kendrick adjusted Kuznets's estimates for consistency with then-current Department of Commerce definitions and published these estimates in *Productivity Trends in the United States.* Annual estimates underlying the moving averages in Kuznets's and Kendrick's published volumes, though never published, were made available to this author. They were used to derive the annual estimates which extend the published Department of Commerce estimates of household expenditure back to 1869. Adjustments made to Kuznets's annual estimates to achieve conceptual and statistical consistency with current Department of Commerce definitions are described in appendix B, to which the interested reader is referred.[8]

Households shifted their spending toward major durable goods after World War I but away from minor durable goods after the turn of this century, as seen from the distribution of total household expenditure over its five subgroups in table 2.3. The share of total expenditure devoted to major durable goods remained relatively stable over the late nineteenth century. It began to increase after World War I, but this growth was arrested by the Great Depression of the 1930s and government-imposed production constraints of World War II.[9] Growth in the share of total household expenditure devoted to major durable goods resumed after World War II and quickly achieved stability above levels reached in the 1920s.

By contrast, minor durable goods commanded a relatively stable share of total household expenditure through the late nineteenth century, but the share then *fell* in the teens and twenties and was temporarily pushed even lower by the Great Depression. During World War II, this share returned to the level first seen in the 1910s and, apart from prosperous years in the late 1950s and early 1960s, has remained at this level into the present.

The estimates in table 2.3 are averages by overlapping decade, 1869 to 1986. This kind of averaging is a common practice when annual estimates are subject to a wide margin of error. Unfortunately, use of overlapping decade averages obscures the experience of the 1920s by blending it with World War I and with the Great Depression. But when the years since 1869 are divided into simply late nineteenth century, pre–World War I, interwar, and post–World War II periods, as in the top panel of table 2.3, the 1920s stand out quite clearly. Major durable goods purchases as a percent of total consumption expenditure averaged 3.9 percent for 1869–97, 4.0 percent for 1898–1916, a much higher 7.6 percent for 1922–29, 6.0 percent for 1930–40, and 9.7 percent for 1948–86. For the full interwar period, 1922–40, expenditure for major durable goods was 6.7 percent of total consumption expenditure. Again by contrast, the share of household spending for minor durable goods fell rather than rose over time. As a share of total consumption expenditure, spending on minor durable goods averaged 5.1 percent for 1869–97, 4.6 percent for 1898–1916, an even lower 4.0 percent for 1922–29, and a still lower 3.3 percent for 1930–40. It then returned to 4.1 percent for 1948–86.

These estimates are all computed using nominal (current price) expenditure estimates. Accordingly they measure the actual distribution of dollars spent by households. Alternatively we can measure household expenditure using real (constant price) estimates. This method essentially measures changes in relative quantities of goods and services purchased by households. If all prices always changed in exactly equal proportion (for example, if every individual product price increased by exactly 1 percent per year), there would be no difference between the distributions of household spending computed using current price and constant price expenditure estimates. Rarely do we observe such lockstep movement in prices, however.

Table 2.3. Average Shares of Total Consumption Expenditure, Current Price Estimates, 1869-1986

Years	Perishable Goods	Semi-Durable Goods	Major Durable Goods	Minor Durable Goods	Services
1869-1897	44.0	16.3	3.9	5.1	30.6
1898-1916	42.4	13.5	4.0	4.6	35.4
1922-1929	35.7	14.1	7.6	4.0	38.6
1930-1940	38.9	12.0	6.0	3.3	39.8
1948-1986	34.1	9.6	9.7	4.1	42.4
1869-1916	43.4	15.2	3.9	4.9	32.5
1922-1940	37.5	12.9	6.7	3.6	39.3

Averages by Overlapping Decades:

Years	Perishable Goods	Semi-Durable Goods	Major Durable Goods	Minor Durable Goods	Services
1869-1878	44.0	17.7	4.3	5.0	29.1
1874-1883	45.2	16.4	3.7	4.8	29.9
1879-1888	44.5	16.0	3.7	5.0	30.7
1884-1893	43.5	15.8	3.9	5.5	31.2
1889-1898	43.7	15.1	3.6	5.3	32.2
1894-1903	44.0	14.0	3.4	5.0	33.5
1899-1908	43.0	13.9	3.6	4.9	34.5
1904-1913	42.0	13.5	4.0	4.6	35.8
1909-1918	42.2	13.5	4.6	4.2	35.5
1914-1923	40.8	14.6	5.7	4.0	34.9
1919-1928	37.5	14.7	7.1	4.0	36.7
1924-1933	35.8	13.1	7.0	3.6	40.6
1929-1938	38.2	12.2	6.0	3.3	40.3
1934-1943	41.1	12.6	5.7	3.7	36.9
1939-1948	42.3	13.9	5.4	4.3	34.1
1944-1953	41.4	13.5	7.8	4.4	33.0
1949-1958	38.7	11.5	10.2	3.9	35.6
1954-1963	36.9	10.3	9.8	3.7	39.4

25

Table 2.3, continued

Years	Perishable Goods	Semi-Durable Goods	Major Durable Goods	Minor Durable Goods	Services
1959-1968	34.8	9.8	9.8	3.9	41.7
1964-1973	32.8	9.5	10.1	4.2	43.4
1969-1978	31.8	8.9	9.8	4.4	45.2
1974-1983	31.1	8.1	9.1	4.4	47.4
1979-1986	29.3	7.6	9.1	4.3	49.8

Sources: Estimates of expenditure for perishable goods, semidurable goods, and services derived as discussed in appendix B, notes 2, 3, and 5. Estimates of expenditure for major durable goods and for minor durable goods derived by first computing the shares of major and minor durable goods expenditure in total durable goods expenditure from table A.6, and then applying these percentage shares to the estimates of durable goods expenditure derived as discussed in appendix B, note 4. Percentage shares should sum to 100, with allowance for rounding error.

Measuring expenditure in constant prices introduces new problems resulting from the choice of base year. If the relative price of a good (or subgroup) is atypically high in the base year, this unusually high relative price will bias upward *all* the annual estimates of that good's (or subgroup's) share of total expenditure. The choice of base year is therefore quite important if we are comparing distribution across groups rather than across years. Years in which relative prices exhibit unusual movements should not be chosen as the base year.

In addition, movement in relative prices over time will change distribution estimates if the base year is periodically updated. The base year for all constant price estimates reported here is 1982, the Department of Commerce's most recent choice of base year. Since World War II, the relative price of major durable goods has consistently declined while that of services has consistently risen. With each post–World War II update of base year, then, the 1920s constant price share of major durables in total consumption expenditure has become smaller while the 1920s constant price share of services has become greater.

The distribution of constant price household expenditure is shown in table 2.4. The share of major durable goods in total expenditure was stable throughout most of the postbellum nineteenth century but dropped to a

Table 2.4. Average Shares of Total Consumption Expenditure, Constant (1982) Price Estimates, 1869-1986

Years	Perishable Goods	Semi-Durable Goods	Major Durable Goods	Minor Durable Goods	Services
1869-1897	44.1	10.5	3.9	3.8	37.7
1898-1916	42.5	9.4	2.8	4.2	41.1
1922-1929	37.6	8.5	4.9	3.5	45.5
1930-1940	41.1	8.2	4.0	2.9	43.8
1948-1986	36.1	6.9	7.7	3.8	45.6
1869-1916	43.5	10.1	3.5	3.9	39.0
1922-1940	39.6	8.3	4.4	3.2	44.5

Averages by Overlapping Decades:

Years	Perishable Goods	Semi-Durable Goods	Major Durable Goods	Minor Durable Goods	Services
1869-1878	42.9	11.0	4.2	3.2	38.8
1874-1883	44.8	10.3	3.7	3.3	37.8
1879-1888	45.2	10.2	3.7	3.8	37.1
1884-1893	44.3	10.3	3.9	4.4	37.1
1889-1898	44.4	10.2	3.7	4.4	37.3
1894-1903	44.6	9.8	3.3	4.3	38.1
1899-1908	43.2	9.5	3.0	4.2	40.1
1904-1913	41.9	9.3	2.7	4.2	41.9
1909-1918	41.2	9.1	2.8	4.1	42.8
1914-1923	40.0	8.6	3.3	3.6	44.5
1919-1928	38.4	8.2	4.5	3.4	45.5
1924-1933	38.1	8.4	4.5	3.2	45.8
1929-1938	40.2	8.2	4.0	2.9	44.7
1934-1943	42.6	8.4	3.9	3.2	41.9
1939-1948	43.8	8.4	3.5	3.5	40.9
1944-1953	42.7	7.7	4.8	3.6	41.2
1949-1958	40.9	7.1	6.6	3.5	41.9
1954-1963	39.8	6.7	6.7	3.2	43.5

Table 2.4, continued

Years	Perishable Goods	Semi-Durable Goods	Major Durable Goods	Minor Durable Goods	Services
1959-1968	38.0	6.7	7.0	3.4	45.0
1964-1973	36.0	6.6	7.7	3.7	46.0
1969-1978	33.9	6.5	8.3	4.0	47.3
1974-1983	31.5	7.0	8.5	4.2	48.7
1979-1986	29.7	7.5	9.3	4.3	49.2

Sources: Except for durable goods, constant dollar estimates of expenditure derived by deflating current dollar estimates of expenditure derived for table 2.3 by the respective implicit price deflators. Durable goods expenditure estimates derived by deflating current dollar expenditure for all durable goods other than horse-drawn vehicles by the implicit price deflator, then combining this with constant dollar estimates of expenditure for horse-drawn vehicles from table A.7. For services and for durable goods, implicit price deflators for 1929 on derived from expenditure estimates in U.S. BEA, *National Income and Product Accounts, 1929-82*, tables 1.1 and 1.2. For perishable and semidurable goods, implicit price deflators for 1929 on derived from expenditure estimates computed from U.S. BEA, *National Income and Product Accounts, 1929-82*, tables 2.4 and 2.5. Except for services, implicit price deflators extended to 1869 using 1929 base implicit price deflators derived from expenditure estimates in Kuznets, "Annual Estimates 1869-1953," tables T-6 and T-7, variant III. For services, the expenditure estimates from Kuznets are first amended using estimates in Kendrick, *Productivity Trends*, tables A-IIa and A-IIb, cols. 2 and 3, as discussed in appendix B, note 5. Constant dollar expenditure for all durable goods is split between major and minor durable goods using the respective percentage shares computed from table A.7. Percentage shares should sum to 100, with allowance for rounding error.

lower level for the first fifteen or so years of the twentieth century. Starting in the late 1910s (but interrupted immediately by World War I) and continuing in the 1920s, the share increased and soon surpassed its nineteenth-century highs. The 1930s depression and especially World War II pushed it back down, but then throughout the post–World War II period, major durables commanded an ever-increasing share of total household purchases of goods and services. Evaluating expenditure in constant prices thus shows that the relatively stable share of actual spending for major durable goods after World War II (table 2.3) masks opposite trends in the relative price of major durables (decreasing over time) and relative purchases of major durables (increasing over time).

Because the relative price of minor durable goods has not fallen over the twentieth century to a similar extent, there is much less difference between the share of expenditure for minor durables that is computed with current price estimates of expenditure and that computed with constant price estimates. Minor durable goods as a share of all goods and services purchased declined gradually from the late nineteenth century through the mid-1930s, and then aside from a decline from the mid-1950s to mid-1960s, has gradually increased into the present, returning in the 1980s to its 1880s highs.

Again, averages by overlapping decades obscure the experience of the 1920s. The share of constant price total consumption expenditure that is for major durable goods fell from 3.9 percent for 1869–97 to 2.8 percent for 1898–1916. It then nearly doubled to 4.9 percent for 1922–29 but fell back to 4.0 percent for 1930–40. Over 1948–86, the share averaged 7.7 percent, though as noted above the share increased steadily through these post–World War II years.

On the other hand, the 1920s are not particularly notable when we look at the behavior of the share of minor durables in total household purchases of goods and services. For minor durable goods, the share of total purchases increased from 3.8 percent for 1869–97 to a high of 4.2 percent for 1898–1916. It then began its decline, falling to 3.5 percent for 1922–29 and 2.9 percent for 1930–40, before beginning its post-Depression climb and averaging 3.8 percent for 1948–86. Figure 2.1 illustrates the contrasting behavior of the shares of expenditure that are for major and minor durable goods.

RELATIVE PRICES OF DURABLE GOODS

Whether evaluated in current or constant prices, the average share of total consumption expenditure that is for major durable goods was greater in the 1920s than for 1898–1916. This observation is not surprising as it is what has given rise to the claim for a Consumer Durables Revolution in the 1920s. But the increase in the share is more pronounced when evaluat-

Figure 2.1. Three-Year Moving Averages of Major and Minor Durable Goods Expenditure as a Share of Total Consumption Expenditure, 1870–1985

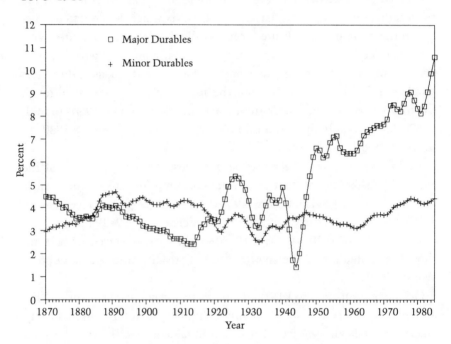

ed with current prices than with constant prices. In current prices, the share increased from 4.0 to 7.6 percent (a ratio of 7.6 to 4.0, or 1.90 to 1), but in constant prices, it increased from 2.8 to 4.9 percent (a ratio of 4.9 to 2.8, or 1.75 to 1). That the larger increase was evident with current price rather than constant price estimates indicates that households spent proportionately more dollars on major durable goods after World War I, due in part to *increases* in the relative price of major durable goods. Compared with 1898–1916, households acquired more major durable goods in the 1920s (as indicated by the constant price estimates), but they also devoted a greater share of their spending to major durable goods because of increases in the relative prices of those goods.

This observation *is* surprising. The received wisdom on this point seems to be that households purchased more major durable goods in the 1920s than they did previously partly because of *declines* in the relative price of major durable goods. Yet if the relative price of major durable goods were lower in the 1920s, the increase in the share of expenditure that was for major durable goods would be less pronounced, not more pronounced, when measured with current prices than when measured with constant prices.

The estimates in table 2.5 resolve this quandary. The relative price of major durable goods did fall *during* the 1920s, but its average level in that decade (155.5) remained 8 percent higher than its average for 1898–1916 (143.6). The rise to this higher level occurred rapidly. Following three decades of stability, the relative price of major durable goods nearly doubled in the fifteen years before World War I. Although the relative price of major durables declined by over 25 percent between 1921 and 1926, it did not return to its pre–World War I level until after World War II and remained above its late nineteenth-century levels until the 1970s. Declining relative prices can help explain rising expenditure for major durables over the course of the 1920s, but they cannot explain the rise in expenditure between the pre–World War I period and the 1920s.

WHICH DURABLE GOODS DID HOUSEHOLDS PURCHASE?

Households spent proportionately more on major durable goods in the 1920s than previously, but specifically which durable goods did they purchase? The answers are in table 2.6.[10] In the late nineteenth century, when just 8 percent of total consumption expenditure was for durable goods, the greatest share of durable goods spending was for furniture; spending for china and tableware, jewelry and watches, and especially house furnishings was also important. Together these four groups accounted for over two-thirds of total spending for durable goods (and about 5 percent of total consumption expenditure) throughout the postbellum nineteenth century. Yet by 1929 only 38 percent of total spending for durable goods (but still over 4.5 percent of total consumption expenditure) went to these four groups of products. The contrast between spending for household goods (furniture, household appliances, radios and musical instruments, china and tableware, and house furnishings) and for transportation goods (automobiles and parts, other motor vehicles, and horse-drawn vehicles) is es-

Table 2.5. Average Relative Price Indexes by Consumption Subgroup, 1869-1986 (1982=100)

Years	Perishable Goods	Semi-Durable Goods	Major Durable Goods	Minor Durable Goods	Services
1869-1897	99.8	155.9	99.9	138.7	81.2
1898-1916	100.0	143.9	143.6	110.1	86.2
1922-1929	94.9	167.2	155.5	114.9	84.7
1930-1940	94.5	146.3	151.5	112.9	90.9
1948-1986	94.6	139.6	130.3	110.0	92.8
1869-1916	99.9	151.1	117.2	127.4	83.2
1922-1940	94.7	155.1	153.2	113.7	88.3
1920	106.5	234.1	178.8	118.8	66.7
1921	95.1	181.7	196.2	137.0	82.7
1922	92.5	172.5	170.2	128.3	85.0
1923	93.2	172.7	160.1	121.4	83.8
1924	91.7	180.3	154.1	122.3	87.0
1925	94.6	164.9	153.8	114.0	84.0
1926	96.5	171.8	144.2	106.6	84.1
1927	95.7	158.8	149.0	110.6	85.5
1928	97.6	160.4	151.9	106.3	84.3
1929	97.5	155.8	160.8	109.9	84.2

Averages by Overlapping Decades:

1869-1878	102.5	161.7	101.7	159.7	75.0
1874-1883	100.8	159.6	100.0	142.5	79.2
1879-1888	98.5	157.4	100.7	132.0	82.8
1884-1893	98.3	153.2	100.3	126.0	84.1
1889-1898	98.5	147.3	97.0	122.0	86.5
1894-1903	98.7	143.8	103.1	118.8	88.0
1899-1908	99.5	146.6	123.2	117.9	86.1

Table 2.5, continued

Years	Perishable Goods	Semi-Durable Goods	Major Durable Goods	Minor Durable Goods	Services
1904-1913	100.3	145.7	150.9	109.5	85.5
1909-1918	102.6	148.3	168.9	101.1	83.0
1914-1923	101.9	172.5	172.2	112.3	78.5
1919-1928	97.6	179.1	162.3	118.0	80.6
1924-1933	93.8	157.6	155.7	111.4	88.5
1929-1938	95.1	147.9	153.6	111.6	90.1
1934-1943	96.6	149.9	147.1	115.1	87.9
1939-1948	96.7	166.4	155.5	121.7	83.4
1944-1953	96.9	174.2	161.7	119.3	80.3
1949-1958	94.7	162.1	154.1	112.8	85.0
1954-1963	92.6	152.8	146.6	113.5	90.3
1959-1968	91.6	146.8	140.9	115.9	92.7
1964-1973	91.1	144.5	130.8	114.2	94.4
1969-1978	93.9	136.7	118.3	108.8	95.5
1974-1983	98.6	116.8	106.5	104.0	97.1
1979-1986	98.8	100.9	98.2	99.5	101.1

Sources: Relative prices equal to ratio of implicit price deflator for that product group to the implicit price deflator for total consumption expenditure. Implicit price deflators for perishable goods, semidurable goods, services, and total consumption expenditure derived from current and constant price expenditure estimates used in tables 2.3 and 2.4. For major and minor durable goods, the implicit price deflators are derived directly from the expenditure estimates in tables A.6 and A.7.

pecially striking. In 1899, 65 percent of durable goods spending (and 5 percent of total consumption expenditure) was for household goods, but just 7 percent (barely 0.5 percent of total consumption expenditure) was for transportation goods, and even this was mostly for horse-drawn vehicles. Thirty years later, transportation goods accounted for 36 percent of total spending for durable goods (and 4.4 percent of total consumption expenditure), while household goods accounted for only 51 percent (but

Table 2.6A. Average Shares of Expenditure for Major Durable Goods, Current Price Estimates, 1869-1986

Years	Autos and Parts	Horse-Drawn Vehicles	Other Motor Vehicles	Subtotal: Transp'n Vehicles	Furniture	Household Appliances	TVs, Radios, and Phono's	Pianos and Musical Instrum'ts	Subtotal: TVs and Musical Instrum'ts	Total: Major Consumer Durables
1869-1897	0.1	7.4	0.0	7.5	23.9	5.9	0.0	5.7	5.8	43.1
1898-1916	8.2	3.3	0.1	11.7	19.3	7.1	1.4	6.7	8.1	46.2
1922-1929	31.7	0.1	0.6	32.4	15.6	8.2	6.7	2.7	9.5	65.6
1930-1940	33.0	0.0	1.4	34.4	13.3	10.2	5.7	0.9	6.6	64.5
1948-1986	37.0	0.0	4.6	41.7	10.5	9.2	n.a.	n.a.	8.8	70.2
1869-1916	3.3	5.8	0.1	9.2	22.1	6.4	0.6	6.1	6.7	44.3
1922-1940	32.4	0.1	1.1	33.5	14.3	9.3	6.1	1.7	7.8	65.0
Averages by Overlapping Decades:										
1869-1878	0.0	8.3	0.0	8.3	25.9	6.5	0.0	5.1	5.1	45.8
1874-1883	0.0	7.6	0.0	7.6	25.0	5.8	0.0	5.5	5.5	43.9
1879-1888	0.0	7.3	0.0	7.3	23.8	5.6	0.0	6.0	6.0	42.6
1884-1893	0.0	7.2	0.0	7.2	22.7	5.4	0.0	6.4	6.5	41.8

Table 2.6A, continued

Years	Autos and Parts	Horse-Drawn Vehicles	Other Motor Vehicles	Subtotal: Transp'n Vehicles	Furniture	Household Appliances	TVs, Radios, and Phono's	Pianos and Musical Instrum'ts	Subtotal: TVs and Musical Instrum'ts	Total: Major Consumer Durables
1889-1898	0.5	6.5	0.0	7.1	21.6	5.6	0.1	6.0	6.2	40.5
1894-1903	1.1	5.4	0.0	6.5	20.2	6.7	0.5	6.4	6.9	40.2
1899-1908	2.7	4.4	0.0	7.1	19.7	7.2	1.0	7.4	8.4	42.4
1904-1913	8.2	3.0	0.1	11.3	19.7	7.2	1.5	7.0	8.5	46.7
1909-1918	17.2	1.7	0.3	19.1	18.1	7.4	2.4	5.4	7.8	52.4
1914-1923	25.2	0.7	0.4	26.3	17.0	7.6	3.8	4.0	7.8	58.7
1919-1928	29.8	0.2	0.5	30.5	16.5	8.1	5.8	3.1	8.9	64.1
1924-1933	33.2	0.1	0.8	34.1	14.2	8.4	7.4	1.8	9.2	65.9
1929-1938	33.2	0.0	1.3	34.6	13.2	9.8	6.2	0.9	7.1	64.7
1934-1943	26.2	0.0	1.3	27.5	15.2	10.5	4.8	0.9	6.4	59.6
1939-1948	17.8	0.0	1.3	19.0	16.9	9.6	n.a.	n.a.	6.8	52.3
1944-1953	26.6	0.0	1.8	28.4	14.2	10.7	n.a.	n.a.	7.1	60.4
1949-1958	39.5	0.0	2.0	41.5	11.5	11.4	n.a.	n.a.	7.8	72.2
1954-1963	41.1	0.0	2.0	43.1	11.5	10.5	n.a.	n.a.	7.6	72.6

Table 2.6A, continued

Years	Autos and Parts	Horse-Drawn Vehicles	Other Motor Vehicles	Subtotal: Transp'n Vehicles	Furniture	Household Appliances	TVs, Radios, and Phono's	Pianos and Musical Instrum'ts	Subtotal: TVs and Musical Instrum'ts	Total: Major Consumer Durables
1959-1968	40.9	0.0	2.4	43.3	11.0	9.0	n.a.	n.a.	8.3	71.6
1964-1973	38.6	0.0	3.9	42.5	10.4	8.3	n.a.	n.a.	9.5	70.7
1969-1978	34.7	0.0	6.6	41.4	10.0	8.2	n.a.	n.a.	9.7	69.2
1974-1983	32.2	0.0	8.0	40.1	9.7	7.7	n.a.	n.a.	9.8	67.3
1979-1986	33.0	0.0	8.5	41.5	9.0	7.2	n.a.	n.a.	10.1	67.8

36

Table 2.6B. Average Shares of Expenditure for Minor Durable Goods, Current Price Estimates, 1869-1986

Years	China and Tableware	House Furnishings	Jewelry and Watches	Medical Products	Books and Maps	Miscellaneous Other Durables	*Total:* Minor Consumer Durables
1869-1897	13.5	19.3	12.9	0.8	5.2	5.2	56.9
1898-1916	13.0	17.0	12.2	1.7	5.0	4.9	53.8
1922-1929	6.8	13.3	6.9	1.6	3.2	2.5	34.4
1930-1940	7.9	13.2	5.3	2.4	3.7	2.9	35.5
1948-1986	4.4	9.6	5.4	2.0	2.6	5.8	29.8
1869-1916	13.3	18.4	12.6	1.2	5.1	5.0	55.7
1922-1940	7.5	13.3	6.0	2.1	3.5	2.7	35.0
Averages by Overlapping Decades:							
1869-1878	14.0	17.6	13.4	0.4	4.1	4.8	54.2
1874-1883	13.9	18.9	12.8	0.5	5.2	4.8	56.1
1879-1888	13.6	19.9	12.8	0.7	5.8	4.6	57.4
1884-1893	13.0	20.5	13.3	1.0	5.8	4.6	58.2

Table 2.6B, continued

Years	China and Tableware	House Furnishings	Jewelry and Watches	Medical Products	Books and Maps	Miscellaneous Other Durables	*Total:* Minor Consumer Durables
1889-1898	12.9	20.3	12.5	1.4	5.9	6.6	59.5
1894-1903	13.5	19.6	12.3	1.5	5.9	6.9	59.8
1899-1908	14.1	18.4	13.1	1.5	5.3	5.0	57.6
1904-1913	13.1	16.7	12.8	1.7	4.7	4.3	53.3
1909-1918	11.4	15.0	10.3	2.4	4.3	4.2	47.6
1914-1923	9.3	14.0	8.2	2.7	3.6	3.5	41.3
1919-1928	7.2	13.5	7.4	1.9	3.3	2.6	35.9
1924-1933	7.3	12.9	6.3	1.7	3.5	2.5	34.1
1929-1938	8.0	13.1	5.4	2.3	3.7	2.8	35.3
1934-1943	8.2	15.0	6.9	3.0	3.9	3.5	40.4
1939-1948	8.5	16.7	10.1	3.4	4.4	4.5	47.7
1944-1953	7.1	13.8	8.2	2.6	3.7	4.2	39.6
1949-1958	4.9	10.0	4.9	1.8	2.5	3.7	27.8
1954-1963	4.3	9.6	4.7	1.8	2.6	4.4	27.4

Table 2.6B, continued

Years	China and Tableware	House Furnishings	Jewelry and Watches	Medical Products	Books and Maps	Miscellaneous Other Durables	*Total:* Minor Consumer Durables
1959-1968	4.0	10.1	4.6	1.9	2.8	5.0	28.4
1964-1973	4.0	9.7	4.8	2.0	2.9	6.0	29.3
1969-1978	4.1	9.0	5.6	2.0	2.8	7.3	30.8
1974-1983	4.2	9.1	6.7	2.1	2.6	8.0	32.7
1979-1986	4.1	8.8	6.7	2.2	2.6	7.9	32.2

Sources: Derived from table A.6.

now over 6 percent of total consumption expenditure). After another fifty years the picture was little different; in 1979 transportation goods constituted 41 percent of total durable goods spending (now 5.5 percent of total consumption expenditure), and household goods constituted 39 percent (still 5.3 percent of total consumption expenditure).

Distribution of constant price expenditure is in table 2.7. The constant price estimates are useful for comparisons over time within commodity groups, but because of the base year problems noted earlier, they are not very useful for comparing the distribution of spending between commodity groups within one time period. From the current price estimates in table 2.6 we see that in the early twentieth century, households shifted their durable goods expenditure toward major durables. This shift was concentrated especially in the 1910s and was effectively completed by 1924: between 1924 and 1929, over 66 percent of durable goods expenditure was for major durable goods; since 1948, this share has ranged between 65 and 75 percent and has averaged just over 70 percent. Such stability in the percentage share also occurred in the nineteenth century (albeit at a much lower level). With this century-long view, it becomes clear that the shift toward major durable goods was not at all gradual but was concentrated in a fifteen-year period that encompassed World War I. An examination of the constant price estimates of table 2.7 reveals the same story.

This rapid shift toward purchases of major durable goods was largely but not exclusively due to purchases of automobiles. Expenditure for automobiles and parts accounted for nearly 32 percent of expenditure for all durable goods in the 1920s. But in 1904, spending for automobiles and parts had been just under 2 percent of total durable goods purchases. After World War I, purchases of major durable goods other than autos also increased. Expenditure for household appliances increased slightly, from a pre–World War I average of 7.1 percent of total expenditure for durable goods to 8.2 percent for 1922–29. Radios and phonographs expenditure also increased relative to other durable goods spending, particularly after the beginning of public radio broadcasting in 1921. Between 1922 and 1929, purchases of radios and phonographs averaged 6.7 percent of total durable goods purchases, almost five times more than the 1898–1916 average of 1.4 percent.

Table 2.7A. Average Shares of Expenditure for Major Durable Goods, Constant (1982) Price Estimates, 1869-1986

Years	Autos and Parts	Horse-Drawn Vehicles	Other Motor Vehicles	Subtotal: Transp'n Vehicles	Furniture	Household Appliances	TVs, Radios, and Phono's	Pianos and Musical Instrum'ts	Subtotal: TVs and Musical Instrum'ts	Total: Major Consumer Durables
1869-1897	0.0	10.4	0.0	10.4	37.2	2.8	0.0	0.7	0.7	51.1
1898-1916	2.6	4.8	0.1	7.5	28.3	3.3	0.2	0.9	1.1	40.2
1922-1929	30.9	0.2	0.7	31.8	21.2	4.0	1.0	0.4	1.5	58.5
1930-1940	29.6	0.0	1.4	31.0	19.2	5.4	1.7	0.3	2.0	57.6
1948-1986	37.1	0.0	4.7	41.7	11.3	7.7	n.a.	n.a.	6.1	66.9
1869-1916	1.0	8.2	0.0	9.2	33.7	3.0	0.1	0.8	0.8	46.8
1922-1940	30.2	0.1	1.1	31.4	20.0	4.8	1.4	0.4	1.8	58.0
Averages by Overlapping Decades:										
1869-1878	0.0	11.9	0.0	11.9	41.4	3.1	0.0	0.6	0.6	57.0
1874-1883	0.0	10.7	0.0	10.7	38.5	2.7	0.0	0.7	0.7	52.6
1879-1888	0.0	10.2	0.0	10.2	35.8	2.6	0.0	0.7	0.7	49.3
1884-1893	0.0	10.0	0.0	10.0	34.2	2.5	0.0	0.8	0.8	47.4

Table 2.7A, continued

Years	Autos and Parts	Horse-Drawn Vehicles	Other Motor Vehicles	Subtotal: Transp'n Vehicles	Furniture	Household Appliances	TVs, Radios, and Phono's	Pianos and Musical Instrum'ts	Subtotal: TVs and Musical Instrum'ts	Total: Major Consumer Durables
1889-1898	0.0	8.9	0.0	8.9	33.9	2.6	0.0	0.7	0.8	46.1
1894-1903	0.1	7.5	0.0	7.5	32.4	3.1	0.1	0.8	0.8	43.8
1899-1908	0.3	6.1	0.0	6.4	30.8	3.3	0.1	0.9	1.0	41.6
1904-1913	1.8	4.2	0.0	6.0	28.6	3.4	0.2	0.9	1.1	39.1
1909-1918	7.5	2.6	0.2	10.3	24.8	3.7	0.4	0.8	1.3	40.0
1914-1923	17.6	1.2	0.4	19.3	23.3	4.0	0.8	0.8	1.5	48.1
1919-1928	27.4	0.3	0.5	28.3	22.5	4.1	1.0	0.6	1.5	56.5
1924-1933	31.1	0.2	0.8	32.1	20.1	4.1	1.4	0.3	1.7	58.0
1929-1938	29.8	0.0	1.3	31.2	19.0	5.1	1.6	0.3	1.9	57.1
1934-1943	24.0	0.0	1.3	25.3	20.6	5.8	1.6	0.3	2.2	53.8
1939-1948	17.8	0.0	1.3	19.2	19.6	5.5	n.a.	n.a.	2.4	46.7
1944-1953	27.3	0.0	2.0	29.2	15.1	6.5	n.a.	n.a.	2.7	53.5
1949-1958	39.2	0.0	2.1	41.3	13.0	7.8	n.a.	n.a.	3.4	65.5
1954-1963	40.0	0.0	2.0	42.0	13.2	8.2	n.a.	n.a.	3.8	67.2

Table 2.7A, continued

Years	Autos and Parts	Horse-Drawn Vehicles	Other Motor Vehicles	Subtotal: Transp'n Vehicles	Furniture	Household Appliances	TVs, Radios, and Phono's	Pianos and Musical Instrum'ts	Subtotal: TVs and Musical Instrum'ts	Total: Major Consumer Durables
1959-1968	39.8	0.0	2.4	42.2	12.6	8.0	n.a.	n.a.	4.7	67.5
1964-1973	39.0	0.0	3.9	42.9	11.1	7.8	n.a.	n.a.	6.0	67.9
1969-1978	36.0	0.0	6.8	42.8	9.9	7.8	n.a.	n.a.	7.0	67.5
1974-1983	33.2	0.0	8.1	41.4	9.5	7.5	n.a.	n.a.	8.4	66.8
1979-1986	32.9	0.0	8.4	41.4	8.9	7.3	n.a.	n.a.	10.6	68.1

43

Table 2.7B. Average Shares of Expenditure for Minor Durable Goods, Constant (1982) Price Estimates, 1869-1986

Years	China and Tableware	House Furnishings	Jewelry and Watches	Medical Products	Books and Maps	Miscellaneous Other Durables	Total: Minor Consumer Durables
1869-1897	14.5	18.4	5.8	0.5	7.7	2.0	48.9
1898-1916	21.1	20.4	7.5	1.2	7.5	2.1	59.8
1922-1929	12.9	14.6	5.2	1.6	5.3	1.9	41.5
1930-1940	14.2	14.5	4.0	2.1	5.6	2.2	42.4
1948-1986	6.3	9.6	5.4	2.3	3.7	5.8	33.1
1869-1916	17.1	19.2	6.5	0.8	7.7	2.0	46.8
1922-1940	13.7	14.5	4.5	1.9	5.5	2.1	42.0
Averages by Overlapping Decades:							
1869-1878	13.7	15.0	6.0	0.3	6.2	1.9	43.0
1874-1883	14.9	16.8	5.7	0.3	7.8	1.9	47.4
1879-1888	15.1	19.0	5.6	0.5	8.7	1.8	50.7
1884-1893	14.7	21.0	5.8	0.6	8.6	1.8	52.6

Table 2.7B, continued

Years	China and Tableware	House Furnishings	Jewelry and Watches	Medical Products	Books and Maps	Miscellaneous Other Durables	*Total:* Minor Consumer Durables
1889-1898	14.8	21.5	5.6	0.9	8.6	2.5	53.9
1894-1903	16.2	21.8	5.8	1.0	8.8	2.7	56.2
1899-1908	19.5	21.1	6.9	1.0	7.9	2.0	58.4
1904-1913	22.5	20.0	8.3	1.1	7.1	1.8	60.9
1909-1918	23.0	18.5	7.8	1.9	6.6	2.2	60.0
1914-1923	19.1	16.2	6.0	2.4	6.1	2.2	51.9
1919-1928	14.0	14.7	5.5	1.9	5.6	1.9	43.5
1924-1933	13.8	14.6	4.8	1.6	5.4	1.8	42.0
1929-1938	14.5	14.6	4.0	2.0	5.7	2.0	42.9
1934-1943	14.5	15.1	4.9	2.8	6.2	2.8	46.2
1939-1948	15.2	15.7	6.9	3.6	7.9	3.9	53.3
1944-1953	13.0	13.3	6.0	3.3	7.0	3.9	46.5
1949-1958	9.1	10.2	4.5	2.4	4.5	3.8	34.5
1954-1963	7.2	9.6	4.7	2.4	4.2	4.6	32.8

Table 2.7B, continued

Years	China and Tableware	House Furnishings	Jewelry and Watches	Medical Products	Books and Maps	Miscellaneous Other Durables	*Total:* Minor Consumer Durables
1959-1968	6.2	9.9	4.8	2.4	4.0	5.2	32.5
1964-1973	5.5	9.5	5.0	2.2	3.9	6.0	32.1
1969-1978	4.9	9.1	5.8	2.1	3.5	7.2	32.5
1974-1983	4.4	9.2	6.7	2.1	2.9	7.9	33.2
1979-1986	4.1	8.8	6.6	2.1	2.5	7.8	31.9

Sources: Derived from table A.7.

46

In absolute terms as well as relative to spending for other durable goods, expenditure for automobiles and parts began to climb in 1903. It might be tempting to conclude, particularly in light of the dramatic shift toward spending for transportation goods, that a "transportation boom" was underway then. Through 1907, however, households were substituting one type of consumer-owned transportation for another, shifting from horse-drawn to motor vehicles. The boom in all transportation vehicles began in 1908, five years after expenditure for automobiles started to increase dramatically. In fact, expenditure for transportation vehicles relative to total durable goods expenditure dropped to its postbellum low in the first years of the 1900s.[11]

WHAT DID HOUSEHOLDS GIVE UP?

After World War I, a greater share of total household purchases were for major durable goods. Transportation vehicles accounted for a large part (but not all) of this shift. Greater purchases of major durable goods reflects not just a reallocation of the household consumption bundle after World War I, however; at the same time, households allocated more disposable income toward consumption in general. Major durable goods substituted for saving in the 1920s. We can see this change in table 2.8, which shows the distribution of disposable personal income over the five consumption subgroups (perishable goods, semidurable goods, major durable goods, minor durable goods, and services) and personal saving.

A comparison of average annual values for 1898–1916 and 1922–29 shows that households used a greater share of their disposable income to purchase major durable goods, semidurable goods, and services in the 1920s. Purchases of perishable goods and of minor durable goods each took a smaller share of disposable income after World War I, as did personal saving. The most pronounced changes were for major durable goods and personal saving. Before the war, only 3.7 percent of disposable income was used on average to purchase major durables, but in the 1920s, fully 7.2 percent, a near doubling, was used for this purpose. Simultaneously, the share of disposable income that was saved nearly halved; the personal saving rate fell from 6.4 to 3.8 percent, a drop in the rate of 42 percent. Evaluated in constant prices (table 2.9), the personal saving rate declined

Table 2.8. Average Shares of Disposable Income (Purchases of Consumer Durables as Consumption Spending), Current Price Estimates, 1869-1986

Years	Perishable Goods	Semi-Durable Goods	Major Durable Goods	Minor Durable Goods	Services	Personal Saving
1869-1897	41.9	15.5	3.7	4.9	29.1	4.2
1898-1916	39.4	12.5	3.7	4.3	32.8	6.4
1922-1929	33.9	13.4	7.2	3.8	36.6	3.8
1930-1940	37.8	11.7	5.8	3.2	38.8	1.4
1948-1986	31.0	8.8	8.8	3.7	38.6	6.8
1869-1916	40.9	14.3	3.7	4.6	30.6	5.1
1922-1940	36.1	12.4	6.4	3.4	37.9	2.4

Averages by Overlapping Decades:

Years	Perishable Goods	Semi-Durable Goods	Major Durable Goods	Minor Durable Goods	Services	Personal Saving
1869-1878	42.3	16.9	4.1	4.8	28.0	3.3
1874-1883	44.4	16.1	3.6	4.7	29.3	1.3
1879-1888	43.0	15.4	3.6	4.9	29.6	2.7
1884-1893	41.8	15.2	3.8	5.2	29.9	3.4
1889-1898	40.4	13.9	3.4	4.9	29.8	6.9
1894-1903	40.7	13.0	3.1	4.7	31.0	6.7
1899-1908	39.7	12.8	3.4	4.6	31.9	6.9
1904-1913	38.7	12.5	3.7	4.2	33.0	6.9
1909-1918	39.0	12.4	4.3	3.8	32.9	6.7
1914-1923	37.5	13.4	5.3	3.7	32.4	6.9
1919-1928	34.9	13.7	6.7	3.7	34.5	5.5
1924-1933	34.5	12.7	6.7	3.4	39.2	1.9
1929-1938	37.2	11.8	5.9	3.2	39.2	1.2
1934-1943	37.5	11.4	5.3	3.3	33.8	7.6
1939-1948	36.4	11.9	4.8	3.7	29.4	12.8
1944-1953	37.0	12.0	7.1	3.9	29.5	9.4
1949-1958	35.6	10.6	9.4	3.6	32.7	6.6
1954-1963	33.8	9.4	9.0	3.4	36.0	6.5

Table 2.8, continued

Years	Perish-able Goods	Semi-Durable Goods	Major Durable Goods	Minor Durable Goods	Services	Personal Saving
1959-1968	31.7	8.9	8.9	3.5	38.0	6.7
1964-1973	29.6	8.5	9.1	3.8	39.1	7.6
1969-1978	28.5	7.9	8.8	3.9	40.5	7.9
1974-1983	28.0	7.3	8.2	4.0	42.7	7.3
1979-1986	26.7	6.9	8.3	3.9	45.4	6.1

Sources: Expenditure estimates derived as for table 2.3. Disposable personal income derived as discussed in appendix B, note 6; equals difference between personal income and personal tax and nontax payments. Personal saving equals difference between disposable personal income and the sum of total consumption expenditure, consumer interest payments to business, and net personal transfer payments to foreigners. Total consumption expenditure equals sum of expenditure for perishable, semidurable, major durable, and minor durable goods, and services. Consumer interest payments derived as discussed in appendix B, note 6. For 1929 on, net transfer payments to foreigners from U.S. BEA, *National Income and Product Accounts, 1929-76*, table 2.1, line 29 (these are consistent with the updated estimates in U.S. BEA, *National Income and Product Accounts, 1929-82*, which are rounded to the nearest tenth of a billion dollars). For 1869-1928, net transfer payments estimated as a constant 1.13 percent of expenditure for services, the ratio of net transfer payments to services in 1929. Percentage shares do not sum to 100 because of interest payments and net transfer payments to foreigners.

by nearly one-third between 1898–1916 and 1922–29, falling from 5.5 to 3.9 percent. Such a sharp decline in the personal saving rate is astounding, particularly since the 1920s were rather prosperous years and we usually expect saving rates to climb, not fall, during periods of prosperity.

The personal saving rate is the ratio of personal saving to disposable personal income. Personal saving is the difference between disposable income and personal outlays; disposable income is the difference between personal income and personal tax payments; personal outlays is the sum of consumption expenditure, consumer interest payments to business, and net personal transfer payments to foreigners.[12] The personal saving rates reported in tables 2.8 and 2.9 are computed from Department of Commerce national income and product account estimates, extended to the nineteenth century as discussed in appendix B. For the national prod-

Table 2.9. Average Shares of Disposable Income (Purchases of Consumer Durables as Consumption Spending), Constant (1982) Price Estimates, 1869-1986

Years	Perish-able Goods	Semi-Durable Goods	Major Durable Goods	Minor Durable Goods	Services	Personal Saving
1869-1897	42.0	9.9	3.7	3.6	35.9	3.2
1898-1916	39.4	8.7	2.6	3.9	38.1	5.5
1922-1929	35.7	8.0	4.7	3.3	43.2	3.9
1930-1940	40.0	8.0	3.9	2.8	42.6	1.6
1948-1986	32.9	6.3	7.0	3.4	41.4	8.6
1869-1916	41.0	9.5	3.3	3.7	36.8	4.2
1922-1940	38.2	8.0	4.2	3.0	42.8	2.6

Averages by Overlapping Decades:

Years	Perish-able Goods	Semi-Durable Goods	Major Durable Goods	Minor Durable Goods	Services	Personal Saving
1869-1878	41.3	10.5	4.0	3.0	37.2	2.4
1874-1883	43.9	10.1	3.7	3.3	37.1	0.3
1879-1888	43.6	9.8	3.6	3.7	35.8	1.8
1884-1893	42.5	9.9	3.8	4.2	35.6	2.4
1889-1898	41.0	9.4	3.5	4.0	34.4	5.8
1894-1903	41.2	9.0	3.1	3.9	35.2	5.7
1899-1908	39.9	8.7	2.8	3.9	37.0	6.0
1904-1913	38.6	8.6	2.5	3.9	38.6	6.2
1909-1918	38.1	8.4	2.5	3.8	39.6	6.1
1914-1923	36.9	7.9	3.1	3.3	41.0	6.5
1919-1928	35.8	7.7	4.2	3.2	42.6	5.3
1924-1933	36.9	8.1	4.3	3.1	44.2	2.2
1929-1938	39.2	8.0	3.8	2.9	43.5	1.5
1934-1943	38.8	7.6	3.6	2.9	38.3	7.7
1939-1948	37.7	7.2	3.1	3.0	35.2	12.7
1944-1953	38.1	6.9	4.4	3.3	36.8	9.6
1949-1958	37.6	6.5	6.1	3.2	38.5	7.5

Table 2.9, continued

Years	Perish-able Goods	Semi-Durable Goods	Major Durable Goods	Minor Durable Goods	Services	Personal Saving
1954-1963	36.4	6.2	6.1	3.0	39.9	7.9
1959-1968	34.6	6.1	6.3	3.1	41.0	8.5
1964-1973	32.5	5.9	7.0	3.3	41.4	9.6
1969-1978	30.4	5.8	7.5	3.6	42.4	10.0
1974-1983	28.4	6.3	7.7	3.8	44.0	9.6
1979-1986	27.1	6.9	8.5	3.9	44.9	8.6

Sources: Following the national income accounts, constant dollar disposable personal income derived by deflating current dollar disposable personal income (derived for table 2.8) by the implicit price deflator for total consumption expenditure. Personal saving equals difference between disposable personal income and the sum of total consumption expenditure, consumer interest payments to business, and net personal transfer payments to foreigners. Expenditure estimates derived as for table 2.4. Nominal values of consumer interest payments to business and net transfer payments to foreigners derived for table 2.8 both deflated by the implicit price deflator for consumer expenditure for services. Percentage shares do not sum to 100 because of interest payments and net transfer payments to foreigners.

uct accounts, the Department of Commerce treats all consumer goods in the same statistical manner: no distinction is made between the product itself and the services it provides.

For all goods, a theoretical distinction can be drawn, however, between the good and the services it provides; a household first purchases a good and subsequently consumes its services. Because a durable good produces services for at least three years, we can make not only a theoretical but also a statistical distinction between a household's annual purchases of durable goods and its annual consumption of the services of durable goods. In making this distinction, we view purchase of a durable good as household investment in a capital asset that produces a stream of services over that asset's productive lifetime. Each year, a household consumes (in effect, purchases from itself) the services "produced" by the durable good within that same year.[13]

Thus for this statistical sketch of the Consumer Durables Revolution, we now break with the Department of Commerce which considers purchase of a durable good an act of household consumption. Instead, recognizing explicitly the difference between purchase and consumption of durable goods, we consider a household's purchase of a durable good as simultaneously an act of investment (increasing the gross stock of capital assets) and an act of personal saving (providing for future consumption of the asset's services).[14]

Saving can be understood in two complementary ways, and the conceptual differences are underscored when we treat durable goods as assets rather than consumer goods. In economic growth models, personal saving (along with the government budget surplus and international trade deficit) provides for investment. In this context, we traditionally think of investment as purchases of producer durable goods and structures, assets that allow an expansion of an economy's total production possibilities. On the other hand, within the context of models of household decision-making, saving provides for a household's future consumption. Here we traditionally think of saving as acquisition of financial assets (stocks, cash, bonds, balances in checking or savings accounts) or physical assets (real estate, art, antiques) that can be liquidated in the future and the proceeds used to purchase consumable goods and services. These two conceptualizations of saving are not at odds, but they do tend to lead to different placement of acquisition of durable goods in an accounting of household spending. Because the services produced by a consumer durable good are typically consumed by only the household that bought the good and not by the whole economy, economic growth models typically exclude acquisition of consumer durable goods from saving and from investment. But because a consumer durable good provides services that can be consumed in the future, household decision-making models include acquisition of consumer durables in saving.[15]

This second treatment of consumer durable goods is analogous to the way the Department of Commerce currently counts purchases of owner-occupied housing in the national expenditure accounts. In effect, the Department of Commerce considers a household to be a business producing services that the household-as-business sells to itself, the household-as-household. Purchases of owner-occupied housing are part of gross private domestic investment, not total consumption expenditure. They are therefore reflected statistically in personal saving.[16] Current consumption of housing services is included in consumer expenditure for services. Adjustments to personal income and to gross national product are made to reflect the income earned by the household-as-business when it sells housing services to the household-as-household. "Gross rental value" of owner-occupied housing (an estimate of the total value of housing services provided by the house) is included in both expenditure for services and in gross national product. "Net rental value" (gross rental value less the values of capital consumption allowance and indirect business tax and nontax liability) is included in personal income. Net rental value also equals the sum of net rental income and mortgage interest payments.

It is possible to make several adjustments to Department of Commerce estimates in order to treat durable good purchases in an analogous manner. (For a complete discussion of the adjustments made, see appendix B, note 7.) Purchase of a durable good is not current consumption but investment expenditure; "adjusted personal saving" thus includes expenditure for durable goods. Gross rental value of durable goods is included with "adjusted expenditure for consumer services." In the national income accounts, consumer interest payments to business (which include payments on debt used to buy major durable goods but do not include mortgage interest) are included in personal income.[17] If we were to follow the statistical treatment of owner-occupied housing strictly and add net rental value of durables (net rental income plus interest payments) to personal income, we would be counting interest payments on durable goods debt twice. To avoid this double counting, only net rental income is included in "adjusted disposable personal income" to measure the income earned by the household-as-business when it rents the services of durable goods to itself, the household-as-household.

Estimates of existing stock of consumer durable goods are necessary for estimates of rental value. The source for our stock estimates, U.S. Bureau of Economic Analysis, *Fixed Reproducible Tangible Wealth, 1925–85*, provides no current price estimates of stock of consumer durable goods. Therefore only constant price estimates of adjusted saving rates can be computed. The adjusted estimates begin in 1900, the first available year of estimates of total stock of all durable goods.

Distribution of adjusted disposable personal income over adjusted saving and the three remaining subgroups of consumption (perishable goods, semidurable goods, and services) is in table 2.10. Recall from table 2.9 that the conventionally defined saving rate falls by nearly one-third between 1898–1916 and 1922–29.[18] When purchase of a durable good is defined as saving and investment, however, this precipitous drop *fully disappears*; the adjusted personal saving rate (in table 2.10) remains constant between 1900–1916 and 1922–29. The difference is illustrated in figure 2.2. The intertemporal behavior of the saving rate changes when purchases of durable goods are included with (rather than excluded from) other saving. We can therefore infer that the share of durable goods in household saving portfolios changed between 1900–1916 and the 1920s. When we view durable goods as assets and their services as consumable products, we see that households did not in fact save *less* in the 1920s than they did previously, but, rather, they saved *differently*. In the 1920s households substituted purchases of durable goods for accumulation of other assets in their saving portfolios.

Figure 2.2. Three-Year Moving Averages of Unadjusted and Adjusted Personal Saving Rates, 1901–1982

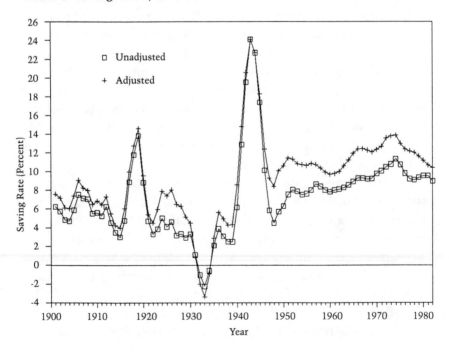

Table 2.10. Average Shares of Disposable Income (Purchases of
Consumer Durables as Investment Spending), Constant (1982) Price
Estimates, 1900-1986

Years	Perishable Goods	Semi-Durable Goods	Services	Adjusted Personal Saving
1900-1916	38.6	8.6	44.6	6.7
1922-1929	34.8	7.8	49.7	6.7
1930-1940	38.8	7.8	50.2	2.4
1948-1983	32.3	6.0	50.8	11.3
1922-1940	37.1	7.8	50.0	4.2

Averages by Overlapping Decades:

1900-1908	39.2	8.6	43.3	7.3
1904-1913	38.1	8.5	44.5	7.3
1909-1918	37.4	8.3	45.7	7.1
1914-1923	36.1	7.7	47.4	7.5
1919-1928	35.0	7.5	48.9	7.5
1924-1933	35.8	7.8	51.6	3.9
1929-1938	38.0	7.8	51.2	2.1
1934-1943	37.9	7.4	45.0	9.0
1939-1948	37.0	7.1	40.7	14.5
1944-1953	37.3	6.7	42.8	12.6
1949-1958	36.6	6.3	46.3	10.7
1954-1963	35.3	6.0	48.6	10.2
1959-1968	33.6	5.9	49.9	11.0
1964-1973	31.4	5.7	50.9	12.5
1969-1978	29.3	5.6	53.3	12.8
1974-1983	27.2	6.0	56.3	11.7
1979-1986	26.3	6.3	58.0	10.7

Sources: Adjusted disposable personal income derived as discussed in
appendix B, note 7. Expenditure for perishable and semidurable goods
derived as for table 2.4. Adjusted expenditure for services equals expendi-

Table 2.10, continued

ture for services in table 2.4 plus imputed gross rental value of consumer durable goods derived as discussed in appendix B, note 7. Adjusted personal saving equals difference between adjusted disposable personal income and sum of expenditure for perishable and semidurable goods, adjusted expenditure for services, adjusted consumer interest payments to business (consumer interest payments from table 2.9 less estimated interest payments for durable goods derived as discussed in appendix B, note 7), and net personal transfer payments to foreigners (derived as for table 2.9). Percentage shares do not sum to 100 because of interest payments and net transfer payments to foreigners.

THE CONSUMER DURABLES REVOLUTION OF THE 1920s

From these estimates we obtain a picture of the Consumer Durables Revolution of the 1920s. After World War I, households shifted their spending toward major durable goods, relatively high-priced and credit-financed goods. The products that accounted for the rise are primarily automobiles but also household appliances and radios. Simultaneously, prices of major durable goods rose relative to prices of other consumer goods and services. Not all durable goods became more popular; households purchased consistently fewer horse-drawn vehicles throughout the early twentieth century. Purchases of china and tableware, house furnishings, jewelry and watches, and other minor durable goods did not climb as fast as purchases of major durable goods, but households did devote a relatively constant share of their total spending for goods and services to these minor durable goods. The 1920s rise in purchases of major durable goods was accomplished partly at the expense of other goods and services but primarily at the expense of conventionally defined personal saving. In the 1920s, households substituted major durable goods for conventional instruments of saving.

AN ECONOMIC
ANALYSIS

o an economist, there are two possible explanations of the changed
role of durable goods in household spending and saving patterns after
the 1910s: in the starkest terms, either the demand for durable goods
shifted, or there was a movement along a stable demand curve. That is,
either households began to react differently to the factors that typically
determine the amount of durable goods spending they wish to undertake
(demand shifted), or the values of those factors changed (demand did not
shift but the quantity demanded changed). In this chapter, economic modeling and econometric analysis are used to sort out which of these two
explanations of the Consumer Durables Revolution is more appropriate.[1]

A PRIOR DEBATE

The question of whether a Consumer Durables Revolution took place was
debated by economists in the 1960s. What began as efforts to apply a thesis
advanced by Harry Oshima to the United States soon evolved into consideration of the existence of a structural shift in consumer tastes toward
durable goods in the 1920s.[2]

Oshima's thesis concerns the role household purchases of durable goods
play in sustaining economic growth. He argued that asset formation by
households (purchases of residential structures and those durable goods
usually bought with credit) is simultaneously a natural outgrowth of capi-

talist development and the sustaining force behind the continued economic growth necessary to prevent economic collapse.[3] In an economy with declining capital-output ratios and therefore declines in the ratio of business investment to gross national product, Oshima noted that the gap between saving and business investment will increase if the saving rate is unchanged. The "excess savings" thus created would, according to Oshima, be channeled to households to finance purchases of household assets. Implicitly assuming households previously had unmet demand for credit, he concluded that households would purchase more durable goods and houses, financing their purchases with credit and thereby absorbing the economy's "excess savings."

Oshima offered no empirical evidence in support of his thesis. Harold Vatter and Robert Thompson evaluated Oshima's thesis with a statistical examination of the United States experience. The thesis would be substantiated, they argued, if household spending for durable goods in the 1920s, widely recognized as the decade of increased expenditure for consumer durables, was proportionately greater than in later periods.[4] Vatter and Thompson evaluated household spending using two measures: the average rate of growth of expenditure for consumer durable goods relative to the average rate of growth of total consumption expenditure, and trend movements in decade-long averages of the share of durables expenditure in total consumption expenditure. They used constant price estimates of expenditure but, due to data limitations, used two different base years: 1929 is the base year for their 1920s estimates; 1954 is the base year for their post-1946 estimates. Despite Oshima's strong emphasis on only those durable goods usually purchased with credit, Vatter and Thompson failed to distinguish between major and minor durable goods when comparing durable goods purchases with total consumption expenditure. When Vatter and Thompson did distinguish between major and minor durable goods, they defined major durable goods differently than Oshima had. They included durable house furnishings and tableware and utensils in major durable goods but excluded radio and television receivers, records, and musical instruments.[5]

Vatter and Thompson concluded that household expenditure patterns of the 1920s do not support Oshima's thesis. The ratio of consumer durables to total consumption expenditures is stable from the 1920s on, and the (constant price) growth rates of consumer durables and total consumption expenditures are similar. In light of this evidence, Vatter and Thompson further submitted that the 1920s pattern of spending for durable goods does not reveal a structural change in consumer preferences in favor of durable goods.

In response, F. Thomas Juster and Robert Lipsey examined the evidence. They used current rather than constant price expenditure estimates. They distinguished between major and minor durable goods based on differences in unit cost, length of service life, and frequency of credit purchase—a distinction that gives product groupings consistent with Oshima's emphasis on debt-financed household investment.[6] Juster and Lipsey arrived at the opposite conclusion of Vatter and Thompson. They concluded the 1920s rise in expenditure for major consumer durables was economically significant and, in particular, partially offset a decline in the ratio of business investment to income.

Harold Vatter addressed the consumer durables issue one more time.[7] Again Vatter argued against the existence of a Consumer Durables Revolution, now defined explicitly as a structural change in consumer tastes in favor of durable goods. Again all durable goods were treated as one mass, with the notable exception of the automobile. And again Vatter invoked statistics similar to those in his earlier article to support his conclusion of no Consumer Durables Revolution.[8]

The debate was never resolved. Vatter conceded the likelihood of an "automobile revolution" but maintained that no Consumer Durables Revolution—that is, no shift toward household purchases of durable goods— took place in the 1920s. Juster and Lipsey, using different statistics, different criteria, and different data, maintained that a significant shift toward purchases of major durable goods did indeed transpire after World War I.

Although definitions and conceptual differences certainly receive partial credit for this lingering disagreement, the debate was also hampered by a lack of suitable data. A single continuous data set spanning a sufficiently long period of time before and after the 1920s was simply not available.[9]

More than by data, though, the debate was hampered by method. Harold Vatter proposed that the condition necessary for the existence of a Consumer Durables Revolution was a change in consumer preferences in favor of durable goods.[10] But he incorrectly argued that such a change would be reflected in a secular rise in decade averages of the ratio of durable goods to total consumption expenditures.

There is no theoretical reason for changes in this ratio and changes in preferences to be related, however. Preferences can change in favor of durable goods but not increase the ratio of durable goods to total consumption expenditures. The converse is also possible; the ratio can increase absent any change in preferences. Using the ratio of durable goods to total consumption expenditures to evaluate whether consumer preferences changed entails at least two implicit assumptions: one, that the income elasticity of demand is equal and constant for all subgroups of total consumption expenditure; and two, that changes in relative prices between subgroups do not reallocate consumer spending between those product groups.[11] If either assumption is false, the method is invalid. For example, when the income elasticity of demand for durable goods is more than that for nondurable goods or services, falling incomes will (all else constant) decrease the ratio of durable goods to total consumption expenditure. Or, if prices of durable goods increase relative to other prices, spending will be reallocated away from durable goods, decreasing the ratio of durable goods to total consumption expenditures. In either case, simultaneous change in consumer preferences in favor of durable goods can simply offset the income- or price-induced decline, yielding no net change in the expenditure ratio.

To resolve the economists' debate over existence of a Consumer Durables Revolution in the United States therefore requires formal economic modeling. In chapter 2 we saw that in the 1920s, the ratio of major (but not minor!) durable goods purchases to both total consumption expenditure and disposable income jumps above previous levels. To discover why; to determine if a Consumer Durables Revolution occurred in the 1920s; to sort out the effects of income, prices, and other factors on household purchases of durable goods, a model of demand is used below to statistically analyze twentieth-century patterns of household purchases of durable goods. I am not attempting to break new theoretical ground in modeling durable goods demand. Rather, a standard and widely accepted economic formulation of household demand for durable goods, the gradual stock-adjustment model, is used. With this model we can see if abnormally large changes in standard demand-determining factors interacted in a normal

way within a standard demand relationship to produce the striking patterns of expenditure for durable goods observed for the twentieth century.
If so, we would have to conclude with Vatter and Thompson that no Consumer Durables Revolution transpired.

A DISCUSSION OF METHOD FOR THE NONSPECIALIST

Like any economic model, the model of demand used here is a formal way
of abstracting from and simplifying complex real-world activity. Here, the
aim is to ascertain what factors determine household demand for durable
goods. Given that aim, we assume that a vast amount of information is
not relevant and can be ignored. Some information is obviously irrelevant.
That Sacramento is the capital of California, for example, is clearly irrelevant to how much money a typical American household wants to spend
on durable goods. Some information is less obviously, even questionably,
irrelevant. The distribution of the population across the United States is
assumed here to be irrelevant, even though some might argue that a shift
of population toward warm and sunny western states would increase demand for some durable goods (like cars) and decrease demand for others
(like heating stoves).

Once the factors that affect durable goods demand are identified, we
use statistical techniques to quantify the influence of each factor on demand. Income and relative price are two factors assumed to affect demand. Economists typically express the extent to which income or a good's
relative price influences demand with the concepts of income elasticity
or own-price elasticity, respectively. Income elasticity measures how
the quantity of a good that is demanded changes in response to a change
in income. Specifically, income elasticity is the ratio of the percentage
change in quantity demanded to the percentage change in income that
generated that change in quantity demanded. Similarly, own-price elasticity is the ratio of the percentage change in quantity demanded to the
percentage change in the good's relative price. An income elasticity of 1
means that a 10 percent increase in income results in a 10 percent increase in quantity demanded. If quantity demanded increases by 20 percent when income increases by only 10 percent, income elasticity is 2.

Values of the income and own-price elasticities can be uncovered with multiple regression analysis. This method allows us to isolate and quantify the influence of the few most important factors that determine typical household demand. A disadvantage to the method, however, is that it does not allow us to identify the diversity of patterns of demand that might be present in just one community. The method provides answers to specific questions—here, the factors that determine a *typical* American household's demand for durable goods. But neither the method nor the data used in this study (aggregate statistics for the entire United States economy) permits discovery of the rich detail of experiences of actual American households.

A MODEL OF DEMAND FOR DURABLE GOODS

Overview

To analyze household expenditure for durable goods, we use a gradual stock-adjustment model of demand for durable goods that is based on one developed in the 1950s by Richard Stone and D. A. Rowe.[12] In this model, households purchase durable goods for two reasons: to replace previously purchased goods that have worn out and to adjust the quantity of durable goods they own toward some desired level. We therefore distinguish between "gross expenditure" for durable goods (total spending for durable goods) and "replacement expenditure" (the amount of spending to replace worn-out goods). The difference between gross and replacement expenditures is called "net expenditure," spending that alters the total value of durable goods that households own. If net expenditure is positive, the total value of durable goods owned by households is increasing. If net expenditure is negative, spending is insufficient to replace worn-out goods, and thus the total value of durable goods owned is decreasing over time.

Net expenditure for durable goods is viewed as the result of a process of gradual adjustment of the actual stock of durable goods owned toward some desired level of stock. A household's decision to purchase a durable good is thus a two-step process: one, forming the desire to own a good, and two, deciding to purchase the now-desired good. Purchase typically does not immediately follow the desire to own a durable good.

The language of economics can be misleading when discussing demand for durable goods. "Demand" normally describes the quantities of a product households are willing and able to purchase at varying prices (and other factors). "Quantity demanded" is the quantity of the product households are willing and able to purchase at some *specific* price (and specified values of other factors). Desire for and demand for durable goods are not the same thing. Demand for durable goods has to do with the second step of the process, households' decisions to purchase a durable good, not the first step of forming the desire to own a durable good. If a household wishes to own an automobile but is not yet willing or able to purchase one, it has zero quantity demanded of autos at existing prices, income, and so on. Only when this household's desire to own an auto becomes willingness and ability to purchase one will they have some positive quantity demanded of autos at existing prices, income, and so on.

Households wish to own durable goods for two reasons: because the good provides a consumable service and because the good is an asset in the household's wealth portfolio.[13] We will call these the "service-desire" and "asset-desire" for durable goods, respectively. In general, both desires to own durable goods depend upon the relative price of the good's services, a long-run income variable, and whether or not the household is newly formed. Households adjust toward their desired stock only gradually because durable goods are lumpy (several years of services are embodied in just one durable good), illiquid (it is sometimes difficult and costly to sell a used durable good), and expensive (the price of some durable goods is six or more months of household income). In general, the speed with which households actually adjust their stock of durable goods depends upon the transactions costs associated with resale and upon the availability of credit financing. As markets for used goods develop, the difficulty and costs of selling a used durable good are lowered, making households less reticent to purchase a good they may subsequently need to sell. If credit financing becomes available, it decreases the amount of saving necessary to purchase an expensive good, allowing a household to make its purchase sooner.

For the statistical analysis, we use a linear demand equation derived from these principles. Gross demand for durable goods is the sum of replacement and net demand. Aggregate replacement demand in each period is, by assumption, equal to aggregate depreciation in that period.[14] Aggregate net demand is a proportion (because adjustment is gradual) of the difference between desired and actual stock of durable goods. Aggregate desired stock of durables depends upon the relative price of the durable good (a proxy for the unmeasurable relative price of the good's services), household disposable income and net wealth (together a proxy for household life-cycle income), and the rate at which new households are formed.

In the next section, the economic model is presented in greater detail. Readers who skip ahead to discussion of the empirical results will not miss anything essential.

The Model in Detail

The gradual stock-adjustment model explicitly allows for gradual adjustment of stock, with only part of the gap between desired and actual stock of a durable good closed in each period.[15] Under stable conditions, the actual level of stock converges to the desired level. To represent the general gradual stock-adjustment model algebraically, let

$Q_{i,t}$ = gross investment expenditure for durable goods by household i during period t

$D_{i,t}$ = depreciation during period t of the stock of durable goods held by household i

$N_{i,t}$ = net investment expenditure for durable goods by household i during period t; equal to $Q_{i,t} - D_{i,t}$

$S_{i,t}$ = actual value of net stock of durable goods held by household i at end of period t[16]

$S^*_{i,t}$ = desired value of net stock of durable goods that household i wishes to hold at end of period t

According to the model, current net investment expenditure closes only some proportion, a, of the gap between $S^*_{i,t}$ and $S_{i,t-1}$.[17] That is,

$$N_{i,t} = Q_{i,t} - D_{i,t} = a \left(S^*_{i,t} - S_{i,t-1}\right) \tag{3.1}$$

where, by assumption of the model, $0 < a < 1$.

The value of the adjustment factor, a, depends in part upon the period of analysis. If one-half the gap between desired and actual stock is closed in one year, with one-eighth of the gap closed each quarter, the adjustment factor will equal 0.5 if one year is the period of analysis but only 0.125 if the period of analysis is one quarter. Since the data are annual, one year is the period of analysis used in this study. The model itself is unchanged when quarterly data are used.

Models of demand for nondurable goods and for services implicitly assume that the adjustment factor of equation 3.1, a, equals 1. A desire to own a nondurable good quickly translates into willingness to purchase the good. Similarly, desire to consume a service translates without delay into willingness to purchase the service. Not so for durable goods. For durable goods, the adjustment factor is less than 1 because durable goods are, as noted above, lumpy, illiquid, and relatively expensive.[18]

Durable goods are lumpy; they are available in large, discrete units only. Absent short-term rental markets, households cannot purchase just one year's worth of a durable good's services. The good they purchase will produce services for at least three years. This implies something of a "threshold effect"; demand for a durable good's service must rise to some threshold level before purchase of the good is triggered.

Durable goods are illiquid assets; a household incurs transactions costs when selling a used durable good. The price of a used durable good is usually less than what the household believes it is "worth," that is, less than the difference between the good's original price and the value the household places on those services of the good that they have already consumed. If resale were costless (if used goods sold for what the owner thought they were "worth"), a household would purchase a durable good when the good's services are demanded and then sell it when the services are no longer demanded. The presence of transactions costs, however, means a household does not fully adjust its existing stock of a durable good to the level associated with its service-desire for the good.[19]

Illiquidity of durable goods also affects a household's asset-desire for durables. Demand for any asset depends upon its rate of return relative to that for other assets. The rate of return on durable goods is derived from the value of the good's services relative to the cost of owning the good. Asset-desire for durable goods depends on the good's ex ante rate of return, a rate that assumes the good will not be resold. But final demand for durable goods reflects the expected ex post rate of return, a rate that takes into account the possibility of resale. Because of transactions costs, resale increases the cost of owning a durable good and therefore lowers the ex post rate of return. With any risk of future resale, a household will not fully adjust its stock to the level associated with its asset-desire.

Durable goods are relatively expensive; the good's price may be a large percentage of a household's annual disposable income. Once a household forms the desire to own a durable good, it takes time to accumulate the resources needed to finance a purchase. The higher the good's price, the more time required. Increases in credit availability can hasten the process; less cash would then be needed before purchase. The less time that elapses between forming a desire to own and purchasing a durable good, the greater the adjustment factor.[20]

Determinants of Desired Stock

In the original and standard formulations of the gradual stock-adjustment model, a household's desired level of stock is derived from only the desire for consumable services, the service-desire. But households not only consume a durable good's services; they also include a durable good's value in savings portfolios. In the present formulation, desired level of stock is also derived from a household's desire for assets, the asset-desire. The two components of total desired stock are not separable; goods desired for their services also satisfy part of a household's asset-desire for durable goods. Distinguishing between service-desire and asset-desire primarily emphasizes differences between consumption and saving, differences that are important in formulating the determinants of desired stock.

Income
A household's desired level of stock should be positively related to income. According to Franco Modigliani's life-cycle hypothesis of saving, a household attempts to smooth consumption over its life cycle by basing each year's consumption on its expected lifetime labor income (life-cycle income) rather than on just that year's income.[21] Current income fluctuations primarily affect saving and have little effect on consumption. A durable good is an asset; its services are consumed. Increases in current income should increase a household's desired stock of durable goods, but its asset-desire for durable goods should be very sensitive to such changes in current income while its service-desire is insensitive to them.

Demand for durable goods is sometimes modeled as being dependent on permanent income rather than life-cycle income.[22] In this context, the two concepts are very similar: permanent income measures long-run (average) income; life-cycle income measures expected lifetime labor income and excludes property income. Using permanent income in empirical analysis introduces the well-known problem of accurately specifying and estimating the unobserved permanent income component from the observed and measured current income variable. Testing for the influence of permanent income on desired level of stock becomes a test of a joint hypothesis: Is permanent income measured correctly, and does income affect desired stock in the expected manner?

These problems are avoided by using life-cycle income as the long-run income variable. The influence of life-cycle income can be approximated with current income and household net wealth, thereby eliminating the specification problem.[23]

Relative Price

In demand models, substitutability between consumable products is normally measured by a relative price effect; the product's price relative to some aggregate price measure (usually one covering all consumer goods and services) should be inversely related to quantity demanded.[24] An *incorrect* extension would be to include simply the relative price of a durable good in our model of demand for durables. But households consume a durable good's services, not the good itself. The good's price is therefore not directly relevant. The relative price of the good's *services* is what matters to the household.

If the good's price is not directly relevant, why then do models of demand for durable goods typically include the relative price of the durable good itself? They do so because the good's price is measurable but the price of the good's services is not. Also, the good's price may be indirectly relevant because in equilibrium, a durable good's price equals the capitalized value of the discounted flow of the good's services. When the good's price is used, however, caution must be exercised in interpreting any empirical results; changes in the good's price can result not only from changes in the price of the good's services but from other sources as well.

Because this point is important but often neglected, in the present study the relationship between a good's price and the price of its services is made explicit. Assume a household is indifferent between consuming a service today and consuming it in the future; that is, assume their rate of time preference is zero. Assume the quantity of services produced by a durable good and made available to the household in each period is predetermined and constant and equal to 1 unit. Assume the household receives the full value of the services produced in each period, whether those services are consumed or foregone.[25] By definition, the total value of services produced in each period equals the product of unit price and quantity of those services. Since the quantity produced in each period is 1 unit, the price of the good's services equals the implicit market value of services produced in each period. Let

P_t = price of the durable good in period t

$PRSER_t$ = implicit price of the good's services in period t; equal to the implicit market value of the services produced in period t

r_t = rate of discount applicable to period t

T = life span of the durable good (number of periods)

Compounding interest once per period (including the initial period), the price of the durable good in equilibrium is[26]

$$P_t = \sum_{i=t}^{t+T} \frac{PRSER_i}{\prod_{j=t}^{i} (1 + r_j)} \tag{3.2}$$

If the discount rate is equal to r in all periods, equation 3.2 becomes

$$P_t = \sum_{i=t}^{t+T} \frac{PRSER_i}{(1 + r)^{i - t + 1}} \tag{3.3}$$

The equation changes slightly if we assume instead that households have a positive rate of time preference, preferring consumption of the durable good's services today over consumption in some future period. The more strongly households prefer consumption today over consumption in the future, the larger the rate of time preference. Let h stand for the rate of time preference. Equation 3.3 becomes

$$P_t = \sum_{i=t}^{t+T} \frac{PRSER_i}{(1 + r + h)^{i-t+1}} \tag{3.4}$$

The price of a durable good, P_t, therefore increases with an increase in the price of its services, $PRSER_t$, an increase in its life span, T, a decrease in the discount rate, r, or a decrease in the rate of time preference, h.

Service-desire for durable goods depends upon the quantity of a good's services that are desired. Under the usual assumptions, the quantity demanded of a good's services is inversely related to the relative price of those services; an increase in the price of services, $PRSER_t$, all else constant, will decrease the quantity of those services that are demanded. But the price of a good's services cannot be observed; only the price of the good itself can be known. If the life span, discount rate, and rate of time preference are all fixed, any change in the good's price must reflect a change in the implicit price of its services. In this case, the relative price of a durable good itself is also inversely related to the quantity of the good's *services* that are demanded. Through the service-desire for durable goods, then, the good's relative price and the desired level of stock of a durable good can be inversely related. Relative price of a durable good and the quantity demanded of that durable good are therefore inversely related with certainty only when life span, discount rate, and the rate of time preference are all fixed.

Unfortunately this situation is the only instance in which the good's price is an adequate proxy for the price of the good's services. If any of the life span, discount rate, or rate of time preference change, the durable good's relative price and the desired level of its stock may *not* be inversely related and can even be positively related. Life span cannot change during a particular good's life, but over time the average life span of goods within a commodity group can change. Taking various combinations of changes in life span and product price, it is a straightforward exercise to show conditions under which a durable good's relative price has no effect or even the "wrong" (positive) effect on quantity demanded of the good. For example, increasing durability will, all else constant, increase a good's price. But increasing durability does not change the price of the good's services. Increasing durability alone therefore will not affect quantity of services demanded nor service-desire for durable goods. The good's price will increase, but quantity demanded of the good will remain unchanged.

Sometimes a good's price remains constant as average durability increases. If the discount rate and rate of time preference are also constant, the implicit price of the good's services must in this instance be falling. The quantity of services demanded and thus the service-desire for durable goods will both increase. Even though the good's price is unchanged, quantity demanded of the good rises.

The rate of discount is the rate at which a household discounts future values to arrive at an equivalent value in today's prices. Discounting future values concerns the effect over time of accumulation of interest on an asset's value. For simplicity but not of necessity, above we assumed a constant rate of discount over the good's life. In fact, though, households may adjust the discount rate as changes occur in market rates of interest on assets that substitute for durable goods in household savings portfolios. If market rates of interest increase and in response the household's discount rate also increases, in equilibrium the good's price will decrease, all else constant. But the price of the good's services is unchanged. So neither the quantity of services demanded nor the service-desire for durable goods will change.

Changes in market interest rates can affect the asset-desire for durable goods. Asset-desire for stock should be inversely related to the good's relative rate of return. In equilibrium, the rate of return earned on a durable good equals the sum of the rate used to discount the good's flow of services, r, and the rate of time preference, h. In the presence of a positive rate of time preference, households are willing to borrow at an interest rate that exceeds the rate of return on liquid assets rather than take time to save up the entire price of a durable good in advance of its purchase.

If market interest rates increase but durable goods' prices do not fall, asset-desire for durable goods should decline as the relative rate of return on durable goods declines. However, an increase in market interest rates matched by an increase in discount rates occasioned by a fall in durable goods' prices will leave relative rates of return and therefore asset-desire for durable goods unchanged. The usual practice of omitting a market interest rate from empirical analysis of durable goods demand reflects an implicit assumption that discount rates and therefore durable goods' prices adjust in response to changes in market interest rates or, equivalently, that the relative rate of return on durable goods is constant over time.

In sum, the price of a durable good is a proxy variable for the relevant price variable, the price of the good's services. It is sometimes a better proxy than others. If durability, the discount rate, and the rate of time preference are all constant, an unambiguous negative relationship between relative price of a durable good and desired stock of that good is expected. But if durability, discount rate, or rate of time preference does change, then the relative price and quantity demanded of a durable good can have no relationship or even a direct relationship.

The durability of many consumer products has increased markedly over the course of this century. Such changes cause measured increases in price of the good to overstate increases in the price of the good's services, and therefore measured price elasticities will understate the responsiveness of demand to changes in the price of the good's services. Some might argue that households' rate of time preference has increased over this century as Americans have become less willing to put off to tomorrow what we can have today. In this case, measured price increases will understate increases in the price of the good's services, and therefore measured price elasticities will overstate "true" price elasticities.[27]

Algebraic Formulation

Demand for durable goods is summarized algebraically as follows. (Full algebraic derivation of the demand equation is presented in appendix C.) For each household, gross expenditure for durable goods, Q, is the sum of replacement and net expenditure. By assumption, replacement expenditure equals current period depreciation, D (which includes allowances for obsolescence as well as accidental damage and destruction). Net expenditure, N, reflects gradual adjustment of actual end-of-previous-period stock toward desired end-of-current-period stock. Desired stock, S^*, is a linear function of a constant term, the relative price of durable goods, personal disposable income, and household net wealth.

Newly formed households may exhibit demand for certain durable goods that results specifically from setting up the household.[28] Strictly this suggests we use cross-section data and examine demand for durable goods at each stage of the household life cycle. With the available aggregate time series data, we instead assume that newly formed households have a different level of desired stock for some goods than previously established households do but respond to changes in price, income, or wealth in the same way as previously established households. In effect, the constant term in the equation for desired stock is different for newly formed households than it is for those established previously.

Aggregating over all households in the economy and deflating by the number of households, H, yields our demand equation

$$\frac{N_t}{H_t} = \frac{Q_t - D_t}{H_t} = a\left(b_0 + b_1 p_t + b_2\frac{Y_t}{H_t} + b_3\frac{W_t}{H_t} + b_4\frac{\Delta H_t}{H_t} - \frac{S_{t-1}}{H_t}\right) \quad (3.5)$$

where H_t is the number of households at the end of period t, p_t is the relative price of the durable good during period t, Y_t is aggregate disposable income during period t, W_t is aggregate net wealth at the end of period t, and S_{t-1} is the aggregate value of existing stock at the end of period $t-1$.

This equation focuses on net expenditure. Replacement expenditure equals depreciation. Estimates of depreciation by commodity group are given in table A.12. For each commodity group, annual depreciation amounts fluctuate very little, and depreciation is a very stable proportion of the value of stock. About 70 percent of gross expenditure is accounted for by depreciation for each group. Short-run fluctuations in gross expenditure are therefore primarily from net expenditure, the focus of the empirical analysis.

Equation 3.5 is the structural form of the demand equation. It explicitly shows the adjustment coefficient, a, separate from the other coefficients that affect desired stock, S^*. To run the regressions, an estimable form of equation 3.5 is used:

$$\frac{N_t}{H_t} = A_0 + A_1 p_t + A_2\frac{Y_t}{H_t} + A_3\frac{W_t}{H_t} + A_4\frac{\Delta H_t}{H_t} + A_5\frac{S_{t-1}}{H_t} \quad (3.6)$$

where the coefficients A_0 through A_5 are to be estimated.

REGRESSION ANALYSIS: PRELIMINARY STEPS

To test for the existence of a Consumer Durables Revolution in the 1920s, we test for shifts in demand. A demand equation based on equation 3.6 is first estimated by commodity group for each of several time periods. The data sources are described in appendix C, where the values of the independent variables are also given.

To the extent that a good's price is an adequate proxy for the price of its services, the relative price coefficient should be negative. When the proxy fails, the coefficient may be zero or even positive.[29]

The coefficient on disposable income per household should be positive.

The wealth coefficient may be positive or negative. An increase in wealth should increase consumption (and thus increase service-desire for durable goods) but decrease saving (and thus decrease asset-desire for durable goods). The sign of the wealth coefficient can indicate whether service-desire or asset-desire dominates for that product group.

If demand by newly formed households is not different from that for previously established households, the household formation rate coefficient should be zero. If setting up a new household requires postponing purchases, the coefficient should be negative. If new households have increased demand for some durable goods, the household formation rate coefficient should be positive.

Finally, if the gradual stock-adjustment model best describes household behavior, the lagged stock coefficient should be negative but greater than −1. If, instead, most households that purchase durable goods are exhibiting habit-formation behavior (where owning stock is largely a force of habit, determined statistically by an autoregressive process), the lagged stock coefficient can be positive.[30]

Wealth per household is highly correlated with lagged stock per household in the post–World War II and full-sample (1902–83) periods as shown in table 3.1. Such multicollinearity does not affect efficiency of parameter estimates but may affect what is often termed their "precision." In particular, the standard error of an estimated coefficient may be quite high and may lead to an incorrect decision to drop one or more of the correlated independent variables from the regression equation. Dropping a theoretically correct but statistically insignificant variable introduces omitted

Table 3.1. Correlation Coefficients of Real Net Wealth per Household with Real Disposable Income per Household and with Lagged Stock per Household by Commodity Group

Correlation of Wealth with	Time Period					
	1902-1919	1920-1941	1947-1983	1902-1941	1920-1983	1902-1983
Income	0.42	0.21	0.93	0.48	0.92	0.94
Correlation of Wealth with Lagged Stock per Household of						
Furniture	-0.05	0.26	0.91	-0.38	0.80	0.48
Household Appliances	0.43	0.37	0.87	0.71	0.92	0.93
China and Tableware	0.38	-0.40	-0.51	-0.43	-0.23	-0.44
House Furnishings	-0.17	0.34	0.80	-0.42	0.85	0.73
Pianos and Musical Instruments	0.40	-0.17	n.a.	-0.26	n.a.	n.a.
TVs, Radios and Phonographs	0.25	0.37	n.a.	0.70	n.a.	n.a.
TVs and Musical Instruments	0.34	0.47	0.77	0.73	0.84	0.84
Jewelry and Watches	0.41	0.05	0.73	-0.26	0.81	0.77
Medical Products	0.36	-0.70	0.84	0.34	0.89	0.92
Books and Maps	-0.40	0.35	0.78	-0.42	0.90	0.83
Miscellaneous Other Durables	-0.41	0.23	0.76	0.29	0.84	0.85
Major Consumer Durables	0.02	0.85	0.87	0.87	0.91	0.92
Minor Consumer Durables	0.38	-0.05	0.75	-0.43	0.84	0.78
All Consumer Durables	0.37	0.69	0.84	0.77	0.90	0.90

Source: Computed from the estimates in tables C.1 and A.13.

variables bias to the remaining parameter estimates, however. Regardless of its statistical significance, the wealth variable is therefore retained in all regressions.

Multicollinearity can also make estimated coefficients very sensitive to a particular data set; adding or deleting a few observations can cause large changes in estimated coefficients. Moreover, a high degree of multicollinearity can make it "difficult to disentangle the relative influences" of the independent variables.[31] Unfortunately this means the estimated sign of the wealth coefficient may not be a statistically reliable measure of the relative strength of the asset-desire and service-desire for durable goods for the post–World War II and full-sample periods. For these two estimation periods, the statistical effects of the wealth and lagged stock coefficients may frequently be "entangled."

Significant autocorrelation of error terms is often present, resulting in inefficient parameter estimates. A Cochrane-Orcutt procedure corrects for this problem. Implementation of the Cochrane-Orcutt procedure requires one continuous sample, so dummy variables DUMWW1 (for 1917–19) and DUMWW2 (for 1942–46) are introduced to account for war-related alterations in household expenditure. Further details on the dummy variables are in appendix C.

Finally, equation 3.6 is theoretically one equation of a simultaneous equations system specifying both demand and supply. Estimation of one equation from a simultaneous equations system with single equation methods (ordinary least squares and Cochrane-Orcutt) can result in biased and inconsistent parameter estimates of the variables that enter more than one equation, here, relative price. The instrumental variables method with a Cochrane-Orcutt correction for serially correlated errors is therefore used to estimate all regression equations. The instruments used are discussed in appendix C.

The equation estimated is

$$\frac{N_t}{H_t} = A_0 + A_1 p_t + A_2 \frac{Y_t}{H_t} + A_3 \frac{W_t}{H_t} + A_4 \frac{\Delta H_t}{H_t} + A_5 \frac{S_{t-1}}{H_t}$$

$$+ A_6 DUMWW1 + A_7 DUMWW2 + e_t \qquad (3.7)$$

where $e_t = (RHO)e_{t-1} + v_t$ and, by assumption, v_t is a serially independent random variable distributed normally with mean zero and constant variance.[32] For each commodity group, the equation is estimated for six periods: pre–World War I (1902–19), interwar (1920–41), post–World War II (1947–83), combined post–World War I (1920–83), combined pre–World War II (1902–41), and full-sample periods (1902–83). The complete set of regression results and summary statistics are in appendix C.

RESULTS OF THE EMPIRICAL ANALYSIS

Did a Consumer Durables Revolution occur in the United States in the 1920s? When Harold Vatter explored this issue in the 1960s, he explicitly defined the condition for existence of a Consumer Durables Revolution to be structural change in consumer tastes in favor of durable goods.[33] Here we generalize Vatter's condition: a "revolution" in consumer durable goods is said to have occurred if there is any sort of structural change in demand for these goods. Structural change in demand can take two forms: absence of stability in estimated elasticities over time or change in the structural form of the demand relationship itself.

Rising household expenditure for many durable goods after World War I may have simply been a normal economic response to abnormally large changes in relative prices and income. This seems to be the profession's received view of the events; increased purchases of durable goods is often linked to 1920s prosperity and declines in relative prices of durable goods. Implicit is stability of the demand relationship itself. If demand *is* stable and dramatic increases in relative expenditure for durable goods are due to income or price changes, this would not constitute a "revolution."

When testing for instability of demand, the proper reference period is the pre–World War I period. If the events of the 1920s represent a revolution in household demand, this revolution is vis-à-vis earlier years.

Two tests for stability of demand across periods are used: an F-test (often called the Chow test) for stability of the entire relationship and a t-test for stability of the estimated price and income elasticities. The F-test uses the standard error of the regression from regressions for each of two periods to calculate an F-statistic.[34] If the value of this F-statistic exceeds some cut-off value, then we can conclude (with some specified level of confidence in our conclusion) that demand is not stable between these two periods. A change in elasticity is deemed statistically significant if the elasticity for one period falls outside the 95 percent confidence interval about the estimated elasticity for the second period, and vice versa.

Elasticities are calculated with respect to gross rather than net expenditure.[35] Because net expenditure is usually around 30 percent of gross expenditure and net expenditure exhibits much more fluctuation than replacement expenditure, this practice lowers the elasticities substantially. Elasticity is the combined effect of change in desired stock and adjustment of actual toward desired stock. A change in either the adjustment coefficient or the structural income or relative price coefficient will give a change in elasticity.

Post-World War II Period

As a standard model of demand for durable goods, equation 3.7 should do a reasonable job of explaining demand for the post–World War II years. It does. The results summarized here are presented in appendix C. Except for the entertainment complex (radios and musical instruments) and for miscellaneous other durable goods, the lagged stock coefficients are negative, greater than −1, and generally statistically significant at the 95 percent level.

Increases in average durability and changes in product quality no doubt account for the failure of the relative price proxy variable for four product groups: automobiles and parts, household appliances, radios and musical instruments, and miscellaneous other durable goods.[36] The relative price coefficient is positive for automobiles and parts, household appliances, and radios and musical instruments but not significantly different from zero at even very low levels of confidence: 20, 45, and 70 percent, respectively. It is positive and statistically significant at the 95 percent level of confidence for miscellaneous other durable goods. For all other groups, the relative price coefficient is negative though sometimes not significantly different from zero at the 95 percent level of confidence.

The household formation rate affects demand for four product groups. Newly formed households have higher demand for household appliances and for china and tableware (significant at 85 to 90 percent levels of confidence). But they have lower demand for radios and musical instruments, and for books and maps (at 85 and 70 percent levels of confidence, respectively).

The R-squared statistic, adjusted to compensate for degrees of freedom, indicates the explanatory power of the regression equation. For these equations, the adjusted R^2 ranges between 0.6 and 0.95 for nearly all commodity groups. This level of explanatory power compares favorably with other studies of post–World War II net expenditure for durable goods.[37] The adjusted R^2 would be much greater (on the order of 0.9 to 0.99 for all groups) if gross expenditure was the dependent variable and depreciation one of the independent variables since depreciation fluctuates so little and accounts for such a large part of gross expenditure for each commodity group.

Demand for durable goods is generally highly income elastic but weakly own-price elastic, as seen in table 3.2. That is, when purchasing durable goods, households respond much more to changes in their income than to changes in the relative price of durable goods. Income elasticity ranges from 0.7 for radios and musical instruments to 3.0 for transportation vehicles. Except for radios and musical instruments, all income elasticities are greater than 1. When the relative price coefficient is negative, price elasticity ranges from -0.1 for transportation vehicles to -1.3 for jewelry and watches. These results are consistent with those obtained in other studies of post–World War II demand for consumer durables.[38]

Comparing Interwar and Post–World War II Periods

If demand for durable goods shifted in the 1920s, a Consumer Durables Revolution occurred then. A fallacious though oft-implied way of testing for existence of a Consumer Durables Revolution in the 1920s is to compare interwar and post–World War II demand. But if demand changed in the early 1920s, it changed with regard to earlier (not later) years. While a comparison of interwar and post–World War II demand cannot therefore determine whether the Consumer Durables Revolution occurred, it is nevertheless important; if the 1920s ushered in a "new era" in household demand for durable goods, then demand should be stable between the interwar and post–World War II periods.

Was the interwar period akin to the post–World War II period with regard to household demand for durable goods? The basis of comparison is the post–World War II period; the household formation rate variable is included when estimating the other demand equations used to conduct

Table 3.2. Estimated Own-Price and Income Elasticities by Commodity Group (Standard Errors in Parentheses)

	Commodity Groups							
	TRA	AUT	FUR	APP	MUS	RAD	PIA	CHI
Pre-World War I Period (1902-1919):								
Own-Price	0.38	0.01	-0.99	-0.21	-0.70	-1.49	-0.58	-1.42
Elasticity	(0.18)	(0.09)	(0.12)	(0.45)	(0.49)	(0.94)	(0.22)	(0.52)
Income	1.84	1.61	0.92	0.94	1.02	0.25	1.16	0.63
Elasticity	(0.74)	(0.59)	(0.16)	(0.24)	(0.32)	(0.50)	(0.25)	(0.29)
Interwar Period (1920-1941):								
Own-Price	0.15	0.13	-0.87	-2.05	-0.27	-0.22	-0.87	-2.16
Elasticity	(0.79)	(0.78)	(0.34)	(0.28)	(0.18)	(0.28)	(0.28)	(0.50)
Income	2.38	2.35	1.62	1.45	1.91	2.73	2.49	0.46
Elasticity	(0.58)	(0.60)	(0.31)	(0.27)	(0.72)	(0.55)	(0.67)	(0.26)
Post-World War II Period (1947-1983):								
Own-Price	-0.08	0.07	-0.93	0.16	0.26	n.a.	n.a.	-0.97
Elasticity	(0.37)	(0.34)	(0.38)	(0.28)	(0.26)			(0.26)
Income	3.05	3.01	1.87	1.99	0.75	n.a.	n.a.	1.12
Elasticity	(0.89)	(0.88)	(0.35)	(0.32)	(0.68)			(0.29)
Post-World War I Period (1920-1983):								
Own-Price	-0.56	-0.09	-0.63	-0.64	0.06	n.a.	n.a.	-2.23
Elasticity	(0.38)	(0.39)	(0.28)	(0.23)	(0.09)			(0.41)
Income	1.40	1.57	1.65	1.36	0.19	n.a.	n.a.	0.68
Elasticity	(0.47)	(0.50)	(0.33)	(0.41)	(0.40)			(0.22)

Table 3.2, continued

	Commodity Groups							
	HSF	JWL	MED	BKS	MIS	MJR	MNR	TOT
Pre-World War I Period (1902-1919):								
Own-Price	-0.85	-1.37	-0.02	-0.34	-2.53	-0.57	-1.09	-0.35
Elasticity	(0.53)	(0.43)	(0.52)	(0.28)	(0.46)	(0.12)	(0.28)	(0.39)
Income	0.84	1.47	0.21	-0.16	0.40	0.81	1.02	0.65
Elasticity	(0.36)	(0.31)	(0.44)	(0.29)	(0.50)	(0.27)	(0.19)	(0.17)
Interwar Period (1920-1941):								
Own-Price	-0.35	-0.97	-1.54	-1.00	-0.58	0.42	-1.22	-0.25
Elasticity	(0.25)	(0.28)	(0.37)	(0.47)	(0.31)	(0.45)	(0.26)	(0.38)
Income	1.81	2.52	0.46	0.95	1.78	2.19	1.58	1.95
Elasticity	(0.11)	(0.26)	(0.34)	(0.31)	(0.24)	(0.26)	(0.12)	(0.18)
Post-World War II Period (1947-1983):								
Own-Price	-0.42	-1.34	-0.86	-0.22	2.08	-0.36	-0.71	-0.71
Elasticity	(0.52)	(0.53)	(0.53)	(0.54)	(0.99)	(0.41)	(0.50)	(0.45)
Income	1.30	1.24	1.29	1.62	2.98	2.17	1.44	1.65
Elasticity	(0.46)	(0.60)	(0.37)	(0.42)	(0.69)	(0.57)	(0.29)	(0.44)
Post-World War I Period (1920-1983):								
Own-Price	-1.44	-0.52	-0.26	-0.51	-0.23	-0.16	-1.42	-0.27
Elasticity	(0.28)	(0.23)	(0.14)	(0.28)	(0.35)	(0.34)	(0.23)	(0.33)
Income	1.44	1.10	0.88	0.86	0.95	1.62	0.91	1.28
Elasticity	(0.27)	(0.38)	(0.30)	(0.33)	(0.47)	(0.28)	(0.20)	(0.26)

Source: Derived from estimations of equation 3.7. Elasticities are calculated with regard to gross expenditure for the commodity group. Full regression results are given in the tables in appendix C.

Note: Three-letter commodity group abbreviations are as follows: TRA, transportation vehicles; AUT, automobiles and parts; FUR, furniture; APP, household appliances; MUS, radios and musical instruments; PIA, pianos and other musical instruments; RAD, radios and phonographs; CHI, china and tableware; HSF, house furnishings; JWL, jewelry and watches; MED, orthopedic and ophthalmic products; BKS, books and maps; MIS, miscellaneous other durable goods; MJR, major durable goods; MNR, minor durable goods; TOT, total durable goods.

the F-test only if it enters the post–World War II equation. The results of the two tests for stability of demand, the F-test and the t-tests, are summarized in table 3.3. (The regression results and the F-statistics are in appendix C.)

Stability of demand between interwar and post–World War II periods is indicated for automobiles and parts, transportation vehicles, radios and musical instruments, house furnishings, jewelry and watches, orthopedic and ophthalmic products, books and maps, miscellaneous other durable goods, and the aggregates major durable goods and total durable goods. Elasticity comparisons but not the F-test also point to post–World War I stability of demand for furniture and the aggregate minor durable goods. Demand shifts between interwar and post–World War II periods for only two product groups: household appliances, and china and tableware.

Comparing Interwar and Pre–World War I Periods

If there were no Consumer Durables Revolution in the 1920s, that is, if increased purchases of durable goods merely resulted from movements along stable demand curves, then demand will be stable between pre–World War I and interwar periods. But in fact very few commodity groups show stable demand between these periods. Only two product groups—china and tableware, and house furnishings—show clear evidence of stable demand. To varying degrees, the statistical tests point to shifts of demand for all other commodity groups.

The F-test (which checks for stability of the entire relationship) rejects the hypothesis of stable demand at the 95 percent level of confidence for transportation vehicles, automobiles and parts, household appliances, pianos and other musical instruments, jewelry and watches, orthopedic and ophthalmic products, books and maps, miscellaneous other durable goods, and the aggregates major durable goods, minor durable goods, and total durable goods. If the test's stringency were weakened just the slightest bit, the stability hypothesis would also be rejected for furniture; its F-value misses the 95 percent cutoff value by just 0.01. Ranking commodity groups by size of the F-statistic, evidence of shifting demand is especially strong for pianos and other musical instruments, jewelry and watches, and household appliances.

Income elasticity of demand increased after World War I for all groups

Table 3.3. Did Demand Shift?

Interwar versus Post-WWII Periods			Pre-WWI versus Post-WWI Periods			Pre-WWI versus Interwar Periods		
Shift	Mixed	No Shift	Shift	Mixed	No Shift	Shift	Mixed	No Shift
		TRA*			TRA^y		TRA	
		AUT*		AUT			AUT	
	FUR		FUR^y					FUR^p
APP^p					APP*	APP^p		
		MUS^y			MUS^p			MUS*
								RAD^p
							PIA	
CHI*				CHI				CHI*
		HSF*			HSF*			HSF^p
		JWL^p		JWL		JWL^y		
		MED*		MED		MED^p		
		BKS*	BKS^y			BKS^y		
		MIS^y	MIS^p			MIS*		
		MJR*	MJR^y			MJR*		
	MNR			MNR		MNR^y		
		TOT*	TOT^y			TOT^y		

Notes:
Shift: F-test and one or both t-tests indicate instability of demand.
Mixed: F-test indicates shift; both t-tests indicate stability.
No Shift: F-test and one or both t-tests indicate stability of demand.
*F-test and both t-tests agree.
^{p}F-test and t-test of own-price elasticity agree.
^{y}F-test and t-test of income elasticity agree.
Three-letter abbreviations are as for table 3.2.

except china and tableware, and orthopedic and ophthalmic products (see table 3.2). The increase is statistically significant at the 90 percent level of confidence for furniture, household appliances, pianos and other musical instruments, radios and phonographs, house furnishings, jewelry and watches, books and maps, miscellaneous other durable goods, and the aggregates major durable goods, minor durable goods, and total durable goods.

Conclusions of the F-test and the t-tests are noted in table 3.3. The F-test of the entire relationship and one or both of the t-tests of the income and price elasticities point to shifting demand between pre–World War I and interwar periods for household appliances, jewelry and watches, ortho-pedic and ophthalmic products, books and maps, miscellaneous other du-rable goods, and the aggregates major durable goods, minor durable goods, and total durable goods. The F-test but neither t-test indicates demand shifts for automobiles and parts, transportation vehicles, and pianos and other musical instruments. Comparing pre–World War I and full post–World War I periods for those products exhibiting stability within 1920–83 confirms the results of the pre–World War I and interwar comparison for all groups except transportation vehicles, jewelry and watches, and ortho-pedic and ophthalmic products.

These results are sensitive to the stringency of the tests applied.[39] We have already noted that the F-test for furniture would indicate a shift of demand if the standards were relaxed ever so slightly. If the elasticity comparisons are conducted at the 90 rather than the 95 percent level of confidence, the conclusions change as follows:

Pianos and other musical instruments: changes to "Shift" for pre–World War I versus interwar comparison (F-test and income elasticity change; price elasticity stable)

Jewelry and watches: changes to "Shift" for pre–World War I versus post–World War I comparison (F-test and price elasticity change; in-come elasticity stable) and thus confirms the comparison of pre–World War I and interwar periods

If a change in elasticity is statistically significant if only one (rather than both) of the estimates falls outside the 95 percent confidence level about the other period's estimate, the conclusions change as follows:

Radios and musical instruments: changes to "Mixed" for pre–World War I versus interwar comparisons (elasticities change; F-test stable)

and to "Mixed" for pre–World War I versus post–World War I comparisons (elasticities change; F-test stable)

Radios and phonographs: changes to "Mixed" for pre–World War I versus interwar comparison (elasticities change; F-test stable)

Pianos and other musical instruments: changes to "Shift" for pre–World War I versus interwar comparison (F-test and income elasticity change; price elasticity stable)

House furnishings: changes to "Mixed" for pre–World War I versus post–World War I comparison (elasticities change; F-test stable)

Jewelry and watches: changes to "Shift" for pre–World War I versus post–World War I comparison (F-test and price elasticity change; income elasticity stable) and thus again confirms the comparison of pre–World War I and interwar periods

Orthopedic and ophthalmic products: changes to "Shift" for pre–World War I versus post–World War I comparison (F-test and income elasticity change; price elasticity stable)

In the gradual stock-adjustment model, the lagged stock coefficient is negative. But positive and statistically significant lagged stock coefficients are present for automobiles and parts, transportation vehicles, and radios and phonographs in the pre–World War I years. These positive coefficients could reflect sustained disequilibrium in these markets; if households had been forced to postpone planned purchases, the delay might produce a positive lagged stock coefficient. The historical evidence disputes this claim, however; automobiles were produced in response to orders until the 1910s, and there is not widespread evidence of the extensive levels of perpetually unfilled orders that would have been necessary to generate a positive lagged stock coefficient. The positive coefficient might reflect a "Jones" effect: if households were trying to "keep up with the Joneses," economy-wide increases in stock of some product in one period may have led to a desire for even more stock in the subsequent period and therefore more net expenditure. Finally, absence of credit for financing purchases of these goods might have produced the positive stock coefficients. Without credit, households must save up the full purchase price of a good before buying it. Cars and phonographs were quite expensive before World War I, and saving up the purchase price could take several years for a typical family. This lengthy time frame means net expenditure may be quite un-responsive to current fluctuations in price or income.[40]

Evidence presented in chapter 2 indicates that households saved differently after World War I, substituting durable goods for other assets in their savings portfolios. Estimated wealth effects confirm this result. Before World War I households demanded the majority of durable goods primarily for their services, not for their value as assets in saving portfolios. But after World War I durable goods were widely viewed as assets; only three types of durables were desired primarily for their service value in the interwar years.[41]

In particular, before World War I the service-desire dominates for furniture, household appliances, radios and musical instruments, radios and phonographs, jewelry and watches, books and maps (though only weakly so), and the aggregate major durable goods. Asset-desire dominates for automobiles and parts, transportation vehicles, house furnishings, china and tableware, and miscellaneous other durable goods, although for the last two groups the effect is only weakly statistically significant. But after World War I only household appliances, radios and musical instruments, and books and maps are demanded primarily for their services—and in each case the effect is only weakly statistically significant. Asset-desire continues to dominate for house furnishings and for miscellaneous other durable goods, and now also dominates for pianos and other musical instruments, jewelry and watches, and the aggregate minor durable goods.

THERE WAS A CONSUMER DURABLES REVOLUTION IN THE 1920s

To the extent that we define existence of a Consumer Durables Revolution to be the existence of shifts in demand for consumer durables, a Consumer Durables Revolution occurred in the United States after World War I. Only demand for china and tableware and for house furnishings clearly remained stable after World War I. For all other product groups and the aggregates, we can say (with varying degrees of confidence) that demand changed. Interwar changes in household expenditure for durable goods cannot be attributed simply to households reacting to changes in income and relative prices within a stable demand environment. Household spending behavior changed after World War I.

A BURGEONING
CREDIT ECONOMY

Accompanying the rise in household purchases of durable goods after World War I was vast expansion of the use of credit for financing such purchases. This expansion was both cause and effect of the Consumer Durables Revolution. Attributes of automobile production led to development of facilities that offered retail credit. The resulting availability of credit allowed thousands of households to enter the auto market. For other products, increased desire to own durable goods led to increased use of consumer credit. A transformation in societal attitudes toward the moral propriety of borrowing facilitated the debt expansion.

USE OF CREDIT

Evidence on household use of credit to finance purchases of durable goods is scattered but uniform in indicating a ballooning of household debt during the 1920s. The figures in table 4.1 are based on the work of Raymond Goldsmith. They cover all short-term nonmortgage consumer debt, of which credit to purchase durable goods is one component. Total debt outstanding approximately doubled in each of the first two decades of the twentieth century. In the 1920s, outstanding debt again doubled, increasing from $3.3 billion in 1920 to over $7.6 billion in 1929. About half as much debt was outstanding in 1933 ($3.9 billion), after which time debt again grew rapidly, doubling in just six years. Per household, outstanding debt nearly tripled between 1900 and 1918 and nearly doubled during the

Table 4.1. Outstanding Short-Term Nonmortgage Consumer Debt, 1900-1939

	Outstanding Consumer Debt Nominal Values		Outstanding Consumer Debt Deflated by Price Index			
Year	Total (Million $)	Dollars per Household	Total (Millions of 1982 $)	1982 Dollars per Household	Additional 1982 Dollars per Household	Debt as a Percentage of Income
1900	659	41.21	7,564	472.98	-32.82	4.46
1901	728	44.54	8,027	491.12	18.13	4.40
1902	812	48.58	8,442	505.04	13.92	4.73
1903	894	52.26	8,905	520.52	15.48	4.95
1904	948	54.11	9,565	545.91	25.39	5.13
1905	1,046	58.31	9,991	556.97	11.06	5.18
1906	1,168	63.50	10,362	563.32	6.35	5.00
1907	1,269	67.27	9,651	511.63	-51.69	5.06
1908	1,257	65.15	9,183	475.96	-35.67	5.60
1909	1,432	72.57	10,982	556.49	80.54	5.37
1910	1,542	76.40	10,737	531.99	-24.50	5.74
1911	1,679	81.43	10,003	485.09	-46.90	6.01
1912	1,817	86.22	9,537	452.55	-32.54	5.91

Table 4.1, continued

Year	Outstanding Consumer Debt Nominal Values		Outstanding Consumer Debt Deflated by Price Index			
	Total (Million $)	Dollars per Household	Total (Millions of 1982 $)	1982 Dollars per Household	Additional 1982 Dollars per Household	Debt as a Percentage of Income
1913	1,927	89.19	9,030	417.92	-34.63	6.03
1914	2,037	92.13	9,749	440.93	23.01	6.91
1915	2,175	96.66	10,044	446.39	5.46	6.96
1916	2,423	105.69	10,799	471.03	24.64	6.22
1917	2,533	108.61	10,254	439.65	-31.38	5.41
1918	2,588	110.04	9,834	418.14	-21.51	4.24
1919	2,918	122.23	8,860	371.13	-47.02	4.64
1920	3,304	135.04	9,510	388.70	17.58	4.68
1921	3,249	129.34	9,678	385.27	-3.43	5.49
1922	3,469	135.05	10,862	422.87	37.60	5.89
1923	3,860	146.78	12,155	462.20	39.33	5.63
1924	4,159	154.37	13,619	505.52	43.32	5.95
1925	4,928	178.94	15,633	567.65	62.13	6.89

Table 4.1, continued

Year	Outstanding Consumer Debt Nominal Values		Outstanding Consumer Debt Deflated by Price Index			Debt as a Percentage of Income
	Total (Million $)	Dollars per Household	Total (Millions of 1982 $)	1982 Dollars per Household	Additional 1982 Dollars per Household	
1926	5,510	196.08	18,069	643.01	75.36	7.25
1927	5,714	199.57	18,839	657.95	14.95	7.54
1928	6,567	225.48	21,043	722.52	64.57	8.68
1929	7,628	257.86	24,096	814.54	92.02	9.34
1930	6,821	227.39	22,174	739.21	-75.34	9.34
1931	5,518	182.28	20,325	671.43	-67.78	8.77
1932	4,085	134.20	16,783	551.36	-120.06	8.51
1933	3,912	127.00	16,210	526.26	-25.11	8.71
1934	4,389	140.20	17,700	565.39	39.13	8.52
1935	5,434	170.39	22,912	718.42	153.03	9.39
1936	6,788	209.16	28,564	880.13	161.72	10.32
1937	7,480	226.06	30,159	911.48	31.35	10.61

Table 4.1, continued

| Year | Outstanding Consumer Debt Nominal Values | | Outstanding Consumer Debt Deflated by Price Index | | | Debt as a Percentage of Income |
	Total (Million $)	Dollars per Household	Total (Millions of 1982 $)	1982 Dollars per Household	Additional 1982 Dollars per Household	
1938	7,047	209.22	28,339	841.33	-70.15	10.88
1939	7,969	231.60	32,571	946.60	105.27	11.43
Averages for:						
1900-1916	1,401	70.31	9,563	496.81	-2.05	5.51
1920-1929	4,839	175.85	15,350	557.02	44.34	6.74
1922-1929	5,229	186.77	16,789	599.53	53.66	7.15
1930-1939	5,944	185.75	23,573	735.16	13.21	9.65

Sources: Outstanding short-term non-mortgage consumer debt (nominal values) from Goldsmith, *Study of Saving,* vol. 1, table D-1. Deflated by an index of prices of major durable goods developed as discussed in appendix A. Number of households from U.S. Bureau of the Census, *Historical Statistics,* Ser. A350, p. 43.

1920s. Before World War I, debt per household increased by an average of $4 per year. In the 1920s, annual increases of $14 per household were average.

Other patterns emerge when total debt is deflated by an index of prices of major durable goods. Doing so provides a rough measure of changes in how many goods were obtained with credit, a concept called "real debt." Because prices of major durables (goods most likely to be purchased with credit) increased before World War I more rapidly than did outstanding debt, real debt per household actually declined slightly between 1900 and 1918, as seen in table 4.1. Households acquired increasing quantities of goods on credit between 1901 and 1906 and again between 1914 and 1916. But their scaling back of the number of goods bought on credit in most other years resulted in an average annual drop in real debt per household between 1900 and 1916. In the 1920s, when prices of major durables were primarily constant and even falling slightly (though falling less rapidly than the prices of other goods and services, as noted in chapter 2), the amount of goods bought with credit increased enormously. Households reduced their debt loads during the Great Depression; by 1933, only two-thirds as much real debt was outstanding. Thereafter the growth of goods bought on credit was often even stronger than it had been in the 1920s.

Comparison of aggregate debt with aggregate annual income indicates the burden of debt on the economy's resources, particularly since all of this debt was under three years in maturity (Goldsmith's cutoff for "short-term" debt) and much of it matured in one year or less.[1] Debt as a percentage of income increased only gradually before World War I, as seen in figure 4.1, but then doubled in the 1920s. Unfortunately these estimates do not reveal the burden of debt on indebted households; the income estimate covers all American households but many households were debt-free. If only one-fifth of aggregate income was earned by indebted households, for instance, the burden of debt on just the indebted households would be five times as large as that indicated by figure 4.1. Similarly, since the number of households with debt probably rose during the 1920s, a doubling of the aggregate debt-to-income ratio does not mean each indebted household found its debt-to-income ratio doubled. Rather, this aggregate doubling reflects at least in part the initiation of many previously debt-free households into the credit economy.

Determining precisely what goods were purchased with all of this new

Figure 4.1. Debt as a Percentage of Income, 1900–1939

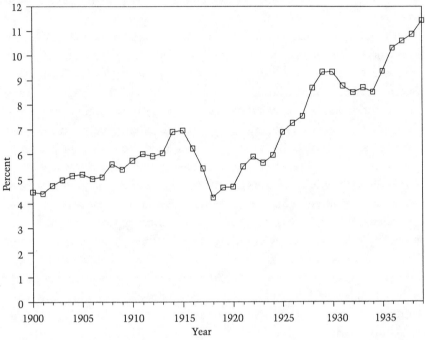

Source: Table 4.1

debt is difficult with the existing data. The Federal Reserve Board disaggregates outstanding debt by purpose of loan, but its figures do not include the pre–World War I years, as seen in table 4.2. Debt for buying cars increased phenomenally in the 1920s, with nearly five times as much debt outstanding in 1929 as in 1922. Since car prices fell somewhat during the 1920s, the increase in the number of cars purchased on credit must be even greater. Extensions of loans for buying cars fell off in each of the years 1930, 1931, and 1932 but then passed the 1929 peak by 1937. The combination of all other consumer goods debt also increased markedly in the 1920s; it more than tripled. When deflated by an index of prices of all major durables, the increase is similar.[2] Repair and modernization loans grew steadily if slowly until 1929 and then fell off each year until 1934, when passage of the National Housing Act first provided federal guarantees for these loans.

The trade association of sales finance companies, the National Associa-

Table 4.2. Outstanding Consumer Debt by Product Group, 1919-1939

Year	Outstanding Automobile Paper		Outstanding Other Consumer Goods Paper		Outstanding Repair and Modernization Loans		Total Outstanding Durable Goods Paper
	Total (Million $)	$ per Household	Total (Million $)	$ per Household	Total (Million $)	$ per Household	(Million $)
1919	304	12.73	409	17.13	5	0.21	718
1920	376	15.37	490	20.03	7	0.29	873
1921	317	12.62	484	19.27	9	0.36	810
1922	295	11.48	619	24.10	10	0.39	924
1923	526	20.00	684	26.01	12	0.46	1,222
1924	670	24.87	779	28.92	16	0.59	1,465
1925	914	33.19	951	34.53	22	0.80	1,887
1926	977	34.77	1,083	38.54	24	0.85	2,084
1927	765	26.72	1,183	41.32	26	0.91	1,974
1928	1,134	38.94	1,331	45.70	28	0.96	2,493
1929	1,384	46.79	1,544	52.19	27	0.91	2,955
1930	986	32.87	1,432	47.74	25	0.83	2,443
1931	684	22.60	1,214	40.10	22	0.73	1,920
1932	356	11.70	834	27.40	18	0.59	1,208

Table 4.2, continued

Year	Outstanding Automobile Paper		Outstanding Other Consumer Goods Paper		Outstanding Repair and Modernization Loans		Total Outstanding Durable Goods Paper (Million $)
	Total (Million $)	$ per Household	Total (Million $)	$ per Household	Total (Million $)	$ per Household	
1933	493	16.01	799	25.94	15	0.49	1,307
1934	614	19.61	889	28.40	37	1.18	1,540
1935	992	31.10	1,000	31.36	253	7.93	2,245
1936	1,372	42.28	1,290	39.75	364	11.22	3,026
1937	1,494	45.15	1,505	45.48	219	6.62	3,218
1938	1,099	32.63	1,442	42.81	218	6.47	2,759
1939	1,497	43.51	1,620	47.08	298	8.66	3,415

Sources: Board of Governors of the Federal Reserve System, "Consumer Credit," table 1, cols. 3, 4, and 5. Number of households from U.S. Bureau of the Census, Historical Statistics, Ser. A350, p. 43.

tion of Finance Companies (NAFC), regularly published estimates of the number of cars and trucks sold on installments. Their figures cover all vehicles—those sold to businesses as well as those sold to households. To estimate how many vehicles were purchased by households only, we follow the Department of Commerce convention in assuming that 30 percent of total vehicle sales are to businesses and the remainder are to households. These estimates for the 1920s and 1930s are reprinted in table 4.3. If we further assume installment selling was allocated similarly and that no household bought more than one auto per year on installments, we find that 5 percent of households purchased an auto on credit in 1919 but fully 15 percent did so just ten years later in 1929. In that same year, nearly one-quarter of all American households purchased a vehicle, whether on time or with cash.[3]

The NAFC estimates in table 4.3 also indicate that up to 70 percent of new cars and 65 percent of used cars were purchased on installments in the 1920s. In a 1927 study commissioned by General Motors, Edwin Seligman estimated that the extent of financing was somewhat higher, with over 75 percent of new autos purchased with credit.[4] Drawing on work by Milan Ayres (staff researcher for NAFC), Seligman further ventured that by 1925 over 70 percent of furniture, 75 percent of radios, 90 percent of pianos, 80 percent of phonographs, 25 percent of jewelry, and about 80 percent of household appliances were purchased with credit.[5]

The Census Bureau surveyed retail establishments in 1929 and again in 1939 to determine the extent of credit selling. Their estimates indicate that by 1929 credit financing of purchases of major durable goods and jewelry was widespread. Table 4.4 gives estimates of the percentage of total retail sales of all types of consumer goods that were made on a credit basis in 1929 and on an installment credit basis in 1939.

NEED FOR CREDIT

Without credit financing, households must purchase expensive goods with cash by decreasing either their other consumption or saving. Cash purchase of many major durable goods commanded a large share of the average household's disposable income. In the 1920s, a Chevrolet cost about 20 percent of annual household income, and a Chrysler could cost over 60

Table 4.3. Sales of Automobiles to Households, 1919-1939

Year	Number of New Cars Sold to Households	Number of Used Cars Sold to Households	Percent Sold on Installments:		Percent of Households Buying on Installments:		Percent of Households Buying Any Car: Cash or Credit
			New Cars	Used Cars	New Cars	All Cars	
1919	1,295,687	760,568	64.9	44.5	3.5	4.9	8.6
1920	1,439,642	935,767	61.6	47.6	3.6	5.4	9.7
1921	1,089,150	766,761	63.9	50.7	2.8	4.3	7.4
1922	1,712,498	1,179,912	63.7	51.6	4.2	6.6	11.3
1923	2,655,248	1,816,190	65.0	54.8	6.6	10.3	17.0
1924	2,322,019	2,117,681	70.4	57.4	6.1	10.6	16.5
1925	2,686,456	2,654,218	68.2	62.8	6.7	12.7	19.4
1926	2,790,199	2,494,437	64.5	65.2	6.4	12.2	18.8
1927	2,098,660	2,486,912	58.0	63.6	4.3	9.8	16.0
1928	2,648,406	3,098,635	58.1	60.8	5.3	11.8	19.7
1929	3,229,005	3,920,840	60.9	64.7	6.6	15.2	24.2
1930	2,064,483	3,164,816	61.1	64.6	4.2	11.0	17.4
1931	1,503,727	2,565,500	62.8	60.4	3.1	8.2	13.4
1932	877,030	1,630,399	54.6	47.0	1.6	4.1	8.2

Table 4.3, continued

| Year | Number of New Cars Sold to Households | Number of Used Cars Sold to Households | Percent Sold on Installments: | | Percent of Households Buying on Installments: | | Percent of Households Buying Any Car: Cash or Credit |
			New Cars	Used Cars	New Cars	All Cars	
1933	936,620	1,316,197	56.8	56.8	1.7	4.2	7.3
1934	1,369,118	1,638,169	54.4	57.9	2.4	5.4	9.6
1935	1,610,000	2,003,834	58.0	62.6	2.9	6.9	11.3
1936	2,193,103	2,819,145	60.9	58.5	4.1	9.2	15.4
1937	2,137,937	2,857,072	57.2	60.1	3.7	8.9	15.1
1938	1,109,231	2,091,833	52	60	1.7	5.4	9.5
1939	1,502,407	2,401,875	54	64	2.4	6.8	11.3

Sources: Sales to households are 70 percent of total sales. Total sales figures for 1919-32 from NAFC, *NAFC News* 65 (May 1933): 4; for 1933-37 from NASFC, "Composite Experience, 1937;" for 1938-39 from NASFC, "Composite Experience, 1939." Percentage sold on installments also given in these three sources. Number of households used to calculate percentages in last three columns from U.S. Bureau of the Census, *Historical Statistics*, Ser. A350, p. 43.

Table 4.4. Retail Sales on Credit, 1929 and 1939 (Percent of Total Sales Volume)

	1929	1939	
Type of Store	Credit Sales (Min. - Max.)	Credit Sales	Installment Credit Sales
TOTAL SALES	30 - 38	34	11
FOOD GROUP:			
Confectionery (Candy)	3 - 5	2	0
Dairy (Milk & Eggs)	20 - 25		
Milk & Dairy Products		65	0
Egg & Poultry		10	0
Delicatessens	4 - 6	4	0
Fruits & Vegetables	8 - 11	6	0
Groceries without Meats	14 - 17	18	0
Groceries & Meats		25	0
Groceries with Meat	24 - 29		
Meats with Groceries	30 - 38		
Fish & Meat Markets		17	0
Fish	19 - 24		
Meats	18 - 24		
Bakeries	8 - 11	10	0
GENERAL MERCHANDISE:			
Department Stores		41	15
Department with Food	32 - 39		
Department without Food	38 - 47		
Dry Goods & General Merchandise		22	4
Dry Goods	14 - 19		
General Merchandise with Food	38 - 47		

Table 4.4, continued

| | 1929 | 1939 | |
Type of Store	Credit Sales (Min. - Max.)	Credit Sales	Installment Credit Sales
General Merchandise without Food	12 - 17		
Variety	0 - 1	0	0
AUTOMOTIVE GROUP:			
Auto Salesrooms	**44 - 54**		
New Autos		**56**	**42**
Used Autos		**51**	**47**
Accessories & Tires		**54**	**15**
Auto Accessories	**20 - 25**		
Tire Shops	**29 - 36**		
Filling Stations		25	1
Filling St (gas & oil)	17 - 24		
Filling St (with tires)	20 - 26		
Filling St (with other)	13 - 18		
Garages	23 - 29		
APPAREL GROUP:			
Men's & Boy's Clothes	8 - 10		
Men's Furnishings	6 - 8	7	1
Men's Clothes & Furnishings	24 - 31	33	7
Family Clothes	39 - 49	47	20
Women's Ready-to-Wear	30 - 37	32	2
Women's Furs	32 - 40	57	20
Women's Millinery	9 - 12	8	0
Custom Tailors		44	4
Shoe Stores		8	0
Men's Shoes	3 - 3		

| | 1929 | 1939 | |
Type of Store	Credit Sales (Min. - Max.)	Credit Sales	Installment Credit Sales
Women's Shoes	11 - 14		
Family Shoes	8 - 11		
FURNITURE & HOUSEHOLD:			
Furniture	**65 - 79**	**79**	**58**
Floor Coverings, Drapes		**41**	**5**
Other Home Furnishings		**55**	**24**
Household Appliances		**78**	**63**
Appliances (Electric only)	**62 - 75**		
Appliances	**63 - 77**		
Radio--Household Appliances		**66**	**48**
Radio Stores--other		**56**	**34**
Radio & Electrical	**51 - 63**		
Radio & Musical Instruments	**64 - 77**		
LUMBER AND BUILDING:			
Lumber, etc.	63 - 78	81	2
Electrical Supply	50 - 61	60	6
Heating & Plumbing		64	14
Heating Appliances	52 - 63		
Plumbing	52 - 65		
Paint, Glass, Wallpaper	45 - 55	56	0
OTHER RETAIL STORES:			
Hardware	**37 - 45**	**44**	**5**
Farm Implements & Hardware		59	28
Feed, Grain, & Hay	34 - 43	47	0

Table 4.4, continued

Type of Store	1929 Credit Sales (Min. - Max.)	1939 Credit Sales	1939 Installment Credit Sales
Book Stores	**42 - 52**	**51**	**21**
Cigar Stores without Fountains	4 - 5	3	0
Fuel, Ice, Fuel Oil		62	2
Coal & Wood Yards	52 - 64		
Drugstores without Fountains	9 - 14	10	0
Drugstores with Fountains	6 - 10	9	0
Florists	39 - 47	47	0
Camera Dealers	**46 - 55**	**38**	**2**
Jewelry Stores		**57**	**34**
Jewelry (install. credit)	**70 - 85**		
Jewelry (other)	**34 - 43**		
Music without Radio	**43 - 53**		
Office Supply & Equipment		81	9
Office Mechanical Appliances	74 - 90		
Office Furniture & Equipment	56 - 69		
Sporting Goods Stores		**34**	**3**
Sport Goods Specialty	**32 - 39**		
Sport with Toys & Stationery	**28 - 36**		
Stationers	46 - 56	43	1
News Dealers		8	0
Opticians		**25**	**5**
Other Retail Stores		42	16
Second-Hand Stores		20	6

Sources: Retail sales on credit, 1929, derived from U.S. Bureau of the Census, *Fifteenth Census: 1930. Retail Distribution, Part I*, table 7A, pp. 72-73, which reports sales volume classified by percentage of business that stores transacted with credit. For example, stores that did 1 to 10 percent

Table 4.4, continued

of their business with credit had net sales of $3,474 million in 1929. Of this amount, between 1 and 10 percent were credit sales (between $34.7 and $347.4 million), and the remainder were cash sales. The "minimum" estimate in this table uses the lower bound percent of credit sales (1 percent in this example) for each classification; the "maximum" estimate uses the upper bound (10 percent in this example) for each classification. There are nine classifications: stores selling entirely for cash, stores conducting 1 to 10 percent of their business on a credit basis, 11 to 20 percent, 21 to 30 percent, . . . , 71 to 80 percent, and over 80 percent of their business on a credit basis. Retail credit sales, 1939, from U.S. Bureau of the Census, *Sixteenth Census: 1940. Retail Trade: 1939, Part I*, table 8A, p. 106, col. 11. Retail installment credit sales, 1939, derived from ibid., table 9A ("Analysis of Credit Sales, by Kinds of Business"), p. 108.

Note: Figures in **bold print** are for durable goods.

percent of a year's pay. These and further examples appear in table 4.5. In general in the 1920s, the advertised price of a car was 20 to 40 percent of the average annual disposable income of a household, a radio or phonograph cost up to 25 percent of annual disposable income, and a piano cost at least 25 percent.

The income estimates in table 4.5 are aggregate disposable income divided by the number of households. Comparing prices with disposable income when income is broken down by income group would more clearly demonstrate the enormous drain that cash purchase of expensive durable goods placed on the economic resources of many households. Income distribution in the United States was far from equal in the 1920s. Average disposable income of the farm population was approximately 40 percent of the economy-wide average throughout the decade; average disposable income of the lower 95 percent of the nonfarm population was about 85 to 90 percent of the averages given in table 4.5.[6] In the 1920s, therefore, advertised car prices equaled, on average, from 20 to 45 percent of annual disposable income of the bulk of nonfarm families but 50 to 100 percent of annual disposable income of farm households.

Suppose an average household decided to purchase a mid-priced car, one costing 30 percent of its annual disposable income. How long would it have taken to save up this much money? The answer depends largely upon saving rates. The number of years of saving required equals the car's price as a percentage of annual disposable income divided by the percentage of disposable income that is saved for purchasing the car.[7] Between 1898 and 1916, the average saving rate in the United States (nominal personal sav-

Table 4.5. Prices of Durable Goods Compared with Disposable Income, Selected Years, 1906-1940

Year	Annual Disposable Income per Household ($)	Product Advertised	Advertised Price(s) or Range of Prices ($)	Product Price as Percent of Annual Household Disposable Income
1906	1,282	Heating stove	10 & up	0.8 & up
		Tiffany jewelry	25 - 150	2.0 - 11.7
1907	1,340	Piano	500 & 750	37.3 & 56.0
		Watch	2 - 36	0.1 - 2.7
1908	1,174	Sewing machine	33	2.8
1909	1,362	Electric car	2,250	165.2
		Hoosier cabinet	1 per week	3.8
		Phonograph	12.50 - 125	0.9 - 9.2
1911	1,367	Cooking stove	6.50 & up	0.5 & up
		Piano	500 & 550	36.5 & 40.0
1913	1,491	Player piano	750	50.3
		Phonograph	10 - 500	0.7 - 33.5
1918	2,619	Electric sewing machine	39.50	1.5
		Phonograph	20 - 2,100	0.8 - 80.0
		Victrola	12 - 950	0.5 - 36.3
1920	2,914	Phonograph	25 - 2,500	0.9 - 86
		Vacuum sweeper	9 - 17.50	0.3 - 0.6
1922	2,312	Dodge auto	980	42.4
		Victrola	25 - 1,500	1.1 - 64.9
		Phonograph	65 - 775	2.8 - 33.5
		Diamond rings	31 - 435	1.3 - 18.8
1923	2,628	Overland auto	525 - 860	20.0 - 32.7
		Dodge auto	880	33.5
		Piano	635 & up	24 & up
		Victrola	250 & 290	9.5 & 11.0

Table 4.5, continued

Year	Annual Disposable Income per Household ($)	Product Advertised	Advertised Price(s) or Range of Prices ($)	Product Price as Percent of Annual Household Disposable Income
1925	2,621	Electric iron	7.50	0.3
		Radio	50 - 460	1.9 - 17.6
1926	2,727	Chevrolet auto	510 - 765	18.7 - 28.0
		Dodge auto	895 - 1,075	32.8 - 39.4
		Chrysler auto	1,075 - 1,275	39.4 - 46.8
		Electric vacuum	34.50 & 39	1.3 & 1.4
1928	2,620	Chevrolet auto	495 - 715	18.9 - 27.3
		Dodge auto	995 - 1,295	38.0 - 49.4
		Chrysler auto	1,040 - 1,655	39.7 - 63.2
		Piano	875 & up	33.4 & up
		Radio	77	1.3
1930	2,461	Plymouth auto	535 - 695	21.7 - 28.2
		Chrysler auto	1,495 - 1,665	60.7 - 67.7
		Buick auto	1,025 - 2,035	41.6 - 82.7
		Electric refrigerator	205	8.3
		Gas cook range	99.75	4.1
1931	2,103	Chevrolet auto	475 - 650	22.6 - 30.9
		Chrysler auto	885 - 3,575	42.1 - 170.0
		Cadillac auto	3,795 & up	180.5 & up
		Electric washer	37.50	1.8
1933	1,479	Dodge auto	595 & up	40.2 & up
1935	1,834	Electric refrigerator	77.50 & up	4.2 & up
1937	2,144	Radio	29.95 - 89.95	1.4 - 4.2

Table 4.5, continued

Year	Annual Disposable Income per Household ($)	Product Advertised	Advertised Price(s) or Range of Prices ($)	Product Price as Percent of Annual Household Disposable Income
1939	2,035	Electric mixer	23.75	1.2
		Diamonds	100 - 1,750	4.9 - 86.0
1940	2,143	Electric range	100 & 129.95	4.7 & 6.1

Sources: Aggregate disposable income from table 2.8. Number of households from U.S. Bureau of the Census, *Historical Statistics*, Ser. A350, p. 43. Prices of durable goods from advertisements in October issues of *Ladies Home Journal*.

ing as a percentage of nominal disposable personal income) was 6.4 percent. If a household saved 6.4 percent of its monthly disposable income and, making the extreme assumption, earmarked all of this saving for the car, 57 months of saving would have been necessary to accumulate enough money to buy the car with cash. A less expensive item costing "only" 20 percent of annual disposable income would, under the same assumptions, have required 38 months of saving. These time frames are only indicative, of course, but more accurate information (the typical ratios between durable goods prices and household income, the saving rate by income class, the share of saving designated for future purchases of durable goods) will no doubt confirm that in the 1920s, a "typical" American household needed to save for two to five years in order to purchase a major durable good with cash.

WHO EXTENDED CREDIT

Before World War I, the options for formal household borrowing included primarily money borrowing through banks, small loan institutes (also known as industrial banks or societies), or pawnbrokers, and installment buying. Installment credit was generally extended only by sellers or manufacturers of consumer goods. Furniture sales were often carried on open account by the seller. Installment sales of pianos were frequently financed by the seller. And installment sales of Singer sewing machines had been offered by Singer since 1856. Banks rarely lent money directly to households wishing to purchase durable goods, although they would extend short-term loans to sellers and manufacturers who were carrying customers' notes.

Merchants who carried open accounts receivables might sell these notes to a credit agent. Credit agents often adopted a non-notification policy under which customers were not notified of transactions between the merchant and the agent. Many merchants in fact insisted upon non-notification, afraid nonbank financing of their accounts receivables might be interpreted by customers and neighbors as a sign of poor business acumen that had led to denial of bank credit.[8] Furniture stores placed great importance on serving as their own collection agents, regardless of the ultimate source of the credit they extended. Furniture merchants argued that a customer's monthly visit to make a payment at the service desk (typically at the very back of the store) provided their sales staff a monthly opportunity to sell an additional piece of furniture.[9]

In the 1920s, the bulk of installment credit extended to households was done so not by sellers nor directly by manufacturers but by sales finance companies, specialized financial institutions that purchase retail time-sales contracts from sellers and sometimes also make wholesale inventory loans to them. Sales finance companies are separate corporate entities from both manufacturers and sellers of products. Their financial activity involves money lending only when they extend inventory loans to sellers. Their retail financing, by contrast, entails absolutely no money lending. In an installment sale, a buyer provides a down payment to the seller and then signs a contract promising to pay the remaining balance (plus charges) in regular, usually monthly, installments. The seller in turn sells this contract to a sales finance company. The buyer has received no money but has issued a promise-to-pay in exchange for current possession of a good. The seller has not borrowed money but has sold an asset (the buyer's promise-to-pay) to a sales finance company. No money has been lent.

Usury limits that apply to money lending rates do not apply to installment financing. Absent legislation particular to installment sales contracts, there are no legal limits on the extent of installment financing charges. The other primary means of buying a good on time is a chattel mortgage, the lending of money with an IOU secured by personal property. Chattel mortgages *are* subject to usury laws.

Not only the application of usury limits but also default consequences differ between chattel mortgages and installment buying. When a borrower fails to make payments on a chattel mortgage, the property securing the loan is sold and the proceeds used to pay off any remaining balance (plus attorney's and other collection fees). Any excess proceeds are returned to the borrower. By contrast, default on an installment contract brings repossession of the good that was being purchased with no financial compensation to the buyer.[10] The loss of wealth upon default can therefore be much greater with installment buying than with borrowing under a chattel mortgage.

Before 1924, sales finance companies bought installment contracts for automobile sales on a "full recourse" basis under which auto dealers were responsible for completing an installment contract if a buyer failed to meet his or her contractual obligation. Beginning in 1924, many independent finance companies began to purchase installment contracts on a "no recourse" basis, relieving dealers of all financial responsibility should a buyer fail to make installment payments. Under this arrangement, finance companies repossessed autos as necessary and bore any resulting financial loss. To guard against dealers writing contracts with poor credit risks, the "repurchase" arrangement soon developed under which a finance company still oversaw any repossession, but dealers were obligated to repurchase any repossessed automobile at a price equal to the remaining balance of the installment contract.[11]

Sales finance companies, which dominated installment credit markets by 1929, are essentially a twentieth-century creation. They are patterned after the credit agents who bought notes from merchants carrying their customers' open accounts. Most independent sales finance companies were established solely to purchase installment contracts and in many cases to also underwrite merchants' inventory financing.

We must look to the 1930s for evidence of the relative extent of consumer financing by finance companies. Reproduced in table 4.6 are David Robbins's estimates of how the volume of installment loans was distributed among each of several types of lending institutions. In 1929, 40 percent of consumer installment loans (which includes installment contracts bought by sales finance companies as well as personal installment loans) were written by finance companies and just over 5 percent by commercial banks. While the volume of lending extended by finance companies nearly

Table 4.6. Installment Loan Volume by Type of Financial Institution

	Millions of Dollars Lent			Share of Total Lending (Percent)	
Year	Commercial Banks	Finance Companies	Total Volume	Commercial Banks	Finance Companies
1929	63	463	1,148	5.5	40.3
1930	66	485	1,130	5.8	42.9
1931	57	494	1,063	5.4	46.5
1932	46	393	812	5.7	48.4
1933	43	322	669	6.4	48.1
1934	69	413	897	7.7	46.0
1935	130	455	1,344	9.7	33.8
1936	248	610	1,929	12.9	31.6
1937	368	662	2,045	18.0	32.4
1938	460	664	2,170	21.2	30.6
1939	680	827	2,686	25.3	30.8
1940	1,017	912	3,293	30.9	27.7
1941	1,198	975	3,631	33.0	26.8
1942	792	784	2,700	29.3	29.0
1943	639	800	2,360	27.1	33.9
1944	749	869	2,548	29.4	34.1
1945	942	956	2,947	32.0	32.4
1946	1,793	1,231	4,593	39.0	26.8
1947	2,636	1,432	6,401	41.2	22.4
1948	3,069	1,534	7,442	41.2	20.6
1949	3,282	1,737	8,132	40.4	21.4

Source: Robbins, Consumer Instalment Loans, tables 3 and 4, pp. 17 and 19.

doubled over the next decade, lending by commercial banks increased tenfold. By 1939, fully 25 percent of the volume of lending was written by commercial banks and only 30 percent by finance companies.[12]

From a customer's perspective, sales financing of durable goods was arranged by the dealer or seller. The practices in the auto industry were typical. Dealers had two prices for every car: a cash price and a higher time price equal to the cash price plus all charges associated with time payment.[13] For cars, the standard cash plus trade-in down payment was one-third of the cash price or 30 percent of the time price for a new car and 40 percent of the cash price for used cars.[14] Added to the amount financed (the cash price minus down payment) were finance charges, dealer and loss reserves, and an insurance premium. Dealer reserves were returned to the dealer to cover losses incurred upon buyer default. Loss reserves were retained by the finance company to cover their repossession costs. Insurance against fire and theft risk was required. Upon receipt of the contract, the sales finance company paid the dealer the amount financed plus dealer reserves but held back a small percentage of this amount to be paid to the dealer only when the buyer completed all payments.[15] Buyers generally made each payment directly to the sales finance company, not to the dealer.

Figure 4.2 is a typical retail installment sales contract.[16] Daniel Harrington purchased a used car for $670 in 1931. He provided a $150 cash down payment plus $100 in trade-in. Added to the $420 remaining to be financed were a $46.00 finance charge (simple interest of 11 percent), $9.00 in reserves, and a $12.50 insurance premium. The total amount due, $487.50, was payable in ten monthly installments. The dealer sold the retail contract to a sales finance company, which paid the dealer $400 after processing the contract and deferred payment of an additional $20 until Mr. Harrington successfully completed all payments.

In 1920, less than 100 sales finance companies were in operation. At the end of 1928, there were well over 1,000.[17] Many of these new companies disappeared within the next several years, though NAFC was quick to note that their disappearance caused little financial loss to the banks who had lent them working capital.[18]

The 1935 NAFC directory lists 207 member companies, many with multiple branch offices. Of these, 92 percent offered motor vehicles fi-

Figure 4.2. A Sample Installment Sales Contract

MAKE	SERIAL NUMBER	MOTOR NUMBER	STYLE	YEAR	MODEL	NEW OR USED	ACCOUNT NUMBER
PONTIAC	1,578,900	1,876,657	coupe	30	6-60	USED	D60-78670

PURCHASER	AGE	OCCUPATION	DAY DUE	CHECK OR DRAFT	PLAN
HARRINGTON, DANIEL H.	30	SALESMAN	15	400.00	R-C-NR

ADDRESS	HOME PHONE	NO. INST.	DEFERRED CERT.	S. S. APPR.
8950 KILPATRICK AVENUE	N C 678	10	20.00	400.00

CITY AND STATE	BUSINESS PHONE	AMT. EA. INST.	INSURANCE COST	SELLING PRICE
NILES CENTER, ILLINOIS	WHI 5700	48.90	12.50	670.00

EMPLOYER AND ADDRESS	FINAL INST.	RESERVE-LOSSES	DOWN PAT.-CASH
NATIONAL TEA CO., 1400 CROSBY ST.	47.40	5.00	150.00

CO. NO.	AMOUNT OF FIRE AND THEFT INSURANCE	RESERVE-DEALER	DOWN PAT.-TRADE
	FIVE HUNDRED - - - - - - - - - DOLLARS	4.00	100.00

SYM.	INSURANCE IN FORCE	GARAGE ☒ PUBLIC ☐ PRIVATE	UNPAID BALANCE
R	FROM NOON 6-15-31 TO NOON 6-15-32	8900 LINCOLN AV	420.00

ACCOUNT NUMBER	DATE PURCHASED	DATE OF NOTE	NET FINANCE CHARGE	FINANCE CHARGE
D60-78670	6-17-31	6-15-32	46.00	67.50

SCHEDULE OF INSTALLMENTS AND DATE PAID — IRREGULAR REMITTANCES — FEES — COLL. MEMO.

	DUE DATES	AMT. EA. INST.	DATE PAID	BALANCE	DATE	REF.	AMOUNT	BALANCE	PD.	AMOUNT	1	2	3	4
	TOTAL AMOUNT OF NOTE			487.50										
1	7-15-31	48.90		438.60										
2	8-15	48.90		389.70										
3	9-15	48.90		340.80										
4	10-15	48.90		291.90										
5	11-15	48.90		243.00										
6	12-15	48.90		194.10										
7	1-15-32	48.90		145.20										
8	2-15	48.90		96.30										
9	3-15	48.90		47.40										
10	4-15	47.40		0.00										

Designed in Cooperation with the National Association of Finance Companies by La Salle-Crittenden Press, Inc., 220 E. Illinois St., Chicago — Form C.M.A.

nancing and 50 percent offered a diversified line that included "financing of mechanical refrigerators, radios, air conditioners, oil burners, automatic stokers, household facilities, pumps, dairy equipment, and other chattels."[19] There were 604 offices of member companies scattered throughout the United States, with at least one office in every state but Wyoming. States with at least ten sales finance company offices in 1935 are shown in table 4.7. The distribution of sales finance company offices across the 48 states mirrors the distribution of population. The ten states with the greatest number of finance companies are all in the top fifteen in terms of population. A simple regression of the distribution of sales finance compa-

Table 4.7. Sales Finance Company Offices by State, 1935 (States with Ten or More Offices Only)

State	Sales Finance Company Offices		State's 1935 Total Population	
	Number	Percent of Total	Thousands	Percent of Total
New York	65	10.8	13,026	10.2
Pennsylvania	49	8.1	9,765	7.7
Illinois	40	6.6	7,763	6.1
Ohio	40	6.6	6,776	5.3
Texas	31	5.1	6,113	4.8
Massachusetts	23	3.8	4,283	3.4
California	22	3.6	6,262	4.9
Indiana	22	3.6	3,332	2.6
New Jersey	22	3.6	4,100	3.2
Tennessee	17	2.8	2,762	2.2
Wisconsin	17	2.8	3,037	2.4
Connecticut	16	2.6	1,657	1.3
Michigan	16	2.6	5,045	4.0
Missouri	16	2.6	3,706	2.9
Florida	13	2.2	1,669	1.3
Iowa	12	2.0	2,504	2.0
Nebraska	12	2.0	1,347	1.1
Kansas	11	1.8	1,841	1.4
Minnesota	11	1.8	2,676	2.1
Georgia	10	1.7	3,015	2.4
Maryland	10	1.7	1,724	1.4
North Carolina	10	1.7	3,365	2.6
Virginia	10	1.7	2,547	2.0

Source: Member sales finance company offices listed in NASFC, *Directory*. Population estimates derived from a geometric interpolation of the 1930 and 1940 state population figures in U.S. Bureau of the Census, *Historical Statistics*, Ser. A195, pp. 24-37.

nies across states on the 1935 distribution of population explains 91 percent of the variance in the distribution of sales finance companies.[20]

DEMAND OR SUPPLY SHIFTS

Does this rise in the use of consumer credit reflect changes in demand for credit only? Again we turn to the economists' demand and supply framework to clarify the issues. Whether it is supply or demand for credit that shifts, increased use of credit results. If credit was a *cause* of the Consumer Durables Revolution, it must be that the supply of credit increased independent of demand for credit. On the other hand, if greater use of credit was simply an *effect* of an otherwise-caused Consumer Durables Revolution, only demand for credit shifted. Figure 4.3 illustrates the point.

Resolution of the issue, as the figures imply, could be obtained by studying the behavior of the price of credit over time. If the price of consumer credit decreased relative to other prices, supply shifts probably explain greater use of credit. If the price rose relative to other prices, demand probably shifted.[21]

Measuring the price of credit is a thorny endeavor, both theoretically and empirically. What "price" do borrowing households consider? A strong contender is monthly borrowing costs. Monthly borrowing costs associated with purchase of some good of fixed price depend jointly on the effective annual interest rate, the required down payment, and the loan or contract maturity. Decreasing effective interest rates unambiguously decreases monthly borrowing costs. Decreasing the down payment reduces the amount of money needed to initiate the credit transaction but increases monthly borrowing costs. Spreading payments over a longer period decreases monthly borrowing costs but for an amortized loan increases total interest charges over the life of the loan.[22] Accurate theoretical specification of the price of credit requires resolving these apparent contradictions.[23]

Theoretical issues aside, empirical evidence on these credit variables is sketchy at best for the early twentieth century. The evidence generally points to an easing of terms after World War I as contract maturities lengthened and to some extent required down payments fell. In response

Figure 4.3. Supply or Demand Shifts?

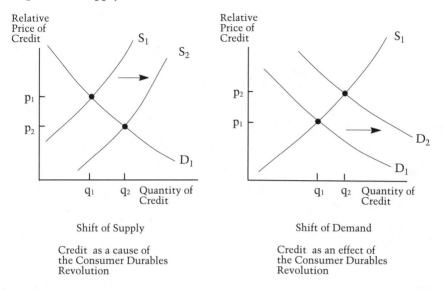

Shift of Supply

Credit as a cause of
the Consumer Durables
Revolution

Shift of Demand

Credit as an effect of
the Consumer Durables
Revolution

to changes in the early 1920s in required down payments and maturity of
installment contracts, NAFC adopted uniform standards for automobile
contracts in 1924: minimum down payments of one-third of the cash price
for new cars and 40 percent for used cars, and maximum contract maturity
of 12 months for all types of cars.[24] Some dealers continued to write new
car contracts with 18-month maturities, however, and by the mid-1930s
this had become the new standard contract length.[25] Down payments for
most other major durable goods averaged 15 percent of the cash purchase
price in the mid-1920s, though the down payment was 10 percent for
washing and sewing machines and 25 percent for radios and phonographs.
Contract maturities ranged from 6 months for radios to 24 months for
pianos; for most products the range was between 12 and 18 months.[26]

By 1934, terms had eased slightly for goods other than autos. NAFC
standards now recommended 10 percent minimum down payment for radios and household appliances; 24-month maximum maturity for refrigerators, stokers, oil burners, and heating equipment; 15-month maximum
maturity for washers and ironers; and 12-month maximum for vacuum
cleaners and radios.[27] A 1932 survey of NAFC members reveals quite a
range in actual practice, however, as noted in table 4.8. Down payments

Table 4.8. Down Payments Required and Maximum Contract Maturity, NAFC Member Companies, 1932

Product	Number of Reports	Percent Down Payment			Months Maturity		
		High	Low	Most Com-mon	High	Low	Most Com-mon
Appliances, Electric	4	25	10	--	12	12	12
Automatic Refrigerators	48	40	0	25	30	12	24
Automobile Tires	2	25	25	25	5	3	--
Coal Stokers	8	33.3	10	10	24	12	24
Furniture and Household Goods	8	33.3	5	20	18	12	18
Home Improvements	13	25	0	5	30	12	24
Musical Instruments	5	20	10	20	18	12	--
Oil Burners	14	25	10	10	24	12	18
Radios	93	40	0	10	24	10	12
Stoves and Ranges	5	50	25	--	18	12	12
Washing Machines	29	25	0	10	24	12	12

Source: NAFC, "Diversified Financing Methods." From a voluntary survey of NAFC member companies. "Number Reports" is the number of companies offering this line of financing that responded to the survey.

on radios range from 0 to 40 percent, with 10 percent most commonly charged. The range is the same for refrigerators, but here a 25 percent down payment is most common. Maturity for radio contracts ranges from 10 to 24 months, with 12 months the most common length. For refrigerators, the range is 12 to 30 months, with 24 months the most common length of contract.[28]

Effective interest rates apparently fell in the late 1920s and then fell further in the 1930s. Assessing interest on the full amount financed but spreading payments over the life of the contract was a common practice in the 1920s. As a result, the effective annual interest rate paid on an installment sales contract was much higher than the rate of the finance charge.

Daniel Harrington made monthly payments of $48.90 on his installment contract, which financed $420 (see figure 4.2). Including insurance, he therefore paid an effective annual interest rate of 34.4 percent on the $420 financed. The effective interest rate is computed assuming each monthly payment covers interest accumulated on the outstanding principal plus a payment to reduce outstanding principal. For example, had Mr. Harrington borrowed $420 at 34.4 percent, his first monthly payment of $48.90 would have covered interest in the amount of $12.04 (420 times 0.344 divided by 12) and principal of $36.86. His second payment of $48.90 would have covered interest of $10.98 (remaining principal of $388.14 [420 less 36.86] times 0.344 divided by 12) and principal of $37.92. His loan would have been paid off after 10 months.

An effective interest rate of 34 percent is consistent with the findings of other studies of interwar consumer finance. For the 1920s, Clyde Phelps cites estimates of annual discount rates of 12 to 24 percent for new automobile purchases.[29] Seligman's estimates are somewhat lower: 10 to 15 percent annual discount rates for the late 1920s.[30] Discount rates are applied to the amount financed; even without additional charges, effective annual interest rates are nearly double these discount rates when (as was the case in the 1920s) the contract is written for 12 months. Evans Clark found effective interest rates (excluding insurance) in 1930 of about 16 percent for new automobiles, 25 percent for household equipment, 20 percent for radios, and 12 percent for pianos.[31] But Margaret Reid's estimates for the early 1930s are sometimes much higher: effective interest rates (including insurance) ranged from 22 to 33 percent for new automobiles, 35 to 47 percent for used automobiles, 6 to 56 percent for furniture, 8 to 52 percent for refrigerators, 0 to 69 percent for cooking ranges, and 12 to 98 percent for radios.[32]

In 1932, NAFC noted that finance charges assessed by their member companies generally increased with maturity of contract, ranging from 6 percent for a 4-month contract to 23.5 percent for 39 months and increasing one-half percentage point with each additional month added to the contract.[33] Effective annual interest rates derived from NAFC's table of standard finance charges are given in table 4.9. For a standard 12-month contract, the finance charges are 10 percent of the amount financed, which reflects an effective annual interest rate of 18 percent. Charges for

Table 4.9. Finance Charges and Effective Interest Rates Assessed by
NAFC Member Companies, 1932

Maturity in Months	Total Finance Charge (%)	Total Amount Due on $100 Contract ($)	Monthly Payments on $100 Contract ($)	Effective Annual Interest Rate (%)
4	6.0	106.00	26.50	28.5
5	6.5	106.50	21.30	25.6
6	7.0	107.00	17.83	23.5
7	7.5	107.50	15.36	22.1
8	8.0	108.00	13.50	21.0
9	8.5	108.50	12.06	20.0
10	9.0	109.00	10.90	19.1
11	9.5	109.50	9.95	18.5
12	10.0	110.00	9.17	18.0
13	10.5	110.50	8.50	17.5
14	11.0	111.00	7.93	17.1
15	11.5	111.50	7.43	16.6
16	12.0	112.00	7.00	16.3
17	12.5	112.50	6.62	16.1
18	13.0	113.00	6.28	15.8
19	13.5	113.50	5.97	15.5
20	14.0	114.00	5.70	15.3
21	14.5	114.50	5.45	15.1
22	15.0	115.00	5.23	15.0
23	15.5	115.50	5.02	14.7
24	16.0	116.00	4.83	14.6
25	16.5	116.50	4.66	14.5
26	17.0	117.00	4.50	14.3
27	17.5	117.50	4.35	14.2
28	18.0	118.00	4.21	14.0
29	18.5	118.50	4.09	14.1
30	19.0	119.00	3.97	13.9

Table 4.9, continued

Maturity in Months	Total Finance Charge (%)	Total Amount Due on $100 Contract ($)	Monthly Payments on $100 Contract ($)	Effective Annual Interest Rate (%)
31	19.5	119.50	3.85	13.7
32	20.0	120.00	3.75	13.7
33	20.5	120.50	3.65	13.6
34	21.0	121.00	3.56	13.5
35	21.5	121.50	3.47	13.4
36	22.0	122.00	3.39	13.4
37	22.5	122.50	3.31	13.3
38	23.0	123.00	3.24	13.3
39	23.5	123.50	3.17	13.2

Source: NAFC, "Diversified Financing Methods." Effective annual interest rate computed assuming $100 principal is repaid in equal monthly installments with interest assessed monthly on the remaining principal balance.

reserves and insurance would be added to these finance charges, further increasing the effective interest rate.

This evidence seems to point to increases in supply of credit as the dominant force in credit markets in the 1920s. But we must be cautious: this analysis presumes credit markets are analogous to product markets. The simple demand and supply framework captured by figure 4.3 assumes that, subject to availability of a product, buyers decide whether or not to purchase the product; sellers do not approve the actions of some buyers but prohibit those of others. Unfortunately, this is not the case for credit markets. Sellers of credit consider a buyer's financial situation (is he or she a poor credit risk?) and the proposed use of the credit (will he or she squander the funds on gambling?). In credit markets, some buyers (borrowers) who view themselves as willing and financially able to buy (borrow) at the market price are prohibited by sellers (lenders) from entering the market. The market price of credit does not capture the price that is implicitly faced by households prohibited from "buying" credit.

In effect, households thus excluded from credit markets face an implicit price of credit that is infinite. Changes in the market price of credit that is available to other households do not affect the (implicit) price of credit faced by households excluded from the market. Moreover, if an institutional change occurs that makes credit available to a group of previously excluded households, the effective price of credit that they face declines from infinity to the market price. Changes in measured credit costs during times when credit is initially unavailable to some potential borrowers therefore cannot capture the price effects of increasing availability of credit. As availability increases, some households face drastic declines in effective credit costs even if absolutely no change in the measured market price of credit takes place.

INCREASED SUPPLY OF CREDIT: FINANCING OF AUTO SALES

The tale of the development of auto sales finance companies is a vivid example of increasing supply of credit leading a revolution in demand for a product. Between 1913 and 1925, availability of credit for financing retail purchases of autos increased greatly as auto sales finance companies were established. In the 1920s and 1930s, auto manufacturers turned to financing companies to market autos to the masses. But the initial establishment of auto sales finance companies was not a response to demand for retail credit but was instead largely a response of auto manufacturers to production problems resulting from adoption of assembly line methods of production.[34]

Distribution in the Auto Industry

During the first decade of auto manufacture, 1900 to 1910, several hundred small companies produced autos.[35] Investors were wary of the industry, so most capital expansion came from reinvestment of retained earnings. Manufacturers required cash payment from dealers upon delivery of an auto, which, together with the thirty- to ninety-day credit received from their parts suppliers, provided most of the manufacturers' working capital. Autos were almost always produced and shipped for specific buyers. Although it was not required, dealers often sent deposits along with their orders because the practice was common among merchants of other products and to do otherwise might signal poor financial standing on the part of the dealers.[36]

By World War I, auto manufacturers had developed a distribution system with hundreds of independent business people serving as local dealers.[37] Autos were now produced and shipped in response to dealers' one-year-in-advance month-by-month forecasts of cars to be sold over a year.[38] Ford's dealer policy was unique in permitting only men of financial means to obtain a dealership. Most other dealers came from the ranks of small merchants with valuable human capital—technical knowledge in an area related to servicing autos—but with little financial capital. Dealers typically placed a $1,000 "good faith" deposit with the manufacturer.[39] Each dealer had a franchise contract with a manufacturer; typically it was an annual, renewable contract granting an exclusive territory, often requiring exclusive representation, and requiring the dealer to keep at least one demonstration car and an adequate supply of parts in stock and to maintain a service department for both warranty and regular servicing of autos. Finally and most importantly for this argument, the contract contained a cancellation clause under which the manufacturer could cancel the franchise contract, with or without cause, with as little as ten and rarely more than thirty days of notice.[40] Upon cancellation, manufacturers were not required to buy back any autos currently in dealer inventory, but without an authorized service department, dealers could expect great difficulty selling those autos.

The Need for Inventory Financing

Assembly line production of autos was essentially nonexistent in 1910 but characterized the industry by World War I. This capital-intensive and expensive production method created a problem for auto manufacturers; to keep average costs down, the assembly line system called for a relatively smooth seasonal production pattern, but demand for cars exhibited tremendous seasonal fluctuations with a strong peak in spring following an extraordinarily slow winter. Throughout the 1920s, nearly 50 percent of annual sales occurred between March 1 and June 30. Sales volume in April was up to four times greater than that for December, January, or February.[41] To produce in lockstep with sales would have driven up fixed costs by requiring in April four times the plant capacity required in January. Idle equipment in winter months would have depreciated more rapidly than equipment in regular use, further increasing costs. Swings in labor demand might have created difficulties acquiring and quickly training skilled laborers needed only during the peak months.[42] For these reasons, production needed to be smoother than sales, thus requiring a large buildup of inventory in winter.

Inventory swings are quite evident in the early 1920s. NAFC estimated the number of cars in inventory of General Motors dealers by month, 1922 to 1928. Their estimates are reproduced in table 4.10. When the patterns of inventory, sales, and production are adjusted to remove an upward time trend, these estimates clearly illustrate the attempts in the early 1920s to smooth production through letting inventory fluctuate, as seen in figure 4.4.[43]

The inventory of finished autos created by smoothing production was quite extensive. Manufacturers could not afford to carry this inventory. The physical storage problem itself would have been enormous; by one estimate the costs of locating and providing storage facilities, quite apart from the opportunity costs of tied-up cash, would have exceeded all gains from smoothing production.[44] Neither were manufacturers in a financial position to carry the inventory on their books due to their continued dependence upon dealer payment at delivery for their working capital. Manufacturers, therefore, wanted dealers to carry the inventory of finished cars.

But dealers were in no better cash position than manufacturers. Until about 1915, dealers financed small inventories internally.[45] But after 1915, the size of inventory increased, and most dealers needed some form of external financing in order to carry inventory.[46] Existing avenues for financing were inadequate. Manufacturers could not afford to offer direct factory credit. Most banks refused to offer adequate inventory financing, citing two reasons: one, autos were not considered necessary items for households; and two, the cancellation clause in the dealers' franchise agreement led to a hands-off policy on the part of bankers.[47]

Individual dealers and the National Automobile Dealers Association (NADA) both tried to overturn the American Bankers Association classification of an auto as a non-necessity good. Dealers had formed their trade

Table 4.10. General Motors Car Production, Sales, and Dealer Inventory, 1922-1928

Month and Year	Beginning-of-Month Dealer Inventory	Production during Month	Sales during Month
January 1922	20,000	15,900	10,900
February 1922	25,000	20,400	14,100
March 1922	31,300	28,100	25,000
April 1922	34,400	43,700	50,000
May 1922	28,100	48,400	53,100
June 1922	23,400	50,000	50,000
July 1922	23,400	34,400	32,800
August 1922	25,000	45,400	43,800
September 1922	26,600	36,600	35,900
October 1922	27,300	44,600	53,100
November 1922	18,800	46,800	37,500
December 1922	28,100	48,500	45,300
January 1923	31,300	53,100	31,300
February 1923	53,100	53,200	34,400
March 1923	71,900	71,900	75,000
April 1923	68,800	68,800	106,300
May 1923	31,300	82,800	92,200
June 1923	21,900	65,600	75,000
July 1923	12,500	56,300	62,500
August 1923	6,300	67,200	59,400
September 1923	14,100	76,500	62,500
October 1923	28,100	75,100	59,400
November 1923	43,800	79,600	48,400
December 1923	75,000	62,500	37,500
January 1924	100,000	59,400	34,400
February 1924	125,000	75,000	50,000
March 1924	150,000	81,300	56,300

Table 4.10, continued

Month and Year	Beginning-of-Month Dealer Inventory	Production during Month	Sales during Month
April 1924	175,000	59,400	90,600
May 1924	143,800	50,000	87,500
June 1924	106,300	40,600	71,900
July 1924	75,000	43,800	62,500
August 1924	56,300	43,800	56,300
September 1924	43,800	53,900	50,800
October 1924	46,900	50,800	46,900
November 1924	50,800	22,600	32,800
December 1924	40,600	25,100	34,400
January 1925	31,300	29,700	26,600
February 1925	34,400	43,700	40,600
March 1925	37,500	78,200	71,900
April 1925	43,800	87,500	96,900
May 1925	34,400	73,400	87,500
June 1925	20,300	71,900	76,600
July 1925	15,600	62,500	65,600
August 1925	12,500	79,700	78,100
September 1925	14,100	89,100	84,400
October 1925	18,800	100,000	87,500
November 1925	31,300	67,900	61,700
December 1925	37,500	57,800	57,800
January 1926	37,500	82,800	54,700
February 1926	65,600	87,500	65,600
March 1926	87,500	112,600	106,300
April 1926	93,800	112,500	137,500
May 1926	68,800	131,300	143,800
June 1926	56,300	112,500	118,800

Table 4.10, continued

Month and Year	Beginning-of-Month Dealer Inventory	Production during Month	Sales during Month
July 1926	50,000	92,200	103,100
August 1926	39,100	137,400	123,400
September 1926	53,100	140,700	118,800
October 1926	75,000	n.a.	n.a.
November 1926	87,500	78,100	103,100
December 1926	62,500	50,000	53,100
January 1927	59,400	109,400	81,300
February 1927	87,500	118,700	103,100
March 1927	103,100	156,300	146,900
April 1927	112,500	170,400	181,300
May 1927	101,600	174,900	173,400
June 1927	103,100	158,600	162,500
July 1927	99,200	139,100	137,500
August 1927	100,800	157,800	159,400
September 1927	99,200	143,000	134,400
October 1927	107,800	126,600	115,600
November 1927	118,800	59,400	81,300
December 1927	96,900	57,800	54,700
January 1928	100,000	135,900	107,800
February 1928	128,100	156,300	134,400
March 1928	150,000	203,200	184,400
April 1928	168,800	200,000	212,500
May 1928	156,300	212,400	228,100
June 1928	140,600	192,200	207,800
July 1928	125,000	169,500	178,100
August 1928	116,400	186,800	189,100
September 1928	114,100	167,200	150,000

Table 4.10, continued

Month and Year	Beginning-of-Month Dealer Inventory	Production during Month	Sales during Month
October 1928	131,300	130,500	143,000
November 1928	118,800	40,600	90,600
December 1928	68,800		32,800

Source: Derived from a graph of monthly sales and inventory in NAFC, *NAFC News* 18 (June 1929): 1. NAFC assumed 20,000 cars were in General Motors dealer inventories as of January 1, 1922. They note that if this assumption is incorrect (though they believed it was not far from the mark), each inventory estimate is off by the same amount, but the seasonal pattern is correct.

Figure 4.4. General Motors Car Production and Dealer Inventory, 1922–1928

(Detrended about Time Trend)

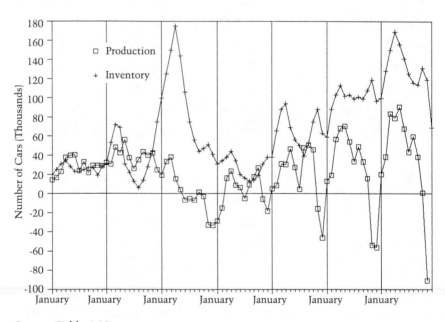

Source: Table 4.10.

association in 1917 in order to coordinate efforts to move autos off of the War Trade Board list of non-necessity items. Successful in this endeavor, they turned after World War I to convincing the banking industry and especially the Federal Reserve that autos were necessities. The national organization lobbied the Fed as well as the members of the American Bankers Association.[48] Individual dealers were advised to place local bankers at the very top of their list of sales prospects.[49] But even when successful in convincing individual bankers of the auto's necessity, the cancellation clause in the dealer's franchise agreement remained an insurmountable obstacle.

Demand for dealerships was so great that manufacturers could adopt a take-it-or-leave-it stance concerning franchise agreements.[50] They viewed the cancellation clause as essential. Not surprisingly, this aspect of the contract caused dealers great concern. At the 1921 annual meeting of NADA, speaker after speaker referred to problems with the agreement. Several dealers emphasized its effect on banking arrangements, noting that many bankers explicitly cited the clause as their reason for refusing inventory loans to franchised dealers.[51] Dealers were in a bind: with the advent of assembly line methods, manufacturers were urging them to carry larger inventories during the slow-selling winter months; dealers could do so only if they could borrow to finance their inventory, but banks generally refused to lend because of the cancellation clause. Without financing, dealers simply could not afford to carry extensive inventory.

Manufacturers could have solved the problem by dropping or changing the cancellation clause. They did not do so. Instead, manufacturers responded by establishing or contracting with a finance company that would carry a franchised dealer's inventory loans and would purchase the dealer's retail installment contracts.[52] Auto sales finance companies were first established therefore not to market cars nor in response to buyer demand for convenient payment schemes, but to preserve manufacturer power over dealers while simultaneously solving the problem of inadequate wholesale inventory financing.

Why did manufacturers not simply lend funds directly to their dealers? A separate finance company, even one owned by a manufacturer, could obtain financial capital not directly available to a manufacturer because assets of manufacturing companies are typically much less liquid than those of financial institutions. Financial markets had set "safe" borrowing ratios (total borrowing to capital-plus-surplus) much higher for financial institutions than for manufacturing concerns.

Who Established Sales Finance Companies?

Two sets of individuals established the early sales finance companies: those with prior experience in retail financing and those in the auto industry. Nearly all of the initial finance companies were "factory-tied" companies, linked to auto manufacturers as subsidiaries or by contract. Alexander Duncan, who apprenticed in a local merchandise business and was briefly employed in the field of credit insurance, established the Commercial Credit Company (later Commercial Credit Corporation [CCC]) in Baltimore in 1912.[53] In 1916, CCC became one of the first finance companies to purchase auto installment contracts.[54] CCC entered into a contractual relationship in 1920 with the company that would become Chrysler Corporation to provide its dealers with adequate financing.[55]

Arthur H. Jones and John L. Little were booksellers around the turn of the century who often accepted notes for monthly payments from their customers. In 1904 they began a business of dealing in accounts receivables in general, adopting a non-notification policy and allowing each client to serve as collecting agent. Following several corporate reorganizations and changes of name, in 1914 the company became the National Bond and Investment Company of Chicago, ultimately an important provider of auto financing.[56] The company was sold to CCC in 1941.

Henry Ittleson formed the Commercial Credit and Investment Company in 1908 in St. Louis to purchase accounts receivables from the chemical companies Monsanto and Dow Chemical.[57] The company later became CIT Financial Corporation, a large auto sales financing concern that contracted with a number of manufacturers.

These companies all began by financing open accounts receivable, and each eventually developed auto installment sales financing as one of its lines of business. The first company founded just to purchase auto installment sales contracts was established in 1913 in San Francisco by an auto dealer, L. F. Weaver.[58] Another company, the Guaranty Securities Company (subsequently incorporated as the Guaranty Securities Corporation

[GSC]), was founded in 1915 with capital provided primarily by John Willys, a prominent auto manufacturer.[59] Its initial plan was to extend credit exclusively to Willys-Overland dealers. The overwhelming number of offers of retail contracts from other dealers led quickly to a change in policy. In a celebrated advertisement in the April 8, 1916, edition of the *Saturday Evening Post*, GSC announced its intention to offer retail sales financing on all makes of autos. Several manufacturers subsequently contracted with GSC to provide wholesale and retail credit to their dealers.[60] In 1922 a controlling interest in GSC (by now named Continental Guaranty Corporation) was acquired by CCC.[61]

General Motors established its sales finance company, the wholly owned subsidiary General Motors Acceptance Corporation (GMAC), in 1919. A principal reason for its establishment was the difficulty General Motors dealers were experiencing in obtaining funds to pay for deliveries from the factory.[62] Contradicting subsequent characterizations of GMAC's birth as primarily a means to market autos, in its 1919 annual report General Motors stated that it established GMAC "to assist dealers in financing their purchase of General Motors' products, and also to finance, to some extent, retail sales."[63]

Henry Ford opposed installment sales of autos and saw no reason to assist his dealers with their inventory financing.[64] Because Ford dealerships were particularly profitable, Henry Ford could risk the ire and possible loss of dealers who could not otherwise obtain inventory financing. Apparently unbeknownst to Henry Ford, however, for many years the Ford Motor Company made substantial deposits of money in banks around the country with the express understanding that the bankers would therefore make financing available to franchised Ford dealers. The practice was initiated by the company treasurer Norval Hawkins sometime in the early 1910s.[65] But Henry Ford's personal opposition to retail credit was so strong that the 1916 franchise contracts prohibited dealers from selling cars for anything but cash.[66] Internal pressure mounted in the early 1920s for some company-sanctioned form of retail financing. In 1923 Henry Ford unveiled the "Ford Weekly Purchasing Plan": customers would receive an auto after it had been fully paid for through regular bank savings deposits.[67] The plan was not wildly successful. In 1928 Ford Motor Company established a subsidiary sales finance company, Universal Credit Corporation, but in 1933 sold a controlling interest in Universal Credit to CIT.[68] As Universal-CIT, the company entered into a contractual relationship with Ford Motor Company.[69]

Hundreds of sales finance companies entered the industry between 1921 and 1925. Nearly all were small local "independents," companies without contracts with any auto manufacturer. Seligman labeled this period "the boom in automobile financing" and noted, ". . . when the would-be purchasers [of autos] came to be predominantly of the middle and lower middle class, and when it became more and more customary for the farmer and even the more prosperous wage-earner to desire a motor car, an opportunity arose to introduce some method to enable purchase on the part of those who had no great stock of accumulated savings or who, at all events, would find it inconvenient to pay in cash."[70]

Indeed, many of these companies specialized in retail financing only. Finance charges on retail contracts are exempt from usury limits that apply to wholesale financing. Contemporary observers believed finance companies earned little or no profit on wholesale financing.[71] Those independents who did offer wholesale financing often did so only as a means of obtaining a dealer's profitable retail contracts.[72]

Only factory-tied sales finance companies operated nationally.[73] Independent sales finance companies operated locally, although a handful had branches throughout the upper Midwest and one, Pacific Finance Corporation, had branches throughout the West. About 90 percent of the volume of financing was written by the few factory-tied companies, which swamped the local independents in both annual earnings and total assets.[74] Of companies listed in *Moody's Manuals*, with rare exception (Pacific Finance being the most glaring) the independent sales finance companies had total assets of under $3 million and gross annual earnings of less than $500,000 in the mid-1920s.[75] By contrast, in 1927 GMAC's assets exceeded $300 million and its annual gross was over $40 million. CCC and CIT both had assets of approximately $100 million and annual earnings between $10 and $15 million. Universal was established in 1928 with initial capital of $11.5 million and quickly grew to the size of CCC and CIT. The Big Four sales finance companies—GMAC, CCC, CIT, and Universal—dominated the field throughout the 1920s and 1930s.

Competition among Finance Companies

Sales finance companies compete with each other for a dealer's business by varying the rates charged on wholesale financing; the size of dealer reserves on retail contracts; the extent of the holdback; the use of a recourse, repurchase, or no-recourse basis for purchasing retail contracts; and the quality of service the finance company offers. Varying rates charged on retail contracts does not directly profit a sales finance company's customers—the dealers. To the extent that retail demand for autos depends upon the costs of financing, however, lower retail financing rates at one dealership can increase that dealer's sales relative to local competitors and may therefore lead the dealer to favor a company that accepted lower retail finance charges.

Compared with independent sales finance companies, in the 1920s factory-tied companies purchased retail contracts written with lower finance charges.[76] Yet dealers did not uniformly prefer the factory-tied companies over the independents; local independents countered their higher retail financing rates with better service. They offered 24-hour turnaround on retail contracts, while mail delays and slower processing meant dealers often waited a week or more for factory-tied finance companies to pay for retail contracts.[77] Since funds from the sale of retail contracts were used to retire a dealer's inventory loans, time was money. Moreover, many local companies purchased retail contracts on a no-recourse basis which eliminated dealer liability in the event of buyer default, but all the national companies used a recourse or repurchase basis.[78] Finally, many dealers desired an ongoing relationship with a local finance company, believing a company owned and operated by a personal acquaintance would be more flexible if the dealer were to encounter difficult times.

Lower rates from factory-tied companies were possible in part because manufacturers paid these companies a fixed amount for each vehicle produced, regardless of how the final sale was financed.[79] Factory-tied companies could also offer lower rates than the independents because their costs of capital were lower. Large, factory-tied finance companies obtained most of their working capital through direct sale of securities (typically collateral trust notes) on capital markets.[80] Size mattered: financial markets considered a "safe" ratio of borrowing to capital-plus-surplus to be 1.5 to 2 for companies with under $500,000 capital but 3 to 5 for larger companies.[81] Furthermore, the costs assessed by the trustee who coordinated the collateral trust note financing varied directly with the size of the note issue but entailed a minimum payment, so small borrowers paid higher rates to finance than large borrowers did. In 1934 borrowers paid trustee fees equal to 0.4 percent per year on the face value of the collateral, but the minimum payment was $1,000 per year, so an issue of less than $250,000 incurred fees in excess of 0.4 percent.[82]

The effects are seen in differences in the liability structures of large and small finance companies. Of companies listed in *Moody's Manuals* for 1928, liabilities of factory-tied companies were largely stock issues and collateral notes, while those of independents were mostly stock issues and bank notes. Banks, still assigning high risk to auto financing despite low consumer default rates even in the 1920–21 depression and unable to rediscount the collateral notes at the Fed, charged lending rates above commercial paper rates.[83] The Fed's discount window was limited to merchandising operations, and sales finance companies produced no merchandise. Believing borrowing rates would fall if banks could rediscount their notes, throughout the 1920s the NAFC urged the Fed to change policy, but to no avail.[84]

THE PROPRIETY OF BORROWING

At least for autos, therefore, expanded use of credit resulted from greater supply of credit. By all accounts, however, a necessary prerequisite to the expansion of credit-financed consumption of not only autos but all other durable goods as well was a fundamental change in society's attitudes toward the propriety of incurring household debt, a change which can have the effect of increasing demand for credit. In 1907 William Jennings Bryan wrote an article for the *Ladies Home Journal* entitled "The First Rule for a Husband and Wife."[85] Its message—Rule #1: live within your means—was typical of the times. Milan Ayres wrote in a 1926 report commissioned by the American Bankers Association, "During the nineteenth century the things that a self-respecting, thrifty American family would buy on the installment plan were a piano, a sewing machine, some expensive articles of furniture, and perhaps sets of books. People who made such purchases didn't talk about them. Installment buying wasn't considered quite respectable."[86] To convey the general attitude of society toward consumer credit, Clyde Phelps wove together several quotes from articles published in popular and professional journals between 1926 and 1928.

> The use of credit, and particularly the instalment type, by consumers was characterized as "an economic sin," as "enervating to character because it leads straight to serfdom," as setting "utterly false standards of living," causing judgment to become "hopelessly distorted," and tending to "break down credit morale." It was attacked as "marking the breakdown of traditional habits of thrift," as tending to "weaken the moral fiber of the Nation," and as dangerous to the economy of the United States. It was accused of "breaking down character and resistance to temptations, to extravagance, and to living beyond one's means, breeding dishonesty," causing "many young people to get their first experience of being dead beats through yielding to temptations that are placed before them," and "creating a new type of criminal or causing professional dead beats to shift to this new and highly lucrative opportunity."[87]

Charles Hardy claims that "changing notions about economy, frugality, saving, and thrift" are an important factor in the rise of credit.[88] He places the beginnings of these changes at the end of the Crisis of the 1890s but notes that "the general collapse of inhibitions against borrowing . . . were particularly conspicuous between 1922 and 1929."[89] Attitudes changed to such an extent in the first twenty years of this century that, according to Frederick Lewis Allen, by the 1920s "people were getting to consider it old-fashioned to limit their purchases to the amount of their cash balances."[90] And Rolf Nugent notes that "in the 1920s it became common practice for dealers in durable household goods to assume that each prospective purchaser was a deferred-payment customer."[91]

LEGISLATIVE CHANGES

Not only had societal norms dictated against the use of consumer credit for purchasing durable goods, but before World War I consumers had had good cause to be wary of that credit which was offered. In her 1938 consumer economics textbook, Margaret Reid states, "During the closing decade of the nineteenth century the practice of installment selling spread more rapidly and came to be widely used by house-to-house sellers without an established place of business. . . . [T]here was much fraud and deception in charges and in repossessions. Installment buying fell into disrepute."[92]

Installment buying was not the only aspect of the credit industry in "disrepute" at the turn of the century; abuses in the small loan business were also legendary then. State usury laws were ineffective; lenders managed to increase effective rates of interest through various fees, penalties, required insurance, and so on. Louis Robinson and Rolf Nugent report that between 1887 and 1922, the actual rates of interest charged by lenders ranged from a low of 3 percent to highs of 200 to 300 percent in northeast and midwest cities and as high as 1,700 percent in southern cities.[93] Surely, the introduction of certain regulatory measures to the consumer credit industry after World War I affected the willingness of households to go into debt.

Regulation of the lending of small sums of money was enacted first. In 1916, a Uniform Small Loan Law that served as a framework for state small loan laws was developed by a national group of small lenders with the aid and sponsorship of the Russell Sage Foundation.[94] An important provision of the law was the requirement that all charges for small loans, assessed for whatever purpose, be legally considered "interest." Usury limits were explicit; the lenders agreed to a maximum monthly interest rate (usually 3 percent per month) that was included in the law.[95] By 1931, twenty-two state legislatures had passed small loan acts conforming to this Uniform Small Loan Law.[96] According to Robinson and Nugent, the legislated changes in conditions surrounding small loans and the legislated decreases in interest charges caused both a general increase in small loan borrowing after 1916 and borrowing "by a better class of borrowers."[97]

State legislative efforts addressing installment credit began around 1935. Within twenty years, fourteen states had enacted bills regulating the installment credit industry, many of which had been sponsored by the finance companies themselves.[98] Involvement of finance companies in regulating their own activities may indicate that they believed the public's perception of the honesty of their lending practices affected the volume of their business. Unlike legislation addressed to the small loan industry, most of the installment sale legislation emphasized disclosure rather than control of the terms of the installment contracts since installment borrowing was typically for discretionary purchase of a durable good while small loan borrowing was due to necessity or emergency.[99]

CREDIT AVAILABILITY AND THE DEMAND FOR DURABLES

Widened credit availability can help explain increases in price and income elasticities between the pre–World War I and interwar periods. Elasticities measure how expenditure responds to changes in price or income. Expenditure for durable goods changes when either desired stock or the adjustment speed changes, as discussed in chapter 3. When credit is available for financing purchases of durable goods, only a down payment rather than the full purchase price is needed to initiate purchase. Because less time is then needed to save up enough money to make a major purchase, households are able to respond more rapidly to changes in price or income. The measured elasticities increase because within each time period a larger part of any desired change in expenditure actually occurs.

In an economy with, broadly stated, two groups of households—well-to-do and middle-income households—greater availability of credit can decrease the aggregate adjustment speed while increasing price and income elasticities. Suppose that with no credit available for anyone, only well-to-do households are able to purchase some durable good. These households adjust their actual to desired stocks rapidly (their adjustment speed is near 1) but respond weakly to changes in price or income (their demand elasticities are small). When credit becomes available, scores of middle-income households enter the market, now able to purchase the goods. They respond quite vigorously to changes in price and especially income (their demand elasticities are large), since the relatively expensive products they are buying are luxury items in their middle-income budgets. They must save up for a down payment, so purchase is not immediate upon forming a desire to own the good. Further caution is exercised in realizing their desire because of the costs associated with resale or under-utilization of durable goods. The adjustment speed for these middle-income households is thus substantially lower than that of the well-to-do. In the aggregate, comparing the periods before and after introduction of credit, adjustment speeds are lower, but price and income elasticities are greater. (See appendix C for a more formal presentation of this point.)

Such a tale is consistent with the estimated demand relationships reported in chapter 3. Within a gradual stock-adjustment framework, adjustment speed decreased between the pre–World War I and interwar periods for furniture, household appliances, china and tableware, house furnishings, jewelry and watches, miscellaneous other durable goods, and for the aggregates major durable goods, minor durable goods, and total durable goods. Simultaneously, elasticities increased. In many cases it appears that the credit-financed move to mass markets was responsible.

A BURGEONING CREDIT ECONOMY

The Consumer Durables Revolution was coincident with a burgeoning credit economy. Most credit extended to households to facilitate purchases of durable goods was installment credit extended by new financial institutions, sales finance companies. Many factors contributed to the growth of that credit industry in the 1910s and 1920s. But an especially important factor in its initial establishment was the desire of auto manufacturers to retain their ability to cancel a dealer's franchise contract while simultaneously coming up with some way to ease dealer financing woes, woes that were making it very difficult for manufacturers to smooth out costly seasonal fluctuations in production in light of strong seasonal patterns of sales. Growing credit availability cleared the path for a Consumer Durables Revolution. In turn, the continuing Consumer Durables Revolution paved the way for further growth in household use of credit.

·5·

ADVERTISING
CONSUMER GOODS

G rowing availability of credit made durable goods, especially expensive major durable goods, more accessible to American households in the interwar years. Advertising strove to make them more desirable. Use of advertising rose substantially after World War I. Over the early twentieth century, new theories of behavioral psychology led to advertising that changed in tone and style, becoming increasingly less informative and reasoned and increasingly more suggestive and persuasive.

Durable goods were advertised more frequently in the 1920s than before World War I, and these advertisements were progressively larger and therefore more difficult to overlook. While households were using credit more and more often after World War I, manufacturers were no more aggressive in marketing their goods with credit; availability of credit terms is mentioned no more frequently in print advertisements of the 1920s than earlier. Nor were manufacturers using price to lure customers; advertisements for durables are somewhat less likely to mention the good's price in the early 1920s than in either the decade before or hence.

Automobiles, electrical household appliances, and radios were all new products; advertising played an important role as it apprised potential customers of the "necessity" of such products. In retrospect, the results of those advertising efforts are sometimes astonishing. Was it successful advertising that led an economist to assert in 1938 that the finance charges incurred to purchase an electric washing machine on installment payments would be more than offset by the decline in medical bills otherwise incurred by the homemaker forced to use a manual washer and wringer?[1]

Perhaps more important than the effects *of* advertising in the Consumer Durables Revolution of the 1920s were the effects *on* advertising. With households able to respond more rapidly to economic stimuli by using credit, producers of major durable goods could expect advertising effects to more readily translate to increased sales. Many advertisers argued that the new mass production methods required mass demand which could only be insured through judicious use of advertising. Advertising nationally compelled firms to standardize their products, but standardization in turn made necessary advertising that could create apparent distinctions between quite similar products offered by different firms within an industry.

BUSINESS EXPENDITURE FOR ADVERTISING

In many ways, World War I marked a watershed for the advertising industry; advertising for consumer goods was greater in volume and more manipulative in nature after the war than just twenty years earlier. According to advertising historian Daniel Pope, "National advertising arose [in the beginning of the twentieth century] to meet the needs of businesses that employed new technologies and sold to new mass consumer markets. Rather quickly, an advertising industry emerged that was capable of meeting these marketing requirements. Advertising practitioners developed professional standards and skills appropriate to the demands businesses placed upon them. By about 1920, the institutional arrangements that still characterize American advertising were already set in place."[2] Characteristic of the rapid changes in the industry, in 1917 the newly formed American Association of Advertising Agencies "forbade its members to engage in practices that were routine for agencies twenty years earlier."[3]

Advertising expenditure was greatest in the 1920s, as seen by the variety of estimates in table 5.1. Estimates of total expenditure for advertising confirm the popular perception that businesses spent much more money for advertising in the 1920s than in any other decade before World War II. The estimates provided by *Printers' Ink* are the basis of all other estimates of total advertising expenditures for the nineteenth and early twentieth centuries. Their estimates should be viewed as indicative of trend only; the exact same figures are repeated in several different years and there is

Table 5.1. Business Expenditure for Advertising, 1880-1935 (Millions of Dollars)

Year	Printers' Ink: Total Volume	Pope: Total Volume	Borden: Newspaper	Borden: Other Periodical	Peterson: General Magazine
1880	200	104			
1890	360	190			
1900	542	256			
1904	821	388			
1909	1,142	540	149	54	
1914	1,302	682	184	72	
1915	1,302				25
1916	1,468				33
1917	1,627				41
1918	1,468				55
1919	2,282	1,409	374	155	87
1920	2,935				120
1921	2,282		522	155	88
1922	2,607				92
1923	2,935		581	213	110
1924	2,935				124
1925	3,099		662	262	143
1926	3,262				156
1927	3,262		725	305	171
1928	3,262				171
1929	3,426	2,987	797	323	186
1930	2,607				182
1931	2,282		625	244	150
1932	1,627				105
1933	1,302		429	141	93
1934	1,627				111
1935	1,690	1,830	500	186	116
1936	1,902				133

Table 5.1, continued

Year	Printers' Ink: Total Volume	Pope: Total Volume	Borden: Newspaper	Borden: Other Periodical	Peterson: General Magazine
1937	2,072		574	236	150
1938	1,904				133
1939	1,980				142
1940	2,088				156
1941	2,236				169

Sources: Printers' Ink, Advertisers' Annual: 1955, p. 58 (reprinted in U.S. Bureau of the Census, Historical Statistics, Ser. T444, p. 856). Pope, Making of Modern Advertising, table 2.2, p. 26. Borden, Economic Effects of Advertising, table 1, p. 48. Peterson, Magazines in the Twentieth Century, table 1, p. 25 (derived by Peterson from records of the Publishers' Information Bureau).

no available explanation of this peculiarity. Pope accepts the *Printers' Ink* estimates (with caution) and uses them as the basis for his revisions.[4]

The estimates by *Printers' Ink* and by Pope cover all advertising—national and local, print and other media. Print advertising includes both newspaper and other periodical advertising. Neil Borden's estimates of expenditure for each of these two print media are also in table 5.1. In the 1920s, print advertising commanded just under one-third of total advertising expenditure. Direct mail and billboard advertising constituted the bulk of the remainder.

Theodore Peterson's estimates of expenditure for national advertising in general magazines are also shown in table 5.1. General magazines include *Ladies Home Journal, Saturday Evening Post, Harper's,* and others. Particularly excluded are farm magazines. Again we see a great increase in advertising expenditure in the 1920s; nearly four to six times more money was spent to advertise in general magazines in each year of the 1920s than in 1915. Peterson further notes that throughout the 1920s, 38 to 43 percent of expenditure for advertising in nationally distributed general and farm magazines was for advertisements in one of the three publications of the Curtis Publishing Company—*Saturday Evening Post, Ladies Home Journal,* and *Country Gentleman.* The weekly *Saturday Evening Post* accounted for much of this expenditure, taking 27 to 31 percent of all national magazine advertising revenue in each year, 1918 to 1929. But the monthly *Ladies Home Journal* was nevertheless one of the top five in magazine advertising revenue in 1920.[5]

These estimates of advertising expenditure are helpful in showing the explosion of such expenditure in the 1920s. But they do not indicate how *many* advertisements there were. The effect of advertising on consumer choices no doubt depends not upon the amount of money businesses spend on advertising but upon the quantity (and perhaps quality or style) of advertisements that a consumer encounters. Adjusting for changes in the price of advertisements would move us closer to estimates of the quantity of advertising, but this endeavor is more complex than it might first appear. In his study of the economics of advertising, Richard Schmalensee devised one such measure of "real" advertising expenditure, taking into account both the amount of space used by advertisements (or time, in the case of broadcast media) and the "exposure" of the advertisements (circulation or audience). For magazines, exposure must include not only subscribers and others who buy an issue, but also other people who look at the issue, whether at home, a library, or the doctor's office.[6] The effort quickly becomes quite complicated.

THE QUANTITY OF PRINT ADVERTISING

As an alternative to seeking the best way to deflate a nominal expenditure series, we can start from scratch and develop a new series that actually measures the quantity of advertising. Measuring the *total* quantity of all advertising in any time period is obviously a Herculean task. But we can measure total quantity of advertising if we reasonably limit the scope of the exercise. For this study, an annual series measuring the quantity of print advertising in *Ladies Home Journal*, a leading women's magazine of the early twentieth century, was developed for the years 1901 to 1941.

Advertisements in October issues of *Ladies Home Journal* were surveyed each year. Every advertisement was measured and then classified by the product advertised. Annual series measuring the total number of advertisements and the total pages of advertisements were constructed, with advertisements for each type of durable good and major categories of non-

durable goods grouped separately. Total pages of advertisements were measured in "full-page equivalent" units: since there are four columns to a
page, a full one-column advertisement is 0.25 page; an advertisement that
is one column wide and one-half page long is 0.25 times 0.5 or 0.125 page
in size; one that is two columns wide and one-quarter page long is also
0.125 page in size.[7] Details regarding construction of the series and placement of advertisements into product groups are in appendix D.

Ladies Home Journal is an especially good magazine to use for such a
survey because its editorial policies and readership were unusually stable
throughout this period.[8] By 1900, its circulation was approaching one million readers, over 4 percent of all women in the United States ages fifteen
and over.[9] Throughout the period studied, the circulation of *Ladies Home
Journal* was always among the top four for all magazines.[10] The magazine
appealed particularly to middle-class rather than poor or working-class
women. A group of Daniel Starch's students surveyed 700 Boston home-
makers in the fall of 1921 and found that nearly one-third of them read
Ladies Home Journal, far outpacing the next most popular women's magazine, *Good Housekeeping,* which was read by only one-fifth of these
women.[11]

Readers of *Ladies Home Journal* saw more pages of advertisements and
larger advertisements in the 1920s than they had previously. The total
number of different advertisements was no greater in the 1920s than in
the pre–World War I years, but the total pages of advertisements shot up in
the late 1910s and peaked at over 162 pages of advertisements in 1926, as
seen in figure 5.1. Because the length of an issue simultaneously increased
from 52 pages in 1901 to a maximum of 268 pages in 1926 and 1929, the
share of each issue devoted to advertising moved less dramatically. As
seen in figure 5.2, advertising occupied around 40 percent of an issue at
the beginning of this century and just over 60 percent in the mid-1920s.
But each advertisement was becoming larger, as shown by figure 5.3. Rising from just under 0.1 pages in 1901, the average size of an advertisement was over 0.6 pages by the 1920s. Advertisements became somewhat
smaller on average in the 1930s but still remained substantially larger
than in the first decade of this century.

A study by Sidney Sherman that was published in 1900 indicates that
the number of magazine advertisements had also jumped at the end of the

Figure 5.1. Total Pages of Advertisements, 1901–1941

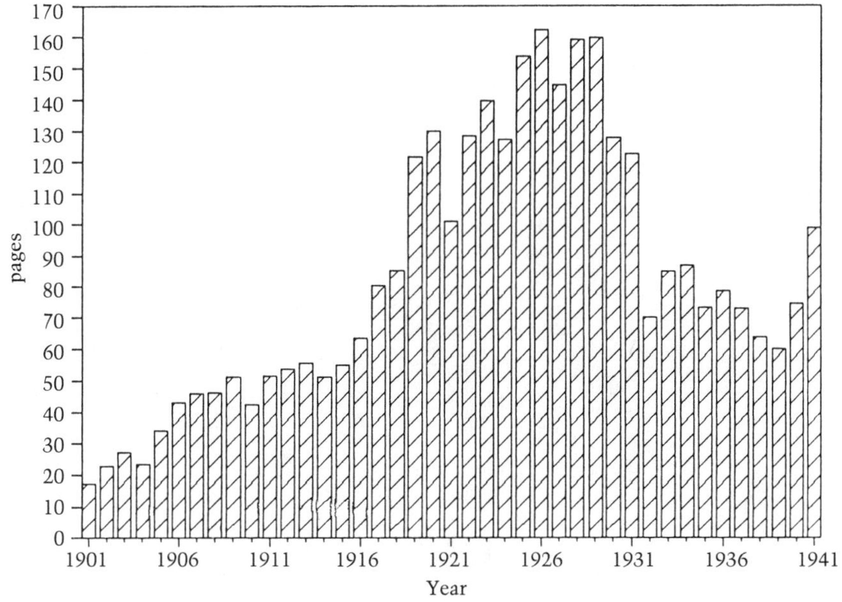

Source: Table D.3. Pages are measured in full-page equivalent units.

1880s, increasing eight-fold in less than ten years.[12] Sherman used October issues of *Harper's Magazine* to measure the number and pages of advertisements during the period 1864–1900. From 1864 to 1886, an issue never contained more than 100 advertisements and usually less than 50. From 1890 to 1900, there were 300 to 400 advertisements per issue. A strict comparison with the *Ladies Home Journal* study reported here would be inappropriate since the two periodicals had different readership, owners, and policies. But Sherman's study does imply that the early twentieth-century changes in the amount of magazine advertising was the continuation of a pattern set at the end of the 1880s.

Increasing size of print advertisements may also have begun in the late 1880s. Sherman's estimates suggest the average size of an advertisement in *Harper's* was steady at between 0.25 and 0.30 page from 1887 to 1898 but had been only about half that size in the early 1870s and 1880s. Albert Poffenberger provides estimates of the average number of lines per print

Figure 5.2. Share of Each Issue Devoted to Advertisements, 1901–1941

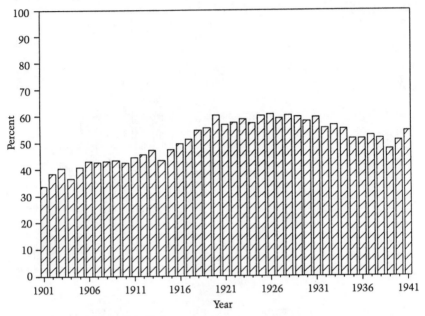

Source: Derived from table D.3.

advertisement in his 1926 text. Before 1900 the average was never more than 61 lines per advertisement, but size rose steadily in the early years of this century, reaching 157 lines per advertisement by 1910.[13] Daniel Starch's estimates show that advertisements began to increase in size in 1898.[14] And Richard Pollay's extensive content analysis of 2,000 print advertisements from the ten largest selling magazines for each decade, 1900–1980, demonstrates that advertisements became larger each decade.[15]

Full-page advertisements became more and more popular as this century progressed. Pollay notes that in the decades of the 1900s and 1910s, 87 percent of advertisements were less than a full page, but in the 1920s only 57 percent were partial page advertisements.[16] Starch notes that in 1917 there was an especially large jump in the use of full-page advertisements in *Ladies Home Journal*.[17] Several studies of the effectiveness of increasing the size of a print advertisement were conducted in the 1910s and 1920s. Most were laboratory experiments designed by behavioral psychol-

Figure 5.3. Average Size of Advertisements, 1901–1941

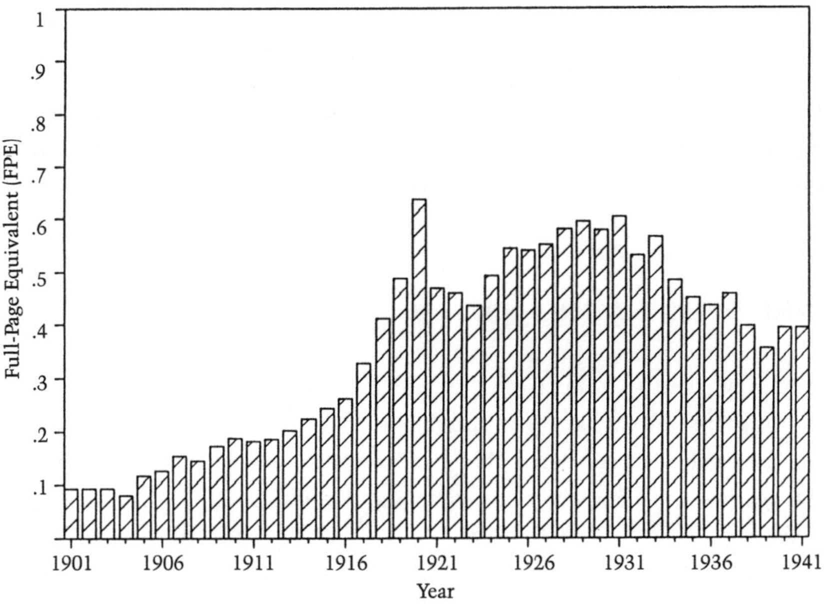

Source: Derived from table D.3.

ogists; the typical experiment tested a subject's recall over time of the existence or content of an advertisement and then correlated recall with the size of the advertisement. An early study is that by Edward Strong, a proponent of the "square root law" in advertising: he concluded that "the value of space in advertising as affecting permanent impressions increases approximately as the square root of the increase in area and not directly with the increase in area."[18] But as several psychology and advertising texts noted by the late 1920s, the assorted experimental results were inconsistent. Nevertheless, the authors of these texts generally advocated larger size advertisements because readers seemed to associate size with prestige, and furthermore, a full-page advertisement would completely avoid any competition for the reader's attention.[19]

Whether all this research was the motivation behind increasing size or justification after the fact is not clear. But one author clearly states that increasing size of advertisements was due to factors other than psychologists' research; Frank Presbrey claims the move to full and double page print advertisements resulted from the excess profits tax first imposed in 1917 by the federal government. "The result was a permanent revision upward in space which has . . . brought a more general use of full pages in the magazines. . . ."[20] Whatever the reason, the move to full-page advertisements was not undertaken to provide consumers with more information about advertised products. Pollay finds that throughout this period, full-page advertisements actually had less overall information content than partial page advertisements.[21]

ADVERTISING AND TOTAL CONSUMPTION

Of money spent to purchase goods, households spent relatively more dollars for major durable and semidurable goods in the 1920s than previously and relatively less for perishable and minor durable goods.[22] Were these changes mirrored in changes in what was advertised?

Not really. Reflecting the larger size of each issue, there were more pages of advertisements for everything, whether households were shifting their spending toward or away from the particular product group. Moreover, the distributions of spending and of national advertising do not seem to bear much relationship to one another when we use these broadly defined product groups. As households shifted their spending toward both semidurable and major durable goods, for instance, there were proportionately fewer pages of advertisements for semidurable goods but proportionately more advertisements for major durables.

Table 5.2 shows the number and pages of advertisements by general product groups—food, clothing, other nondurable, major durable, and minor durable goods. Advertising for clothing, a semidurable good, is a proxy for advertising for all semidurable goods. A few semidurable goods (particularly semidurable house furnishings) are included with advertisements for "other nondurable" goods, but the bulk of "other nondurable" advertisements are for perishable goods, particularly personal toiletries or house cleaning products.

There were more advertisements for food in the 1920s than at any other time but only somewhat more advertisements for other nondurables and just half as many advertisements for clothing. Food advertisements became much larger between 1901 and the 1920s, increasing from one-tenth

Table 5.2. Volume of Advertising by General Product Type, 1901-1941

| Year | Number of Advertisements | | | | | Pages of Advertisements | | | | | Total Pages in Issue |
| | Nondurables | | | Durables | | Nondurables | | | Durables | | |
	Food	Clothing	Other	Major	Minor	Food	Clothing	Other	Major	Minor	
1901	20	62	60	27	20	2.4	5.0	5.5	1.7	2.8	52
1902	24	92	76	27	28	3.6	8.7	6.9	1.8	2.0	60
1903	34	101	93	33	35	5.8	7.8	8.0	2.9	3.1	68
1904	28	116	85	35	30	3.9	8.8	4.6	2.9	3.1	64
1905	33	91	107	26	36	5.7	10.2	9.5	5.1	3.7	84
1906	34	109	117	39	45	7.2	11.9	13.1	7.2	3.8	100
1907	21	103	97	41	36	7.5	15.5	9.9	7.7	5.4	108
1908	26	124	108	36	27	8.8	18.3	11.8	5.3	2.2	108
1909	28	113	99	34	25	8.5	20.0	13.5	7.2	2.0	118
1910	34	57	85	29	22	11.1	11.7	11.5	5.1	3.2	100
1911	38	107	86	26	27	12.6	20.5	9.6	5.0	3.7	116
1912	46	93	103	28	20	14.1	18.0	14.0	4.2	3.5	118
1913	35	100	84	27	30	10.8	20.5	15.3	3.8	5.3	118
1914	33	66	87	19	25	10.1	16.2	16.0	3.6	5.3	118

Table 5.2, continued

Year	Number of Advertisements					Pages of Advertisements					Total Pages in Issue
	Nondurables			Durables		Nondurables			Durables		
	Food	Clothing	Other	Major	Minor	Food	Clothing	Other	Major	Minor	
1915	30	74	86	15	21	10.2	16.3	18.9	5.9	3.8	116
1916	36	70	93	20	24	14.3	18.9	16.6	6.3	7.4	128
1917	32	72	98	25	18	16.9	21.7	24.0	11.3	6.2	156
1918	33	71	74	14	15	22.2	24.9	25.6	6.4	6.1	156
1919	48	78	81	24	19	31.6	34.2	33.4	12.8	9.8	220
1920	43	50	61	29	21	29.9	25.5	38.1	24.3	12.3	216
1921	30	64	89	15	18	19.6	28.1	38.3	7.2	7.8	178
1922	44	63	110	32	31	27.9	29.8	43.3	16.5	11.3	224
1923	45	72	123	47	33	23.4	30.9	50.1	22.0	13.4	238
1924	42	56	106	30	24	28.3	24.2	44.0	18.2	12.5	222
1925	47	51	120	37	28	34.6	26.4	50.6	25.3	16.8	256
1926	54	55	133	33	25	41.3	28.7	57.8	21.5	12.9	268
1927	50	41	119	33	19	37.7	15.9	55.7	22.4	12.9	244
1928	59	42	125	29	19	42.2	19.2	62.7	24.2	10.9	264
1929	59	39	115	32	24	41.4	19.6	56.4	26.6	15.8	268

Table 5.2, continued

Year	Number of Advertisements					Pages of Advertisements					Total Pages in Issue
	Nondurables			Durables		Nondurables			Durables		
	Food	Clothing	Other	Major	Minor	Food	Clothing	Other	Major	Minor	
1930	43	26	117	18	17	32.6	15.4	55.6	13.6	10.6	220
1931	44	14	114	19	12	34.9	8.1	59.2	14.1	6.2	206
1932	29	16	71	9	7	17.8	6.7	34.6	5.3	5.6	126
1933	38	15	80	7	10	25.3	5.5	41.8	6.0	6.4	150
1934	41	27	92	8	12	27.5	9.7	38.1	4.6	7.1	158
1935	35	26	86	5	10	23.0	7.2	35.0	2.7	5.1	142
1936	32	30	100	5	13	21.3	10.6	36.3	2.1	7.8	152
1937	30	25	86	6	12	21.9	10.2	29.8	3.9	7.0	138
1938	33	24	92	3	9	19.5	10.8	28.2	2.1	3.2	124
1939	30	29	90	8	12	18.0	10.4	21.8	5.0	4.8	126
1940	34	36	90	11	18	18.9	13.5	29.9	5.6	6.5	146
1941	50	37	130	14	20	26.7	10.2	43.5	8.1	10.3	182

Sources: Analysis of October issues of *Ladies Home Journal.* Pages of advertisements measured in "full-page equivalent" units. See appendix D.

147

to three-quarters of a page, as did clothing advertisements, which increased from one-tenth to one-half of a page. There were therefore many more pages of advertisements for food; from under three pages in 1901, the number of pages of food advertisements rose to well over thirty pages in the 1920s. Advertisements for other nondurable goods (especially toiletries and home cleaners) also occupied many more pages, tripling between 1916 and the mid-1920s. Clothing advertisements were most evident in the 1920s, though they filled progressively fewer pages after 1926.

The number of advertisements for major durables was no greater in the 1920s than two decades earlier, though there had been quite a drop in the meantime as advertising for major durable goods decreased around the time of World War I (between 1914 and 1921). But because the advertisements were much bigger, there were almost five times more pages of advertisements for major durables in the 1920s than before World War I. Minor durable goods were advertised most often in the early years of this century; there were no more advertisements for minor durable goods in the 1920s than in the 1910s. There are more *pages* of advertisements for minor durable goods in the 1920s than earlier, however, but even this increase was much less noticeable than increases for any of the other product groups.

The number of pages in an issue was increasing through the mid-1920s, so increases in the number of pages of advertisements is not surprising. But as table 5.3 shows, the composition of advertising was changing. The most marked change was in clothing advertisements. National advertisements for clothing increased so slowly into the 1920s that the share of pages that were for clothing advertisements fell by more than half between 1913 and 1925. There was little movement in the share of pages devoted to food advertisements until the 1930s, when, as household incomes fell and a greater share of the family budget went toward buying food and other essential items, proportionately more pages of advertising were for food advertisements. Especially notable is the post–World War I increase in the share of advertising that was for other nondurable goods, with the rise continuing into the 1930s. Advertisements for toiletries (mouthwash, soap, and so on) accounted for most of this increase.

Changes in what was advertised are more clearly evident when we look at the distribution of pages of advertisements in just a few selected years

Table 5.3. Share of Advertising by General Product Type, 1901-1941

| | Percent of Number of Advertisements | | | | | Percent of Pages of Advertisements | | | | | |
| | Nondurables | | | Durables | | Nondurables | | | Durables | | Share of |
Year	Food	Clothing	Other	Major	Minor	Food	Clothing	Other	Major	Minor	Issue in Ads
1901	11	33	32	14	11	14	29	32	10	16	34
1902	10	37	31	11	11	15	38	30	8	9	38
1903	11	34	31	11	12	21	28	29	10	11	40
1904	10	39	29	12	10	17	38	20	13	13	37
1905	11	31	37	9	12	17	30	28	15	11	41
1906	10	32	34	11	13	17	28	30	17	9	43
1907	7	35	33	14	12	16	34	22	17	12	43
1908	8	39	34	11	8	19	39	25	11	5	43
1909	9	38	33	11	8	17	39	26	14	4	43
1910	15	25	37	13	10	26	27	27	12	8	43
1911	13	38	30	9	10	24	40	19	10	7	44
1912	16	32	36	10	7	26	33	26	8	6	46
1913	13	36	30	10	11	19	37	27	7	9	47
1914	14	29	38	8	11	20	32	31	7	10	43

Table 5.3, continued

| | Percent of Number of Advertisements | | | | | Percent of Pages of Advertisements | | | | | |
| | Nondurables | | | Durables | | Nondurables | | | Durables | | Share of |
Year	Food	Clothing	Other	Major	Minor	Food	Clothing	Other	Major	Minor	Issue in Ads
1915	13	33	38	7	9	18	30	34	11	7	47
1916	15	29	38	8	10	23	30	26	10	12	50
1917	13	29	40	10	7	21	27	30	14	8	51
1918	16	34	36	7	7	26	29	30	8	7	55
1919	19	31	32	10	8	26	28	27	10	8	55
1920	21	25	30	14	10	23	20	29	19	9	60
1921	14	30	41	7	8	19	28	38	7	8	57
1922	16	23	39	11	11	22	23	34	13	9	57
1923	14	23	38	15	10	17	22	36	16	10	59
1924	16	22	41	12	9	22	19	35	14	10	57
1925	17	18	42	13	10	23	17	33	16	11	60
1926	18	18	44	11	8	25	18	36	13	8	61
1927	19	16	45	13	7	26	11	39	15	9	59
1928	22	15	46	11	7	26	12	39	15	7	60

Table 5.3, continued

| | Percent of Number of Advertisements | | | | | Percent of Pages of Advertisements | | | | | |
| | Nondurables | | | Durables | | Nondurables | | | Durables | | Share of |
Year	Food	Clothing	Other	Major	Minor	Food	Clothing	Other	Major	Minor	Issue in Ads
1929	22	14	43	12	9	26	12	35	17	10	60
1930	19	12	53	8	8	26	12	43	11	8	58
1931	22	7	56	9	6	29	7	48	12	5	59
1932	22	12	54	7	5	25	10	49	8	8	56
1933	25	10	53	5	7	30	6	49	7	7	57
1934	23	15	51	4	7	32	11	44	5	8	55
1935	22	16	53	3	6	32	10	48	4	7	51
1936	18	17	56	3	7	27	14	46	3	10	51
1937	19	16	54	4	8	30	14	41	5	10	53
1938	20	15	57	2	6	31	17	44	3	5	52
1939	18	17	53	5	7	30	17	36	8	8	48
1940	18	19	48	6	10	25	18	40	8	9	51
1941	20	15	52	6	8	27	10	44	8	10	54

Sources: Analysis of October issues of *Ladies Home Journal.* Pages of advertisements measured in "full-page equivalent" units. See appendix D.

151

using the figures in table D.3. In 1935, 32 percent of advertisements in *Ladies Home Journal* were for food, 27 percent for personal care items (toiletries), 13 percent for home care items, 11 percent for durable goods, and 10 percent for clothing.[23] This composition of advertising is quite different from that at the beginning of this century. In *Ladies Home Journal*, advertisements for clothing were by far the greatest percentage of advertisements before World War I. In 1902, clothing advertisements were 38 percent of total advertisements; personal care items, 14 percent; food, 16 percent; household cleaners, 7 percent; and durable goods, about 17 percent. By 1915, the emphasis was shifting away from personal items and toward household and family products: clothing advertisements still constituted 30 percent of the total, but personal care items were now only 10 percent; food, 18 percent; household cleaners, 12 percent; and durable goods, still 18 percent. And by 1929, clothing advertisements were only 12 percent of total advertisements; personal care items were again 18 percent; food advertisements had risen to 26 percent; household cleaners were 10 percent; and durable goods were now 26 percent. These changes in what was advertised should be contrasted with the usual stability of advertisers in the magazine. In an October 1915 appeal to advertisers, the editors of the *Ladies Home Journal* claimed that the "great volume of advertising is stable and permanent. Last year more than 86 percent of it came from firms that had also used the *Journal* the year before."[24]

Richard Pollay's analysis of 2,000 advertisements in the ten top circulation magazines reveals similar patterns. Pollay finds little change in the share of advertisements for durable goods through the 1930s, but he documents a big jump in food advertisements in the 1910s, a comparable jump in personal care advertisements in the 1920s and 1930s, and a continual decline in apparel advertisements from the beginning of the century into the 1930s.[25]

ADVERTISING OF DURABLE GOODS

Advertisements for durable goods were never more than 30 percent of all advertisements. Even so, this percentage was substantially more than the share of household spending that went to durable goods; before World War II, never more than 12 percent of total consumption expenditure was for major and minor durable goods. There was no obvious trend in the representation of minor durable goods in advertisements; about 7 to 10 percent of advertising pages were for minor durable goods from 1910 on, though this was less than the share for 1900–1907. For major durable goods, the decades of the 1920s and 1900s were comparable; about 12 to 15 percent of advertising pages were for major durable goods in each decade. This share was somewhat greater than in the 1910s, and in the 1930s advertising for major durable goods all but disappeared.

The composition of advertising for major durable goods was changing after World War I even as the share held steady, as seen in table 5.4. Automobiles were advertised on relatively more pages (up to a maximum of 5 percent of advertising pages in 1926); pianos were advertised relatively less (falling from a maximum of almost 4 percent of advertising space in 1903 to no advertisements at all for pianos or other musical instruments after 1929). There was little appreciable trend in national advertising for appliances, though what cannot be seen from the table is a pronounced movement toward more advertising of electrical appliances after 1914. Among minor durable goods, advertising for china and for house furnishings (especially rugs, wool blankets, and linoleum) consistently made up the bulk of advertising.

Automobile manufacturers had a spotty history with national advertising campaigns before World War II. Ford sold more autos than any other manufacturer but did not consistently have the highest advertising budget. Ford advertised "aggressively" from 1903 to 1911 but then began to discover other, far less costly ways to obtain "advertising" for the Model T; Allan Nevins and Frank Hill note that Henry Ford's institution of the five-dollar day gave the company "more than 2,000,000 lines of favorable advertising on the front pages of newspapers and thousands and thousands of editorial endorsements."[26] Relying on this and other publicity, Ford's corporate advertising department essentially closed down from 1917 to 1922. In the words of Daniel Pope, Ford "would have sooner painted a Model T chartreuse than have undertaken a major national advertising campaign."[27] The company shifted the burden of advertising onto their dealers who purchased primarily newspaper advertising that featured copy that was often provided by the company itself. But in the summer of 1923, Ford Motor Company reestablished its advertising department, and in

Table 5.4. Share of Advertising for Durable Goods by Product, 1901-1941

	Percent of Total Number of Advertisements										
Year	AUT	FUR	APP	PIA	RAD	CHI	HSF	JWL	MED	BKS	MIS
1901	--	6.9	5.8	1.6	--	3.7	2.1	2.1	--	1.1	1.6
1902	--	4.0	2.8	3.6	--	4.5	1.6	2.8	0.8	0.4	1.2
1903	0.3	4.1	3.0	3.7	--	4.1	3.4	2.0	0.7	1.0	0.7
1904	--	6.1	2.0	3.1	0.7	3.4	3.1	2.0	0.7	0.3	0.7
1905	--	4.4	2.4	2.0	--	5.5	4.1	1.7	0.7	--	0.3
1906	--	4.7	3.8	2.3	0.6	5.2	3.8	2.0	0.3	0.9	0.9
1907	--	4.7	5.4	3.4	0.3	5.0	3.0	2.0	1.0	--	1.0
1908	--	5.3	3.7	1.9	0.3	2.8	3.7	0.6	0.3	0.6	0.3
1909	0.3	6.0	2.7	2.0	0.3	3.3	2.3	1.0	0.3	1.0	0.3
1910	0.4	4.8	5.7	1.8	--	4.0	4.4	0.9	--	0.4	--
1911	0.4	3.9	3.5	1.1	0.4	4.2	2.1	2.8	0.4	--	--
1912	0.3	2.8	4.5	1.7	0.3	3.1	2.4	1.0	0.3	--	--
1913	--	3.6	4.7	1.1	0.4	5.1	2.9	1.1	--	1.8	--
1914	--	2.6	3.9	1.3	0.4	5.7	3.0	1.7	--	0.4	--
1915	0.9	0.4	4.0	0.9	0.4	3.5	1.8	1.8	0.4	1.8	--
1916	0.8	2.9	2.9	1.2	0.4	3.7	2.5	2.5	--	0.8	0.4
1917	0.8	4.1	3.3	0.8	1.2	2.4	2.9	0.8	--	1.2	--
1918	0.5	1.9	3.4	--	1.0	1.9	3.9	--	--	1.4	--
1919	0.8	2.8	4.4	--	1.6	4.0	1.2	1.2	--	0.8	0.4
1920	1.5	2.5	6.9	0.5	2.9	4.9	2.5	1.5	--	1.0	0.5
1921	--	3.2	2.8	--	0.9	3.2	4.2	0.5	--	0.5	--
1922	1.1	4.3	5.0	0.4	0.7	5.4	3.9	0.7	--	1.1	--
1923	1.9	5.0	6.6	0.9	0.3	4.7	3.1	1.3	--	0.9	0.3
1924	1.2	3.5	5.8	--	1.2	4.3	3.9	0.8	--	--	--
1925	2.1	4.6	4.9	0.4	1.1	4.9	4.6	--	--	0.4	--
1926	2.7	3.0	4.0	0.3	1.0	4.0	3.7	--	--	0.7	--
1927	2.3	3.1	4.6	0.8	1.9	3.1	3.4	--	--	0.4	--
1928	2.2	2.6	3.6	1.5	0.7	2.2	3.3	0.4	--	1.1	--
1929	1.9	2.2	5.9	0.4	1.5	3.7	4.1	0.4	--	0.7	--

Table 5.4, continued

	Percent of Total Number of Advertisements									
Year	AUT	FUR	APP	PIA	RAD	CHI	HSF	JWL	MED	BKS	MIS
1930	2.7	0.9	4.5	--	--	3.2	4.1	--	--	--	--
1931	2.5	0.5	5.9	--	0.5	1.0	4.4	--	--	0.5	--
1932	0.8	0.8	4.5	--	0.8	2.3	3.0	--	--	--	--
1933	1.3	1.3	2.0	--	--	2.0	4.7	--	--	--	--
1934	0.6	1.1	2.8	--	--	2.2	4.4	--	--	--	--
1935	--	0.6	2.5	--	--	1.9	4.3	--	--	--	--
1936	--	--	2.2	--	0.6	2.2	5.0	--	--	--	--
1937	--	1.3	1.9	--	0.6	3.8	3.8	--	--	--	--
1938	--	0.6	1.2	--	--	3.1	2.5	--	--	--	--
1939	--	1.2	3.6	--	--	4.1	2.4	0.6	--	--	--
1940	0.5	0.5	4.2	--	0.5	6.3	3.2	--	--	--	--
1941	--	2.4	2.8	--	0.4	4.0	3.2	0.4	--	0.4	--

Table 5.4. Share of Advertising for Durable Goods by Product, 1901-1941

	Percent of Total Number of Advertisements										
Year	AUT	FUR	APP	PIA	RAD	CHI	HSF	JWL	MED	BKS	MIS
1901	--	6.9	5.8	1.6	--	3.7	2.1	2.1	--	1.1	1.6
1902	--	4.0	2.8	3.6	--	4.5	1.6	2.8	0.8	0.4	1.2
1903	0.3	4.1	3.0	3.7	--	4.1	3.4	2.0	0.7	1.0	0.7
1904	--	6.1	2.0	3.1	0.7	3.4	3.1	2.0	0.7	0.3	0.7
1905	--	4.4	2.4	2.0	--	5.5	4.1	1.7	0.7	--	0.3
1906	--	4.7	3.8	2.3	0.6	5.2	3.8	2.0	0.3	0.9	0.9
1907	--	4.7	5.4	3.4	0.3	5.0	3.0	2.0	1.0	--	1.0
1908	--	5.3	3.7	1.9	0.3	2.8	3.7	0.6	0.3	0.6	0.3
1909	0.3	6.0	2.7	2.0	0.3	3.3	2.3	1.0	0.3	1.0	0.3
1910	0.4	4.8	5.7	1.8	--	4.0	4.4	0.9	--	0.4	--
1911	0.4	3.9	3.5	1.1	0.4	4.2	2.1	2.8	0.4	--	--
1912	0.3	2.8	4.5	1.7	0.3	3.1	2.4	1.0	0.3	--	--
1913	--	3.6	4.7	1.1	0.4	5.1	2.9	1.1	--	1.8	--
1914	--	2.6	3.9	1.3	0.4	5.7	3.0	1.7	--	0.4	--
1915	0.9	0.4	4.0	0.9	0.4	3.5	1.8	1.8	0.4	1.8	--
1916	0.8	2.9	2.9	1.2	0.4	3.7	2.5	2.5	--	0.8	0.4
1917	0.8	4.1	3.3	0.8	1.2	2.4	2.9	0.8	--	1.2	--
1918	0.5	1.9	3.4	--	1.0	1.9	3.9	--	--	1.4	--
1919	0.8	2.8	4.4	--	1.6	4.0	1.2	1.2	--	0.8	0.4
1920	1.5	2.5	6.9	0.5	2.9	4.9	2.5	1.5	--	1.0	0.5
1921	--	3.2	2.8	--	0.9	3.2	4.2	0.5	--	0.5	--
1922	1.1	4.3	5.0	0.4	0.7	5.4	3.9	0.7	--	1.1	--
1923	1.9	5.0	6.6	0.9	0.3	4.7	3.1	1.3	--	0.9	0.3
1924	1.2	3.5	5.8	--	1.2	4.3	3.9	0.8	--	--	--
1925	2.1	4.6	4.9	0.4	1.1	4.9	4.6	--	--	0.4	--
1926	2.7	3.0	4.0	0.3	1.0	4.0	3.7	--	--	0.7	--
1927	2.3	3.1	4.6	0.8	1.9	3.1	3.4	--	--	0.4	--
1928	2.2	2.6	3.6	1.5	0.7	2.2	3.3	0.4	--	1.1	--
1929	1.9	2.2	5.9	0.4	1.5	3.7	4.1	0.4	--	0.7	--

Table 5.4, continued

	Percent of Total Pages of Advertisements									
Year	AUT	FUR	APP	PIA	RAD	CHI	HSF	JWL	MED	BKS	MIS
1930	3.7	1.0	5.9	--	--	4.3	3.8	--	--	--	--
1931	4.1	0.8	6.2	--	0.4	0.6	4.0	--	--	0.4	--
1932	0.1	1.4	4.6	--	1.4	4.6	3.4	--	--	--	--
1933	2.4	2.4	2.4	--	--	2.1	5.4	--	--	--	--
1934	1.1	1.2	2.9	--	--	2.3	5.9	--	--	--	--
1935	--	1.4	2.3	--	--	2.1	5.0	--	--	--	--
1936	--	--	2.6	--	0.1	2.7	7.3	--	--	--	--
1937	--	2.7	2.2	--	0.3	4.2	5.5	--	--	--	--
1938	--	1.6	1.8	--	--	2.7	2.3	--	--	--	--
1939	--	3.3	5.0	--	--	2.4	4.0	1.7	--	--	--
1940	0.7	1.3	5.2	--	0.3	4.5	4.2	--	--	--	--
1941	--	3.9	4.0	--	0.3	3.7	5.1	1.0	--	0.5	--

Notes: Pages measured in "full-page equivalent" units. See appendix D.

Three-letter abbreviations for the commodity groups are as follows: AUT, automobiles and parts; FUR, furniture; APP, household appliances; PIA, pianos and other musical instruments; RAD, radios and phonographs; CHI, china and tableware; HSF, house furnishings; JWL, jewelry and watches; MED, orthopedic and ophthalmic products; BKS, books and maps; MIS, miscellaneous other durable goods. Major durable goods are the sum of automobiles and parts, furniture, household appliances, pianos and other musical instruments, radios and phonographs, and horse-drawn vehicles (not shown in table; there was just one advertisement for horse-drawn vehicles between 1901 and 1941, appearing in the October 1902 issue). Minor durable goods are all other durable goods, including tombstones (not shown in table; advertisements for tombstones appeared in October 1924, 1927, and 1930 issues only).

1925, attempting to bolster sales of the Model T, Ford spent more money on advertising than did any other company in the United States.

George Hotchkiss captures the dilemma of those who believed in the necessity of advertising but were struck by Ford's no-advertising success. Hotchkiss notes that Ford achieved leadership in the automobile industry "without much advertising. It merely gave efficient low-cost transportation." But even though advertising was not credited with Ford's sales success, its apparent ineffectiveness in reversing declines in sales is nevertheless lamented when Hotchkiss goes right on to note that advertising was unable to "persuade the great body of consumers to accept the familiar old Model T."[28] The Ford roller coaster continued: the company eliminated nearly all advertising expenditure in mid-1926 but undertook a massive campaign when it unveiled the new Model A in 1927.[29]

Noting that both auto production and auto advertising increased by 800 percent between 1910 and 1916, Frank Presbrey all but asserts that the rise in production resulted directly from this advertising boom.[30] Auto advertising continued to grow in the 1920s; Roland Vaile reports that auto manufacturers spent $4 million for national magazine advertising in 1921 but fully $10 million in 1925.[31] In the years before World War I, automobile advertising had focused on the uses and mechanical reliability of autos. By the 1920s, as the market became increasingly one for replacement rather than first-time purchases, advertising had to focus on the need to replace one's auto "every year or two."[32] Corporate identity was also to be established in the public consciousness through advertising; in 1922 General Motors initiated a campaign to advertise the parent company after a company-sponsored consumer survey demonstrated that virtually no one knew "GM."[33]

Presbrey's enthusiasm for automobile advertising seems almost unbounded. In his 1929 book, he trumpets:

> When advertising shall have had fifty years more of development and the practitioner of 1978 looks back over its history he doubtless will regard as unimportant all progress made up to the time advertising was given the automobile to employ itself upon. . . . Successful advertising of the motor car set at rest all doubts as to the ability of the average American to acquire an article of luxury when the pleasure of possession is convincingly pictured to him, and opened the way for a class of advertising that has in a quarter of a century revolutionized American living habits and given us the highest standard of living any people ever enjoyed.[34]

Not only had advertising provided such a grand standard of living, but it seemed nearly all the commercial success of the automobile industry was to be credited to advertising.

Leaders in the automobile industry who recall the difficulty experienced early in the century in securing a wide acceptance of the automobile by the public have no doubts as to what it was that created demand. This demand made possible mass production and low price. "Advertising," said President Alfred P. Sloan, Jr., of the General Motors Company in 1928, "has reduced the cost of many articles, such as automobiles, as no other business force could." John N. Willys in 1926 put it thus: "Today sixty-nine cents will buy, in an automobile, what cost a dollar on the pre-war basis; advertising has done the big thing." In 1927 E. T. Strong, president of the Buick Motor Company, said: "We all know it [advertising] to be the one great force in the merchandising scheme upon which depends the success of every other element in the process."[35]

The president of General Motors may have believed advertising allowed production costs to be lowered, but the economist Roland Vaile disputed the claim. Vaile wrote in 1927:

During that period [1914 to 1925] there was little advertising effort devoted to the advantages of owning automobiles. There was much quarreling as to which automobile was the "best," but that was all. It hardly seems reasonable to credit any large part of the increased efficiency of manufacture to the public bickerings of salesmen, especially during years when everyone was forced to realize the existence of automobiles at every turn; if one were not aware of them he was promptly run down! . . . Something else must be responsible for the increased effectiveness of labor.[36]

Studying advertising of refrigerators, Neil Borden repeated but qualified the claim that advertising facilitated the adoption of large-scale, low-cost production methods. Noting that both advertising and "persuasive" personal selling of mechanical refrigerators intensified after 1924, Borden claims that without these active efforts, demand would have risen much more slowly.[37] Furthermore, firms could not exploit economies of scale in production until demand rose to a sufficiently high level. While he explicitly credits technological advances rather than advertising with decreasing production costs, Borden's argument implies that advertising was at least a catalyst to lowering costs: advertising spurred demand which allowed adoption of large-scale production methods that could take advantage of new technology.[38]

ADVERTISING CREDIT'S AVAILABILITY

If availability of financing terms had been used to market major durable goods, we would expect to see such availability mentioned (even featured) in advertisements for major durable goods. Especially for nationally distributed products where the manufacturer rather than an individual seller made arrangements for retail financing—products like automobiles—it seems availability of credit ought to have been part of the advertisement.

Yet throughout the 1920s and 1930s, when a total of sixty-one different automobile advertisements were printed in *Ladies Home Journal*, only four advertisements mentioned the availability of credit: a 1925 Willys-Knight advertisement, which mentioned time payments in the text of the ad; two Chrysler advertisements, one in 1927 and one in 1929, both noting credit availability in a footnote; and a 1931 Cadillac advertisement with "GMAC terms available" in small print. A 1924 Ford advertisement published elsewhere did feature Ford's Weekly Purchasing Plan, announcing "Buy your Ford now or start weekly payments on it."[39] Lest the public incorrectly conclude Henry Ford had finally granted his approval to credit buying, they had only to read the company's November 1926 advertisement: "Despite confusion, in the minds of many, of extravagance with progress, a vast majority [of the American people] cling to the old-fashioned idea of living within their incomes. From these came and are coming the millions of Ford owners."[40]

Before World War I, "easy payment plans" were mentioned most often in advertisements for pianos. As seen in table 5.5, credit was mentioned in at least one piano advertisement in each year between 1901 and 1917. After World War I, easy payment plans were instead mentioned most often in advertisements for appliances, especially electrical appliances, yet even here rarely more than 25 percent of appliances were advertised as available on the installment plan. If manufacturers were offering credit as a means to market their products, they certainly were not making it a part of their advertising strategy!

Table 5.5. Shares of Number of Advertisements That Mention Credit, 1901-1941 (Percent)

Year	AUT	HDV	OMV	FUR	APP	PIA	RAD	CHI	HSF	JWL	MED	BKS	MIS	TMB	Major	Minor
1901	--	--	--	0	0	79	--	0	0	0	--	0	0	--	10.3	0.0
1902	--	0	--	0	0	35	--	0	0	0	0	0	0	--	12.6	0.0
1903	0	--	--	0	0	65	--	0	0	22	0	90	0	--	23.3	23.0
1904	--	--	--	0	0	55	0	0	0	0	0	0	0	--	15.5	0.0
1905	--	--	--	5	0	80	--	0	0	0	0	--	0	--	12.5	0.0
1906	--	--	--	0	0	47	0	0	0	0	0	0	0	--	4.7	0.0
1907	--	--	--	0	10	27	0	0	0	0	0	--	0	--	7.9	0.0
1908	--	--	--	0	14	19	0	0	6	0	0	0	0	--	7.7	1.5
1909	0	--	--	22	0	48	0	0	0	0	0	0	0	--	20.6	0.0
1910	0	--	--	15	0	61	--	0	0	0	--	0	--	--	15.4	0.0
1911	0	--	--	23	0	42	0	0	0	0	0	--	--	--	13.6	0.0
1912	0	--	--	32	17	29	0	0	0	0	0	--	--	--	16.4	0.0
1913	--	--	--	0	15	69	0	0	0	0	--	--	--	--	20.9	0.0
1914	--	--	--	0	21	18	0	0	0	0	--	0	--	--	10.2	0.0
1915	0	--	--	100	7	30	0	0	0	0	0	0	--	--	5.3	0.0
1916	0	--	--	2	30	100	0	0	0	0	--	0	0	--	12.1	0.0

161

Table 5.5, continued

Year	AUT	HDV	OMV	FUR	APP	PIA	RAD	CHI	HSF	JWL	MED	BKS	MIS	TMB	Major	Minor
1917	0	--	--	42	49	100	0	0	0	0	--	0	--	--	23.0	0.0
1918	0	--	--	0	0	--	0	0	0	--	--	0	--	--	0.0	0.0
1919	0	--	--	0	37	--	0	0	0	0	--	0	0	--	13.1	0.0
1920	0	--	--	36	27	0	0	0	0	0	--	0	0	--	16.5	0.0
1921	--	--	--	0	26	--	0	0	0	0	--	0	--	--	6.9	0.0
1922	0	--	--	18	7	0	0	0	0	0	--	0	--	--	9.1	0.0
1923	0	--	--	32	22	12	0	0	6	0	--	0	0	--	17.6	1.9
1924	0	--	--	21	30	--	33	0	0	0	--	--	--	0	23.3	0.0
1925	17	--	--	25	26	0	0	12	0	--	--	0	--	--	19.9	5.9
1926	0	--	--	20	28	0	20	6	0	--	--	0	--	--	14.4	3.9
1927	17	--	--	0	12	0	38	0	0	--	--	0	--	0	13.4	0.0
1928	0	--	--	0	1	63	0	0	0	0	--	20	--	--	5.5	2.3
1929	32	--	--	0	13	100	25	0	0	0	--	33	--	--	19.7	1.6
1930	0	--	--	0	26	--	--	0	21	--	--	--	--	0	14.7	9.4
1931	20	--	--	0	43	--	0	0	0	--	--	0	--	--	30.1	0.0
1932	0	--	--	0	8	--	0	0	0	--	--	--	--	--	4.8	0.0

Table 5.5, continued

Year	AUT	HDV	OMV	FUR	APP	PIA	RAD	CHI	HSF	JWL	MED	BKS	MIS	TMB	Major	Minor
1933	0	--	--	0	0	--	--	0	0	--	--	--	--	--	0.0	0.0
1934	0	--	--	94	0	--	--	0	10	--	--	--	--	--	21.8	7.0
1935	--	--	--	100	0	--	--	0	0	--	--	--	--	--	37.5	0.0
1936	--	--	--	--	0	--	0	0	0	--	--	--	--	--	0.0	0.0
1937	--	--	--	0	0	--	0	0	0	--	--	--	--	--	0.0	0.0
1938	--	--	--	0	89	--	--	29	0	--	--	--	--	--	47.0	15.4
1939	--	--	--	50	0	--	--	0	0	100	--	--	--	--	20.0	20.7
1940	0	--	--	100	0	--	0	0	0	--	--	--	--	--	17.8	0.0
1941	--	--	--	0	0	--	0	27	0	100	--	0	--	--	0.0	19.4

Source: Derived from table D.6. HDV stands for horse-drawn vehicles; OMV stands for other motor vehicles; TMB stands for tombstones. Other commodity group abbreviations as for table 5.4.

163

ADVERTISING A GOOD'S PRICE

Readers *were* likely to learn of a durable good's price in an advertisement, however. And while a reader might have to search carefully to find mention of the availability of credit financing tucked away in a tiny note at the end of an advertisement, prices of durable goods could rarely be missed even with a casual glance; they were generally announced in large type, bold print, or both.[41] Throughout the sample period 1901–41, over 40 percent of *Ladies Home Journal* advertisements for durable goods included a reference to price, either noting the explicit price of the good or making a general reference such as "low prices."

Daniel Pope notes that in the first years of this century, advertising agencies advised against mentioning price in advertisements.[42] Their advice must have been followed; price was mentioned less frequently in the first decade of this century than in any other decade before World War II. We might expect that price would have been mentioned more often after World War I than before, when (according to the analysis in chapter 3) households were more sensitive to changes in durable goods' prices. But as table 5.6 shows, the experience of the 1920s stands out only in relation to the early 1930s, not to the 1910s. Prices of minor and particularly major durable goods were less likely to be included in advertisements between 1918 and 1924, and much more likely to have been included in those published in the early 1930s.[43]

Throughout 1901–41, nearly every advertisement for a radio or phonograph noted the good's price. Before 1920, 13 of the 14 advertisements for automobiles noted the price. But in the 1920s, only 18 of 46 auto advertisements (39 percent) mentioned how much the car cost. The trend reversed again in the 1930s, when 10 of 15 auto advertisements included the car's price. After about 1923, advertisements for china were more likely to include price, but advertisements for the other heavily advertised minor durable good, various house furnishings, were less likely to include price.

Most noteworthy is the experience of October 1921, an issue distributed in the midst of the 1920–21 recession and price deflation. Suddenly it was twice as likely that advertisements for durable goods would mention the good's price; while there were fewer advertisements for durable goods (33 in 1921 as opposed to 50 in 1920), price was mentioned in more of them (17 in 1921 as opposed to only 15 in 1920). Starch also notes much more

Table 5.6. Shares of Number of Advertisements That Mention Price, 1901-1941 (Percent)

Year	AUT	HDV	OMV	FUR	APP	PIA	RAD	CHI	HSF	JWL	MED	BKS	MIS	TMB	Major	Minor
1901	--	--	--	68	37	55	--	24	0	54	--	5	90	--	53.3	29.0
1902	--	100	--	35	40	0	--	38	14	6	0	0	100	--	26.0	35.2
1903	100	--	--	34	18	47	--	22	50	11	0	100	0	--	36.0	39.5
1904	--	--	--	70	33	25	100	13	61	15	0	100	53	--	51.9	27.6
1905	--	--	--	53	10	26	--	35	52	100	0	--	0	--	33.0	50.5
1906	--	--	--	43	10	26	0	21	36	96	0	85	33	--	23.6	40.7
1907	--	--	--	16	7	26	100	37	58	71	61	--	0	--	25.1	43.1
1908	--	--	--	40	33	0	0	29	32	74	0	0	0	--	29.4	28.5
1909	100	--	--	71	38	37	100	21	30	82	0	82	0	--	63.4	27.7
1910	0	--	--	48	19	80	--	44	50	11	--	100	--	--	40.3	44.1
1911	0	--	--	47	51	71	100	49	29	1	0	--	--	--	58.3	32.0
1912	100	--	--	25	22	4	0	33	37	91	0	--	--	--	19.7	51.8
1913	--	--	--	57	52	55	100	27	66	52	--	53	--	--	66.4	36.6
1914	--	--	--	49	23	0	100	44	91	75	--	0	--	--	46.0	55.5
1915	100	--	--	0	15	70	100	56	100	63	0	26	--	--	65.8	59.1
1916	100	--	--	14	67	74	100	48	89	96	--	74	0	--	70.1	70.9

Table 5.6, continued

Year	AUT	HDV	OMV	FUR	APP	PIA	RAD	CHI	HSF	JWL	MED	BKS	MIS	TMB	Major	Minor
1917	67	--	--	28	45	67	67	41	38	100	--	52	--	--	53.0	44.7
1918	100	--	--	27	47	--	100	43	23	--	--	94	--	--	71.0	33.4
1919	0	--	--	37	0	--	71	43	0	100	--	100	100	--	27.4	49.0
1920	0	--	--	0	2	0	46	26	43	100	--	100	100	--	13.4	49.0
1921	--	--	--	8	26	--	100	66	68	100	--	100	--	--	38.4	68.6
1922	25	--	--	9	6	0	100	33	65	77	--	100	--	--	20.6	47.6
1923	33	--	--	16	21	44	100	54	33	49	--	57	100	--	27.1	47.3
1924	0	--	--	47	15	--	67	54	37	100	--	--	--	0	29.6	48.0
1925	33	--	--	25	55	100	33	63	26	--	--	0	--	--	37.8	43.4
1926	63	--	--	1	44	0	100	55	39	--	--	8	--	--	46.6	48.5
1927	50	--	--	40	37	0	100	59	28	--	--	0	--	0	48.1	42.7
1928	50	--	--	24	0	63	33	100	26	100	--	0	--	--	28.3	55.3
1929	48	--	--	100	10	100	75	61	40	100	--	0	--	--	50.7	52.4
1930	58	--	--	80	60	--	--	99	29	--	--	--	--	0	61.3	64.9
1931	80	--	--	100	30	--	100	100	48	--	--	0	--	--	54.9	50.1
1932	100	--	--	100	14	--	100	100	95	--	--	--	--	--	47.7	98.0

Table 5.6, continued

Year	AUT	HDV	OMV	FUR	APP	PIA	RAD	CHI	HSF	JWL	MED	BKS	MIS	TMB	Major	Minor
1933	50	--	--	50	0	--	--	86	22	--	--	--	--	--	33.3	39.3
1934	0	--	--	94	1	--	--	49	49	--	--	--	--	--	22.3	49.1
1935	--	--	--	100	63	--	--	67	59	--	--	--	--	--	76.6	61.3
1936	--	--	--	--	25	--	100	52	4	--	--	--	--	--	28.9	17.1
1937	--	--	--	50	0	--	100	47	25	--	--	--	--	--	32.2	34.4
1938	--	--	--	100	0	--	--	68	0	--	--	--	--	--	47.0	36.6
1939	--	--	--	50	58	--	--	83	42	100	--	--	--	--	55.0	66.4
1940	0	--	--	100	87	--	0	70	4	--	--	--	--	--	77.8	38.2
1941	--	--	--	52	31	--	100	55	25	100	--	0	--	--	43.1	41.6

Source: Derived from table D.7. Commodity group abbreviations as for table 5.5.

frequent mention of prices in advertisements published between 1920 and 1922, as the postwar price adjustment occurred.[44]

Pollay found a similar temporal pattern to the frequency with which advertising copy included price, although his results are for all advertisements and not just durable goods. About 50 percent of his advertisements noted price in the decades of the 1900s, 1910s, and 1920s; 43 percent did so in the 1930s; and only 25 to 35 percent included price in the 1940s, 1950s, 1960s, and 1970s.[45] Pollay's result for the 1930s—that price was mentioned less often than in the 1920s—contrasts not only with those for durable goods advertised in *Ladies Home Journal* but also with the observations of contemporary scholars who noted that advertising copy in the depression years increasingly stressed price as a selling point.[46]

Pollay also found that advertisements for durable goods were more likely to include price information than were those for other consumer goods. For his entire sample period, 1900–1980, only 39 percent of all advertisements included price, while 46 percent of advertisements for durable goods did so.[47] The difference may be attributable to the relative frequency with which households purchase durable goods. Buyers rely on advertisements for product information more heavily for goods purchased only once every few years than for goods purchased weekly or monthly.[48]

Comparing *Ladies Home Journal* advertisements for different durable goods, in general we find that price was featured relatively more often in advertisements for minor rather than major durable goods, though the difference was small. In addition, the frequency with which price was mentioned varied more between decades than between major and minor durable goods.[49] As seen from table 5.6, in some years price information was advertised much more frequently for minor than for major durable goods. These exceptions occurred in the mid-1900s and mid-1910s, though even they are dwarfed by the substantial differences observed for 1919–24. In 1919, 1920, and 1922, barely 20 percent of advertisements for major durable goods mentioned price, but around 50 percent of advertisements for minor durable goods did.

WHY WAS THERE MORE ADVERTISING?

Why did the volume of advertising increase, and why did the composition of what was advertised change? A variety of arguments have been offered.

The boom in post–World War I advertising is variously associated with the rise of big business and adoption of mass production methods in consumer goods industries; the large inventory buildups of the 1920–21 recession, which underscored the need to maintain consumer demand; the need to counter underconsumption or overproduction tendencies, which first transpired in the 1920s; the success of the World War I propaganda campaign and especially the Liberty and Victory Bond campaigns; and the wartime imposition of a federal excess profits tax (sometimes called the wartime profits tax), which defined advertising as a fully deductible, legitimate business expense.

Evidence from one advertising agency, N. W. Ayer and Son, lends support to an emphasis on the rise of big business. Between 1921 and 1930, as total advertising volume exploded throughout the economy, the agency experienced a rapid drop in the number of accounts but quite an increase in their total dollar volume of business as advertising became overwhelmingly the bailiwick of only large accounts.[50] But we should quickly note that these changes also support an emphasis on the role of the excess profits tax.

It was often presumed that the expense of advertising actually *lowered* business costs. Indeed, advertisers themselves used this argument in trying to woo clients. Advertising would increase demand, enabling the firm to increase production and exploit (presumed) economies of scale, thereby lowering the unit cost of production and permitting the firm to lower the price of the product without lowering profit.[51] In the 1920s there were few voices of dissent to this rosy scenario.[52] One economist even claimed that if all advertising were suddenly eliminated, prices would actually rise because demand and therefore the size of firms would be smaller.[53]

Others argue not that advertising allowed mass production but that mass production necessitated advertising. Technological advances permitted new production methods, which required high levels of output in order to be profitable. Daniel Pope asserts that high fixed costs inherent in capital-intensive production and the related importance of avoiding large production swings meant "advertising could be a strategy to match demand to the conditions of capitalist production required by the new technologies."[54] Roland Vaile made a related point. Modern industry expands not in smooth, continuous units but in large, discrete chunks, as expensive pieces of machinery or additional plants are obtained. The "periodic unused capacity" that is therefore part and parcel of modern industry is a "principal urge behind advertising."[55]

President Calvin Coolidge emphasized the interdependence of advertising, mass production, and mass demand in a speech delivered to the American Association of Advertising Agencies in 1926.

> Under the stimulation of advertising, the country has gone from the old hand methods of production which were so slow and laborious with high unit costs and low wages to our present great factory system and its mass production with the astonishing results of low unit costs and high wages.... Mass production is only possible where there is mass demand. Mass demand has been created almost entirely through the development of advertising. . . . Modern business . . . constantly requires publicity. It is not enough that goods are made—a demand for them must also be made. It is on this foundation of enlarging production through the demands created by advertising that very much of the success of the American industrial system rests.[56]

That advertising became so much more prevalent in the 1920s in particular is sometimes viewed as a side effect of the 1920–21 recession. Although the recession was short-lived (only nineteen months according to the NBER), it was intense and distinctive for its unusually large swings in inventory holdings.[57] Some credit advertising with facilitating the selling off of inventory.[58] Alfred Chandler argues not that advertising saved the day in 1921 but that by focusing the attention of business management on consumer demand and thereby on advertising and other marketing efforts, these inventory buildups were an indirect boon to the advertising industry.[59]

If businesses recognized advertising's usefulness because of the 1920–21 recession, they certainly did not uniformly do so *during* that recession. In a widely cited study, Roland Vaile looked specifically at advertising practices and sales of over 200 "well-known" firms during the recession. While close to sixty firms in his sample increased advertising expenditure during the recession, the general tendency was for firms to increase advertising during prosperity but decrease it during economic downturns. Studies of advertising today typically presume that a firm's sales determine its advertising.[60] But in the 1920s the presumed direction of causality was reversed; that high sales and high advertising expenditure tended to go hand in hand was "proof" of the efficacy of advertising, not evidence that firms followed a "percentage-of-sales rule" in setting their advertising budgets.[61] So it is less surprising that Vaile concludes from his study that "where intensive advertising during depression was a part of the sales technique, sales were maintained in better volume than where advertising appropriations were cut. . . . Advertising is a form of sales effort, and its reduction at a time of depression seems to have resulted in a greater loss of sales than was experienced by the firms which constantly depended on other types of distribution."[62]

More generally, the boom in advertising may have resulted from increased recognition in the 1920s of the role of advertising in increasing demand, particularly after the "passing of the so-called seller's market" in 1921.[63] Firms may have undertaken additional advertising to avoid the immediate perils of an economy-wide tendency toward underconsumption that first arose in the 1920s.[64] Even U.S. Secretary of Labor James Davis claimed in 1927 that "unemployment and business depression can be avoided by increases in advertising."[65]

The 1920–21 recession may well have inspired a number of firms to begin or broaden their advertising efforts, but to attribute all responsibility for the boom in advertising either to the recession or to the relative abundance of goods in the 1920s overlooks earlier moves toward greater advertising volume. Figure 5.1 clearly shows that the boom in advertising volume began as early as 1917. *Ladies Home Journal* quickly moved from devoting 50 percent of an issue to advertising in 1916 to using fully 60 percent of its pages for advertising in 1920.

Many attribute this earlier growth of advertising expenditure and volume to what was widely perceived as the success of advertising in the World War I effort. American advertising sounded a patriotic pitch as it sought to sell Liberty and Victory Bonds, raise money for the Red Cross, and more. Otis Pease writes, "Advertising men took pride in the success with which they had helped to persuade a nation at war to invest in Liberty Bonds, to forego sugar and meat, to drive its women into munitions plants, and to think of the unpleasant work of trench warfare as a crusade. . . ."[66] Frank Presbrey goes so far as to credit advertising with shortening the war and saving lives: "Without doubt employment of advertising by the United States and the Allies brought an earlier amassing of resources that shortened the war by many months and saved millions of lives, besides those saved by Red Cross work that funds raised through advertising made possible."[67]

Advertising's success in the war effort had a variety of effects. Advertisers were quite impressed with themselves. In 1919 at the fiftieth anniversary celebration of the founding of N. W. Ayer and Son, the founder's son proclaimed:

> Can you conceive a more remarkable demonstration [of advertising as a social force] than has been the war use of advertising to sell Liberty Loans, to create favorable opinion toward America, to develop our own morale, to undermine the morale of our enemies? These more recent uses of advertising clearly point the way toward the field of its greater future usefulness in the extension of goodwill advertising for private commercial business, as well as for the more efficient service of the community at large and the country as a whole.[68]

Bankers noted the enormous sales of Liberty Bonds, associated the success with advertising, and subsequently initiated their own advertising campaigns to bring in additional deposits.[69] And other business executives granted new respect and credibility to the entire advertising industry, whose members before the war had been "in a class with side-show barkers and check-suited salesmen, socially rejected, morally suspect; the trade was hardly worthy of recognition by a government agency, to say nothing of a respectable business firm. . . ."[70]

But even the most successful war propaganda campaign might not have generated such an explosion in advertising expenditure had it not been for the federal government's imposition of an excess profits tax. The government set the top corporate tax rate at 2 percent in 1916 and then increased it to 6 percent in 1917 and 12 percent in 1918. In March 1917, the government initiated a tax on profit in excess of 8 percent of invested capital. The tax was originally set at 8 percent, but just seven months later the excess profits tax rate was capped at 60 percent, and early in 1919 the top rate was raised further to 65 percent.[71]

Advertising expenses were fully deductible business costs. For highly profitable companies, the excess profits tax alone meant a dollar spent on advertising was sixty and then sixty-five cents saved in taxes. Put another way, a business could buy a dollar's worth of advertising for only thirty-five or forty cents net cost (and this calculation ignores the effect of the corporate tax, which lowers the net cost of advertising even further to about twenty-three cents).[72] Firms bought larger and larger advertisements and, with few if any products to sell, they purchased "good will" advertising to keep their name in the public eye.[73]

CHANGES IN STYLE AND TONE

Not only was the quantity of advertising greater after World War I than before, but its appearance and tone were different too. This change can also be seen as a consequence of World War I advertising and the excess profits tax: more goodwill rather than product advertising together with the successful Liberty and Victory Bond campaigns inspired advertising copy that increasingly emphasized ideas over product characteristics.[74] Describing the changes in advertising's tone, Frederick Lewis Allen writes:

> [In the 1920s], no longer was it considered enough to recommend one's goods in modest and explicit terms and to place them on the counter in the hope that the ultimate consumer would make up his or her mind to purchase. . . . [T]he copywriter was learning to pay less attention to the special qualities and advantages of his product, and more to the study of what the mass of unregenerate mankind wanted—to be young and desirable, to be rich, to keep up with the Joneses, to be envied. The winning method was to associate the product with one or more of these ends, logically or illogically, truthfully or cynically. . . .[75]

Quantifying Allen's observations, Pollay analyzed the "tactical focus" of advertisements by decade, noting for each of his 2,000 advertisements which of three tactics predominates: product features, benefits to gain, or risks to avoid. In the first decade of this century, 59 percent of advertisements emphasized product features and 40 percent emphasized benefits of use. By the 1920s only 29 percent of advertisements emphasized the good's features and fully 62 percent emphasized the benefits of its use. This emphasis on benefits continued into the 1930s (63 percent of advertisements featuring benefits), but suddenly and for that decade only, advertisements focused increasingly on the risks to avoid (17 percent of advertisements did so).[76]

Roland Marchand, in a fascinating study of advertisements of the 1920s and 1930s replete with hundreds of actual advertisements, also notes that advertising copy after World War I increasingly focused on the consumer rather than on products. Advertisements began to tell parables: the Parable of the First Impression (Will body odor ruin that crucial first impression others have of you? Use our product.); the Parable of the Democracy of Goods (You too can live like royalty. Buy this affordable product that even the wealthy enjoy.); the Parable of Civilization Redeemed (Until our product came along, people lived uncivilized lives.); and the Parable of the Captivated Child (Are you forced to nag your child into eating? Be a good parent by offering your child our product.).[77] Sanford Dornbusch and Lauren Hickman found further evidence of significant change in the nature of advertisements after 1920, when advertising themes increasingly emphasized "other-directedness"—increasing someone else's happiness rather than your own through use of the advertised product.[78]

These changes in tone reflect in part the early twentieth-century marriage of psychology and advertising. With the blessings of leaders in the advertising industry, academic psychologists had begun applying principles of psychology to advertising content in the very early years of this century.[79] The courtship began in earnest in 1901, when Walter Dill Scott addressed a gathering of businessmen regarding the psychology of advertising.[80] Scott's book *The Theory of Advertising* appeared in 1903. Advertisers were initially skeptical, and acceptance of Scott's thesis—that psychological principles, especially the concept of suggestion, could be effectively applied to advertising—was slow in coming. But by about 1910 the relationship was in full bloom. According to David Kuna, by that year "the concept of suggestion had become deeply entrenched in the thinking of professional advertising men."[81] Any remaining skeptics were surely won over by the success of the World War I propaganda efforts which demonstrated the powerful effects persuasive advertising could have upon the American populace.[82] By the 1920s, writes Pope, "psychologists were bringing the new gospel of behaviorism to the study of advertising."[83] According to Pollay, advertising's full acceptance of psychology into the fold was "most dramatically symbolized by the hiring of the famous behaviorist, J. B. Watson, as vice president of a major New York agency in the late 1920s."[84]

A number of psychology and advertising texts appeared in the 1920s, authored by professors of psychology many of whose academic affiliations were with schools of business.[85] Edward Strong expressed succinctly the purpose of these texts in the preface to his 1925 textbook: "Selling in terms of permanent satisfaction, developing goodwill, converting potential prospects into regular customers, are all real psychological problems. They result when certain definite changes have taken place in the minds of prospects so that they come to think and feel in a new way. . . . The purpose of this book is to supply a working formula in terms of which a seller may . . . tend steadily to convert buyers into customers. A few years ago there would have been little interest in this subject."[86] Similarly, Darrell Lucas and C. E. Benson claimed that the four "aims of psychology in advertising" were to understand human reactions, to provide a scientific basis for advertising appeals, to assess the effects of various mechanical aspects of advertisements (such as color, typeface, size, and so on), and to construct audience profiles so that advertisements were appropriately designed for each intended medium.[87]

Much of this could only be accomplished by first identifying the fundamental wants or desires of human beings. Every text included therefore a list of anywhere from fifteen to forty-five such desires. Daniel Starch ranked his list, claiming the top ten human wants or motives for action were: appetite (hunger), love of offspring, health, sex attraction, parental affection, ambition, pleasure, bodily comfort, possession, and approval by others.[88] Copywriters responded. A 1923 study found the following appeals contained in print advertisements:[89]

Direction of Appeal	Number of Cases
Appeal to vanity	39
Appeal to shame	22
Appeal to sex curiosity	17
Appeal to cupidity	17
Appeal to fear	8
Palpably false	44
Harmful products	28
All others	69
Total	244

Changes in advertising copy inspired by the counsel of behavioral psychologists set up an ongoing conflict in the early twentieth century between two types of advertising: "reason-why" and "atmosphere" advertising.[90] Reason-why advertising usually consisted of long, detailed discourses on the features of a product; atmosphere advertising emphasized "mental images, illustrations, attractive girls, healthy children, and prosperous family scenes."[91]

In the late nineteenth century, reason-why advertising was dominant as advertisers sought to distinguish themselves in the public's eye from "patent medicine vendors and confidence men" by invoking what historian T. J. Jackson Lears calls the "rhetoric of sincerity": "For advertising men, . . . truth was insufficient and sometimes irrelevant. The important job was . . . making the Truth 'Sound True.' Sincerity had become at once a moral stance and a tactic of persuasion."[92]

Atmosphere advertising made an appearance early in this century with the introduction of psychological principles into the field but was at first almost completely dominated by reason-why advertising. The conflict between the two types of advertising was especially intense in the decade before World War I. In 1909, the advertisers of Colgate toothpaste even took this conflict directly to consumers, giving them the opportunity to decide "Which is the Better Ad?"—the one that offered a detailed explanation of the health advantages of Colgate toothpaste, or the one that used illustrations to associate the use of Colgate with a happy family life. Contemporaries seemed surprised when the responses were equally divided; the public looked more favorably upon the suggestive copy than had been expected.[93]

By the mid-1920s, the two approaches coexisted "in a sniping stalemate."[94] It was becoming clear that no one form should completely hold sway. Each had its place. Reason-why copy was appropriate for industrial advertising, where decision making rested on a "rational" profit motive. Starch argued that reason-why copy was also appropriate for advertising consumer durable goods; because these goods were purchased infrequently, buyers needed advertisements that contained more information about the goods' characteristics.[95] Similarly, Lucas and Benson concluded in 1930 that "Reason, emotions, and habits all enter into each purchase, but in varying degrees. Reasoning efforts probably lead the publisher to buy an improved printing press in order to increase the output. Emotions lead some men to burden themselves with a heavy load of life insurance, or to buy extravagant clusters of roses for their fiancées. Habits predominate in our regular purchases, keeping Bon Ami on the shelf and Camels in the pocket."[96]

Lears associates the rise of atmosphere advertising with increasing similarity of different brands of the same product: "Confronted by standardization born of technological advances, advertisers sought to make a particular beer seem 'special' (1907) or to establish that 'Bread Isn't Just Bread' (1930)."[97] Similarly, Pope argues that effective advertising required creation of a "distinctive, differentiated product, one that promised real or imagined advantages over rival brands or unbranded goods."[98] With increasing standardization of consumer products eliminating many of the real differences between brands, the emphasis of advertising shifted to the "imagined" advantages.

By contrast, contemporaries claimed not that standardization created a need for advertising but that advertising created the need for products to be standardized. Technological advances allowing standardization were responses to needs *created by* advertising. Starch claimed, "Standardized packages and brands might have developed and no doubt would have developed quite apart from advertising. However, it is quite certainly true that this development has been much more rapid and far more widespread through the aid of printed publicity than it would otherwise have been."[99] Similarly, Hotchkiss wrote that "national advertising stimulated the practice of standardizing and trade-marking commodities."[100]

Changes in the tone and style of advertising also reflected advertisers' changing attitudes toward consumers. Advertisers increasingly looked upon themselves as quite set apart from the consumers who saw their ads. Twentieth-century consumers were viewed as having little time to spare and therefore valuing brevity in advertisements, and as having "irrational impulses."[101] More to the point, copywriters were male, and consumers were female. From studying advertising agency archives, Marchand finds that advertisers were predominately male, white, Christian, upper-class, well-educated New Yorkers who frequently employed servants and even chauffeurs and whose cultural tastes ran to modern art, opera, and symphonies. These men saw their audience as female; fickle; debased; emo-

tional; possessing a natural inferiority complex; having inarticulate long-
ings, low intelligence, and bad taste; and being culturally backward.[102]

Their public pronouncements were more charitable. In a discourse on
the advertising business written by one of its executives, the author argued that advertising should be consciously directed toward women since
they were the "purchasing agents" of the family: "Advertising is . . . the
business of housekeeping. . . . [Women] need information on which to base
their selections, and advertising supplies that information."[103] Indeed,
Vaile commented that men, not women, were "especially susceptible to
brand advertising because they do not care to 'shop,' and because they are
willing to accept the same article time after time."[104]

The importance of women as the "purchasing agents" of the home was
apparent in advertising copy. Winifred Wandersee notes that in the 1920s,
"Advertising . . . changed qualitatively, playing upon the emotions, fears,
and anxieties of Americans."[105] What better example of this emphasis
than the advertisement headline judged in 1929 as the most effective:
"The Call That Will Wake Any Mother." "A curious reader," Lucas and
Benson comment, "would want to know the cause of the distress."[106]

Ruth Schwartz Cowan surveyed advertisements and articles that appeared in national women's magazines in the 1920s and found that "appli-
ance ads specifically suggested that the acquisition of one gadget or another would make it possible to fire the maid, spend more time with the
children, or have the afternoon free for shopping."[107] To summarize her
findings, Cowan writes, "If I had to choose one word to characterize the
temper of the women's magazines during the 1920s, it would be 'guilt.'
Readers of the better quality women's magazines are portrayed as feeling
guilty a good lot of the time, and when they are not guilty they are em-
barrassed."[108]

These approaches to advertising the products that women purchased
were no secret, of course. In her 1938 consumer economics textbook, Margaret Reid politely wrote, "Consumers should find it very enlightening to
look at themselves through the eyes of sellers, to see the rating sellers
place on their intelligence and their emotional stability and to become
aware of the influences which will lead them to make initial purchases
and to come back for more. An enlightened consumer is one who sees
through the methods and techniques."[109]

ADVERTISING AND THE CONSUMER DURABLES REVOLUTION

Did advertising change consumer tastes, increasing the desire to own consumer durable goods and leading to the Consumer Durables Revolution? Or would the Consumer Durables Revolution have transpired even in the absence of the developments in advertising? It appears we can answer both yes and no to both questions.

Keep in mind that the Consumer Durables Revolution, as it has been defined here, is not characterized simply by greater household expenditure for durables over time. A Consumer Durables Revolution occurred in this century because demand for most but not all durable goods changed—households responded more aggressively to changes in relative prices and income (elasticities increased), or some more general change occurred in household demand. Even though households bought more china and more house furnishings in the 1920s than previously, the Consumer Durables Revolution did not extend to these product groups; we can explain rising expenditure for these two groups of products as standard household responses to changes in prices and income.

That many consumer durables were new products in the early part of this century is particularly relevant when assessing the role of advertising in the Consumer Durables Revolution. Advertising can hasten the adoption of new products. Buyers must learn of the availability and characteristics of the products, and advertising is an effective means by which to do so.[110] Without advertising or, as illustrated by Ford's success, other forms of publicity, dissemination of new products relies upon word of mouth, a much slower process of informing the public. The marked changes in household demand for automobiles, household appliances (especially electrical appliances), and radios and phonographs no doubt reflects advertising's ability to put these products squarely in the public eye.

Consistent with the empirical results of chapter 3, Neil Borden notes that advertising can increase demand elasticities for new products. When products are new and consumers are accordingly skeptical, changes in product price or household income have little effect on demand so long as that skepticism remains. To the extent that advertising leads to acceptance of a new good and resultant increases in its use throughout the economy, skepticism erodes, and consumers begin to respond to changes in price or income.[111]

A similar scenario is implied by what is called the "Griliches effect." Zvi Griliches studied hybrid corn, a far cry from automobiles and electrical appliances.[112] But Griliches's findings generalize to temporal patterns of adoption of new technology or products. Griliches found that a sometimes lengthy initial period of very slow adoption is followed by a period of rapid dissemination and then culminates in an extended "steady state" in which the technology or product makes few further gains in its rate of adoption. The questions become: What determines the onset of the dissemination stage and what determines its pace? In these terms, advertising can speed the dissemination process, moving an industry to that steady state position all the more quickly.

Not all products that were part of the Consumer Durables Revolution were new products. Jewelry certainly was not new. There was in fact less advertising for jewelry and watches after the war, but its demand still changed then. Moreover, not all durable goods for which advertising became more prevalent were part of the Consumer Durables Revolution. There were many more pages of advertising for china and tableware and for house furnishings after World War I, but demand for these product groups remained stable.

Some changes in demand—some aspects of the Consumer Durables Revolution—transpired without advertising's help. Others, and particularly those for new goods, appear to have benefited from advertising.

In facilitating the Consumer Durables Revolution, did advertising change consumer tastes or just alert consumers to the characteristics of new products? The answer depends largely on how broadly or narrowly we define "tastes." Broadly defined, consumers have a taste or desire for transportation services; narrowly defined, the taste might be for automobiles; more narrowly, for six-cylinder, closed automobiles with electric starters and sleek styling. While President Coolidge was willing to proclaim that advertising "makes new thoughts, new desires, and new actions," others were less bold.[113] Businesses certainly did not depend only on advertising but made it just one component of their overall marketing efforts.[114]

Our conceptualization of "tastes" relates in turn to the ability of advertising to alter aggregate consumption and saving rates. By and large, economists today conclude that advertising engenders brand loyalty but does not affect allocation of disposable income between consumption and saving.[115] A striking characteristic of the 1920s, however, was the drop in the personal saving rate, a drop due (as seen in chapter 2) entirely to households' substitution of durable goods for conventional saving instruments. Aggregate consumption as usually measured by the federal government jumped because households changed the form in which they purchased certain services; they bought cars rather than trolley tickets, washers rather than laundry services. Households had no greater demand for these *services*; they merely bought them in a new, different and, most importantly, longer-lasting form. To the extent that advertising influenced these substitutions in the 1920s, advertising indeed increased aggregate consumption.[116]

A CHANGED
ECONOMY

T hrough all its twists and turns, this study has told essentially one tale. Interwar American households bought many more durable goods than did prewar households. They let a greater share of their total spending go to major durables. But while buying more durables and undeniably spending more of their disposable income on currently produced products, households were not really saving any less of their disposable income. They were saving differently—providing for their future transportation needs by buying a car today rather than setting aside a few dollars each week for trolley fare, for example—but they were not saving less.

Contrary to received wisdom, in buying so many more durable goods households were not simply responding to lower relative prices and higher incomes. In fact, when we compare the 1920s with the prewar years, we find that major durable goods were *more* expensive relative to everything else after World War I, though less so as the 1920s progressed. Households were responding to changes in relative prices and income more vigorously than in previous decades. Bluntly put, demand for most durable goods shifted after World War I.

As demand shifted and sales of durable goods soared, households also embraced a new economic philosophy: buy now, pay later. Contrary again to conventional wisdom, more household borrowing was not simply a reflection of greater purchases of expensive durable goods inducing greater demand for credit. Indeed, in the auto industry—which accounted for much of the 1920s boom in household indebtedness—consumer financing was initially made available by auto manufacturers not so they could market cars or respond to consumer demands for financing schemes but so they could resolve a production problem: the need to finance seasonally fluctuating finished goods inventory in order to allow cost-reducing smoothing of seasonal fluctuations in production without abandoning an important tool of power over dealers, the manufacturer's ability to cancel a dealer's franchise contract. Moreover, households became increasingly willing to buy now and pay later as moral inhibitions against being in debt weakened. But surprisingly, despite its growing availability and these weakening societal prohibitions, manufacturers did not aggressively use credit as a marketing device in the 1920s. Only pianos were consistently advertised as available on time payments, and these efforts were focused in the years before World War I. Not until the 1930s did advertising campaigns for durable goods zero in on the availability of credit financing as a means of marketing the product.

Although not advertising credit's availability, firms certainly spent much more money to advertise in the 1920s than in either neighboring decade. More money meant more advertisements, and in the 1920s households were barraged with these advertisements, most of them larger than ever before. There were proportionately fewer advertisements for clothing and more for major durable goods. That manufacturers sought to protect and increase their markets through advertising is indisputable; in fact, self-interested advertisers and even supposedly objective economists argued that advertising actually *lowered* retail prices through increasing demand which called forth increased production and exploitation of presumed economies of scale in production. But World War I seems to have played the deciding role in advertising's boom. Wartime propaganda campaigns highlighted advertising's power; the government's use of private advertising agencies granted advertisers professional status; and perhaps most importantly war-related federal budgetary needs generated an excess profits tax that, by defining advertising expense as fully deductible, lowered the effective cost of advertising by more than any advertiser could have even dreamt possible.

A Consumer Durables Revolution occurred in the United States in the 1920s as demand for most consumer durable goods changed. Households became more responsive to changes in prices and income. While we have by no means explored all possible causes of this revolution—such vital factors as electrification, suburbanization, and the entire phenomenon of consumerism have gone wholly unmentioned—we have pointed to two interrelated factors: consumer credit availability and advertising.[1] Increased availability of consumer credit coupled with declining social dictates against household borrowing led to greater effective demand for consumer durable goods. Magazines awash with print advertisements for new products (and old) kept many households keenly aware of what goods were available to meet their needs.

IMPLICATIONS OF THE TALE

For the economist, if the quantity of durable goods purchased by households changes but these changes are due simply to changes in household income or in the relative price of durable goods, that in itself is a largely uninteresting tale. If the 1920s boom in consumer durables were so readily explained, it would be simply another example of how markets function—which is nice but neither interesting nor earthshaking.

Here, however, we have something more. Households purchased many more major durable goods after World War I because demand for these goods shifted. Households responded differently to those standard economic stimuli, relative prices and income.[2] What does viewing the Consumer Durables Revolution as a result of such changes in demand add to our understanding of other issues?

Saving
Saving—traditionally measured as that portion of a household's disposable income that is not used to purchase currently produced goods and services—matters because its level affects the pace of economic growth. The identity that many former students of economics recall, that $I = S$ or Investment = Saving, is the simplest version of an identity readily derived from a Keynesian aggregate demand model of the macroeconomy. When we also incorporate the government and foreign sectors, the identity becomes in equilibrium[3]

$$I + BD = S + TD \tag{6.1}$$

Investment spending (I, which equals construction, business purchases of new machinery, and inventory investment) plus the size of the government budget deficit (BD, which equals government outlays less government revenues) equals saving (S, which equals disposable income less consumption) plus the size of the international trade deficit (TD, which equals imports less exports). All else constant, the smaller saving is, the smaller will be the level of investment and therefore the smaller the size of the nation's capital stock (structures and machines) and the slower the pace of economic growth.

The effects of variation in the level of saving are therefore captured ultimately in concern for economic growth. Saving is a household's way of providing for future consumption. A household's purchase of a durable good—an act that provides consumable services for the next several years—is clearly an act of saving. But if this act is saving, it is therefore also investment; like a business's purchase of a piece of machinery, a household's purchase of a durable good adds to the nation's physical stock of capital goods that allow production of other goods or services in the future.

Regardless of what factors determine the *level* of household saving, households may alter the *form* of their saving in response to institutional or other changes. When households increased their demand for major durable goods in the 1920s, the form of saving changed (more durable goods and less other assets in their saving portfolios), but as we saw in chapter 2, this increase in demand did not alter the overall personal saving rate. Similarly, David and Scadding have demonstrated that the 1920s change in purchases of consumer durables altered the form but not the rate of gross private saving (corporate and personal saving where the latter includes purchases of consumer durable goods).[4] But such changes in the form of saving despite unchanging rates of saving do not leave economic growth unaffected.

Substitution of consumer durable goods for more conventional forms of saving is accompanied by an increase in investment: investment in consumer durable goods. So as saving changes its form, so too does investment. All else constant, there are fewer economic resources available for all other forms of investment. To the extent that the change in the form of household saving in the 1920s resulted from changes in financial institutions providing consumer credit, these institutional changes had the power to alter the face and pace of economic growth.

The Household Economy

Without settling the issues, this study of the Consumer Durables Revolution provides additional grist for the mill in debates over two issues that each address the role of women in the interwar household economy: the connections between purchases of appliances and the employment of servants, and the connections between purchases of appliances and married women's labor force participation.

Were household appliances substituted for servants? Some advertisements for household appliances suggested that purchase of the product would allow the buyer to do the work previously done by a maid. The data in chapter 2 and appendix A clearly demonstrate the growth in purchases of household appliances in the 1920s and especially the 1930s. The analysis of chapter 3 shows that demand for appliances was different in the interwar years than earlier, with price and income elasticities both higher. But did households buy more appliances so they could fire the maid, or because the maid had quit, or so the maid could use those appliances in her work? Even if we were to add data on employment of household servants (which most people would interpret as ruling out the third possibility), we could not yet decide the issue.

This study, however, points to one avenue to pursue: What caused the change in demand for household appliances? If households purchased appliances so they could let the maid go, this does not necessarily imply a change in demand for appliances. A change in the relative prices of maids' labor and appliances plus one's own labor could have induced an increase in purchases of appliances within a stable demand framework. On the other hand, if labor opportunities or relative wages changed such that fewer women were willing to work as maids, this drop in the supply of maids' services could have induced an increase in purchases of appliances that was accompanied by a change in demand. We must therefore determine what caused the change in demand for appliances. That the price elasticity rose so much more than did the income elasticity might contain some clues. Whatever the case, this point remains for others to pursue.

Did households purchase more household appliances because the increase in women's labor force participation increased household income?

The analysis of chapter 3 suggests this story is incomplete. More household appliances were purchased in part because income *elasticity* increased, not just because income increased; households were responding more vigorously to changes in their disposable income. Did increases in women's labor force participation cause increased income elasticity of demand? Or, taking our lead from Harry Oshima's 1961 argument, did increases in elasticity of demand lead to more debt-financed purchases of appliances and thereby push married women into the labor force so the family could more readily meet its new financial obligations? The question becomes: What caused income elasticity of demand for appliances to increase? Was it increased women's labor force participation, increases in the availability of consumer credit, or something else altogether? Again, it remains for others to pursue these questions.

The Great Depression of the 1930s
Consumption fell precipitously in the early 1930s and, according to Peter Temin, fell disproportionately when compared with consumption patterns in the two neighboring recessions.[5] Contrary to Temin's oft-repeated conclusion that the drop in consumption in 1930 was "truly autonomous, which in this case means also unexplained," others have shown that the 1930 fall in consumption is well explained by income and wealth effects and that the absence of similar declines in 1920–21 and 1937–38 is the "unexplained" feature of interwar consumption behavior.[6]

Frederic Mishkin accounts for the drop in purchases of consumer durable goods in the Great Depression with his liquidity preference theory.[7] He argues that increases in real contractual obligations (debt, lease agreements, and so on) coupled with declines in real financial asset holdings of households increases a household's subjective assessment of the likelihood of future financial distress (defined as an inability to readily pay all bills), leading households to cut back on their tangible asset acquisitions (real estate and durable goods purchases) since a "distress sale" of such illiquid assets would involve quite high transactions costs. Mishkin notes that a one-dollar increase in debt has five times the effect of a one-dollar decrease in financial asset holdings, and thus the relatively small declines in purchases of consumer durables in 1920–21 and 1937–38 are expected since in both episodes real financial asset declines accounted for the bulk of observed changes in household net wealth.[8]

Mishkin's analysis leaves unexplained the behavior of nondurable consumption, which also exhibited a disproportionate decline in the early years of the Great Depression. Christina Romer argues that consumption of both durable and semidurable goods fell in 1930 as households responded to the stock market crash of October 1929 by adopting a wait-and-see attitude and putting off purchases easily postponed.[9]

Both Mishkin and Romer focus on the illiquidity of consumption goods and the resultant transactions costs incurred upon resale. But the vast majority of purchases of major consumer durables were financed with installment credit in the late 1920s and early 1930s. Absence of government income guarantee programs in the early years of the Great Depression, the institutional characteristics of credit markets that require households to build up equity in goods purchased on installments, the maturation of the auto market such that in 1930 most demand was replacement demand, the increase in real debt burdens through deflation, and the threat of lost take-home pay as production declined all led households to severely reduce their demand for major durables and may have led indebted households to restrict all consumption in the early years of the Great Depression.

Milan Ayres noted (with regard to the 1920 recession, but he argued with applicability to the Great Depression) that when layoffs began in 1920, "Other employees, observing these dismissals, began to feel nervous. They may not have sensed the fact that a general depression was coming, but many began to doubt the security of their own jobs, and abstained from costly purchases, while those who felt secure in their positions or had other sources of income made no change in their buying habits."[10] Those with debt made every effort to pay up "rather than lose what they had already put in."[11] Indeed, the 1930s default rate on consumer credit was extremely low. "Consumer credit was a safer investment in 1933 than cash in banks. Consumers did not repudiate their debts en masse . . . but merely tightened their belts until they could pay what they owed and then buy more."[12]

Goods were repossessed if a payment was as little as thirty days late. Households were usually not compensated for the difference between the resale value of the repossessed good and the remaining balance on the installment contract. As most contracts were only eighteen months long (and usually shorter) but the goods provided their services for several additional years, repossession represented loss of wealth. Not only was wealth lost upon repossession but the household had to then provide the now-missing service (transportation, entertainment, clean clothes, and so on) through other means. When faced with the possibility of a protracted decline in income (a possibility that would have become more evident as the Great Depression wore on), indebted households could protect their debt-laden durable goods from repossession by cutting back on all consumption spending—durable goods, semidurable goods, perishable goods, and services.[13]

To decide the issue—were households avoiding costly resale of goods or were they protecting these goods from repossession?—will require analysis that is conducted with disaggregated data. Were the households in debt those with financial assets? If so, they were less likely to worry about the risk of default and repossession. Were those in debt the households without financial assets at their disposal? Then actions to avoid repossession are more reasonably expected. These crucial questions must be pursued.

PARTING WORDS

If there is but one message contained in all these words, it must be the message that will surprise no historian but might intrigue a few economists: Institutions matter. Institutions can alter our economic behavior in fundamental and consequential ways.

In much of economic theory, institutions are essentially irrelevant. Banks, brokerage companies, even courts of law do not alter long-run economic outcomes. Indeed, institutions are often perceived as having been created by rational economic actors in response to perceived market imperfections. Without denying such an understanding of why institutions are created, this study illustrates that the effects of such rationally created institutions might well extend beyond the imperfection they are designed to correct. Sales finance companies, designed to correct a production problem, vastly increased the availability of consumer credit, thereby contributing to the creation of a Consumer Durables Revolution in the United States—a revolution that, because it was accompanied by a "buy now, pay later" philosophy, had a profound impact on the economy of the 1930s.

♦ APPENDIX A ♦

TECHNICAL NOTES:
ESTIMATING DURABLE GOODS
EXPENDITURE AND STOCK

Development of the estimates of real and nominal expenditure for consumer durable goods, their price deflators, and real existing stock of consumer durable goods is described in this appendix. All estimates are annual. Those for expenditure and price begin with 1869. Stock estimates begin no later than 1899, earlier for most commodity groups. Previously available estimates of expenditure for or stock of consumer durable goods that are broken down by commodity group are only for partial periods: William Shaw estimated output destined for domestic consumption, 1869, 1879, and 1889–1933; Simon Kuznets estimated output destined for domestic consumption, 1919–33; Raymond Goldsmith estimated expenditure and stock, 1897–1949; the national product accounts include estimates of expenditure, 1929 on; and the U.S. Bureau of Economic Analysis (BEA) provides estimates of stock, 1925 on, and estimates of expenditure, 1922 (and often earlier) on.[1]

The estimates of expenditure and stock presented here link directly to those published in U.S. Bureau of Economic Analysis, *Fixed Reproducible Tangible Wealth, 1925–85* (henceforth, the BEA-Wealth estimates). The sources used to develop the estimates are primarily: Shaw, *Value of Commodity Output*; Kuznets, "Annual Estimates, 1869–1953"; Kuznets, *Commodity Flow and Capital Formation*; and Goldsmith, *Study of Saving*. The new estimates augment the BEA-Wealth estimates as follows:

- Included are consumer expenditure for and stocks of horse-drawn vehicles. The BEA implicitly includes these goods in the producer durable category "Agricultural Machinery."
- "Radio and Television Receivers" is split into "Phonographs, Records, Radios, and Televisions" and "Pianos and Other Musical Instruments" for 1869–1942.
- Estimates of expenditure begin in 1869 and link to the BEA-Wealth estimates.
- Estimates of stock begin no later than 1899 and link to the BEA-Wealth estimates.

ESTIMATES OF NOMINAL EXPENDITURE

To extend the BEA-Wealth estimates of expenditure to 1869, ideally we would simply duplicate the BEA's methodology. Unfortunately, the full description of the methodology the BEA used to develop its pre-1929 estimates of expenditure is: "the [1929 on] flows were extrapolated by data from William H. Shaw, *Value of Commodity Output Since 1869.*"[2] Therefore, extensive data analysis was necessary to determine methods that replicate the published BEA-Wealth estimates. Based upon this analysis, it appears that the BEA essentially followed the methodology that Raymond Goldsmith used to develop estimates of consumer expenditure for durable goods, 1897–1928. Goldsmith provides very complete documentation, and thus we begin by discussing his methodology.[3]

Methodology: Estimating Nominal Expenditure

Goldsmith used Shaw, *Value of Commodity Output*, as the primary source material to develop annual estimates of consumer expenditure for durable goods.[4] To move from Shaw's estimates of value of commodity output to Goldsmith's estimates of consumer expenditure involves five steps.

First, because Shaw's estimates are total output *destined* for domestic consumption rather than total output actually *purchased* for domestic consumption, Goldsmith adjusted Shaw's 1919–29 estimates to compensate for differences between production and sales as reflected by inventory changes. The inventory adjustment factors are not commodity group-specific though they are particular to consumer durable goods; Goldsmith derived the factors from Kuznets's estimates of "Net changes in distributive inventories, final approximation, wholesale and retail expressed in terms of wholesale and retail prices" and "Adjusted estimate of flow to ultimate consumers at cost to them" for the sector consumer durable goods.[5] No inventory adjustment is made before 1919 due to absence of data; Goldsmith assumed that inventory changes were negligible before 1919.[6] Values of the inventory adjustment factors are given in table A.1.

Second, since Shaw's output estimates are valued with producer (wholesale) rather than consumer (retail) prices, Goldsmith adjusted for changes in the markup of retail over wholesale prices. The retail markup factors are commodity group-specific but are constant within decade long periods, thus ignoring any annual fluctuations within each period. Quoting Goldsmith, "the practical necessity of applying the same percentage markup for long periods unjustifiably smoothens the cyclical variations in margins. As a result expenditures and hence saving are probably somewhat understated in boom years and overstated in depression years. This shortcoming is particularly important in the case of automobiles and other goods in the marketing of which trade-ins play an important role."[7] The retail markup factors Goldsmith used are in table A.2.

Goldsmith's retail markup factors are compared with those derived from Harold Barger's study of retail and wholesale margins in table A.3.[8] Goldsmith's estimates are generally lower than Barger's but they do follow a similar temporal pattern. This temporal pattern is of primary concern; the methodology used to derive expenditure estimates makes differences in levels irrelevant.

Third, Goldsmith accounts for the fact that some "consumer" durable goods are actually purchased by institutions, businesses, and government agencies. These commodity group-specific consumer allocation factors are given in table A.4.

Fourth, Goldsmith compensates for a break in Shaw's estimates at 1919. Shaw provides two estimates of output for 1919: one consistent with his 1869–1918 estimates and a second consistent with his 1920–33 estimates. Those for 1920–33 are based upon Kuznets's estimates of "Value of Finished Commodities Destined for Domestic Consumption," 1919–33.[9] Goldsmith multiplies the 1869–1918 estimates by a constant factor to

Table A.1. Inventory Adjustment Factor, 1919-1933

Year	Inventory Adjustment Factor
1919	0.940
1920	0.967
1921	1.114
1922	0.967
1923	0.940
1924	0.994
1925	0.993
1926	0.979
1927	1.026
1928	0.973
1929	0.988
1930	1.110
1931	1.096
1932	1.137
1933	0.972

Sources: For 1919-29, Goldsmith, *Study of Saving*, 1:notes to table Q-5, p. 678; derived by Goldsmith from Kuznets, *Commodity Flow and Capital Formation*, table V-6, p. 307. For 1930-33, computed from Kuznets, *Commodity Flow and Capital Formation*, table V-6, p. 307.

splice them onto the 1919–33 estimates, yielding just one estimate for 1919, the estimate derived from Kuznets's work.

Finally, Goldsmith links everything to a set of 1929 benchmarks. The adjusted and spliced Shaw series (derived by making the first four adjustments) are multiplied by a constant final adjustment factor, thereby extrapolating the 1929 estimate back into the earlier years.

In summary, Goldsmith derives estimates of consumer expenditure as follows:

Adjustments 1, 2, and 3: Shaw to Adjusted Shaw:

$$\left.\begin{array}{c} 1897 \\ \text{to} \\ 1929 \end{array}\right\} \begin{array}{c} \text{Adjusted} \\ \text{Shaw}_t \end{array} = \begin{array}{c} \text{Shaw's} \\ \text{Original} \\ \text{Estimate}_t \end{array} \times \begin{array}{c} \text{Inventory} \\ \text{Adjustment} \\ \text{Factor}_t \end{array} \times \begin{array}{c} \text{Retail} \\ \text{Markup} \\ \text{Factor}_t \end{array} \times \begin{array}{c} \text{Consumer} \\ \text{Allocation} \\ \text{Factor}_t \end{array}$$

Table A.2. Retail Markup Factors, 1867-1929

Commodity Group	1867-1900	1901-1910	1911-1920	1921-1929
Automobiles	1.45	1.45	1.45	1.45
Automobile Accessories	2.23	2.23	2.23	2.40
Furniture	1.45	1.52	1.59	1.66
Household Appliances	1.62	1.69	1.79	1.88
China, Jewelry, etc.	1.77	1.85	1.93	2.00
House Furnishings	1.48	1.55	1.63	1.70
Musical Instruments, Radios	1.82	1.95	2.08	2.21
Ophthalmic Products, etc.	3.74	3.74	3.74	3.74
Books and Maps	1.56	1.60	1.76	1.86
Miscellaneous Durable Goods:				
Luggage	1.82	1.91	2.00	2.09
Wheel Goods, Durable Toys, and Sports Equipment	1.70	1.70	1.70	1.90
Pleasure Craft	1.20	1.20	1.20	1.20

Source: Goldsmith, *Study of Saving*, 1:table Q-10, pp. 686-87.

Adjustment 4: Adjusted Shaw to Spliced Adjusted Shaw:

$$
\begin{matrix} 1897 \\ \text{to} \\ 1918 \end{matrix} \Bigg\} \quad \begin{matrix} \text{Spliced} \\ \text{Adjusted} \\ \text{Shaw}_t \end{matrix} = \text{Adjusted Shaw}_t \times \frac{\text{Shaw's second 1919 figure (Table I-2)}}{\text{Shaw's first 1919 figure (Table I-1)}}
$$

$$
\begin{matrix} 1919 \\ \text{to} \\ 1929 \end{matrix} \Bigg\} \quad \begin{matrix} \text{Spliced} \\ \text{Adjusted} \\ \text{Shaw}_t \end{matrix} = \text{Adjusted Shaw}_t
$$

Adjustment 5: Spliced Adjusted Shaw to Goldsmith:

$$
\begin{matrix} 1897 \\ \text{to} \\ 1928 \end{matrix} \Bigg\} \quad \begin{matrix} \text{Goldsmith} \\ \text{estimate}_t \end{matrix} = \begin{matrix} \text{Spliced} \\ \text{Adjusted} \\ \text{Shaw}_t \end{matrix} \times \frac{\text{1929 benchmark}}{\text{Spliced Adjusted Shaw 1929 estimate}}
$$

Table A.3. Retail Markup Factors: Comparing Barger and Goldsmith, Decennial Estimates, 1869-1947

	1869	1879	1889	1899	1909	1919	1929	1939	1947
Automobiles									
Barger	136.6	137.7	132.6	138.3	139.3	139.7	138.9	141.6	141.6
Goldsmith	145	145	145	145	145	145	145		
Automobile Accessories									
Barger				157.2	170.6	165.3	172.7	173.0	171.8
Goldsmith	223	223	223	223	223	223	240		
Furniture (independent stores)									
Barger	159.5	161.6	162.3	163.9	164.7	186.6	198.0	185.2	181.5
Goldsmith	145	145	145	145	152	159	166		
Furniture (chain stores)									
Barger				178.6	178.6	178.6	178.6	178.6	178.6
Goldsmith				145	152	159	166		
Household Appliances									
Barger	190.5	186.2	190.1	185.9	187.3	186.9	188.0	188.0	188.0
Goldsmith	162	162	162	162	169	179	188		

Table A.3, continued

	1869	1879	1889	1899	1909	1919	1929	1939	1947
Musical Instruments									
Barger	159.5	161.6	162.3	163.9	164.7	186.6	198.0	185.2	181.5
Goldsmith	182	182	182	182	195	208	221		
Jewelry									
Barger	188.3	186.2	186.6	186.9	193.0	207.0	223.2	217.9	212.3
Goldsmith	177	177	177	177	185	193	200		
Drugs (Medical)									
Barger	166.1	171.2	179.2	187.6	197.6	204.5	198.4	190.8	192.3
Goldsmith	374	374	374	374	374	374	374		
Books									
Barger	157.5	155.3	156.2	160.8	164.5	172.7	179.2	185.9	186.2
Goldsmith	156	156	156	156	160	176	186		

Table A.3, continued

	1869	1879	1889	1899	1909	1919	1929	1939	1947
Wheel goods, etc. (Cameras, luggage, toys, and sporting goods)									
Barger	177.9	187.6	176.4	186.2	185.5	185.2	189.4	186.2	184.5
Goldsmith	171	171	171	171	173	182	189		

Sources: Derived from Barger, *Distribution's Place in the American Economy*; equal to one over the difference between 100 and Barger's estimates of "Distributive Spread" from table 26, p. 92 (ratio then increased by a factor of 10,000). Goldsmith's estimates from *Study of Saving*, 1:table Q-10, pp. 686-87. Barger does not include estimates of the markups for china, durable house furnishings, or radios.

Table A.4. Consumer Allocation Adjustment Factors, 1867-1929

Commodity Group	1867-1919	1920-1928	1929
Automobiles	0.70	0.70	0.70
Automobile Accessories	0.10	0.30	0.40
Furniture	0.97	0.97	0.97
Household Appliances	0.92	0.92	0.92
China, Jewelry, etc.	0.90	0.90	0.90
House Furnishings	0.70	0.70	0.70
Musical Instruments, Radios	0.90	0.90	0.90
Ophthalmic Products, etc.	1.00	1.00	1.00
Books and Maps	0.74	0.74	0.74
Miscellaneous Durable Goods:			
Luggage	0.92	0.92	0.92
Wheel Goods, Durable Toys, and Sports Equipment	0.70	0.995	0.995
Pleasure Craft	1.00	1.00	1.00

Source: Goldsmith, Study of Saving, 1:table Q-11, pp. 686-87.

Annual Estimates of Nominal Expenditure, 1869, 1879, 1889–1986

The BEA-Wealth estimates of expenditure for consumer durable goods can be replicated using an almost identical methodology. The inventory adjustment factors for 1919–29 are those in table A.1. The retail markup factors are generally those in table A.2; however, the BEA breaks the final subperiod at 1919/1920 rather than 1920/1921, and for two groups—china and tableware, and jewelry and watches—the BEA substitutes different values of the factors altogether. The consumer allocation factors are those in table A.4. Finally, the BEA's 1929 benchmarks are from the 1981 and 1986 editions of the national product accounts though they are not in general identical to those estimates.[10]

The commodity groups used in the BEA-Wealth study occasionally differ from those used by Goldsmith and by Shaw. Table A.5 shows the correspondences between the categories used by the BEA, those given in the national product accounts, those used by Goldsmith, and those used by Shaw. The primary differences between Goldsmith and the BEA-Wealth

Table A.5. Correspondences between Commodity Groups

BEA-Wealth	1986 NIPA	1947 NIPA	Goldsmith	Shaw
Automobiles (includes tires, tubes, accessories, and other parts) (2)	New Automobiles (65) Net Purchases of Used Autos (66) Tires, Tubes, Accessories, and Parts (68)	New Cars and Net Purchases of Used Cars (VIII-1a) Tires and Tubes (VIII-1b) Parts and Accessories (VIII-1c)	New Passenger Cars (8) Used Car Markups (table P-16: cols. 2 and 4) Passenger Car Accessories (9)	Passenger Vehicles, Motor (20a) Motor Vehicle Accessories (20b) Tires and Tubes (11)
Other Motor Vehicles (3)	Other Motor Vehicles (67)	Unknown	Unknown	Unknown
Furniture, including mattresses and bedsprings (4)	Furniture, including mattresses and bedsprings (29)	Furniture (V-1)	New Furniture (2)	Household Furniture (12)
Kitchen and Other Household Appliances (5)	Kitchen and Other Household Appliances (30)	Refrigerators, Washing Machines, Sewing Machines (V-3) Misc. Electrical Appliances, except Radios (V-4) Cooking and Portable Heating Equipment (V-5)	Household Appliances (3)	Heating and Cooking Apparatus and Household Appliances, not Electrical (13a) Electrical Household Appliances and Supplies (13b)

Table A.5, continued

BEA-Wealth	1986 NIPA	1947 NIPA	Goldsmith	Shaw
China, Glassware, Tableware, and Utensils (6)	China, Glassware, Tableware, and Utensils (31)	China, Glassware, Tableware, and Utensils (V-6)	China, Tableware, Utensils, Jewelry, and Watches (part of 5)	China and Household Utensils (15)
Other Durable House Furnishings (7)	Other Durable House Furnishings (includes floor coverings, clocks, writing equipment, and tools) (32)	Floor Coverings (V-2) Durable House Furnishings, n.e.c. (V-7) Products of Custom Establishments, n.e.c. (V-8) Writing Equipment (V-9) Tools (VII-2)	House Furnishings (4)	Floor Coverings (14a) Misc. Housefurnishings (14b) Housefurnishings (14)
Radio and Television Receivers, Records, and Musical Instruments (8)	Radio and Television Receivers, Records, and Musical Instruments (87)	Radios, Phonographs, Parts, and Records (IX-5h) Pianos and other Musical Instruments (IX-5i)	Musical Instruments Radios (6)	Musical Instruments (16) Radios (13c)
Jewelry and Watches (9)	Jewelry and Watches (18)	Jewelry and Watches (II-12)	China, Tableware, Utensils, Jewelry, and Watches (part of 5)	Jewelry, Silverware, Clocks, and Watches (17)
Ophthalmic Products and Orthopedic Appliances (10)	Ophthalmic Products and Orthopedic Appliances (46)	Ophthalmic Products and Orthopedic Appliances (VI-2)	Ophthalmic Products and Orthopedic Appliances (10)	Ophthalmic Products and Artificial Limbs (23)

Table A.5, continued

BEA-Wealth	1986 NIPA	1947 NIPA	Goldsmith	Shaw
Books and Maps (11)	Books and Maps (83)	Books and Maps (IX-5a)	Books (7)	Printing and Publishing: Books (18)
Wheel Goods, Durable Toys, Sports Equipment, Boats, and Pleasure Aircraft (12)	Wheel Goods, Durable Toys, Sports Equipment, Boats, and Pleasure Aircraft (86)	Wheel Goods, Durable Toys and Sports Equipment (IX-5e) Boats and Pleasure Craft (IX-5f) Luggage (VIII-4)[a]	Miscellaneous Consumer Durables (includes luggage, wheel goods, durable toys, sports equipment, and pleasure craft) (11)	Motorcycles and Bicycles (21) Pleasure Craft (22)[a] Luggage (19)[a] Toys, Games, and Sporting Goods (10)[b]
PART: Agricultural Machinery, except Tractors (table B2, column 5)	PART: Agricultural Machinery, except Tractors (table 5.6, line 24)	PART: Agricultural Machinery, except Tractors (table 32, line 7)	PART: Farm Machinery (tables A-16 and A-17)	Passenger Vehicles, Horse-Drawn, and Accessories (20c)

Sources: BEA-Wealth: U.S. BEA, *Fixed Reproducible Tangible Wealth, 1925-85*, table B10, p. 361, except where noted. 1986 NIPA: U.S. BEA, *National Income and Product Accounts, 1929-82*, table 2.4, pp. 106-12, except where noted. 1947 NIPA: U.S. Office of Business Economics, "National Income: 1947 Edition," table 30, except where noted. Goldsmith: Goldsmith, *Study of Saving*, 1:table Q-5, pp. 678, 680, and 1:table A-24, pp. 780, 784, except where noted. Shaw: Shaw, Value of Commodity Output, table I-1, pp. 30-65 and table I-2, pp. 66-69.

Notes: Number in parentheses indicates column, series, or line number in associated document.

[a]Later reclassified as a nondurable good. Included here for correspondence with Goldsmith and Shaw.
[b]Not used by Goldsmith.

study are: separate consideration of china and of jewelry by the BEA; combination by the BEA of automobiles, automobile accessories, and tires (tires and tubes are not considered durable goods by Goldsmith); exclusion of luggage from the BEA-Wealth estimates, following earlier reclassification of luggage from a durable to a nondurable good in the national product accounts; and inclusion by the BEA of the category "Other Motor Vehicles," a relatively recent addition to the national product accounts.[11]

The specific adjustment factors and the methodology followed to extend the BEA-Wealth estimates back to 1869 are considered below, taking each BEA-Wealth commodity group in turn.

Automobiles and Parts

This category combines expenditure for new automobiles (line 65 in the national product accounts), net expenditure for used automobiles (line 66), and expenditure for automobile parts, accessories, and tires (line 68).[12] The BEA-Wealth estimates of expenditure for automobiles and parts begin in 1918. Their estimates are derived not from Shaw but instead from annual state data that is tabulated by the R. L. Polk Company and covers the number and ages of automobiles in use.[13] The BEA does not describe their procedures; presumably their estimates of gross investment in automobiles (flows) are derived from the stock estimates which are themselves based on the Polk Company data. Since it was impossible to replicate the BEA-Wealth estimates, I used the methodology outlined above to extend these expenditure estimates back to 1869.

There are three steps to developing estimates of expenditure for automobiles and parts: one, developing initial estimates of expenditure for each of the four component parts (new autos, used autos, auto accessories, and tires); two, summing these expenditure estimates to derive an initial estimate of total expenditure for automobiles and parts; and three, adjusting this sum by a constant multiplicative factor to link it to the BEA-Wealth estimate for 1918.[14]

Estimates of expenditure for new automobiles are derived from Shaw's series "passenger vehicles, motor" (#20a), using the inventory, markup, and consumer allocation factors in tables A.1, A.2, and A.4 and a final adjustment factor of 0.9935.[15] The 1929 benchmark value, $2,557 million, is from the 1981 national product accounts; the 1986 revision of the product accounts rounds this figure to $2.6 billion.

Estimates of net expenditure for used automobiles are based on those provided by Goldsmith.[16] Goldsmith assumes businesses' share of net purchases of used automobiles is one-half their share of new automobile purchases. However, he first increases the consumers' share of total new car expenditure from the Department of Commerce estimate of 70 percent to his own estimate of 90 percent. Goldsmith was studying saving; he contended that automobile purchases by consumers for business use were best treated as personal rather than business saving. For studying determinants of spending, the Department of Commerce approach is more appropriate; presumably automobiles purchased by consumers for business use are subject to different behavioral factors than are automobiles purchased for personal use. Using Goldsmith's methodology but the Department of Commerce allocation, 30 percent of expenditure for new autos and therefore 15 percent of net expenditure for used autos are from the business sector. Following Goldsmith, the remaining 85 percent of Goldsmith's estimate of total nonfarm net expenditure for used cars is expenditure for used cars by nonfarm consumers. This estimate is combined with net expenditure by farmers, giving total net consumer expenditure for used cars. Note that the estimate for 1929 derived in this way, $336 million, is more than ten times greater than that given in the national product accounts, $31 million; the estimates are based on the best available information, Goldsmith's work on used car margins, and should be used here with this discrepancy in mind.

For automobile accessories, Goldsmith's estimates of consumer expenditure for motor vehicle accessories can be used. The estimates can be replicated with Shaw's series "motor vehicle accessories" (#20b), the adjustment factors of tables A.1, A.2, and A.4, and a final adjustment factor of 0.531.

Estimates of expenditure for tires are derived from Shaw's estimates of output of "tires and tubes" (#11), the inventory factors of table A.1, the markup factors for motor vehicle accessories in table A.2, the consumer allocation factors for motor vehicles in table A.4, and a 1929 benchmark of $419 million, which is taken from the 1947 edition of the national product accounts (the last year in which tires were separately listed). Use of the consumer allocation factor for motor vehicles rather than the possibly more obvious motor vehicle accessories allocation factor requires comment. Goldsmith assumed consumers purchased only 10 percent of all motor vehicle parts before 1919 and only 30 percent in the 1920s. The present study assumes 70 percent of autos were purchased directly by consumers. The choice of which of these two consumer allocation factors to use for tire purchases was based in part on casual empiricism—there are many more advertisements in national magazines for tires than for other automobile parts—and on the belief that consumers are more likely to directly purchase replacement tires than other replacement parts for their automobiles. Using the accessories allocation factor would reduce the final estimates of expenditure for tires by 25 percent between 1919 and 1928 and by 75 percent between 1869 and 1918.

The final estimate of expenditure for automobiles and parts is the sum of expenditures for new automobiles, net used automobiles, automobile accessories, and tires, multiplied by a constant 0.84, thereby linking the derived estimates to the first available BEA-Wealth estimate, that for 1918.[17]

Other Vehicles
Other motor vehicles are such items as motor homes, dune buggies, and other recreational vehicles. For this study, purchases of horse-drawn vehicles are also estimated and included with other motor vehicles in a new, expanded category, "Other Vehicles."

For 1869, 1879, and 1889–1919, Shaw provides estimates of "passenger vehicles, horse-drawn, and accessories" (#20c) output destined for domestic (nonbusiness) consumption. Following Kuznets, after 1919 Shaw incorporates all horse-drawn vehicles into the category "farm equipment" (#27) and thus provides no separate estimates of output of just horse-drawn vehicles for 1920 on.[18] For 1919–33, however, Kuznets breaks down his category "farm equipment," using biennial estimates of output (before adjustment for net exports) from the Census of Manufactures.[19] Interpolating linearly between Kuznets's biennial estimates of the share of horse-drawn vehicles in total farm equipment, annual estimates of consumer horse-drawn vehicles are derived from Shaw's annual series of "farm equipment" (#27), 1919–33. This process yields two estimates of consumer expenditure for horse-drawn vehicles for 1919: the first from Shaw's estimates for 1869–1919, the second from applying Kuznets's 1919 share of horse-drawn vehicles in total farm equipment output to Shaw's farm equipment estimate for 1919. The two estimates differ substantially, the first equaling $26,387 thousand and the second equaling $48,165 thousand.

This discrepancy arises because Shaw and Kuznets allocate total horse-drawn vehicles between business and nonbusiness use differently. Their estimates of total output of all horse-drawn vehicles in 1919, business and nonbusiness, are nearly identical; Shaw's estimate is $69,643 thousand and Kuznets's is $68,892 thousand. But for 1919, Shaw estimates the consumer share of total output of horse-drawn vehicles at 39 percent while Kuznets estimates it at 88 percent.[20] Neither Shaw nor Kuznets defends their estimates. I therefore follow the lead of the Department of Commerce and assume (as with motor vehicle output) that 70 percent of horse-drawn vehicle output is allocated to consumers and 30 percent to businesses. The resulting revised estimates of consumer expenditure for horse-drawn vehicles as a share of total expenditure for farm equipment, 1919–33, are applied to Shaw's estimates of total farm equipment. The resulting series is annual estimates, 1889–1933, of horse-drawn vehicle output destined for domestic consumption by consumers.

This series is then adjusted with the inventory factors from table A.1 and a constant retail markup factor of 1.24.[21] The 1929 benchmark is $6.40 million, derived by multiplying the national product accounts estimate of total farm equipment expenditure in 1929 by the 1929 Kuznets share of carriages output in farm equipment output. The final adjustment factor is 0.560. Horse-drawn vehicle expenditure by consumers falls to less than $2 million by 1933; I assume it equals zero in subsequent years.

The BEA extended the national product account estimates of expenditure for other motor vehicles back to 1922. Their estimates could not be replicated. Estimates of expenditure for other motor vehicles for the years before 1922 are therefore derived from estimates of expenditure for automobiles, new and net used. Other motor vehicle expenditure, 1889–1921, is simply equal to 2.23 percent of automobile expenditure where the adjustment factor, 0.0223, is based on the average ratio of other motor vehicles to total automobile expenditure, 1922–26.

Furniture

Estimates of nominal expenditure for furniture use Shaw's series "furniture" (#12), the adjustment factors from tables A.1, A.2, and A.4, and a final adjustment factor of 1.269.

Kitchen and Other Household Appliances

Expenditure estimates are from Shaw's series "heating and cooking apparatus and household appliances, except electrical" (#13c) and "electrical household appliances and supplies" (#13b), the adjustment factors from tables A.1, A.2, and A.4, and a final adjustment factor of 0.861.

China, Glassware, Tableware, and Utensils

The BEA-Wealth estimates of expenditure for china and tableware can only be replicated using a slightly different retail markup factor than that used by Goldsmith. The BEA apparently used a retail markup factor of 2.125 for 1903–19 and 2.0 for 1920–29, rather than Goldsmith's factors of 1.85 for 1903–10, 1.93 for 1911–19, and 2.0 for 1920–29. The surprising aspect of the BEA's retail markup factor is its temporal decrease; none of Goldsmith's retail markup series decrease over time. Unfortunately, the source of the BEA's markup series remains unknown. In the absence of an alternative, the retail markup factor for china is held constant at 2.125 for 1869–1919.

Expenditure estimates are derived with Shaw's series "china and household utensils" (#15), a retail markup factor of 2.125 for 1869–1919 and 2.0 for 1920–29, the inventory and consumer allocation factors of tables A.1 and A.4, and a final adjustment factor of 1.285.

Other Durable House Furnishings

The BEA-Wealth series and Goldsmith's estimates of consumer expenditure for durable house furnishings are identical.[22] The estimates for 1915–29 cannot be replicated; the final adjustment factor varies between 1.40 and 1.56 with no obvious temporal pattern. But this is of no matter since the expenditure estimates for 1897–1914 can be replicated with Shaw's "floor coverings" series (#14a) and "miscellaneous durable housefurnishings" series (#14b), the adjustment factors of tables A.1, A.2, and A.4, and a final adjustment factor of 1.369. The estimates are extended to 1869 with these factors.

Radio and Television Receivers

This category includes radio and television receivers, phonographs, records, and musical instruments. The BEA-Wealth estimates are replicated with a final adjustment factor of 1.076 for 1905–12 and 1.086 for 1913–29 and the inventory, markup, and consumer allocation factors of tables A.1, A.2, and A.4. To extend the BEA-Wealth estimates to 1869, a final adjustment factor of 1.076 is used with Shaw's "musical instruments" series (#16).

In the 1947 and 1951 national income and product accounts, this single category is split into two categories: radios, phonographs, parts, and records; and pianos and other musical instruments. For 1919 on, Shaw's estimates of output of radios are separate from those of musical instruments; however, he still includes output of phonographs and records with output of pianos and other musical instruments. Quinquennially, 1899–1919, Shaw provides a breakdown of musical instruments versus phonographs and records output; Kuznets provides the same breakdown biennially, 1919–33. Setting the share of phonographs and records in total output of phonographs, records, and musical instruments at 0 percent for 1889 and interpolating the share linearly between benchmark years produces estimates of the share of phonographs and records output in total "musical instruments" output, 1889–1933.

For 1919–29, I apply these shares to Shaw's estimates of "musical instruments output destined for domestic consumption" to derive annual estimates of phonographs and records output. Combined with Shaw's estimates of "radio output destined for domestic consumption," this yields estimates of the share of total musical instrument and radio output attributable to radios, phonographs, records, and parts.

There are two initial estimates of the 1919 share of radios and phonographs in total radios and musical instruments output: one derived from Shaw's 1899–1919 output estimates and a second from Kuznets's 1919–33 estimates. The 1869–1918 estimates are therefore spliced onto the 1919–29 estimates, which increases the annual estimates of the share of radios, phonographs, records, and parts in total musical instruments output by 4.6 percent for 1869–1918. One final adjustment using a factor of 1.023 links the 1869–1929 estimates to the 1929 values derived from the 1951 national product accounts estimates of nominal expenditure of $905 million for radios, phonographs, records, and parts (89.43 percent of total), and $107 million for pianos and musical instruments (10.57 percent of total). The annual estimates of total radio and musical instruments expenditure are then split between the two components using these final estimates of the share of radios and phonographs expenditure in total musical instruments, phonograph, and radio expenditure, 1869, 1879, and 1889–1929.

For 1929–42, the BEA-Wealth estimates of total nominal expenditure for musical instruments, phonographs, radios, and televisions are allocated to the two subcategories on the basis of estimated nominal expenditures for "radios, phonographs, parts, and records" (group IX-5h) and for "pianos and other musical instruments" (group IX-5i) published in the 1951 national product accounts.[23] Absence of data prohibits this separation after 1942.

Jewelry and Watches
The BEA-Wealth estimates can be replicated using a retail markup factor of 1.915 for the full period 1901–18 and 2.0 for 1919–29, rather than Goldsmith's factors of 1.85 for 1901–10, 1.93 for 1911–19, and 2.0 for 1920–29. To extend this series requires values of the retail markup factor for the years before 1901. I set the retail markup factor for jewelry at 1.85 for 1869–99 and 1.915 for 1900; these factors hold the same statistical relationship to one another as do the markup factors for 1899 and 1909 derived from Barger's estimates of margins. Expenditure estimates are derived with this retail markup series, Shaw's series "jewelry" (#17), the inventory and consumer allocation factors from tables A.1 and A.4, and a final adjustment factor of 0.789.

Ophthalmic Products and Orthopedic Appliances
Expenditure is estimated with Shaw's series "ophthalmic products and artificial limbs" (#23), the adjustment factors from tables A.1, A.2, and A.4, and a final adjustment factor of 0.680.

Books and Maps
Estimates of expenditure use Shaw's series "printing and publishing: books" (#18), the adjustment factors from tables A.1, A.2, and A.4, and a final adjustment factor of 1.186.

Wheel Goods, Durable Toys, Sports Equipment,
Boats, and Pleasure Aircraft

Despite numerous and creative attempts, it was impossible to replicate the BEA-Wealth estimates of expenditure for this category. Nor was it possible to replicate Goldsmith's estimates of expenditure for miscellaneous consumer durable goods. The statistical relationship between Goldsmith's miscellaneous consumer durable series and the sum of Shaw's categories "motorcycles and bicycles" (#21), "luggage" (#19), and "pleasure craft" (#22), adjusted by the factors of tables A.1, A.2, and A.4, is stable for 1919–29 only. Goldsmith's final adjustment factor is 1.639 for 1919–29, but between 1897 and 1918 this factor varies from 1.88 to 3.69 with no obvious temporal pattern. Inclusion of Shaw's category "passenger vehicles, horse-drawn, and accessories" (#20c) for 1897–1919 yields a final adjustment factor that ranges between 1.64 and 1.72 again with no obvious temporal pattern.

Comparing the BEA-Wealth estimates with the sum of Shaw's series "motorcycles and bicycles" (#21), "pleasure craft" (#22), and "passenger vehicles, horse-drawn, and accessories" (#20c), adjusted by the factors of tables A.1, A.2, and A.4, produces final adjustment factors ranging from 1.90 to 6.18 with no temporal pattern. Exclusion of horse-drawn vehicles results in a final adjustment factor that varies between 3.58 and 11.02. Because the BEA-Wealth estimates cannot be replicated, I accept their estimate for 1929 and develop independent estimates for 1869–1928.

Shaw does not include separate estimates of output of *durable* toys and sports equipment; he classifies all toys and sports equipment as semidurable goods. The breakdown of Shaw's category "toys, games, and sporting goods" (#10) shows, however, that items such as billiard tables, children's sleds and carriages, pocketknives, and firearms are included there.[24] I reclassify these items as durable goods and divide Shaw's estimates of toys, games, and sporting goods output destined for domestic consumption into two categories—semidurable toys and sporting goods, and durable toys and sporting goods—based on the shares of total output accounted for by the combination of billiard tables, children's sleds and carriages, pocketknives, and firearms.

For 1869, 1879, and quinquennially for 1889–1919, the shares of total output (before adjustment for net exports) of toys, games, and sporting goods accounted for by output of billiard tables, children's sleds and carriages, pocketknives, and firearms are calculated from Shaw's estimates of output. For 1919–29, Kuznets's biennial estimates of output are used to calculate the same percentage shares.[25] The percentage shares are then interpolated linearly between benchmarks. The resulting annual estimates of the percentage of *total* toys and sporting goods output accounted for by output of *durable* toys and sporting goods are then applied to Shaw's estimates of total "toys and sporting goods" (#10), yielding estimates of durable toys and sporting goods output.

Output of durable toys and sporting goods is adjusted by the inventory factors of table A.1, the markup series for wheel goods given in table A.2, and the consumer allocation factor for wheel goods given in table A.4. Similarly, Shaw's series "motorcycles and bicycles" (#21) and "pleasure craft" (#22) are adjusted using the factors given in tables A.1, A.2, and A.4. These three adjusted series are then summed for 1869, 1879, and 1889–1929.

Shaw omits annual estimates of bicycles for 1890–94. To compensate, I determine the share of bicycles in the aggregate series in 1889 and 1895, interpolate this percentage share linearly for the intervening years, and estimate annual figures for bicycles that bear the resulting indicated percentage relationships to the aggregate which includes this estimate of bicycles. For 1869 and 1879, absent any alternative estimates, I assume bicycle production is zero.

This process results in a series that combines bicycles, durable toys and sports equipment, and pleasure aircraft. This sum is then adjusted by a final factor of 1.326, yielding estimates of nominal consumer expenditure that directly link to the BEA-Wealth estimate at 1929.

Extension of Annual Estimates to 1869

Shaw does not construct annual estimates for the years before 1889 but does provide estimates for the census years 1869 and 1879. To interpolate between the estimates for 1869, 1879, and 1889, I use Kuznets's unpublished annual estimates of total nominal consumer expenditure for durable goods, 1869–89, that serve as the basis for the five-year moving averages published in *Capital in the American Economy*.[26]

The annual estimates for 1870–78 and 1880–88 are developed as follows. First, Kuznets's annual estimates of total nominal expenditure for consumer durable goods are used to interpolate my estimates of total expenditure annually, 1870–78 and 1880–88. To do this, separate linear equations are estimated for each of these two periods using the two estimates of total expenditure from the census years 1869, 1879, and 1889; these equations are then used to estimate total expenditure for the intercensus years.[27] Second, for each commodity group, the percentage of total expenditure accounted for by that group in 1869, 1879, and 1889 is calculated from my estimates of nominal expenditure. These percentages are interpolated linearly for the intervening years. Finally, for each commodity group, these estimated annual percentages are multiplied by the annual estimates of total expenditure.

The annual estimates of nominal expenditure, by commodity group, 1869–1986, are presented in table A.6. The first year of the BEA-Wealth estimates is in **bold print**.[28]

ESTIMATES OF REAL EXPENDITURE

To extend the BEA-Wealth estimates of real expenditure (1982 base) back to 1869, I first develop annual price indexes for 1869, 1879, and 1889 on that link to the BEA's implicit price deflators and then deflate the nominal expenditure estimates by these price indexes.

Methodology: Estimating Price Indexes

The BEA-Wealth commodity group-specific implicit price deflators can be replicated using the methodology Goldsmith used to estimate price index numbers.[29] Goldsmith's price indexes are based on commodity group-specific price indexes published in Shaw, *Value of Commodity Output*. It is again helpful to begin by outlining Goldsmith's methodology.

When Shaw's and Goldsmith's commodity group classifications are identical, Goldsmith first recomputes Shaw's 1913 base price indexes to a 1929 base. Then, since Shaw's price indexes are based on producer rather than consumer prices, Goldsmith adjusts each annual price index number by the ratio of that year's retail markup factor to the 1929 retail markup

Table A.6. Nominal Expenditure by Commodity Group, 1869-1986 (Millions of Dollars)

Year	AUT	HOR	OMV	OTH	FUR	APP	CHI	HSF
1869	0	36	0	36	107	30	56	65
1870	0	35	0	35	106	29	56	66
1871	0	37	0	37	112	30	59	71
1872	0	48	0	48	147	38	78	96
1873	0	44	0	44	137	35	74	92
1874	0	39	0	39	122	30	66	84
1875	0	39	0	39	125	30	68	88
1876	0	36	0	36	115	27	63	83
1877	0	35	0	35	116	27	64	85
1878	0	32	0	32	108	24	60	81
1879	0	35	0	35	120	26	67	92
1880	0	46	0	46	153	34	86	120
1881	0	46	0	46	152	34	86	122
1882	0	49	0	49	162	37	92	132
1883	0	48	0	48	159	37	91	132
1884	0	47	0	47	153	36	88	129
1885	0	48	0	48	156	38	90	134
1886	0	53	0	53	169	41	97	148
1887	0	54	0	54	171	43	99	153
1888	0	54	0	54	170	43	98	154
1889	0	55	0	55	172	44	100	159
1890	0	61	0	61	175	43	106	169
1891	0	63	0	63	185	44	112	187
1892	0	64	0	64	211	44	114	183
1893	0	59	0	59	184	40	94	163
1894	0	51	0	51	151	35	85	145
1895	6	46	0	46	172	40	99	167
1896	8	40	0	40	165	52	110	147
1897	15	41	0	41	162	58	110	156

Table A.6, continued

Year	AUT	HOR	OMV	OTH	FUR	APP	CHI	HSF
1898	15	44	0	44	164	53	112	155
1899	14	54	0	54	191	69	131	188
1900	11	51	0	51	**196**	73	150	206
1901	12	65	0	65	228	**87**	158	219
1902	12	59	0	60	249	97	169	250
1903	13	57	0	58	269	98	**196**	**260**
1904	24	58	0	59	275	91	198	249
1905	39	62	1	63	310	108	234	267
1906	66	63	1	64	367	132	264	316
1907	93	64	2	66	356	132	260	311
1908	133	49	3	52	294	109	202	250
1909	157	50	3	53	370	125	222	313
1910	211	54	4	58	390	135	246	333
1911	225	46	4	50	410	151	253	333
1912	325	42	6	48	444	190	262	356
1913	401	41	7	48	477	184	280	375
1914	434	36	8	44	448	162	271	342
1915	565	31	10	41	427	179	271	332
1916	898	31	16	48	547	230	348	443
1917	1,152	39	19	58	605	316	477	551
1918	**676**	36	9	45	663	357	426	650
1919	1,422	25	22	47	936	410	466	719
1920	1,436	14	22	36	1,227	617	595	1,014
1921	1,984	11	33	44	1,062	414	431	748
1922	1,583	6	**28**	34	991	429	375	820
1923	2,300	11	39	50	1,113	558	521	1,018
1924	2,259	9	39	48	1,248	601	417	983
1925	2,495	10	47	57	1,264	669	552	1,080
1926	2,774	9	45	54	1,277	732	616	1,044
1927	2,525	7	36	43	1,313	742	542	1,079

Table A.6, continued

Year	AUT	HOR	OMV	OTH	FUR	APP	CHI	HSF
1928	2,733	6	38	44	1,252	677	621	1,108
1929	3,240	6	125	131	1,204	702	628	1,148
1930	2,425	5	91	96	939	614	442	937
1931	1,803	2	65	67	798	516	429	783
1932	1,427	1	38	39	510	314	406	562
1933	1,660	2	42	44	463	373	364	472
1934	1,518	0	65	65	515	473	404	573
1935	1,741	0	80	80	667	562	407	617
1936	1,922	0	103	103	850	670	456	827
1937	2,062	0	106	106	925	773	515	885
1938	1,379	0	77	77	829	650	472	800
1939	2,044	0	103	103	951	707	475	908
1940	2,696	0	108	108	1,062	806	510	991
1941	3,214	0	151	151	1,324	1,059	623	1,214
1942	145	0	7	7	1,288	739	658	1,266
1943	164	0	9	9	1,245	266	612	1,369
1944	112	0	11	11	1,318	157	643	1,398
1945	147	0	16	16	1,563	331	800	1,519
1946	2,197	0	387	387	2,254	1,640	1,256	2,185
1947	4,867	0	440	440	2,559	2,880	1,341	2,444
1948	6,227	0	518	518	2,793	3,149	1,442	2,742
1949	9,698	0	456	456	2,709	2,846	1,391	2,679
1950	11,891	0	589	589	3,100	3,596	1,498	3,121
1951	10,757	0	644	644	3,259	3,543	1,593	3,468
1952	10,601	0	642	642	3,521	3,498	1,557	3,156
1953	13,123	0	662	662	3,761	3,662	1,614	3,109
1954	14,043	0	573	573	3,877	3,715	1,628	2,905
1955	16,395	0	768	768	4,437	4,103	1,732	3,326
1956	15,256	0	873	873	4,663	4,356	1,790	3,600
1957	16,115	0	785	785	4,537	4,340	1,726	3,770

Table A.6, continued

Year	AUT	HOR	OMV	OTH	FUR	APP	CHI	HSF
1958	14,121	0	695	695	4,518	4,169	1,697	3,766
1959	16,745	0	786	786	4,824	4,441	1,741	4,088
1960	17,727	0	840	840	4,792	4,311	1,739	4,150
1961	16,425	0	779	779	4,798	4,304	1,756	4,262
1962	19,585	0	993	993	5,135	4,343	1,859	4,596
1963	22,809	0	1,129	1,129	5,529	4,532	1,900	5,058
1964	22,725	0	1,295	1,295	6,183	4,896	2,125	5,783
1965	27,034	0	1,553	1,553	6,556	4,923	2,371	6,252
1966	24,685	0	1,828	1,828	7,086	5,369	2,738	6,865
1967	26,682	0	2,012	2,012	7,323	5,563	2,947	7,239
1968	31,346	0	2,704	2,704	7,977	6,254	3,254	7,912
1969	31,638	0	3,230	3,230	8,531	6,840	3,418	8,044
1970	29,853	0	3,155	3,155	8,654	7,291	3,471	7,901
1971	36,569	0	4,442	4,442	9,284	7,981	3,640	8,114
1972	37,965	0	6,109	6,109	10,529	9,039	3,978	8,952
1973	43,384	0	7,623	7,623	11,908	9,942	4,594	10,330
1974	37,118	0	7,170	7,170	12,638	10,383	5,079	11,477
1975	40,466	0	8,694	8,694	12,945	10,631	5,586	12,027
1976	50,157	0	13,161	13,161	14,195	11,560	6,345	13,467
1977	57,506	0	16,932	16,932	16,464	12,785	7,134	15,213
1978	64,137	0	20,413	20,413	18,325	14,054	7,882	16,938
1979	68,038	0	18,864	18,864	20,516	15,623	8,626	18,756
1980	65,796	0	13,576	13,576	21,087	16,450	9,262	19,765
1981	70,317	0	14,618	14,618	22,288	17,567	10,037	21,075
1982	76,662	0	17,731	17,731	21,780	17,802	10,394	21,517
1983	90,331	0	23,528	23,528	23,998	19,713	11,183	24,372
1984	107,953	0	30,006	30,006	26,721	21,724	12,237	27,142
1985	120,551	0	35,576	35,576	28,334	23,635	12,755	28,300
1986	131,997	0	39,326	39,326	30,855	24,842	13,400	30,300

Table A.6, continued

Year	RAD	PIA	MUS	JWL	MED	BKS	MIS	TOT
1869	0	20	20	57	1	12	19	403
1870	0	20	20	56	1	13	19	400
1871	0	21	21	59	2	14	20	424
1872	0	28	28	77	2	21	27	562
1873	0	27	27	71	2	21	25	528
1874	0	24	24	63	2	20	23	473
1875	0	25	25	64	2	22	23	487
1876	0	24	24	59	2	21	22	452
1877	0	24	24	58	2	23	22	457
1878	0	23	23	54	2	22	21	427
1879	0	26	26	59	2	26	23	478
1880	0	34	34	77	3	34	30	618
1881	0	35	35	78	4	35	29	622
1882	0	39	39	85	4	38	31	669
1883	0	39	39	85	5	38	31	665
1884	0	39	39	83	5	38	29	649
1885	0	41	41	86	5	40	30	668
1886	0	46	46	95	6	44	32	732
1887	0	48	48	98	7	46	32	750
1888	0	49	49	99	7	46	32	752
1889	0	51	51	102	8	48	32	770
1890	0	60	60	124	9	47	35	829
1891	1	59	60	119	10	46	41	866
1892	1	62	63	124	11	48	43	905
1893	1	41	42	98	11	47	52	790
1894	1	35	36	80	11	39	44	678
1895	2	49	51	95	12	49	59	796
1896	2	40	42	80	13	48	59	762
1897	2	43	45	87	13	46	82	815
1898	3	48	51	102	14	56	83	848

Table A.6, continued

Year	RAD	PIA	MUS	JWL	MED	BKS	MIS	TOT
1899	3	59	62	133	16	62	71	992
1900	6	71	77	142	16	61	59	1,042
1901	9	87	95	**147**	17	67	65	1,160
1902	12	100	112	167	19	69	62	1,266
1903	16	111	127	171	19	**73**	60	1,344
1904	16	97	113	171	19	76	56	1,329
1905	19	119	**138**	204	23	80	68	1,535
1906	22	136	158	246	26	79	73	1,792
1907	24	147	171	257	31	80	93	1,851
1908	18	105	123	183	31	76	63	1,515
1909	22	127	149	249	34	89	77	1,839
1910	27	124	151	264	35	85	81	1,989
1911	35	135	170	264	36	92	87	2,072
1912	48	151	199	272	**35**	103	90	2,324
1913	59	160	219	279	41	120	114	2,538
1914	58	134	192	219	51	106	102	2,371
1915	68	121	189	204	66	114	100	2,488
1916	102	142	244	315	78	119	140	3,409
1917	135	147	282	311	120	140	204	4,216
1918	162	140	302	278	234	154	143	3,928
1919	292	198	490	570	139	186	163	5,548
1920	334	253	587	527	166	220	220	6,645
1921	233	196	429	417	132	221	166	6,049
1922	240	208	448	450	120	198	141	5,590
1923	290	249	539	519	140	201	192	7,152
1924	443	239	682	513	123	236	185	7,295
1925	477	254	731	542	117	243	188	7,938
1926	597	240	837	554	116	249	206	8,459
1927	591	202	793	561	130	289	205	8,222
1928	788	152	940	548	120	285	205	8,533

Table A.6, continued

Year	RAD	PIA	MUS	JWL	MED	BKS	MIS	TOT
1929	912	108	1,020	565	131	310	**220**	9,299
1930	846	82	928	518	133	265	173	7,470
1931	422	61	482	331	117	254	160	5,740
1932	234	36	270	254	93	154	111	4,140
1933	172	24	196	174	92	153	93	4,084
1934	200	31	231	200	124	166	119	**4,388**
1935	208	42	250	235	131	184	137	5,011
1936	280	55	335	267	140	209	172	5,951
1937	325	63	388	336	165	244	211	6,610
1938	280	62	342	326	157	222	211	5,465
1939	359	64	423	358	172	227	229	6,597
1940	421	77	498	413	186	235	255	7,760
1941	515	97	612	555	227	256	315	9,550
1942	547	92	639	729	258	292	307	6,328
1943	n.a.	n.a.	406	944	307	368	272	5,962
1944	n.a.	n.a.	313	1,013	333	452	324	6,074
1945	n.a.	n.a.	347	1,193	349	522	402	7,189
1946	n.a.	n.a.	1,124	1,440	396	591	797	14,267
1947	n.a.	n.a.	1,408	1,408	400	533	959	19,239
1948	n.a.	n.a.	1,461	1,387	431	586	969	21,705
1949	n.a.	n.a.	1,688	1,310	454	630	840	24,701
1950	n.a.	n.a.	2,439	1,330	486	677	873	29,600
1951	n.a.	n.a.	2,258	1,431	546	779	904	29,182
1952	n.a.	n.a.	2,378	1,551	580	791	1,000	29,275
1953	n.a.	n.a.	2,626	1,595	604	833	1,105	32,694
1954	n.a.	n.a.	2,773	1,676	595	809	1,193	33,787
1955	n.a.	n.a.	2,920	1,790	592	871	1,408	38,342
1956	n.a.	n.a.	2,991	1,861	655	955	1,597	38,597
1957	n.a.	n.a.	2,877	1,865	674	987	1,745	39,421
1958	n.a.	n.a.	2,865	1,898	663	1,026	1,871	37,289

Table A.6, continued

Year	RAD	PIA	MUS	JWL	MED	BKS	MIS	TOT
1959	n.a.	n.a.	3,079	1,969	778	1,092	2,032	41,575
1960	n.a.	n.a.	3,061	1,951	758	1,144	2,001	42,474
1961	n.a.	n.a.	3,221	1,920	767	1,217	1,968	41,417
1962	n.a.	n.a.	3,413	2,063	935	1,292	2,039	46,253
1963	n.a.	n.a.	3,733	2,179	986	1,419	2,204	51,478
1964	n.a.	n.a.	4,341	2,446	1,064	1,621	2,550	55,029
1965	n.a.	n.a.	5,138	2,724	1,157	1,659	2,921	62,288
1966	n.a.	n.a.	6,326	3,229	1,296	1,854	3,663	64,939
1967	n.a.	n.a.	7,086	3,495	1,211	1,863	4,134	69,555
1968	n.a.	n.a.	7,665	3,862	1,408	2,024	4,789	79,195
1969	n.a.	n.a.	8,052	4,053	1,628	2,318	5,232	82,984
1970	n.a.	n.a.	8,604	4,133	1,861	2,934	5,215	83,072
1971	n.a.	n.a.	8,980	4,452	1,884	2,988	5,651	93,985
1972	n.a.	n.a.	10,126	4,828	2,151	2,956	7,400	104,033
1973	n.a.	n.a.	11,360	6,067	2,375	3,066	8,658	119,307
1974	n.a.	n.a.	12,186	7,060	2,568	3,205	9,240	118,124
1975	n.a.	n.a.	13,590	8,172	2,862	3,585	10,562	129,120
1976	n.a.	n.a.	14,958	9,934	3,042	3,591	12,133	152,543
1977	n.a.	n.a.	15,855	11,085	3,231	4,091	13,777	174,073
1978	n.a.	n.a.	17,079	12,521	3,727	4,774	15,776	195,626
1979	n.a.	n.a.	18,967	13,401	4,272	5,174	17,357	209,594
1980	n.a.	n.a.	20,037	15,520	4,669	5,618	17,264	209,044
1981	n.a.	n.a.	22,185	16,896	4,998	6,199	18,813	224,993
1982	n.a.	n.a.	24,700	16,806	5,541	6,578	19,425	238,936
1983	n.a.	n.a.	28,430	18,114	5,948	7,214	20,532	273,363
1984	n.a.	n.a.	31,757	20,026	6,743	7,800	24,961	317,070

Table A.6, continued

Year	RAD	PIA	MUS	JWL	MED	BKS	MIS	TOT
1985	n.a.	n.a.	36,395	20,932	7,400	8,200	26,068	341,846
1986	n.a.	n.a.	41,133	23,649	8,300	8,700	27,175	379,677

Source: Derived as discussed in appendix A.

Note: A figure in **bold print** is the first year of the BEA-Wealth estimates. See text. Three-letter abbreviations for the commodity groups are as follows: AUT, automobiles and parts; HOR, horse-drawn vehicles; OMV, other motor vehicles; OTH, other vehicles; FUR, furniture; APP, household appliances; CHI, china and tableware; HSF, house furnishings; RAD, radios and phonographs; PIA, pianos and other musical instruments; MUS, radios and musical instruments; JWL, jewelry and watches; MED, orthopedic and ophthalmic products; BKS, books and maps; MIS, miscellaneous other durable goods; TOT, total of all durable goods.

factor, yielding a 1929 base price index in consumer prices. When Goldsmith's commodity group is a combination of two or more of Shaw's commodity groups, Goldsmith first develops a composite price index series for his commodity group by calculating a weighted harmonic mean of the relevant price indexes, using the corresponding nominal expenditure estimates as weights.[30] The resulting series is then recomputed to a 1929 base and adjusted by the ratio of the retail markup factors. When Shaw's price index series does not extend back far enough, Goldsmith estimates the missing values using the price index for all consumer durable goods as an extrapolator.

Annual Estimates of Price Deflators and Real Expenditure, 1869, 1879, 1889–1986

To develop price indexes by commodity group, I use Shaw's price indexes, 1869, 1879, and 1889 on, without initial modification for those commodity groups for which there is a one-to-one correspondence between Shaw's categories and the BEA's (see table A.5). When more than one of Shaw's commodity groups corresponds to a single BEA-Wealth commodity group, a composite price index is constructed using a weighted harmonic mean of the relevant price indexes, with weights corresponding to Shaw's estimates of output destined for domestic consumption.[31] If Shaw's price index does not extend to 1869, the existing price index numbers are extrapolated back using a price index for all consumer durable goods that is equal to the harmonic mean of Shaw's price index series by commodity groups, 1869, 1879, and 1889–1929, with weights corresponding to Shaw's estimates of output destined for domestic consumption.

For each commodity group, these producer price series are then adjusted by the ratio of the current year retail markup factor to the 1913 retail markup factor, resulting in a 1913 base price index that is implicitly in consumer prices. Using these indexes, the BEA-Wealth implicit price deflators are extrapolated back to 1869, yielding commodity group-specific price series in a 1982 base for 1869, 1879, and 1889–1986. The estimates of nominal expenditure by commodity group are then deflated by the corresponding price series, resulting in annual estimates of real expenditure, 1982 dollars, by commodity group for 1869, 1879, and 1889–1986.

To summarize, the price index numbers are developed as follows:

$$\text{Price}_{1982,t} = \text{Price}_{1913,t} \times \frac{\text{BEA-Wealth Price}_{1982,T}}{\text{Price}_{1913,T}}$$

where T is the first year of the BEA-Wealth price series, and

$$\text{Price}_{1913,t} = \text{Shaw}_{1913,t} \times \frac{\text{retail markup}_t}{\text{retail markup}_{1913}}$$

The specific methodology followed to extend the BEA-Wealth price series back to 1869 is discussed below, taking each commodity group in turn.

Automobiles and Parts
The BEA's implicit price deflator for automobiles and parts can be derived from Shaw's price index for "motor vehicles" (#20a). To use one price index to deflate the aggregate automobiles and parts would be inappropriate, however, because Shaw's price index for "tires and tubes" (#11) differs from his index for "motor vehicles" (#20a). Accordingly, four individual price series are developed, and each of the four nominal expenditure series are individually deflated.

For new automobiles, Shaw's price index for "motor vehicles" (#20a), unadjusted since the retail markup for automobiles is constant throughout, is used to extrapolate the 1918 value of the BEA-Wealth implicit price deflator for automobiles and parts.

Implicitly assuming that used and new car prices follow the same temporal pattern, the price index for new autos is also used to deflate net expenditure for used automobiles. Use of this procedure follows Goldsmith, who deflated nominal used car markups by the price index for new automobiles.[32]

Shaw indicates that the price index for motor vehicles should be used for motor vehicle accessories as well.[33] Adjusting this index by the retail markup factor for automobile accessories gives a 1913 base consumer price index for automobile accessories. The benchmark used to recompute this 1913 base price index to a 1982 base is derived from the national product accounts. For 1929 on, the national product accounts provide annual price index numbers by commodity group, 1982 base.[34] Shaw used the price index for automobiles as the index for automobile accessories; the 1929 value of the price index for new automobiles is 16.0. The retail markup patterns for automobiles and for automobile accessories differ, and so this value (16.0) is increased by a factor of 1.076, the ratio of the automobile accessories retail markup factor for 1929 to that for 1913. The resulting 1929 benchmark value, 17.216, is used to convert the 1913 base price index for automobile accessories to a 1982 base.

Shaw's price index for "tires and tubes" (#11) begins in 1900. It is extended back with the price index for all consumer durable goods and then adjusted by the retail markup factor ratios for automobile accessories, yielding a 1913 base price index for tires.[35]

To convert the tires price index to a 1982 base, a 1929 benchmark is again derived from the national product accounts. The 1929 price index number for automobile accessories and tires is 36.9. Using the value above (17.216) as the 1929 price index number for automobile accessories, and using as weights the 1929 estimates of nominal expenditures for automobile accessories ($221 million) and for tires ($419 million), the value of the 1929 price index number for tires is computed as follows: the 1929 price index number for automobile accessories and tires, 36.9, is equal to the weighted harmonic mean of the price index values for automobile accessories (17.216 with a weight of 221) and for tires (unknown value with a weight of 419).[36] The resulting 1929 price index value for tires, 92.961, is used to convert the 1913 base index to a 1982 base.

Estimating real expenditure for automobiles and parts, 1869, 1879, and

1889–1917, follows the procedure used to develop nominal expenditure estimates. First, nominal expenditure estimates (by component) are each multiplied by 0.84, following the adjustment of the original estimates of nominal expenditure for automobiles and parts. Then each of the four resulting series is deflated by its corresponding price index, 1869, 1879, and 1889–1917. The sum of these four series is the estimate of real expenditure for automobiles and parts for 1869, 1879, and 1889–1917, supplementing the BEA-Wealth series, which begins in 1918.

Other Vehicles

Two price series are required to estimate real expenditure for other vehicles: one for horse-drawn vehicles and one for other motor vehicles. The price index for horse-drawn vehicles is derived from four sources. Shaw's 1907–19 price index for "carriages and wagons" (#20c) is extended back to 1869 using the price index for all consumer durable goods. For 1919–29, Shaw's price index for "farm equipment" (#27) is used to extrapolate forward his index for "carriages and wagons." The retail markup factor for horse-drawn vehicles is constant throughout, so no adjustment for changes in markup is needed. The price index for 1869, 1879, and 1889–1929 is converted to a 1982 base and extended to 1933 using the national product accounts price index for farm equipment.[37] The resulting price index is used to deflate the estimates of nominal expenditure for horse-drawn vehicles.

For the years before 1922, Shaw's price index for "motor vehicles" (#20a) is used to extrapolate back the BEA-Wealth implicit price deflator for other motor vehicles. The retail markup factor (that for automobiles) is constant throughout, so no adjustment to compensate for changes in the retail markup is necessary. Estimated real expenditure for other motor vehicles is derived by deflating nominal expenditure.

Finally, the estimates of real expenditures for horse-drawn vehicles and for other motor vehicles are summed, and the implicit price deflator for all other vehicles is derived as the ratio of nominal to real expenditures for all other vehicles.

Furniture

The price index for furniture is derived from Shaw's price index for "furniture" (#12), adjusted by the retail markup factor for furniture from table

A.2, and linked to the BEA-Wealth implicit price deflator for furniture at 1895.

Kitchen and Other Household Appliances

Shaw provides no price index for electrical appliances. For nonelectrical appliances, his price index begins in 1913. Following Goldsmith, Shaw's price index for nonelectrical appliances is extended from 1913 back to 1869 using the price index for all consumer durable goods as an extrapolator; the index for all consumer durable goods is used as a proxy for the price index for electrical appliances; and a composite price index for household appliances is then computed by taking the weighted harmonic mean of these two indexes, with weights corresponding to Shaw's estimates of output destined for domestic consumption, adjusted by splicing each output series at 1919.[38] This series is adjusted by the ratio of the retail markup factors and then used to extrapolate the BEA-Wealth implicit price deflator for household appliances back of 1901.

China, Glassware, Tableware, and Utensils

The price index uses Shaw's price index for "china and household utensils" (#15), adjusted by the retail markup factor used to estimate nominal expenditure, and then linked to the BEA-Wealth implicit price deflator at 1903.

Other Durable House Furnishings

A composite price index for 1869, 1879, and 1889–1919 is first derived from Shaw's price indexes for "floor coverings" (#14a) and "miscellaneous housefurnishings" (#14b) by taking the weighted harmonic mean of these two price indexes, with weights corresponding to Shaw's estimates of output destined for domestic consumption. For 1919–29, Shaw's composite index for "durable housefurnishings" (#14) is used. These price indexes are adjusted by the ratio of the retail markup factors and then used to extrapolate the BEA-Wealth implicit price deflator back of 1903.

Radio and Television Receivers

Shaw provides price index numbers for "musical instruments" (#16) only. Therefore there is only one price index for this commodity group, and it is used to deflate nominal expenditure for both radios and phonographs, and pianos and other musical instruments. Shaw's price index for "musical instruments" begins in 1889. It is extended to 1869 and 1879 with the price index for all consumer durable goods, then adjusted by the ratios of the retail markup factors, and finally linked to the BEA-Wealth implicit price deflator at 1904.

Jewelry and Watches

To develop the price index for jewelry and watches, Shaw's price index for "jewelry, silverware, clocks, and watches" (#17) is first extended back from its initial year of 1890 to 1869 and 1879 with the price index for all consumer durable goods and then adjusted by the ratios of the retail markup factors used to estimate nominal expenditure for jewelry and watches. The resulting price index is linked to the BEA-Wealth implicit price deflator at 1901.

Ophthalmic Products and Orthopedic Appliances

Shaw provides no price index for this commodity group. Following Goldsmith, the price index for all consumer durable goods is used as a proxy.[39] The retail markup factor for medical appliances is constant throughout, so no further adjustment to the 1913 base price index is necessary. The price index for all consumer durable goods is linked to the BEA-Wealth implicit price deflator for medical appliances at 1913.

Books and Maps

Again, Shaw provides no price index for this commodity group, and, following Goldsmith, the price index for all consumer durable goods is used as a proxy.[40] This index is adjusted by the ratios of the retail markup factor for books and then used to extrapolate the BEA-Wealth implicit price deflator back of 1903.

Wheel Goods, Durable Toys, Sports Equipment, Boats, and Pleasure Aircraft

Because the estimates of nominal expenditure for this commodity group use the BEA-Wealth estimates for 1929 on only, the price series is also developed independently and links to the BEA-Wealth implicit price deflator at 1929.

Shaw provides no price indexes for "motorcycles and bicycles" (#21) or for "toys, games, and sporting goods" (#10). Following Goldsmith, the price index for all consumer durable goods is therefore used as a proxy for each of these two subgroups.[41] Following Shaw, the price index for "ships and boats" (#31) is used as the price index for pleasure craft.[42] Since the retail markup factors for these three commodity subgroups differ, each price index is first adjusted by the ratio of its respective retail markup factors, and then a weighted harmonic mean is computed from these three adjusted price indexes. The weights for "durable toys" are my estimates of durable toys output. For "motorcycles and bicycles," the weights for 1890–94 are derived from my estimates of expenditure for bicycles: the estimates for 1890–94 are multiplied by the inverse of the product of the adjustment factors of tables A.1, A.2, and A.4, and by the ratio of Shaw's second 1919 estimate of output destined for domestic consumption ($23,951 thousand) to Shaw's first 1919 estimate of the same ($18,981 thousand). The weights for the remaining years for "bicycles" and for "pleasure craft" are Shaw's estimates of output.

This process yields a 1913 base price index, which is then used to extrapolate the BEA-Wealth implicit price deflator for this commodity group back of 1929.

Extension of Annual Estimates to 1869

To develop annual estimates of real expenditure for the intercensus years 1870–78 and 1880–88, Kuznets's unpublished estimates of total real expenditure for consumer durable goods, 1929 prices, are used to interpolate between the 1869, 1879, and 1889 census-year values of total real expenditure for consumer durable goods.[43] The percentage shares of total real expenditure accounted for by each commodity group are computed for 1869, 1879, and 1889 and then interpolated linearly, 1870–78 and 1880–88. The annual estimates by commodity group, 1870–78 and 1880–88, are the product of the annual percentage shares and estimated total real expenditure for consumer durable goods.

The annual estimates of real expenditure by commodity group, 1869–1986, are presented in table A.7. The first year of the BEA-Wealth estimates is in **bold print**. The price series, 1869–1986, are in table A.8. Asterisks (*) indicate those numbers that are estimated price index numbers. All other values are implicit price deflators, derived by taking the ratio of nominal to real expenditure in that year.

Table A.7. Real Expenditure by Commodity Group, 1869-1986 (Millions of 1982 Dollars)

Year	AUT	HOR	OMV	OTH	FUR	APP	CHI	HSF
1869	0	361	0	361	1,212	100	338	370
1870	0	345	0	345	1,166	94	338	370
1871	0	333	0	333	1,135	90	342	374
1872	0	441	0	441	1,518	118	475	520
1873	0	458	0	458	1,589	121	516	565
1874	0	399	0	399	1,397	104	471	515
1875	0	460	0	460	1,627	119	569	623
1876	0	456	0	456	1,626	116	590	646
1877	0	493	0	493	1,779	124	670	732
1878	0	478	0	478	1,741	118	680	743
1879	0	556	0	556	2,049	136	829	906
1880	0	585	0	585	2,132	144	870	983
1881	0	639	0	639	2,306	159	949	1,107
1882	0	680	0	680	2,426	171	1,008	1,213
1883	0	682	0	682	2,404	173	1,008	1,251
1884	0	677	0	677	2,359	173	999	1,277
1885	0	750	0	750	2,584	194	1,104	1,454
1886	0	836	0	836	2,846	218	1,228	1,665
1887	0	882	0	882	2,965	232	1,292	1,803
1888	0	879	0	879	2,920	234	1,286	1,845
1889	0	864	0	864	2,835	232	1,261	1,860
1890	0	877	0	877	2,944	205	1,359	1,991
1891	0	907	0	907	3,105	212	1,429	2,152
1892	0	956	0	956	3,554	218	1,500	2,211
1893	0	934	0	934	3,340	210	1,237	1,934
1894	0	843	0	843	2,797	191	1,139	1,843
1895	2	801	0	801	3,470	234	1,380	2,337
1896	2	735	0	735	3,718	317	1,569	2,066
1897	4	773	0	773	3,678	357	1,723	2,190

Table A.7, continued

Year	AUT	HOR	OMV	OTH	FUR	APP	CHI	HSF
1898	4	768	0	768	3,330	304	1,753	2,141
1899	10	908	0	908	3,755	386	1,995	2,599
1900	12	776	0	777	**3,417**	371	2,159	2,578
1901	15	986	0	987	3,822	**421**	1,998	2,720
1902	17	878	0	878	4,021	457	2,130	3,042
1903	20	820	1	820	4,192	442	**2,492**	**2,985**
1904	43	826	1	827	4,246	409	2,638	2,736
1905	49	851	1	852	4,746	484	3,314	2,969
1906	74	828	2	830	5,339	569	3,739	3,272
1907	92	773	3	775	4,642	529	3,658	3,043
1908	135	568	4	571	3,892	461	2,897	2,713
1909	263	573	7	580	5,010	538	3,289	3,356
1910	375	610	10	621	4,869	549	3,743	3,487
1911	411	533	11	544	4,295	563	4,072	3,277
1912	723	482	20	502	4,225	665	4,249	3,428
1913	897	466	24	490	3,998	609	4,443	3,462
1914	1,149	420	31	451	3,774	534	4,126	3,223
1915	1,654	370	45	415	3,596	593	4,126	3,179
1916	2,847	367	78	445	4,478	720	4,607	3,361
1917	3,220	413	88	500	4,864	877	4,580	2,903
1918	**2,139**	273	39	312	4,228	811	3,242	2,609
1919	3,894	168	78	246	4,681	847	3,499	2,812
1920	3,424	100	69	170	5,999	1,212	4,253	3,947
1921	5,391	73	117	190	5,052	776	2,949	2,894
1922	5,049	51	**123**	174	4,603	771	2,504	3,157
1923	7,798	93	157	250	5,012	960	3,408	3,895
1924	8,153	74	143	217	6,086	1,000	2,752	3,770
1925	8,656	80	194	274	6,077	1,140	3,656	4,154
1926	10,312	73	183	256	6,322	1,271	4,219	4,031

Table A.7, continued

Year	AUT	HOR	OMV	OTH	FUR	APP	CHI	HSF
1927	9,267	55	144	199	6,665	1,309	3,790	4,248
1928	9,774	51	150	201	6,421	1,207	4,404	4,504
1929	11,265	52	471	523	6,271	1,267	4,518	4,803
1930	8,983	43	352	395	5,048	1,161	3,274	4,146
1931	6,800	17	268	285	4,866	1,055	3,516	3,915
1932	5,417	11	164	175	3,806	741	3,561	3,267
1933	6,530	13	200	213	3,355	935	3,279	2,682
1934	6,060	0	300	300	3,433	1,174	3,285	2,894
1935	7,219	0	373	373	4,537	1,419	3,015	3,085
1936	8,096	0	478	478	5,592	1,667	3,591	4,054
1937	8,682	0	485	485	5,572	1,854	4,023	3,969
1938	5,695	0	332	332	5,086	1,555	3,688	3,687
1939	8,512	0	456	456	5,944	1,712	3,711	4,127
1940	10,917	0	480	480	6,556	2,025	3,984	4,309
1941	11,993	0	631	631	7,397	2,527	4,756	4,856
1942	405	0	26	26	6,104	1,533	4,446	4,538
1943	423	0	28	28	4,960	498	3,687	4,388
1944	486	0	32	32	4,379	276	3,439	3,994
1945	479	0	45	45	4,611	549	4,124	4,051
1946	7,005	0	1,305	1,305	6,629	2,729	6,508	5,827
1947	14,532	0	1,260	1,260	7,229	4,357	6,807	6,141
1948	17,046	0	1,360	1,360	7,428	4,511	7,174	6,804
1949	24,176	0	1,111	1,111	7,442	4,198	6,688	6,782
1950	29,296	0	1,520	1,520	8,378	5,375	6,935	7,557
1951	25,456	0	1,539	1,539	7,892	4,941	6,750	7,523
1952	21,916	0	1,481	1,481	8,504	4,879	6,434	7,029
1953	23,220	0	1,486	1,486	9,107	5,143	6,508	6,848
1954	28,577	0	1,220	1,220	9,343	5,300	6,460	6,413
1955	35,276	0	1,749	1,749	10,768	6,052	6,739	7,246
1956	34,798	0	1,900	1,900	11,155	6,733	6,439	7,579

Table A.7, continued

Year	AUT	HOR	OMV	OTH	FUR	APP	CHI	HSF
1957	32,768	0	1,604	1,604	10,599	6,803	5,891	7,725
1958	27,542	0	1,383	1,383	10,557	6,702	5,619	7,654
1959	31,307	0	1,505	1,505	11,272	7,151	5,784	8,259
1960	33,146	0	1,670	1,670	11,170	7,044	5,592	8,153
1961	31,618	0	1,548	1,548	11,056	7,186	5,575	8,292
1962	36,877	0	1,936	1,936	11,778	7,412	5,755	8,943
1963	42,175	0	2,190	2,190	12,624	7,896	5,689	9,821
1964	43,466	0	2,497	2,497	14,117	8,620	6,250	11,164
1965	52,403	0	3,043	3,043	14,866	8,870	6,974	12,116
1966	51,361	0	3,638	3,638	15,677	9,852	7,890	13,151
1967	51,335	0	3,962	3,962	15,615	10,189	8,255	13,556
1968	59,160	0	5,201	5,201	16,180	11,228	8,452	14,491
1969	59,326	0	6,124	6,124	16,374	12,000	8,524	14,625
1970	54,621	0	5,846	5,846	15,967	12,485	8,384	14,210
1971	65,845	0	7,934	7,934	16,609	13,392	8,545	14,594
1972	67,857	0	10,942	10,942	18,537	15,091	8,939	15,986
1973	77,567	0	13,613	13,613	20,252	16,597	9,774	18,187
1974	63,689	0	12,189	12,189	19,809	16,480	9,565	18,692
1975	64,750	0	13,657	13,657	18,789	15,187	8,995	18,250
1976	76,072	0	19,397	19,397	19,881	15,643	9,599	19,433
1977	82,816	0	23,728	23,728	22,219	16,690	10,369	21,129
1978	85,349	0	26,674	26,674	23,524	17,458	10,797	22,584
1979	84,094	0	22,933	22,933	24,688	18,402	10,933	23,682
1980	75,884	0	15,349	15,349	23,404	18,462	10,622	22,850
1981	74,315	0	15,700	15,700	23,241	18,629	10,466	22,396
1982	78,424	0	18,347	18,347	21,780	17,802	10,394	21,517
1983	89,964	0	23,639	23,639	23,393	19,210	10,985	23,731
1984	103,695	0	29,285	29,285	25,511	21,121	11,997	25,850
1985	113,972	0	33,283	33,283	26,418	23,434	12,456	26,300
1986	122,732	0	35,283	35,283	28,132	24,742	12,800	27,900

Table A.7, continued

Year	RAD	PIA	MUS	JWL	MED	BKS	MIS	TOT
1869	0	17	17	179	6	124	52	2,760
1870	0	17	17	172	6	131	51	2,688
1871	0	16	16	167	6	139	50	2,652
1872	0	22	22	223	9	202	68	3,597
1873	0	24	24	232	10	228	72	3,817
1874	0	22	22	203	9	216	65	3,402
1875	0	26	26	236	12	270	76	4,018
1876	0	26	26	235	12	289	77	4,074
1877	0	29	29	256	14	338	86	4,520
1878	0	29	29	250	15	352	85	4,490
1879	0	35	35	292	18	440	102	5,362
1880	0	38	38	311	21	471	106	5,661
1881	0	43	43	344	25	524	114	6,209
1882	0	46	46	370	28	566	120	6,629
1883	0	48	48	375	31	577	119	6,666
1884	0	49	49	376	32	582	117	6,641
1885	0	55	55	422	38	656	128	7,385
1886	0	63	63	475	45	743	141	8,261
1887	0	68	68	507	51	796	147	8,743
1888	0	69	69	510	53	806	145	8,747
1889	0	70	70	507	55	805	141	8,631
1890	0	83	83	558	57	714	142	8,932
1891	1	84	85	536	64	706	164	9,362
1892	1	81	82	614	73	765	181	10,155
1893	1	55	57	542	80	795	228	9,356
1894	1	51	52	465	83	682	202	8,298
1895	3	80	82	552	98	917	287	10,162
1896	3	65	67	467	107	941	301	10,291
1897	3	68	72	553	113	926	426	10,815
1898	4	78	83	602	114	1,045	403	10,546

Table A.7, continued

Year	RAD	PIA	MUS	JWL	MED	BKS	MIS	TOT
1899	5	89	94	764	123	1,110	332	12,075
1900	8	100	108	787	111	998	252	11,569
1901	11	112	123	**744**	121	1,059	273	12,283
1902	14	117	131	837	128	1,065	256	12,962
1903	18	129	148	863	127	**1,084**	240	13,413
1904	19	115	134	848	122	1,077	219	13,298
1905	22	131	**153**	1,010	149	1,150	263	15,139
1906	25	150	175	1,292	158	1,060	270	16,777
1907	27	160	187	1,297	171	1,011	317	15,723
1908	19	113	132	1,055	171	1,071	212	13,311
1909	23	139	162	1,527	207	1,231	277	16,440
1910	29	136	165	1,614	204	1,154	284	17,065
1911	38	147	185	1,614	205	1,099	300	16,565
1912	52	163	215	1,603	**200**	1,161	310	17,281
1913	63	168	231	1,547	223	1,282	378	17,560
1914	65	150	215	1,204	276	1,121	358	16,431
1915	76	135	211	1,139	350	1,172	365	16,800
1916	115	159	274	1,490	381	1,128	508	20,240
1917	146	160	306	1,048	503	1,132	672	20,605
1918	147	126	273	771	842	1,082	389	16,699
1919	218	148	366	1,506	492	1,143	392	19,878
1920	245	185	430	1,330	579	1,359	410	23,112
1921	167	140	307	1,005	454	1,372	353	20,743
1922	170	146	316	1,064	407	1,240	372	19,657
1923	183	157	340	1,209	476	1,245	525	25,118
1924	252	136	388	1,281	423	1,409	502	25,981
1925	261	139	400	1,489	416	1,405	532	28,199
1926	319	128	447	1,620	422	1,465	596	30,960
1927	310	106	416	1,665	473	1,710	577	30,318
1928	411	79	490	1,636	430	1,667	575	31,309

Table A.7, continued

Year	RAD	PIA	MUS	JWL	MED	BKS	MIS	TOT
1929	507	60	567	1,687	465	1,813	**598**	33,777
1930	616	59	675	1,556	475	1,606	468	27,787
1931	435	63	498	1,000	419	1,618	455	24,427
1932	329	51	380	817	350	1,020	355	19,889
1933	266	37	303	559	361	1,070	313	19,600
1934	288	45	333	664	486	1,169	399	**20,197**
1935	304	62	366	813	514	1,296	469	23,106
1936	412	82	494	870	551	1,462	621	27,476
1937	468	91	559	1,124	647	1,671	733	29,319
1938	418	92	510	1,168	616	1,500	710	24,547
1939	557	100	657	1,239	664	1,523	787	29,332
1940	646	118	764	1,350	713	1,577	847	33,522
1941	767	145	912	1,595	866	1,695	1,036	38,264
1942	682	115	797	1,719	977	1,934	898	23,377
1943	n.a.	n.a.	501	2,165	1,129	2,272	866	20,917
1944	n.a.	n.a.	358	2,042	1,198	2,707	903	19,814
1945	n.a.	n.a.	397	2,358	1,238	3,017	1,086	21,955
1946	n.a.	n.a.	1,271	2,939	1,375	3,283	2,081	40,952
1947	n.a.	n.a.	1,292	2,697	1,338	2,747	2,262	50,662
1948	n.a.	n.a.	1,259	2,741	1,386	2,764	2,222	54,695
1949	n.a.	n.a.	1,378	2,604	1,410	2,788	1,931	60,508
1950	n.a.	n.a.	2,002	2,725	1,500	2,943	2,074	70,305
1951	n.a.	n.a.	1,872	2,741	1,606	3,315	1,970	65,605
1952	n.a.	n.a.	2,146	2,988	1,686	3,164	2,173	62,400
1953	n.a.	n.a.	2,447	3,045	1,782	3,192	2,413	65,191
1954	n.a.	n.a.	2,732	3,306	1,776	3,064	2,640	70,831
1955	n.a.	n.a.	3,029	3,639	1,741	3,238	3,179	82,656
1956	n.a.	n.a.	3,097	3,759	1,899	3,511	3,534	84,404
1957	n.a.	n.a.	2,872	3,829	1,877	3,380	3,777	81,125
1958	n.a.	n.a.	2,806	3,946	1,831	3,299	3,938	75,277

Table A.7, continued

Year	RAD	PIA	MUS	JWL	MED	BKS	MIS	TOT
1959	n.a.	n.a.	3,168	4,085	2,126	3,456	4,399	82,512
1960	n.a.	n.a.	3,149	4,055	2,021	3,542	4,258	83,800
1961	n.a.	n.a.	3,366	3,992	1,977	3,677	4,100	82,387
1962	n.a.	n.a.	3,666	4,279	2,373	3,822	4,170	91,011
1963	n.a.	n.a.	4,066	4,501	2,490	4,137	4,471	100,060
1964	n.a.	n.a.	4,802	4,759	2,653	4,617	5,140	108,085
1965	n.a.	n.a.	5,846	5,458	2,829	4,673	5,843	122,921
1966	n.a.	n.a.	7,487	6,784	3,078	5,135	7,239	131,292
1967	n.a.	n.a.	8,466	7,250	2,746	5,034	8,058	134,466
1968	n.a.	n.a.	9,158	7,770	3,088	5,231	9,104	149,063
1969	n.a.	n.a.	9,643	7,719	3,427	5,753	9,779	153,294
1970	n.a.	n.a.	10,292	7,740	3,715	6,986	9,675	149,921
1971	n.a.	n.a.	10,690	8,184	3,548	6,776	9,984	166,101
1972	n.a.	n.a.	12,012	8,667	3,897	6,511	12,914	181,353
1973	n.a.	n.a.	13,459	10,514	4,152	6,578	14,649	205,342
1974	n.a.	n.a.	14,007	11,573	4,196	6,475	14,348	191,023
1975	n.a.	n.a.	15,083	12,495	4,336	6,713	15,242	193,497
1976	n.a.	n.a.	16,384	14,695	4,340	6,423	16,945	218,812
1977	n.a.	n.a.	17,328	16,182	4,354	6,695	18,468	239,978
1978	n.a.	n.a.	18,365	17,342	4,778	7,094	20,330	254,295
1979	n.a.	n.a.	19,882	17,006	5,197	7,078	21,065	254,960
1980	n.a.	n.a.	20,551	15,756	5,205	6,970	19,076	234,129
1981	n.a.	n.a.	22,230	16,500	5,223	6,927	19,577	235,204
1982	n.a.	n.a.	24,700	16,806	5,541	6,578	19,425	241,314
1983	n.a.	n.a.	29,338	17,913	5,725	6,649	20,230	270,777
1984	n.a.	n.a.	34,681	19,624	6,296	7,000	24,055	309,115

Table A.7, continued

Year	RAD	PIA	MUS	JWL	MED	BKS	MIS	TOT
1985	n.a.	n.a.	42,343	20,731	6,700	6,800	24,860	337,297
1986	n.a.	n.a.	52,021	23,247	7,300	7,000	25,967	367,124

Source: Derived as discussed in appendix A.

Notes: A figure in **bold print** is the first year of the BEA-Wealth estimates. See text. Commodity group abbreviations as for table A.6.

ESTIMATES OF REAL NET STOCK

For each type of consumer durable good, the BEA-Wealth study includes four sets of stock estimates: gross and net stock, each calculated under constant- and current-cost valuation.[44] Gross stock does not take account of depreciation that occurs during the life of the good; net stock does.[45] Constant-cost stock estimates are derived from estimates of real expenditure; current-cost estimates are derived after first revaluing nominal expenditure in all previous years to their current-year equivalent values using the ratios of price deflators. I extended only the constant-cost net stock estimates to the years prior to 1925.

The method used to extend the depreciation and stock estimates replicates the BEA-Wealth estimates. Again due to absence of detailed documentation, extensive data analysis was required. The methodology that replicates the BEA-Wealth estimates requires several assumptions (noted in the text and notes below) evidently made by the BEA.[46]

Methodology: Estimating Depreciation

The BEA uses a straight-line method of depreciation: the annual depreciation rate is the inverse of the good's estimated life length, with life length measured in years.[47] For example, a good with an expected life length of eight years will depreciate at a rate of 12.5 percent per year in each of the eight years, with the rate applied to the original acquisition price. The good is fully depreciated by the end of its expected lifetime.

The average life length that the BEA associates with each commodity group is shown in table A.9, together with life length estimates drawn from other sources. The life lengths that the BEA uses range from three years for automobile accessories and tires to fourteen years for furniture.

Table A.8. Price Deflators by Commodity Group, 1869-1986 (1982=100)

Year	AUT	HOR	OMV	OTH	FUR	APP	CHI	HSF
1869	n.a.	10.0*	n.a.	10.0	8.9*	30.1*	16.6*	17.6*
1870	n.a.	10.2	n.a.	10.2	9.1	30.8	16.5	17.8
1871	n.a.	11.0	n.a.	11.0	9.8	33.2	17.3	19.0
1872	n.a.	10.8	n.a.	10.8	9.7	32.6	16.5	18.5
1873	n.a.	9.6	n.a.	9.6	8.6	28.9	14.3	16.3
1874	n.a.	9.7	n.a.	9.7	8.7	29.2	14.1	16.3
1875	n.a.	8.5	n.a.	8.5	7.7	25.6	12.0	14.1
1876	n.a.	7.8	n.a.	7.8	7.1	23.5	10.7	12.8
1877	n.a.	7.2	n.a.	7.2	6.5	21.6	9.6	11.7
1878	n.a.	6.8	n.a.	6.8	6.2	20.4	8.8	10.9
1879	n.a.	6.4*	n.a.	6.4	5.8*	19.2*	8.1*	10.2*
1880	n.a.	7.8	n.a.	7.8	7.2	23.5	9.9	12.2
1881	n.a.	7.1	n.a.	7.1	6.6	21.6	9.1	11.0
1882	n.a.	7.2	n.a.	7.2	6.7	21.7	9.1	10.9
1883	n.a.	7.1	n.a.	7.1	6.6	21.4	9.0	10.5
1884	n.a.	7.0	n.a.	7.0	6.5	21.0	8.8	10.1
1885	n.a.	6.4	n.a.	6.4	6.0	19.4	8.1	9.2
1886	n.a.	6.3	n.a.	6.3	5.9	19.0	7.9	8.9
1887	n.a.	6.1	n.a.	6.1	5.8	18.4	7.7	8.5
1888	n.a.	6.1	n.a.	6.1	5.8	18.4	7.7	8.3
1889	n.a.	6.3*	n.a.	6.3	6.0*	19.1*	7.9*	8.5*
1890	n.a.	7.0*	n.a.	7.0	5.9*	21.0*	7.8*	8.5*
1891	n.a.	6.9*	n.a.	6.9	5.9*	21.0*	7.8*	8.7*
1892	n.a.	6.7*	n.a.	6.7	5.9*	20.2*	7.6*	8.3*
1893	n.a.	6.3*	n.a.	6.3	5.5*	19.1*	7.6*	8.4*
1894	n.a.	6.1*	n.a.	6.1	5.4*	18.4*	7.4*	7.8*
1895	364.4	5.7*	n.a.	5.7	5.0*	17.2*	7.2*	7.1*
1896	345.9	5.4*	n.a.	5.4	4.4*	16.3*	7.0*	7.1*
1897	342.2	5.3*	n.a.	5.3	4.4*	16.1*	6.4*	7.1*
1898	366.5	5.7*	n.a.	5.7	4.9*	17.3*	6.4*	7.2*

Table A.8, continued

Year	AUT	HOR	OMV	OTH	FUR	APP	CHI	HSF
1899	139.9	6.0*	37.2*	6.0	5.1*	18.0*	6.6*	7.2*
1900	96.8	6.5*	37.2*	6.5	5.7	19.7*	6.9*	8.0*
1901	79.9	6.6*	37.2*	6.6	6.0	20.7	7.9*	8.1*
1902	71.6	6.8*	36.7*	6.8	6.2	21.2	7.9*	8.2*
1903	64.0	7.0*	36.8*	7.0	6.4	22.2	7.9	8.7
1904	54.2	7.1*	33.5*	7.1	6.5	22.2	7.5	9.1
1905	79.8	7.3*	50.7*	7.3	6.5	22.3	7.1	9.0
1906	89.7	7.6*	58.8*	7.7	6.9	23.2	7.1	9.7
1907	101.1	8.3*	67.7*	8.5	7.7	25.0	7.1	10.2
1908	98.2	8.7*	67.7*	9.1	7.6	23.6	7.0	9.2
1909	59.8	8.8*	41.0*	9.2	7.4	23.2	6.7	9.3
1910	56.3	8.8*	37.8*	9.3	8.0	24.6	6.6	9.5
1911	54.8	8.7*	35.9*	9.3	9.5	26.8	6.2	10.2
1912	45.0	8.7*	29.9*	9.5	10.5	28.6	6.2	10.4
1913	44.7	8.7*	28.8*	9.7	11.9	30.2	6.3	10.8
1914	37.8	8.6*	24.4*	9.7	11.9	30.3	6.6	10.6
1915	34.1	8.4*	22.6*	9.9	11.9	30.2	6.6	10.4
1916	31.5	8.6*	21.0*	10.7	12.2	31.9	7.6	13.2
1917	35.8	9.5*	21.6*	11.6	12.4	36.0	10.4	19.0
1918	31.6	13.1*	23.6*	14.4	15.7	44.0	13.1	24.9
1919	36.5	14.9*	27.8*	19.0	20.0	48.4	13.3	25.6
1920	41.9	14.2*	31.4*	21.2	20.5	50.9	14.0	25.7
1921	36.8	15.8*	28.0*	23.3	21.0	53.4	14.6	25.8
1922	31.4	12.2*	22.8	19.7	21.5	55.6	15.0	26.0
1923	29.5	12.2*	24.8	20.1	22.2	58.1	15.3	26.1
1924	27.7	12.7*	27.3	22.3	20.5	60.1	15.2	26.1
1925	28.8	12.5*	24.2	20.8	20.8	58.7	15.1	26.0
1926	26.9	12.6*	24.6	21.2	20.2	57.6	14.6	25.9
1927	27.2	12.6*	25.0	21.6	19.7	56.7	14.3	25.4
1928	28.0	12.5*	25.3	22.1	19.5	56.1	14.1	24.6

Table A.8, continued

Year	AUT	HOR	OMV	OTH	FUR	APP	CHI	HSF
1929	28.8	12.4*	26.5	25.1	19.2	55.4	13.9	23.9
1930	27.0	12.6*	25.9	24.4	18.6	52.9	13.5	22.6
1931	26.5	12.6*	24.3	23.6	16.4	48.9	12.2	20.0
1932	26.3	12.4*	23.2	22.5	13.4	42.4	11.4	17.2
1933	25.4	13.5*	21.0	20.6	13.8	39.9	11.1	17.6
1934	25.0	n.a.	21.7	21.7	15.0	40.3	12.3	19.8
1935	24.1	n.a.	21.4	21.4	14.7	39.6	13.5	20.0
1936	23.7	n.a.	21.5	21.5	15.2	40.2	12.7	20.4
1937	23.8	n.a.	21.9	21.9	16.6	41.7	12.8	22.3
1938	24.2	n.a.	23.2	23.2	16.3	41.8	12.8	21.7
1939	24.0	n.a.	22.6	22.6	16.0	41.3	12.8	22.0
1940	24.7	n.a.	22.5	22.5	16.2	39.8	12.8	23.0
1941	26.8	n.a.	23.9	23.9	17.9	41.9	13.1	25.0
1942	35.8	n.a.	26.9	26.9	21.1	48.2	14.8	27.9
1943	38.8	n.a.	32.1	32.1	25.1	53.4	16.6	31.2
1944	23.0	n.a.	34.4	34.4	30.1	56.9	18.7	35.0
1945	30.7	n.a.	35.6	35.6	33.9	60.3	19.4	37.5
1946	31.4	n.a.	29.7	29.7	34.0	60.1	19.3	37.5
1947	33.5	n.a.	34.9	34.9	35.4	66.1	19.7	39.8
1948	36.5	n.a.	38.1	38.1	37.6	69.8	20.1	40.3
1949	40.1	n.a.	41.0	41.0	36.4	67.8	20.8	39.5
1950	40.6	n.a.	38.8	38.8	37.0	66.9	21.6	41.3
1951	42.3	n.a.	41.8	41.8	41.3	71.7	23.6	46.1
1952	48.4	n.a.	43.3	43.3	41.4	71.7	24.2	44.9
1953	56.5	n.a.	44.5	44.5	41.3	71.2	24.8	45.4
1954	49.1	n.a.	47.0	47.0	41.5	70.1	25.2	45.3
1955	46.5	n.a.	43.9	43.9	41.2	67.8	25.7	45.9
1956	43.8	n.a.	45.9	45.9	41.8	64.7	27.8	47.5
1957	49.2	n.a.	48.9	48.9	42.8	63.8	29.3	48.8
1958	51.3	n.a.	50.3	50.3	42.8	62.2	30.2	49.2

Table A.8, continued

Year	AUT	HOR	OMV	OTH	FUR	APP	CHI	HSF
1959	53.5	n.a.	52.2	52.2	42.8	62.1	30.1	49.5
1960	53.5	n.a.	50.3	50.3	42.9	61.2	31.1	50.9
1961	51.9	n.a.	50.3	50.3	43.4	59.9	31.5	51.4
1962	53.1	n.a.	51.3	51.3	43.6	58.6	32.3	51.4
1963	54.1	n.a.	51.6	51.6	43.8	57.4	33.4	51.5
1964	52.3	n.a.	51.9	51.9	43.8	56.8	34.0	51.8
1965	51.6	n.a.	51.0	51.0	44.1	55.5	34.0	51.6
1966	48.1	n.a.	50.2	50.2	45.2	54.5	34.7	52.2
1967	52.0	n.a.	50.8	50.8	46.9	54.6	35.7	53.4
1968	53.0	n.a.	52.0	52.0	49.3	55.7	38.5	54.6
1969	53.3	n.a.	52.7	52.7	52.1	57.0	40.1	55.0
1970	54.7	n.a.	54.0	54.0	54.2	58.4	41.4	55.6
1971	55.5	n.a.	56.0	56.0	55.9	59.6	42.6	55.6
1972	55.9	n.a.	55.8	55.8	56.8	59.9	44.5	56.0
1973	55.9	n.a.	56.0	56.0	58.8	59.9	47.0	56.8
1974	58.3	n.a.	58.8	58.8	63.8	63.0	53.1	61.4
1975	62.5	n.a.	63.7	63.7	68.9	70.0	62.1	65.9
1976	65.9	n.a.	67.9	67.9	71.4	73.9	66.1	69.3
1977	69.4	n.a.	71.4	71.4	74.1	76.6	68.8	72.0
1978	75.1	n.a.	76.5	76.5	77.9	80.5	73.0	75.0
1979	80.9	n.a.	82.3	82.3	83.1	84.9	78.9	79.2
1980	86.7	n.a.	88.4	88.4	90.1	89.1	87.2	86.5
1981	94.6	n.a.	93.1	93.1	95.9	94.3	95.9	94.1
1982	97.8	n.a.	96.6	96.6	100.0	100.0	100.0	100.0
1983	100.4	n.a.	99.5	99.5	102.6	102.6	101.8	102.7
1984	104.1	n.a.	102.5	102.5	104.7	102.9	102.0	105.0
1985	105.8	n.a.	106.9	106.9	107.3	100.9	102.4	107.6
1986	107.5	n.a.	111.5	111.5	109.7	100.4	104.7	108.6

Table A.8, continued

Year	MUS[a]	JWL	MED	BKS	MIS	TOT	MJR	MNR
1869	116.2*	31.8*	21.5*	9.4*	35.9*	14.6	11.4	19.6
1870	119.0	32.5	22.0	9.6	36.7	14.9	11.7	19.7
1871	128.4	35.1	23.9	10.4	39.6	16.0	12.7	20.8
1872	126.2	34.4	23.4	10.2	38.9	15.6	12.5	20.1
1873	112.1	30.6	20.9	9.1	34.6	13.8	11.1	17.5
1874	113.3	30.9	21.1	9.2	35.0	13.9	11.2	17.4
1875	99.2	27.1	18.4	8.0	30.6	12.1	9.8	15.0
1876	91.3	24.9	16.9	7.4	28.2	11.1	9.1	13.5
1877	83.6	22.8	15.5	6.8	25.8	10.1	8.3	12.2
1878	78.9	21.6	14.6	6.4	24.4	9.5	7.9	11.3
1879	74.3*	20.3*	13.7*	6.0*	23.0*	8.9	7.5	10.5
1880	90.7	24.8	16.8	7.3	28.0	10.9	9.2	12.7
1881	83.2	22.8	15.4	6.7	25.7	10.0	8.5	11.6
1882	83.8	22.9	15.5	6.8	25.9	10.1	8.6	11.6
1883	82.7	22.6	15.3	6.7	25.6	10.0	8.6	11.3
1884	80.9	22.1	14.9	6.5	25.0	9.8	8.5	11.0
1885	74.9	20.5	13.8	6.0	23.2	9.0	7.9	10.1
1886	73.3	20.0	13.5	5.9	22.7	8.9	7.8	9.8
1887	70.9	19.4	13.1	5.7	21.9	8.6	7.6	9.4
1888	71.0	19.4	13.1	5.7	21.9	8.6	7.7	9.4
1889	73.6*	20.1*	13.6*	5.9*	22.7*	8.9	8.0	9.7
1890	71.8*	22.2*	15.0*	6.5*	24.9*	9.3	8.2	10.2
1891	70.2*	22.2*	15.0*	6.5*	24.8*	9.2	8.2	10.2
1892	76.5*	20.2*	14.4*	6.3*	24.0*	8.9	7.9	9.8
1893	74.4*	18.1*	13.6*	5.9*	22.7*	8.4	7.2	9.7
1894	68.8*	17.2*	13.1*	5.7*	21.9*	8.2	7.1	9.1
1895	61.7*	17.2*	12.3*	5.3*	20.5*	7.8	6.9	8.6
1896	61.8*	17.2*	11.6*	5.1*	19.5*	7.4	6.3	8.4
1897	62.3*	15.8*	11.5*	5.0*	19.3*	7.5	6.6	8.3

Year	MUS[a]	JWL	MED	BKS	MIS	TOT	MJR	MNR
1898	61.3*	16.9*	12.3*	5.4*	20.6*	8.0	7.3	8.6
1899	66.2*	17.4*	12.8*	5.6*	21.5*	8.2	7.6	8.7
1900	71.5*	18.0*	14.0*	6.1*	23.5*	9.0	8.7	9.2
1901	77.7*	19.8	14.1*	6.3*	23.7*	9.4	9.1	9.7
1902	85.2*	20.0	14.6*	6.5*	24.4*	9.8	9.6	9.9
1903	85.9*	19.8	15.1*	6.7	25.1*	10.0	10.0	10.0
1904	84.1*	20.2	15.3*	7.1	25.4*	10.0	9.9	10.1
1905	90.2	20.2	15.7*	7.0	26.0*	10.1	10.5	9.9
1906	90.3	19.0	16.4*	7.5	27.2*	10.7	11.3	10.3
1907	91.4	19.8	18.0*	7.9	29.4*	11.8	13.1	10.9
1908	93.2	17.3	17.9*	7.1	29.5*	11.4	13.7	9.9
1909	92.0	16.3	16.6*	7.2	27.7*	11.2	13.0	10.0
1910	91.5	16.4	17.1*	7.4	28.5*	11.7	14.4	10.0
1911	91.9	16.4	17.5*	8.4	29.2*	12.5	16.8	10.1
1912	92.6	17.0	17.5	8.9	29.2*	13.5	19.1	10.2
1913	94.8	18.0	18.4	9.4	30.2*	14.5	21.3	10.7
1914	89.3	18.2	18.5	9.5	28.5*	14.4	20.9	10.6
1915	89.6	17.9	18.9	9.7	27.4*	14.8	21.7	10.5
1916	89.1	21.1	20.5	10.5	27.5*	16.8	22.4	12.6
1917	92.2	29.7	23.9	12.4	30.4*	20.5	24.7	16.6
1918	110.6	36.1	27.8	14.2	36.6*	23.5	26.3	21.1
1919	133.9	37.8	28.3	16.3	41.7*	27.9	32.9	22.8
1920	136.5	39.6	28.7	16.2	53.6*	28.7	34.7	23.1
1921	139.7	41.5	29.1	16.1	47.1*	29.2	33.6	23.4
1922	141.8	42.3	29.5	16.0	38.0*	28.4	31.9	24.1
1923	158.5	42.9	29.4	16.1	36.6*	28.5	31.8	24.1
1924	175.8	40.0	29.1	16.7	36.8*	28.1	30.5	24.2
1925	182.8	36.4	28.1	17.3	35.3*	28.2	31.5	23.4
1926	187.2	34.2	27.5	17.0	34.6*	27.3	30.5	22.5

Table A.8, continued

Year	MUS[a]	JWL	MED	BKS	MIS	TOT	MJR	MNR
1927	190.6	33.7	27.5	16.9	35.6*	27.1	30.3	22.5
1928	191.8	33.5	27.9	17.1	35.7*	27.3	31.2	21.8
1929	179.9	33.5	28.2	17.1	**36.8**	27.5	31.7	21.6
1930	137.5	33.3	28.0	16.5	37.0	26.9	30.8	21.4
1931	96.8	33.1	27.9	15.7	35.2	23.5	27.1	19.0
1932	71.1	31.1	26.6	15.1	31.3	20.8	24.3	16.9
1933	64.7	31.1	25.5	14.3	29.7	20.8	24.1	16.3
1934	69.4	30.1	25.5	14.2	29.8	21.7	24.8	17.8
1935	68.3	28.9	25.5	14.2	29.2	21.7	23.7	18.6
1936	67.8	30.7	25.4	14.3	27.7	21.7	23.8	18.6
1937	69.4	29.9	25.5	14.6	28.8	22.5	24.8	19.4
1938	67.1	27.9	25.5	14.8	29.7	22.3	24.9	19.2
1939	64.4	28.9	25.9	14.9	29.1	22.5	24.5	19.7
1940	65.2	30.6	26.1	14.9	30.1	23.1	24.9	20.3
1941	67.1	34.8	26.2	15.1	30.4	25.0	27.1	21.5
1942	80.2	42.4	26.4	15.1	34.2	27.1	31.8	24.2
1943	81.0	43.6	27.2	16.2	31.4	28.5	32.6	26.7
1944	87.4	49.6	27.8	16.7	35.9	30.7	34.6	29.1
1945	87.4	50.6	28.2	17.3	37.0	32.7	39.5	30.1
1946	88.4	49.0	28.8	18.0	38.3	34.8	40.1	30.3
1947	109.0	52.2	29.9	19.4	42.4	38.0	42.4	32.2
1948	116.0	50.6	31.1	21.2	43.6	39.7	44.8	32.7
1949	122.5	50.3	32.2	22.6	43.5	40.8	45.4	32.9
1950	121.8	48.8	32.4	23.0	42.1	42.1	46.4	33.6
1951	120.6	52.2	34.0	23.5	45.9	44.5	49.1	36.5
1952	110.8	51.9	34.4	25.0	46.0	46.9	53.0	36.8
1953	107.3	52.4	33.9	26.1	45.8	50.2	57.6	37.2
1954	101.5	50.7	33.5	26.4	45.2	47.7	53.0	37.2
1955	96.4	49.2	34.0	26.9	44.3	46.4	50.3	37.7

Table A.8, continued

Year	MUS[a]	JWL	MED	BKS	MIS	TOT	MJR	MNR
1956	96.6	49.5	34.5	27.2	45.2	45.7	48.8	39.1
1957	100.2	48.7	35.9	29.2	46.2	48.6	52.4	40.7
1958	102.1	48.1	36.2	31.1	47.5	49.5	53.8	41.5
1959	97.2	48.2	36.6	31.6	46.2	50.4	54.9	41.6
1960	97.2	48.1	37.5	32.3	47.0	50.7	54.7	42.5
1961	95.7	48.1	38.8	33.1	48.0	50.3	53.9	43.1
1962	93.1	48.2	39.4	33.8	48.9	50.8	54.3	43.6
1963	91.8	48.4	39.6	34.3	49.3	51.4	54.7	44.2
1964	90.4	51.4	40.1	35.1	49.6	50.9	53.7	45.1
1965	87.9	49.9	40.9	35.5	50.0	50.7	53.2	45.1
1966	84.5	47.6	42.1	36.1	50.6	49.5	51.5	45.4
1967	83.7	48.2	44.1	37.0	51.3	51.7	54.3	46.5
1968	83.7	49.7	45.6	38.7	52.6	53.1	55.4	48.3
1969	83.5	52.5	47.5	40.3	53.5	54.1	56.3	49.6
1970	83.6	53.4	50.1	42.0	53.9	55.4	58.0	50.3
1971	84.0	54.4	53.1	44.1	56.6	56.6	58.8	51.8
1972	84.3	55.7	55.2	45.4	57.3	57.4	59.3	53.2
1973	84.4	57.7	57.2	46.6	59.1	58.1	59.5	55.0
1974	87.0	61.0	61.2	49.5	64.4	61.8	63.0	59.6
1975	90.1	65.4	66.0	53.4	69.3	66.7	67.7	64.8
1976	91.3	67.6	70.1	55.9	71.6	69.7	70.6	67.9
1977	91.5	68.5	74.2	61.1	74.6	72.5	73.4	70.6
1978	93.0	72.2	78.0	67.3	77.6	76.9	78.2	74.3
1979	95.4	78.8	82.2	73.1	82.4	82.2	83.5	79.5
1980	97.5	98.5	89.7	80.6	90.5	89.3	89.1	89.6
1981	99.8	102.4	95.7	89.5	96.1	95.7	95.4	96.2
1982	100.0	100.0	100.0	100.0	100.0	99.0	98.5	100.0
1983	96.9	101.1	103.9	108.5	101.5	101.0	100.2	102.5
1984	91.6	102.0	107.1	111.4	103.8	102.6	101.8	104.3

Table A.8, continued

Year	MUS[a]	JWL	MED	BKS	MIS	TOT	MJR	MNR
1985	86.0	101.0	110.4	120.6	104.9	103.2	102.1	105.9
1986	79.1	101.7	113.7	124.3	104.7	103.4	102.0	107.0

Sources: Values marked with asterisk (*) are price index numbers derived as discussed in appendix A. All other values are implicit price deflators, derived by taking the ratio of nominal to real expenditures.

Notes: A figure in **bold print** is the first year of the BEA-Wealth estimates. MJR stands for major durable goods; MNR stands for minor durable goods. All other commodity group abbreviations as for table A.6.

[a]Used as the price index for PIA (pianos and other musical instruments) and RAD (radios and phonographs) as well.

The BEA assumes that while an "average" life length can be associated with each commodity group, goods within that group have expected life lengths that may differ from the overall average. For each commodity group, the variety of expected life lengths are determined by applying a Winfrey L-2 distribution (which the BEA first modifies) to the average life length of goods within that group.[48] Relative to Winfrey's original distribution, the BEA decreases the range of expected service lives by condensing the distribution and decreases the number of different service lives associated with each commodity group by increasing the size of the increment.[49] The original Winfrey L-2 distribution and the BEA's modified Winfrey L-2 distribution are presented in table A.10.

Using the modified distribution, the BEA then determines what percentage of annual expenditure is associated with each expected service life. As seen from table A.10, in each year, 1.5 percent of total expenditure will be for goods with an expected service life that is 25 percent of the average life length, 2.1 percent will be for goods with an expected service life that is 35 percent of the average, and so on.[50] The BEA then apparently rounds each expected service life to its nearest integer value, with 2.5 years rounded down to 2 years, 3.5 years rounded down to 3 years, and so on.[51] The distributions of expected service lives by commodity group are in table A.11.

Annual depreciation is estimated using these distributions of expected service lives and the straight-line method of depreciation. Expenditure is

Table A.9. Average Service Lives (Years)

Commodity Group	BEA	Ruffin and Tippett	Goldsmith (1962)	Goldsmith (1955)	Epstein	Cox and Breyer
New Autos	10		15	6,9,12[a]		8
Auto Parts and Accessories	3		5	5		3
Tires and Tubes	3[b]		c	c		3
Other Motor Vehicles	8					
Horse-Drawn Vehicles				8		
Farm Machinery, except Tractors	14		15	15		
Furniture	14		15	20	12	15
Kitchen and Other Household Appliances	11		12	12	13	
Refrigerators, Washing and Sewing Machines					16	14
Refrigerators		15				
Freezers		20				

Table A.9, continued

Commodity Group	BEA	Ruffin and Tippett	Goldsmith (1962)	Goldsmith (1955)	Epstein	Cox and Breyer
Washing Machines		11				
Miscellaneous Electrical Appliances					8	12
Cooking and Portable Heating Equipment					12	14
Electric Ranges		12				
Gas Ranges		13.5				
China, Glassware, Tableware, and Utensils	10		10	10	11	
Other Durable House Furnishings	10		10	10		
Floor Coverings					9	9
Tools					6	
Other Durable House Furnishings					8	

247

Table A.9, continued

Commodity Group	BEA	Ruffin and Tippett	Goldsmith (1962)	Goldsmith (1955)	Epstein	Cox and Breyer
Radios, TVs, Pianos, and Other Musical Instruments	9		10	10,15,20[a]	10	
Radios, Phonographs, Televisions		11			9	7
Televisions						
Pianos and Other Musical Instruments					16	23
Jewelry and Watches	11		15	10	13	15
Ophthalmic Products and Orthopedic Appliances	6		4	5	4	
Books and Maps	10		6	10	6	

Table A.9, continued

Commodity Group	BEA	Ruffin and Tippett	Goldsmith (1962)	Goldsmith (1955)	Epstein	Cox and Breyer
Wheel Goods, Toys, Boats, Aircraft	10		10	10		
Wheel Goods, Toys, and Sports Equipment					4	
Boats and Pleasure Aircraft					14	

Sources: BEA: U.S. BEA, Fixed Reproducible Tangible Wealth, 1925-85, table B, "Service Lives Used to Derive BEA Wealth Estimates," p. xxii. Ruffin and Tippett: Ruffin and Tippett, "Service-Life Expectancy of Household Appliances," p. 169. Goldsmith (1962): Goldsmith, National Wealth, table B-31, p. 252. Goldsmith (1955): Goldsmith, Study of Saving, 1:table Q-12, pp. 638-39. Epstein: Epstein, "Consumers' Tangible Assets," p. 442. Cox and Breyer: Cox and Breyer, Consumer Plant and Equipment, pp. 56-58.

Notes:
[a]Service life estimates vary over time.
[b]The BEA-Wealth study includes "Tires and Tubes" with "Automobile Accessories."
[c]Assumed to have a service life less than 3 years.

Table A.10. Original Winfrey and Modified Winfrey L-2 Retirement Patterns

AGE: Given as Percent of Average Service Life	WINFREY: Percent of Original Purchases Surviving (1)	WINFREY: Percent of Original Purchases Discarded since Previous Age (2)	BEA: Cumulative Percent of Original Purchases Discarded (3)	BEA: Percent of Original Purchases with Age Indicated (4)
0	100.00000			
5	99.98516	0.01484		
10	99.88940	0.09576		
15	99.64732	0.24208		
20	99.20930	0.43802		
25	98.53977	0.66953	1.5	1.5
30	97.61555	0.92422		
35	96.41791	1.19764	3.6	2.1
40	94.85656	1.56135		
45	92.77820	2.07836	7.2	3.6
50	90.07738	2.70082		
55	86.72860	3.34878	13.2	6.0
60	82.78113	3.94747		
65	78.33876	4.44237	21.6	8.4
70	73.53626	4.80250		
75	68.51802	5.01824	31.4	9.8
80	63.42158	5.09644		
85	58.36648	5.05510	41.6	10.2
90	53.44823	4.91825		
95	48.73660	4.71163	51.2	9.6
100	44.27685	4.45975		

Table A.10, continued

AGE: Given as Percent of Average Service Life	WINFREY: Percent of Original Purchases Surviving (1)	WINFREY: Percent of Original Purchases Discarded since Previous Age (2)	BEA: Cumulative Percent of Original Purchases Discarded (3)	BEA: Percent of Original Purchases with Age Indicated (4)
105	40.09316	4.18369	59.8	8.6
110	36.19309	3.90007		
115	32.57226	3.62083	67.3	7.5
120	29.21877	3.35349		
125	26.11696	3.10181	73.7	6.4
130	23.25024	2.86672		
135	20.60301	2.64723	79.2	5.5
140	18.16176	2.44125		
145	15.91540	2.24636	83.9	4.7
150	13.85508	2.06032		
155	11.97372	1.88136	87.9	4.0
160	10.26528	1.70844		
165	8.72414	1.54114	91.1	3.2
170	7.34447	1.37967		
175	6.11983	1.22464	93.7	2.6
180	5.04292	1.07691		
185	4.10549	0.93743	95.7	2.0
190	3.29841	0.80708		
195	2.61180	0.68661	97.2	1.5
200	2.03522	0.57658		
205	1.55792	0.47730	98.2	1.0

Table A.10, continued

AGE: Given as Percent of Average Service Life	WINFREY: Percent of Original Purchases Surviving (1)	WINFREY: Percent of Original Purchases Discarded since Previous Age (2)	BEA: Cumulative Percent of Original Purchases Discarded (3)	BEA: Percent of Original Purchases with Age Indicated (4)
210	1.16899	0.38893		
215	0.85763	0.31136	100.0	1.8
220	0.61326	0.24437		
225	0.42576	0.18750		
230	0.28560	0.14016		
235	0.18396	0.10164		
240	0.11287	0.07109		
245	0.06525	0.04762		
250	0.03501	0.03024		
255	0.01706	0.01795		
260	0.00731	0.00975		
265	0.00261	0.00470		
270	0.00071	0.00190		
275	0.00012	0.00059		
280	0.00001	0.00011		
285	0.00000	0.00001		

Sources: Column 1: Winfrey, *Industrial Property Retirements*, table 21, p. 103. Column 2: First difference of column 1. Column 3: U.S. BEA, *Fixed Reproducible Tangible Wealth, 1925-85*, table C, "Modified Winfrey Retirement Patterns," p. xxiv. Column 4: First difference of column 3.

Table A.11. Distribution of Expected Service Lives, by Commodity Group (Years)

Percent of Original Purchases	Auto Accessories and Tires	Medical Products	Radios and TVs	Horse-drawn Vehicles, Other Motor Vehicles	Radios and Pianos	Autos, China, House-furnishings, Books, Wheel Goods	Household Appliances, Jewelry	Furniture	Pianos
1.5	1	1	2	2	2	2	3	3	4
2.1	1	2	3	3	3	3	4	5	6
3.6	1	3	3	4	4	4	5	6	7
6.0	2	3	4	4	5	5	6	8	9
8.4	2	4	5	5	6	6	7	9	10
9.8	2	4	6	6	7	7	8	10	12
10.2	3	5	6	7	8	8	9	12	14
9.6	3	6	7	8	9	9	10	13	15
8.6	3	6	8	8	9	10	12	15	17
7.5	3	7	9	9	10	11	13	16	18
6.4	4	7	9	10	11	12	14	17	20
5.5	4	8	10	11	12	13	15	19	22
4.7	4	9	11	12	13	14	16	20	23
4.0	5	9	12	12	14	15	17	22	25

Table A.11, continued

Percent of Original Purchases	Auto Accessories and Tires	Medical Products	Radios and TVs	Horse-drawn Vehicles, Other Motor Vehicles	Radios and Pianos	Autos, China, House-furnishings, Books, Wheel Goods	Household Appliances, Jewelry	Furniture	Pianos
3.2	5	10	12	13	15	16	18	23	26
2.6	5	10	13	14	16	17	19	24	28
2.0	6	11	14	15	17	18	20	26	30
1.5	6	12	15	16	18	19	21	27	31
1.0	6	12	15	16	18	20	23	29	33
1.8	6	13	16	17	19	21	24	30	34

Sources: Derived from the distribution in column 4 of table A.10. Each row is the product of the average life length of the goods indicated with the "age as a percent of average service life" in table A.10 that corresponds to the "percent of original purchases" in the first column of this table, then rounded to the nearest integer value. When the fractional part of the product is 0.5, the value is rounded down. For example, from table A.10 we see that 1.5 percent of goods will have a life length that is 25 percent of the average. When the average life length is 3 years, 1.5 percent of goods will have an average life length of 25 percent of 3 years, 0.75 years, which is rounded up to 1 year. Average life length assumptions as follows: automobile accessories and tires, 3 years; medical products (orthopedic appliances and ophthalmic products), 6 years; radios and televisions, 7.5 years; horse-drawn vehicles and other motor vehicles, 8 years; radios, phonographs, pianos, and other musical instruments, 9 years; automobiles, china and tableware, house furnishings, books, and miscellaneous other durable goods (wheel goods, durable toys, etc.), 10 years; household appliances, jewelry and watches, 11 years; furniture, 14 years; pianos and other musical instruments, 16 years.

assumed to be evenly distributed over the year.[52] For a given expected service life, Y_i, depreciation in year t is therefore equal to

$$D_{i,t} = \frac{p_i}{Y_i} \left(\frac{Q_t}{2} + \sum_{j=i}^{Y_i - 1} Q_{t-j} + \frac{Q_{t-Y_i}}{2} \right) \qquad (A.1)$$

where $D_{i,t}$ is depreciation in year t of goods with service life Y_i, p_i is the percent of expenditure with expected service life Y_i, and Q_t is total expenditure in year t.[53] For each commodity group, total depreciation in year t is the sum of the depreciation amounts associated with each expected service life; that is,

$$D_t = \sum_{i=1}^{20} D_{i,t} = \sum_{i=1}^{20} \frac{p_i}{Y_i} \left(\frac{Q_t}{2} + \sum_{j=i}^{Y_i - 1} Q_{t-j} + \frac{Q_{t-Y_i}}{2} \right) \qquad (A.2)$$

where the index, $i = 1, 2, \ldots 20$, reflects the maximum twenty different expected service lives as indicated in table A.11.

Annual estimates of expenditure begin in 1869. Any estimate of depreciation of necessity therefore takes into account only those goods purchased in 1869 and later, not goods purchased earlier. For each commodity group, the first year in which the depreciation estimate is "complete"— that is, the first year in which all existing goods are taken into account in the determination of depreciation—is the year when every good purchased in 1868 and earlier has already reached the end of its expected service life. The first year in which the depreciation estimates are complete is therefore 1869 plus the maximum expected life length for that commodity group.

Methodology: Estimating Net Stock

The perpetual inventory method is used to calculate stock: current end-of-year stock equals previous end-of-year stock plus current-year purchases less current-year depreciation. That is,

$$S_t = S_{t-1} + Q_t - D_t \qquad (A.3)$$

where S_t is existing stock at the end of year t, Q_t is expenditure in year t, and D_t is depreciation in year t.

Goods are fully depreciated by the end of their expected service lives. Therefore, if only those goods that have passed the end of their lifetimes are considered, cumulative expenditure and cumulative depreciation will be equal. If we sum both expenditure and depreciation from 1869 (including therefore the "incomplete" depreciation estimates which theoretically should reflect pre-1869 expenditure but due to data limitations do not), then only those goods that are still "alive" at the end of the current year will actively contribute to the difference between cumulative expenditure and cumulative depreciation. Let t_0 represent the first year in which the depreciation estimates are complete. Then for $t = t_0, t_0+1, \ldots, 1983$, equation A.3 is equivalent to[54]

$$S_t = \sum_{i = 1869}^{t} Q_i - \sum_{i = 1869}^{t} D_i, \quad \text{for } t = t_0, t_0 + 1, \ldots \quad (A.4)$$

Extension of the BEA-Wealth depreciation and net stock estimates to the years before 1925 uses equations A.2 and A.4 and the estimates of real expenditure in table A.7. This procedure essentially replicates the BEA-Wealth depreciation estimates for 1925–83. However, an estimation error of 0.02 percent in depreciation—an error due merely to rounding the expenditure estimates—results in a stock estimation error of up to 0.20 percent. When the BEA-Wealth 1925 stock estimate and my initial 1925 stock estimate differ, the new pre-1925 estimates are multiplied by a constant factor equal to the ratio of the two 1925 stock estimates. The values of these factors are noted below.

Treatment of Used Goods

For most commodity groups, the BEA modifies the estimates of nominal expenditure in the national product accounts to revalue consumer expenditure for used durable goods previously owned by private business or government to the original acquisition prices of those goods as determined by the age of the goods at the time of resale. Quoting from the BEA-Wealth study, "In the NIPA's [National Income and Product Accounts], consumer purchases of used durable goods from private business or government are valued at purchase prices. For purposes of stock estimation, these transfers are revalued to original acquisition prices by raising the used sales prices for each type of good by a factor determined by the estimated age of the goods at the time of purchase by consumers. These factors are based on data from the BEA's input-output tables."[55]

An example illustrates the statistical implications. Suppose a good with an estimated ten-year life length is purchased by a private business at an original acquisition price of $10,000. Under the straight-line method of depreciation, the good will be depreciated $1,000 per year. Suppose further that when the good is six years old, this private business sells the good to a consumer at a resale price of $3,600. In the national product accounts, $3,600 will be entered as consumer expenditure for a used durable good in the year of consumer purchase.

At the time of resale, the good has a remaining lifetime of four years. If no adjustment is made to the resale price, the good will then be depreciated at a rate of 25 percent, or $900 per year. However, total depreciation of the good over its lifetime, aggregating the business and consumer sectors, will then total only $9,600 ($6,000 by the business and $3,600 by the consumer), falling short of the original acquisition price of $10,000. For the BEA-Wealth estimates, the BEA would revalue consumer expenditure in the year of resale to $4,000, reflecting the original acquisition price of $10,000 and the passing of six of the ten years of the good's expected lifetime. Depreciation then continues to be $1,000 per year.

The estimates of nominal expenditure in table A.6 and of real expenditure in table A.7 reflect this adjustment. The BEA-Wealth estimates of nominal expenditure exceed the national product accounts estimates as follows: furniture, increased 1.0 percent; household appliances, increased 0.5 percent; radios and television receivers, increased 0.75 percent; jewelry and watches, increased 0.9 percent; books and maps, increased 0.4 percent; and wheel goods, durable toys, etc., increased 0.45 percent.

Annual Estimates of Depreciation and Stock

Development of the annual estimates of depreciation and of existing net stock is discussed below, considering each commodity group in turn.

Automobiles and Parts

The BEA uses the Polk Company annual estimates of the number and age distribution of automobiles in use to estimate net automobile stock.[56] They also derive annual estimates of depreciation from the Polk Company data, with depreciation equal to the number of automobiles in each age group times an average depreciation amount per automobile in that age group. Average depreciation amounts were determined with the straight-line method and a ten-year life span. For automobiles more than ten years old, the BEA uses a "nominal net unit value" to determine depreciation.[57]

This method cannot be used to extend the automobile depreciation and stock estimates to the years before 1925, so equations A.2 and A.4 are used instead. Separate estimates of the stock of automobiles and of automobile accessories and tires are summed for an initial estimate of the stock of automobiles and parts, 1895–1983.[58] A multiplicative adjustment factor is then applied to derive the final estimates of real stock of automobiles and parts, 1895 on.

Estimated stock of automobiles is derived using an assumed ten-year average life length and the distribution of table A.11.[59] The estimates begin in 1899, the first year in which estimated expenditure for automobiles is greater than zero. For automobile accessories and tires, an average life length of three years is used with the distribution of table A.11.

Summing the estimates of stock of automobiles and of automobile accessories and tires provides initial estimates of net stock of automobiles and parts that exceed the BEA-Wealth estimates by an average of 2.32 percent. An adjustment factor of 0.980 is applied to the 1895–1924 estimates.[60] Allocating total stock between the two subgroups, automobiles, and automobile accessories and tires, 1895–1983, uses the annual shares of total stock in the initial stock estimates for these two subgroups.

Other Vehicles

Horse-drawn vehicles are included with "Agricultural Machinery, except Tractors," in the BEA-Wealth estimates. The BEA assumes an average life length of fourteen years for "Agricultural Machinery, except Tractors."[61] Goldsmith assumes horse-drawn vehicles had an average life length of eight years.[62] Since the BEA's assumption applies to a wide range of agricultural machinery and equipment, but Goldsmith's applies to horse-drawn vehicles in particular, I follow Goldsmith and assume an average life length of eight years for horse-drawn vehicles. The stock estimates therefore begin in 1886.

The BEA-Wealth estimates of stock of other motor vehicles are apparently derived directly from the Polk Company data.[63] To extend the estimates of depreciation and net stock of other motor vehicles, I use equations A.2 and A.4 and an average life length of eight years.[64] The estimates are first complete in 1886. The initial net stock estimates for other motor vehicles average 13.03 percent more than the BEA-Wealth estimates for 1925–83. An adjustment factor of 0.889 is applied to my initial estimates.

Furniture
The estimates are first complete in 1899, since the average life length is fourteen years. The initial stock estimates are approximately 0.11 percent less than the BEA-Wealth estimates; an adjustment factor of 1.001 is used.

Kitchen and Other Household Appliances
An average life length of eleven years is used. The first year in which the estimates are complete is 1893. No final adjustment was necessary.

China, Glassware, Tableware, and Utensils
An average life length of ten years is used. The estimates are first complete in 1890. The initial stock estimates for 1925–83 average 0.15 percent less than the BEA-Wealth estimates. An adjustment factor of 1.001 is used.

Other Durable House Furnishings
The assumed average life length is ten years. The first year in which the estimates are complete is 1890. The initial stock estimates average 0.16 percent less than the BEA-Wealth estimates for 1925–83. A final adjustment factor of 1.002 is used.

Radio and Television Receivers
The estimates for the full commodity group use the BEA's average life length of nine years. The estimates are therefore first complete in 1888. No final adjustment factor is needed.

The BEA's average life length assumption of nine years applies to the full commodity group: radios, televisions, phonographs, and pianos and other musical instruments. The subgroup of radios, phonographs, and televisions constitutes over 80 percent of total expenditure by 1929. These goods are generally presumed to be less durable than pianos and other musical instruments. Goldsmith assumes the life length of the full commodity group decreases over time as the share of expenditure devoted to pianos and other musical instruments declines; from a high of twenty years for 1897–1919, the expected life length decreases to fifteen years for

1920–29 and then to ten years for 1930–49.[65] Lenore Epstein estimates the average life length of pianos and musical instruments as sixteen years and the average life length of radios, televisions, and so on as nine years.[66] If we assume the BEA's average life length of nine years is the weighted average of the average life lengths of the two subgroups with weights determined by their respective shares in total expenditure, and if sixteen years is the average life length for pianos and other musical instruments, then an average life length of 7.25 years for radios, phonographs, and televisions is indicated when weights of 20 and 80 are used. With weights of 15 and 85, an average life length of 7.76 years for radios, phonographs, and televisions yields a weighted average of nine years for the entire group.

For the years before 1942, I generated a second set of depreciation and stock estimates with each subgroup considered separately. The average life length of pianos and other musical instruments is assumed to be sixteen years; the estimates are therefore not complete until 1903. An average life length of 7.5 years is used for radios, phonographs, and televisions; all estimates are complete since expenditure is zero until 1890. These initial stock estimates are summed. For 1903–42 the annual proportions of total stock accounted for by each subgroup are then computed. For 1903–42, these annual proportions are applied to the BEA-Wealth stock estimates (as extended to 1888) for the full commodity group, yielding revised stock estimates by subgroup. For 1888–1902, an adjustment factor equal to the 1903 ratio of the revised-to-initial net stock estimates for radios, phonographs, and so on is applied to the initial estimates of net stock for this subgroup to derive revised stock estimates. These radio stock estimates are then subtracted from total stock to derive revised stock estimates for pianos and other musical instruments, 1888–1902.

Jewelry and Watches
An average life length of eleven years is used, and thus the estimates are first complete in 1893. No final adjustment was needed.

Ophthalmic Products and Orthopedic Appliances
The average life length is six years. The first year in which the estimates are complete is 1882. The initial stock estimates for 1925–83 average 0.25 percent less than the BEA's estimates. A final adjustment factor of 1.003 is used.

Books and Maps

The estimates are first complete in 1890, reflecting an average life length of ten years. The initial stock estimates average 0.16 percent less than the BEA-Wealth estimates for 1925–83. A final adjustment factor of 1.002 is used.

Wheel Goods, Durable Toys, Sports Equipment,
Boats, and Pleasure Aircraft

The average life length is assumed to be ten years. The estimates are therefore first complete in 1890. The BEA-Wealth estimates of expenditure are used for 1929 on only. Therefore, the new stock estimates link with the BEA-Wealth stock estimates at 1950, not 1925. For 1950–83, the initial stock estimates average 0.17 percent less than the BEA-Wealth estimates. An adjustment factor of 1.002 is used. Note again: the BEA-Wealth stock estimates are used for 1950–83 only.

Summary Tables

The depreciation estimates are in table A.12. The depreciation estimates for the years before 1924 are those from which the initial stock estimates are derived; those for 1925 on are from the BEA-Wealth study. The stock estimates are in table A.13. In both tables, only the "complete" estimates are given. The first year of the BEA-Wealth estimates is in **bold print**.

Table A.12. Depreciation by Commodity Group, Various Years to 1983
(Millions of 1982 Dollars)

Year	AUT	HDV	OMV	OTH	FUR	APP	CHI	HSF
1886	n.a.	649	0	649	n.a.	n.a.	n.a.	n.a.
1887	n.a.	689	0	689	n.a.	n.a.	n.a.	n.a.
1888	n.a.	728	0	728	n.a.	n.a.	n.a.	n.a.
1889	n.a.	761	0	761	n.a.	n.a.	n.a.	n.a.
1890	0	789	0	789	n.a.	n.a.	1,119	1,505
1891	0	814	0	814	n.a.	n.a.	1,169	1,607
1892	0	840	0	840	n.a.	n.a.	1,222	1,711
1893	0	864	0	864	n.a.	203	1,257	1,788
1894	0	876	0	876	n.a.	205	1,262	1,829
1895	0	874	0	874	n.a.	207	1,271	1,884
1896	1	861	0	861	n.a.	215	1,303	1,944
1897	2	844	0	844	n.a.	229	1,352	1,986
1898	3	830	0	830	n.a.	242	1,410	2,023
1899	4	827	0	827	3,140	257	1,480	2,080
1900	4	825	0	825	3,206	274	1,571	2,159
1901	5	831	0	831	3,265	292	1,657	2,238
1902	6	846	0	846	3,342	313	1,733	2,340
1903	8	849	0	849	3,432	334	1,831	2,450
1904	11	848	0	848	3,527	350	1,951	2,531
1905	17	848	1	848	3,633	366	2,111	2,601
1906	24	847	1	848	3,779	389	2,326	2,693
1907	33	840	1	841	3,918	412	2,548	2,779
1908	46	815	1	816	3,987	429	2,697	2,818
1909	69	775	2	777	4,060	443	2,804	2,865
1910	107	739	3	742	4,171	459	2,943	2,953
1911	153	704	5	708	4,244	475	3,112	3,028
1912	218	664	6	671	4,277	496	3,290	3,089
1913	310	625	9	634	4,291	517	3,470	3,154
1914	424	586	13	598	4,282	529	3,623	3,199

Table A.12, continued

Year	AUT	HDV	OMV	OTH	FUR	APP	CHI	HSF
1915	579	545	17	562	4,240	538	3,737	3,218
1916	834	507	25	532	4,224	555	3,862	3,238
1917	1,178	478	35	513	4,267	586	3,998	3,236
1918	1,452	447	42	489	4,294	620	4,030	3,181
1919	1,762	403	47	450	4,303	651	3,975	3,117
1920	2,136	353	53	406	4,389	700	3,973	3,138
1921	2,552	301	61	362	4,497	743	3,932	3,168
1922	3,017	250	71	322	4,538	760	3,775	3,147
1923	3,595	209	84	293	4,575	784	3,647	3,191
1924	4,336	176	97	273	4,682	815	3,544	3,277
1925	**4,378**	148	**73**	221	**4,825**	**852**	**3,466**	**3,375**
1926	5,203	126	97	223	4,964	899	3,489	3,487
1927	5,999	109	114	223	5,131	951	3,534	3,597
1928	6,688	95	125	220	5,301	998	3,602	3,726
1929	7,445	83	163	246	5,433	1,039	3,717	3,878
1930	8,082	74	215	289	5,495	1,073	3,764	3,995
1931	8,325	64	244	308	5,503	1,093	3,745	4,042
1932	8,215	53	251	304	5,448	1,085	3,731	4,018
1933	7,988	44	245	289	5,308	1,064	3,697	3,905
1934	7,766	36	246	282	5,147	1,063	3,644	3,760
1935	7,585	28	260	288	5,035	1,086	3,571	3,637
1936	7,538	21	288	309	5,004	1,134	3,519	3,591
1937	7,600	16	322	338	5,013	1,205	3,534	3,611
1938	7,531	11	342	353	5,014	1,271	3,563	3,621
1939	7,468	8	358	366	5,038	1,328	3,580	3,649
1940	7,742	6	384	390	5,123	1,407	3,616	3,721
1941	8,253	4	419	423	5,274	1,523	3,716	3,841
1942	6,030	2	415	417	5,416	1,607	3,845	3,973
1943	5,114	2	359	361	5,464	1,574	3,903	4,068

Table A.12, continued

Year	AUT	HDV	OMV	OTH	FUR	APP	CHI	HSF
1944	4,158	1	302	303	5,435	1,464	3,889	4,118
1945	3,249	1	251	252	5,379	1,349	3,889	4,133
1946	4,990	0	316	316	5,409	1,362	4,071	4,250
1947	6,254	0	447	447	5,545	1,575	4,414	4,485
1948	7,055	0	589	589	5,715	1,886	4,792	4,774
1949	8,256	0	712	712	5,887	2,188	5,144	5,088
1950	9,871	0	841	841	6,088	2,531	5,452	5,426
1951	11,191	0	968	968	6,298	2,907	5,733	5,784
1952	12,849	0	1,083	1,083	6,507	3,245	5,945	6,079
1953	14,807	0	1,154	1,154	6,765	3,563	6,102	6,293
1954	18,729	0	1,168	1,168	7,050	3,855	6,220	6,427
1955	21,883	0	1,201	1,201	7,388	4,150	6,321	6,548
1956	25,181	0	1,275	1,275	7,776	4,479	6,394	6,707
1957	26,026	0	1,319	1,319	8,140	4,819	6,397	6,872
1958	26,697	0	1,333	1,333	8,461	5,134	6,336	7,020
1959	27,550	0	1,332	1,332	8,782	5,438	6,258	7,181
1960	28,202	0	1,359	1,359	9,104	5,723	6,176	7,356
1961	29,331	0	1,382	1,382	9,394	5,978	6,083	7,516
1962	30,040	0	1,417	1,417	9,681	6,221	6,005	7,706
1963	31,554	0	1,492	1,492	10,001	6,463	5,942	7,968
1964	32,942	0	1,605	1,605	10,390	6,736	5,920	8,346
1965	34,333	0	1,775	1,775	10,839	7,030	5,987	8,841
1966	35,731	0	2,023	2,023	11,329	7,363	6,162	9,428
1967	38,218	0	2,324	2,324	11,831	7,742	6,421	10,063
1968	40,013	0	2,699	2,699	12,321	8,168	6,710	10,730
1969	43,997	0	3,207	3,207	12,807	8,658	7,002	11,401
1970	47,032	0	3,724	3,724	13,254	9,179	7,267	11,985
1971	49,542	0	4,308	4,308	13,678	9,734	7,505	12,489
1972	51,640	0	5,183	5,183	14,167	10,379	7,744	13,021
1973	55,736	0	6,401	6,401	14,766	11,145	8,025	13,698

Table A.12, continued

Year	AUT	HDV	OMV	OTH	FUR	APP	CHI	HSF
1974	57,282	0	7,597	7,597	15,381	11,930	8,311	14,472
1975	58,947	0	8,676	8,676	15,895	12,582	8,517	15,180
1976	61,450	0	10,103	10,103	16,371	13,122	8,692	15,853
1977	64,686	0	12,059	12,059	16,942	13,669	8,918	16,618
1978	66,633	0	14,386	14,386	17,617	14,240	9,193	17,497
1979	68,328	0	16,435	16,435	18,354	14,831	9,477	18,449
1980	70,517	0	17,388	17,388	19,054	15,405	9,720	19,322
1981	69,199	0	17,543	17,543	19,645	15,923	9,904	20,013
1982	69,848	0	17,655	17,655	20,103	16,346	10,043	20,514
1983	71,296	0	18,156	18,156	20,513	16,743	10,185	20,995

Table A.12, continued

Year	RAD	PIA	MUS	JWL	MED	BKS	MIS	TOT
1882	n.a.	n.a.	n.a.	n.a.	19	n.a.	n.a.	n.a.
1883	n.a.	n.a.	n.a.	n.a.	22	n.a.	n.a.	n.a.
1884	n.a.	n.a.	n.a.	n.a.	24	n.a.	n.a.	n.a.
1885	n.a.	n.a.	n.a.	n.a.	27	n.a.	n.a.	n.a.
1886	0	n.a.	n.a.	n.a.	31	n.a.	n.a.	n.a.
1887	0	n.a.	n.a.	n.a.	35	n.a.	n.a.	n.a.
1888	0	n.a.	51	n.a.	40	n.a.	n.a.	n.a.
1889	0	n.a.	54	n.a.	44	n.a.	n.a.	n.a.
1890	0	n.a.	58	n.a.	48	662	129	n.a.
1891	0	n.a.	63	n.a.	51	680	133	n.a.
1892	0	n.a.	67	n.a.	56	696	140	n.a.
1893	1	n.a.	69	481	61	714	149	n.a.
1894	1	n.a.	68	490	67	723	160	n.a.
1895	1	n.a.	69	498	73	737	173	n.a.
1896	1	n.a.	70	504	80	765	191	n.a.
1897	2	n.a.	70	508	88	792	217	n.a.
1898	2	n.a.	71	518	96	822	248	n.a.
1899	3	n.a.	73	537	102	862	270	9,632
1900	3	n.a.	77	566	107	897	281	9,966
1901	4	n.a.	83	593	111	924	285	10,283
1902	6	n.a.	89	621	115	951	287	10,643
1903	8	80	98	654	118	977	285	11,035
1904	10	84	105	686	120	998	278	11,407
1905	12	88	113	722	124	1,021	273	11,828
1906	15	93	122	779	131	1,038	271	12,398
1907	17	99	132	846	139	1,044	272	12,965
1908	19	103	139	898	148	1,048	270	13,295
1909	20	107	143	957	158	1,064	267	13,606
1910	21	110	147	1,041	170	1,084	268	14,087
1911	24	114	153	1,125	180	1,094	271	14,544

Table A.12, continued

Year	RAD	PIA	MUS	JWL	MED	BKS	MIS	TOT
1912	27	119	161	1,202	188	1,102	275	14,968
1913	33	124	171	1,268	195	1,120	284	15,415
1914	39	128	180	1,304	208	1,135	296	15,778
1915	46	131	187	1,311	232	1,141	307	16,052
1916	55	133	196	1,326	264	1,146	326	16,502
1917	69	136	211	1,330	307	1,146	364	17,136
1918	85	138	225	1,292	391	1,143	392	17,508
1919	104	139	241	1,272	464	1,140	400	17,774
1920	129	142	266	1,280	500	1,153	406	18,348
1921	148	144	285	1,266	520	1,181	408	18,913
1922	158	145	295	1,239	509	1,200	406	19,208
1923	165	146	305	1,222	497	1,210	412	19,730
1924	177	147	317	1,220	485	1,230	426	20,603
1925	193	147	**332**	**1,233**	**466**	**1,257**	439	20,844
1926	211	146	347	1,265	453	1,287	457	22,075
1927	232	144	362	1,308	448	1,332	477	23,362
1928	258	140	379	1,352	445	1,386	495	24,592
1929	296	135	402	1,394	445	1,443	512	25,954
1930	347	129	436	1,431	449	1,492	521	27,026
1931	388	123	464	1,432	449	1,524	518	27,403
1932	400	116	470	1,388	438	1,513	506	27,117
1933	394	109	460	1,314	419	1,464	485	26,393
1934	380	103	445	1,230	415	1,418	465	25,635
1935	366	97	433	1,159	429	1,385	457	25,064
1936	359	92	430	1,101	451	1,373	463	24,913
1937	367	90	439	1,066	486	1,387	487	25,166
1938	378	88	449	1,053	523	1,407	518	25,303
1939	397	87	465	1,055	557	1,421	551	25,479
1940	433	87	499	1,074	593	1,440	593	26,198
1941	484	89	549	1,117	641	1,470	648	27,454

Table A.12, continued

Year	RAD	PIA	MUS	JWL	MED	BKS	MIS	TOT
1942	534	92	601	1,181	709	1,521	702	26,002
1943	n.a.	n.a.	622	1,274	794	1,604	740	25,517
1944	n.a.	n.a.	610	1,380	889	1,730	772	24,748
1945	n.a.	n.a.	588	1,492	981	1,897	813	24,022
1946	n.a.	n.a.	620	1,645	1,072	2,090	922	26,747
1947	n.a.	n.a.	709	1,809	1,155	2,255	1,099	29,747
1948	n.a.	n.a.	792	1,954	1,220	2,371	1,275	32,423
1949	n.a.	n.a.	876	2,080	1,277	2,470	1,417	35,395
1950	n.a.	n.a.	1,001	2,191	1,329	2,561	**1,538**	**38,829**
1951	n.a.	n.a.	1,153	2,294	1,388	2,668	1,645	42,029
1952	n.a.	n.a.	1,305	2,395	1,456	2,771	1,740	45,375
1953	n.a.	n.a.	1,481	2,498	1,529	2,853	1,846	48,891
1954	n.a.	n.a.	1,680	2,605	1,598	2,917	1,963	54,212
1955	n.a.	n.a.	1,892	2,730	1,651	2,971	2,114	58,849
1956	n.a.	n.a.	2,103	2,868	1,701	3,043	2,305	63,832
1957	n.a.	n.a.	2,283	3,009	1,753	3,114	2,520	66,252
1958	n.a.	n.a.	2,420	3,148	1,788	3,165	2,744	68,246
1959	n.a.	n.a.	2,551	3,286	1,837	3,210	2,985	70,410
1960	n.a.	n.a.	2,681	3,416	1,896	3,263	3,223	72,399
1961	n.a.	n.a.	2,802	3,527	1,932	3,322	3,417	74,684
1962	n.a.	n.a.	2,936	3,634	1,994	3,393	3,578	76,605
1963	n.a.	n.a.	3,096	3,753	2,093	3,484	3,732	79,578
1964	n.a.	n.a.	3,310	3,884	2,211	3,617	3,920	82,881
1965	n.a.	n.a.	3,620	4,053	2,349	3,775	4,170	86,772
1966	n.a.	n.a.	4,083	4,317	2,504	3,954	4,525	91,419
1967	n.a.	n.a.	4,690	4,662	2,628	4,142	4,993	97,714
1968	n.a.	n.a.	5,365	5,045	2,726	4,319	5,548	103,644
1969	n.a.	n.a.	6,065	5,434	2,861	4,522	6,171	112,125
1970	n.a.	n.a.	6,778	5,796	3,034	4,810	6,783	119,642
1971	n.a.	n.a.	7,487	6,152	3,199	5,139	7,348	126,581

Table A.12, continued

Year	RAD	PIA	MUS	JWL	MED	BKS	MIS	TOT
1972	n.a.	n.a.	8,224	6,519	3,351	5,413	8,043	133,684
1973	n.a.	n.a.	9,049	6,970	3,527	5,644	8,952	143,913
1974	n.a.	n.a.	9,905	7,532	3,704	5,837	9,877	151,828
1975	n.a.	n.a.	10,761	8,155	3,867	6,008	10,753	159,341
1976	n.a.	n.a.	11,664	8,899	4,008	6,145	11,685	167,992
1977	n.a.	n.a.	12,610	9,794	4,117	6,252	12,715	178,380
1978	n.a.	n.a.	13,577	10,780	4,242	6,375	13,850	188,390
1979	n.a.	n.a.	14,597	11,746	4,422	6,502	15,029	198,170
1980	n.a.	n.a.	15,643	12,551	4,620	6,606	16,007	206,833
1981	n.a.	n.a.	16,715	13,237	4,794	6,684	16,763	210,420
1982	n.a.	n.a.	17,922	13,882	4,962	6,724	17,404	215,403
1983	n.a.	n.a.	19,434	14,507	5,143	6,736	17,962	221,670

Sources: Derived as discussed in appendix A.

Notes: Only "complete" estimates of depreciation are shown. A figure in **bold print** is the first year of the BEA-Wealth estimates. See text. Commodity group abbreviations as for table A.6.

Table A.13. Net Stock by Commodity Group, Various Years to 1986
(Millions of 1982 Dollars)

Year	AUT	HOR	OMV	OTH	FUR	APP	CHI	HSF
1886	n.a.	2,944	0	2,944	n.a.	n.a.	n.a.	n.a.
1887	n.a.	3,137	0	3,137	n.a.	n.a.	n.a.	n.a.
1888	n.a.	3,287	0	3,287	n.a.	n.a.	n.a.	n.a.
1889	n.a.	3,390	0	3,390	n.a.	n.a.	n.a.	n.a.
1890	0	3,479	0	3,479	n.a.	n.a.	5,993	8,316
1891	0	3,572	0	3,572	n.a.	n.a.	6,253	8,861
1892	0	3,688	0	3,688	n.a.	n.a.	6,531	9,362
1893	0	3,758	0	3,758	n.a.	1,206	6,511	9,508
1894	0	3,725	0	3,725	n.a.	1,192	6,388	9,522
1895	1	3,653	0	3,653	n.a.	1,220	6,498	9,976
1896	3	3,527	0	3,527	n.a.	1,323	6,765	10,097
1897	5	3,456	0	3,456	n.a.	1,451	7,136	10,302
1898	6	3,393	0	3,393	n.a.	1,513	7,479	10,420
1899	12	3,474	0	3,475	24,169	1,642	7,995	10,940
1900	19	3,425	0	3,426	24,381	1,739	8,583	11,361
1901	29	3,581	1	3,581	24,938	1,869	8,924	11,843
1902	39	3,613	1	3,614	25,617	2,013	9,321	12,547
1903	52	3,584	1	3,585	26,378	2,121	9,983	13,083
1904	83	3,562	2	3,564	27,098	2,180	10,671	13,288
1905	115	3,565	3	3,567	28,212	2,298	11,876	13,657
1906	164	3,546	4	3,550	29,774	2,478	13,291	14,237
1907	222	3,478	5	3,484	30,498	2,595	14,403	14,502
1908	310	3,231	7	3,239	30,403	2,627	14,603	14,397
1909	500	3,030	12	3,042	31,354	2,722	15,089	14,889
1910	762	2,901	18	2,919	32,053	2,812	15,889	15,424
1911	1,015	2,731	24	2,755	32,104	2,900	16,851	15,674
1912	1,510	2,548	36	2,584	32,052	3,069	17,810	16,014
1913	2,086	2,389	49	2,439	31,759	3,162	18,785	16,322
1914	2,796	2,224	66	2,290	31,250	3,167	19,288	16,346

Table A.13, continued

Year	AUT	HOR	OMV	OTH	FUR	APP	CHI	HSF
1915	3,850	2,049	91	2,140	30,605	3,222	19,678	16,307
1916	5,824	1,909	139	2,048	30,860	3,387	20,424	16,430
1917	7,825	1,844	185	2,029	31,458	3,678	21,007	16,097
1918	8,498	1,670	183	1,853	31,391	3,869	20,218	15,524
1919	10,589	1,435	211	1,645	31,770	4,065	19,741	15,219
1920	11,852	1,182	225	1,407	33,381	4,578	20,021	16,029
1921	14,635	954	275	1,229	33,937	4,611	19,037	15,755
1922	16,626	754	321	1,075	34,002	4,622	17,765	15,764
1923	20,747	639	386	1,025	34,440	4,799	17,526	16,469
1924	24,489	538	427	964	35,846	4,984	16,732	16,964
1925	**27,612**	469	**456**	925	**37,097**	**5,272**	**16,922**	**17,742**
1926	32,722	415	543	958	38,455	5,645	17,652	18,286
1927	35,990	361	573	934	39,989	6,002	17,908	18,937
1928	39,077	317	598	915	41,109	6,211	18,710	19,715
1929	42,897	286	906	1,192	41,947	6,440	19,511	20,641
1930	43,798	255	1,044	1,299	41,500	6,528	19,022	20,791
1931	42,272	209	1,069	1,278	40,863	6,490	18,793	20,664
1932	39,474	166	981	1,147	39,220	6,146	18,624	19,914
1933	38,014	135	935	1,070	37,267	6,016	18,206	18,691
1934	36,309	99	989	1,088	35,553	6,127	17,847	17,825
1935	35,943	72	1,102	1,174	35,056	6,460	17,291	17,273
1936	36,501	51	1,291	1,342	35,644	6,993	17,363	17,736
1937	37,584	35	1,454	1,489	36,203	7,641	17,852	18,093
1938	35,747	24	1,444	1,468	36,276	7,925	17,976	18,159
1939	36,791	16	1,542	1,558	37,181	8,309	18,107	18,637
1940	39,966	10	1,639	1,649	38,613	8,927	18,475	19,225
1941	34,966	6	1,850	1,856	40,736	9,932	19,514	20,240
1942	29,341	4	1,461	1,465	41,425	9,858	20,116	20,805
1943	24,650	2	1,131	1,133	40,921	8,782	19,899	21,125

Year	AUT	HOR	OMV	OTH	FUR	APP	CHI	HSF
1944	20,978	1	861	862	39,865	7,594	19,449	21,001
1945	18,208	1	655	656	39,097	6,793	19,683	20,918
1946	20,222	0	1,502	1,502	40,318	8,161	22,119	22,495
1947	26,966	0	2,293	2,293	42,001	10,942	24,513	24,151
1948	35,248	0	3,043	3,043	43,715	13,568	26,895	26,180
1949	48,343	0	3,397	3,397	45,270	15,578	28,439	27,875
1950	66,421	0	3,918	3,918	47,560	18,421	29,922	30,006
1951	78,810	0	4,361	4,361	49,153	20,455	30,939	31,744
1952	86,638	0	4,496	4,496	51,150	22,089	31,428	32,694
1953	98,172	0	4,549	4,549	53,492	23,669	31,833	33,249
1954	106,003	0	4,423	4,423	55,784	25,114	32,074	33,235
1955	119,522	0	4,742	4,742	59,165	27,016	32,492	33,933
1956	124,636	0	5,071	5,071	62,544	29,270	32,537	34,805
1957	128,870	0	5,165	5,165	65,004	31,254	32,030	35,658
1958	127,083	0	5,047	5,047	67,100	32,822	31,314	36,293
1959	129,185	0	5,087	5,087	69,590	34,535	30,840	37,371
1960	132,772	0	5,198	5,198	71,656	35,856	30,256	38,168
1961	132,511	0	5,146	5,146	73,318	37,064	29,747	38,944
1962	137,140	0	5,468	5,468	75,415	38,255	29,497	40,180
1963	144,995	0	5,999	5,999	78,038	39,688	29,244	42,034
1964	153,565	0	6,709	6,709	81,765	41,571	29,574	44,852
1965	168,514	0	7,797	7,797	85,792	43,412	30,561	48,127
1966	182,153	0	9,221	9,221	90,140	45,901	32,289	51,850
1967	192,527	0	10,589	10,589	93,924	48,348	34,123	55,343
1968	208,658	0	12,848	12,848	97,783	51,408	35,865	59,104
1969	222,285	0	15,507	15,507	101,351	54,751	37,387	62,328
1970	226,846	0	17,289	17,289	104,064	58,056	38,504	64,554
1971	238,774	0	20,509	20,509	106,994	61,714	39,543	66,658
1972	253,560	0	25,904	25,904	111,365	66,425	40,739	69,623
1973	271,058	0	32,622	32,622	116,851	71,877	42,489	74,111

Table A.13, continued

Year	AUT	HOR	OMV	OTH	FUR	APP	CHI	HSF
1974	273,235	0	36,688	36,688	121,279	76,427	43,743	78,331
1975	274,475	0	41,004	41,004	124,173	79,032	44,221	81,402
1976	283,658	0	49,553	49,553	127,684	81,553	45,128	84,982
1977	296,285	0	60,525	60,525	132,961	84,574	46,578	89,494
1978	309,226	0	71,975	71,975	138,867	87,792	48,183	94,580
1979	318,472	0	77,700	77,700	145,202	91,363	49,638	99,813
1980	318,122	0	74,993	74,993	149,551	94,420	50,539	103,341
1981	320,598	0	72,260	72,260	153,147	97,126	51,101	105,724
1982	322,790	0	71,816	71,816	154,824	98,582	51,453	106,727
1983	335,244	0	75,745	75,745	157,707	100,974	52,253	109,463
1984	360,500	0	83,900	83,900	162,200	104,801	53,800	113,663
1985	390,400	0	93,900	93,900	167,000	110,200	55,600	117,900
1986	424,500	0	103,600	103,600	172,800	116,200	57,400	122,900

Table A.13, continued

Year	RAD	PIA	MUS	JWL	MED	BKS	MIS	TOT
1882	n.a.	n.a.	n.a.	n.a.	69	n.a.	n.a.	n.a.
1883	n.a.	n.a.	n.a.	n.a.	77	n.a.	n.a.	n.a.
1884	n.a.	n.a.	n.a.	n.a.	85	n.a.	n.a.	n.a.
1885	0	n.a.	n.a.	n.a.	96	n.a.	n.a.	n.a.
1886	0	n.a.	n.a.	n.a.	111	n.a.	n.a.	n.a.
1887	0	n.a.	n.a.	n.a.	126	n.a.	n.a.	n.a.
1888	0	n.a.	269	n.a.	140	n.a.	n.a.	n.a.
1889	0	n.a.	285	n.a.	151	n.a.	n.a.	n.a.
1890	0	n.a.	310	n.a.	161	3,535	676	n.a.
1891	1	n.a.	332	n.a.	174	3,561	707	n.a.
1892	2	n.a.	347	n.a.	192	3,630	748	n.a.
1893	2	n.a.	335	2,951	210	3,710	827	n.a.
1894	3	n.a.	320	2,926	226	3,669	870	n.a.
1895	4	n.a.	334	2,980	251	3,849	984	n.a.
1896	5	n.a.	331	2,944	278	4,025	1,094	n.a.
1897	6	n.a.	333	2,989	303	4,160	1,304	n.a.
1898	7	n.a.	344	3,073	321	4,382	1,459	n.a.
1899	9	n.a.	365	3,300	342	4,630	1,520	58,390
1900	12	n.a.	396	3,520	346	4,731	1,492	59,994
1901	16	n.a.	436	3,672	357	4,867	1,481	61,996
1902	21	n.a.	477	3,888	370	4,981	1,450	64,318
1903	28	499	527	4,097	379	5,089	1,405	66,699
1904	34	521	556	4,259	380	5,167	1,345	68,591
1905	41	555	596	4,547	405	5,297	1,335	71,905
1906	48	601	649	5,060	432	5,319	1,334	76,288
1907	55	648	703	5,511	464	5,286	1,379	79,047
1908	54	642	697	5,668	488	5,308	1,321	79,060
1909	56	660	716	6,238	537	5,475	1,331	81,893
1910	61	672	734	6,810	571	5,545	1,348	84,868

Table A.13, continued

Year	RAD	PIA	MUS	JWL	MED	BKS	MIS	TOT
1911	71	694	766	7,299	595	5,551	1,377	86,885
1912	88	732	820	7,700	607	5,610	1,412	89,189
1913	110	771	880	7,979	635	5,772	1,505	91,323
1914	128	788	916	7,878	703	5,758	1,566	91,960
1915	149	791	940	7,706	822	5,789	1,625	92,684
1916	193	825	1,018	7,870	939	5,771	1,807	96,378
1917	252	860	1,113	7,588	1,136	5,757	2,116	99,804
1918	299	861	1,161	7,067	1,588	5,696	2,114	98,980
1919	392	893	1,285	7,301	1,616	5,699	2,106	101,037
1920	493	955	1,449	7,351	1,695	5,906	2,110	105,778
1921	512	959	1,470	7,090	1,629	6,097	2,055	107,545
1922	525	967	1,491	6,915	1,527	6,137	2,021	107,947
1923	543	984	1,527	6,902	1,506	6,172	2,134	113,246
1924	609	988	1,598	6,963	1,444	6,352	2,210	118,546
1925	672	994	**1,666**	**7,218**	**1,394**	**6,499**	2,304	124,651
1926	770	996	1,766	7,573	1,362	6,677	2,443	133,539
1927	844	976	1,820	7,930	1,387	7,056	2,542	140,495
1928	988	943	1,931	8,214	1,372	7,336	2,622	147,213
1929	1,195	902	2,097	8,507	1,391	7,706	2,708	155,037
1930	1,468	867	2,335	8,631	1,417	7,819	2,655	155,796
1931	1,540	829	2,369	8,199	1,387	7,913	2,592	152,820
1932	1,498	781	2,279	7,628	1,299	7,420	2,440	145,592
1933	1,398	724	2,122	6,873	1,240	7,026	2,268	138,793
1934	1,330	680	2,010	6,308	1,311	6,777	2,202	133,357
1935	1,288	655	1,943	5,963	1,396	6,687	2,214	131,400
1936	1,354	653	2,007	5,731	1,496	6,776	2,372	133,961
1937	1,466	661	2,127	5,789	1,657	7,060	2,619	138,114
1938	1,517	671	2,188	5,904	1,750	7,153	2,812	137,357
1939	1,690	690	2,380	6,088	1,857	7,256	3,048	141,211

Table A.13, continued

Year	RAD	PIA	MUS	JWL	MED	BKS	MIS	TOT
1940	1,919	726	2,645	6,364	1,977	7,393	3,302	148,536
1941	2,220	788	3,008	6,842	2,202	7,618	3,691	150,605
1942	2,386	818	3,204	7,380	2,470	8,031	3,888	147,982
1943	n.a.	n.a.	3,083	8,272	2,805	8,699	4,014	143,383
1944	n.a.	n.a.	2,831	8,934	3,113	9,676	4,145	138,449
1945	n.a.	n.a.	2,639	9,800	3,370	10,797	4,419	136,380
1946	n.a.	n.a.	3,291	11,094	3,673	11,990	5,580	150,445
1947	n.a.	n.a.	3,874	11,981	3,856	12,483	6,746	169,806
1948	n.a.	n.a.	4,341	12,769	4,022	12,875	7,695	190,351
1949	n.a.	n.a.	4,843	13,293	4,155	13,193	8,209	212,595
1950	n.a.	n.a.	5,844	13,827	4,326	13,575	**8,747**	**242,567**
1951	n.a.	n.a.	6,563	14,275	4,544	14,222	9,072	264,138
1952	n.a.	n.a.	7,404	14,868	4,774	14,615	9,504	279,660
1953	n.a.	n.a.	8,370	15,415	5,027	14,953	10,072	298,801
1954	n.a.	n.a.	9,422	16,116	5,205	15,101	10,749	313,226
1955	n.a.	n.a.	10,558	17,024	5,295	15,368	11,814	336,929
1956	n.a.	n.a.	11,551	17,915	5,493	15,837	13,043	352,702
1957	n.a.	n.a.	12,140	18,736	5,617	16,102	14,299	364,875
1958	n.a.	n.a.	12,526	19,534	5,661	16,237	15,494	369,111
1959	n.a.	n.a.	13,142	20,333	5,950	16,482	16,908	379,423
1960	n.a.	n.a.	13,611	20,971	6,075	16,761	17,943	389,267
1961	n.a.	n.a.	14,174	21,437	6,120	17,116	18,625	394,202
1962	n.a.	n.a.	14,904	22,082	6,499	17,546	19,218	406,204
1963	n.a.	n.a.	15,875	22,831	6,895	18,199	19,957	423,755
1964	n.a.	n.a.	17,367	23,705	7,337	19,199	21,177	446,821
1965	n.a.	n.a.	19,593	25,110	7,817	20,097	22,850	479,670
1966	n.a.	n.a.	22,996	27,577	8,391	21,277	25,563	517,358
1967	n.a.	n.a.	26,772	30,165	8,509	22,169	28,629	551,098
1968	n.a.	n.a.	30,565	32,890	8,870	23,081	32,185	593,257
1969	n.a.	n.a.	34,142	35,175	9,436	24,312	35,793	632,467

Table A.13, continued

Year	RAD	PIA	MUS	JWL	MED	BKS	MIS	TOT
1970	n.a.	n.a.	37,656	37,120	10,117	26,488	38,686	659,380
1971	n.a.	n.a.	40,859	39,152	10,466	28,125	41,321	694,115
1972	n.a.	n.a.	44,647	41,300	11,012	29,223	46,192	739,990
1973	n.a.	n.a.	49,058	44,844	11,636	30,158	51,889	796,593
1974	n.a.	n.a.	53,159	48,885	12,128	30,796	56,360	831,031
1975	n.a.	n.a.	57,481	53,225	12,598	31,500	60,849	859,960
1976	n.a.	n.a.	62,201	59,020	12,929	31,779	66,109	904,596
1977	n.a.	n.a.	66,919	65,408	13,166	32,222	71,862	959,994
1978	n.a.	n.a.	71,707	71,970	13,703	32,942	78,343	1,019,288
1979	n.a.	n.a.	76,992	77,231	14,477	33,518	84,379	1,068,785
1980	n.a.	n.a.	81,900	80,436	15,063	33,883	87,448	1,089,696
1981	n.a.	n.a.	87,414	83,699	15,492	34,125	90,262	1,110,948
1982	n.a.	n.a.	94,192	86,623	16,070	33,979	92,282	1,129,338
1983	n.a.	n.a.	103,820	90,059	16,652	33,893	94,491	1,170,301
1984	n.a.	n.a.	116,700	94,620	17,583	34,197	99,800	1,241,764
1985	n.a.	n.a.	134,500	99,500	18,600	34,300	105,000	1,326,900
1986	n.a.	n.a.	157,600	105,900	19,900	34,400	110,400	1,425,600

Sources: Derived as discussed in appendix A.

Notes: Only "complete" estimates are shown. A figure in **bold print** is the first year of the BEA-Wealth estimates. See text. Commodity group abbreviations defined as for table A.6.

◆ APPENDIX B ◆

TECHNICAL NOTES:
DEVELOPMENT OF ESTIMATES
UNDERLYING CHAPTER 2 TABLES

NOTE I: SOURCES FOR ESTIMATES OF CONSUMPTION EXPENDITURES

Annual estimates of nominal expenditures for perishable goods, semidurable goods, durable goods, and services, 1869–1929, are from Simon Kuznets, "Annual Estimates, 1869–1953," table T-6, variant III. These annual estimates, themselves unpublished, were used to produce the averages published in Kuznets, *Capital in the American Economy*, tables R-18, R-27, and related tables. Professor Kuznets granted his permission to use these annual estimates with the understanding that the estimates themselves remain unpublished.

For perishable goods, semidurable goods, and durable goods, the 1929 expenditure benchmarks used by Kuznets are from U.S. Office of Business Economics, *National Income: 1954 Edition*. Kuznets's original estimates of expenditure for services rely upon a conceptual basis that differs from the Department of Commerce basis. His estimates were therefore adjusted by John Kendrick (*Productivity Trends*), who took both the conceptual basis and the 1929 benchmark for his estimates from *National Income: 1954 Edition*.

Since 1954, the Department of Commerce has revised the national income and product accounts several times, introducing both statistical revisions and conceptual changes.[1] As a result, the Kuznets-Kendrick estimates and the Department of Commerce estimates of consumption expenditure in 1929 are no longer equal. To develop one continuous series of consumption expenditure, 1869 to the present, that is conceptually consistent with the present day national product account estimates and that replicates those estimates beginning with 1929, the Kuznets-Kendrick estimates are adjusted as discussed in notes 2 through 5 below.

The Department of Commerce does not distinguish between perishable and semidurable goods; these two categories are combined in "nondurable goods" in the national product accounts. Using Kuznets's definitions from *Capital in the American Economy*, notes to table R-3, but the current commodity group descriptions from the national product accounts, nondurable goods are distributed as shown in table B.1.

NOTE 2: EXPENDITURE FOR PERISHABLE GOODS

Kuznets's 1929 benchmark for perishable goods expenditure was $27,245 million. Due to statistical revisions of the imputed value of food produced and consumed on farms, the 1929 estimate of perishable goods expenditure is now $27,254 million.[2] To compensate, Kuznets's estimates of expenditure for perishable goods, 1869–1928, are therefore multiplied by a constant adjustment factor of 1.003 (27,254/27,245). This adjustment yields one continuous series, 1869–1986, that links to the national product accounts estimate at 1929.

NOTE 3: EXPENDITURE FOR SEMIDURABLE GOODS

No statistical or conceptual revisions have occurred for these product groups. Kuznets's estimates of nominal expenditure for semidurable goods, 1869–1928, are therefore used without further adjustment.

NOTE 4: EXPENDITURE FOR DURABLE GOODS

Kuznets's 1929 benchmark was $9,212 million; the current national product accounts estimate of expenditure in 1929 for durable goods is $9,243 million. The change reflects statistical revisions of expenditures for furniture and household appliances and introduction of the commodity group "other motor vehicles."

Table B.1. Distribution of Nondurable Goods between Perishable and Semidurable Goods

Perishable Goods

line 2:	Food and tobacco
line 21:	Toilet articles and preparations
line 34:	Cleaning preparations, household paper products, etc.
line 35:	Stationery and writing supplies
line 40:	Fuel oil and coal
line 45:	Drug preparations and sundries
line 70:	Gasoline and oil
line 84:	Magazines, newspapers, and sheet music
line 89:	Flowers, seeds, and potted plants
1/2 of line 105:	Expenditures abroad by U.S. residents
less	
1/2 of line 107:	Personal remittances in kind to foreigners

Semidurable Goods

line 12:	Shoes and other footwear
line 13:	Clothing and accessories except footwear
line 16:	Standard clothing issued to military personnel
line 33:	Semidurable house furnishings
line 85:	Nondurable toys and sport supplies
1/2 of line 105:	Expenditures abroad by U.S. residents
less	
1/2 of line 107:	Personal remittances in kind to foreigners

Note: Line numbers are from U.S. BEA, National Income and Product Accounts, 1929-82, table 2.4, pp. 106-12.

To compensate for the statistical revisions, Kuznets's estimates are multiplied by an adjustment factor of 0.9915 (9,134/9,212), where the 1929 benchmark of $9,134 million excludes expenditure for other motor vehicles. To compensate for introduction of other motor vehicles, the estimates of nominal expenditure for other motor vehicles, 1869–1928, in table A.6 are added in after first multiplying them by a constant factor of 0.8720 (109/125) to adjust for the difference between the national product account and *Fixed Reproducible Tangible Wealth* estimates of expenditure in 1929. The resulting two series (adjusted Kuznets's series and other motor vehicles) are then combined with estimates of expenditure for horse-drawn vehicles from table A.6 to yield estimates of total expenditure for durable goods.

NOTE 5: EXPENDITURE FOR SERVICES

Kendrick adjusted Kuznets's estimates of expenditure for services to make them conceptually consistent with the *National Income: 1954 Edition* estimates. These Kuznets-Kendrick estimates of consumer expenditure for services (published in Kendrick, *Productivity Trends*, tables A-IIa and A-IIb) link directly to the *National Income: 1954 Edition* estimates at 1929. Statistical revisions and conceptual changes have altered the national product accounts estimate of expenditure for services in 1929. The Kuznets-Kendrick estimates, 1869–1928, are therefore adjusted so that they link directly with the current national product accounts 1929 estimate.

Statistical revisions affect eight commodity groups and result in a net increase of $82 million in expenditure for services in 1929, as shown in the top panel of table B.2. Conceptual changes affect three additional commodity groups: interest payments to brokers have been separated from investment counseling expenses and combined with interest on personal debt to yield a new expenditure group, consumer interest payments to business; and consumer interest payments to business and personal cash remittances to foreigners have been removed from consumer expenditure for services and are now included with consumer outlays. The effect of these changes is indicated in the lower panel of table B.2.

Table B.2. Changes Made to 1929 Expenditure for Services

Commodity Group	1929 Expenditure (Millions of Dollars)		
	1954 Edition	Current Edition	Change
Statistical Revisions:			
Tenant-occupied nonfarm dwellings--rent	4500	4542	42
Rental value of farm dwellings	829	913	84
Housing--Other (motels, hotels, etc.)	249	355	106
Private hospital and sanitariums	403	410	7
Services of financial intermediaries	1278	1104	-174
Higher education	219	222	3
Elementary and secondary schools, private	162	166	4
Religious and welfare activities	1196	1206	10
Net change:	8836	8918	82
Conceptual Changes:			
Brokerage charges and interest, investment counseling	1707	756	-951
Interest on personal debt	584	---	-584
Net personal cash remittances to foreigners	288	---	-288
Net change:	2579	756	-1823

Sources: Figures in 1954 edition are from U.S. Office of Business Economics, *National Income: 1954 Edition*. Figures in current edition are from U.S. BEA, *National Income and Product Accounts, 1929-82*.

The first adjustment made to the Kuznets-Kendrick estimates of expenditure for services simultaneously compensates for both the statistical revisions and the revised treatment of personal cash remittances to foreigners. Absent data on which to base the pre-1929 estimates of personal cash remittances to foreigners, no separate adjustment is made for this item. The sum of the national product accounts estimates of expenditure for services in 1929 ($30,322 million) and of consumer interest payments to business in 1929 ($1,532 million) is used as the 1929 benchmark. The Kuznets-Kendrick estimates of expenditure for services, 1869–1928, are multiplied by 0.9935 (31,854/32,063), yielding "adjusted Kuznets-Kendrick" estimates of expenditure for services.

Use of this constant adjustment factor for 1869–1928 reflects the assumption that personal cash remittances to foreigners are a constant proportion of total service expenditure over the period. Such an assumption is not valid for consumer interest payments to business; largely because of the debt-financed stock market boom, consumer interest payments do not bear a constant statistical relationship to total expenditure for services in the interwar years. Interest payments to brokers and investment counselors were especially large in 1929, reflecting the relatively high incidence of borrowing to buy stock. We can see this pattern by looking at the data for the 1930s. Interest payments to stockbrokers averaged less than 5 percent of total consumer interest payments to business for 1933–39 but had been 9 percent of the total in 1932, 15 percent in 1931, 30 percent in 1930, and over 60 percent of total interest payments to business in 1929.[3]

The national product accounts estimates of consumer interest payments to business for 1929 are extrapolated back to 1897 with Raymond Goldsmith's estimates of outstanding short-term consumer debt (*Study of Saving*, 1:table D-1). The national product accounts estimate of total consumer interest paid to business in 1929 (when brokerage debt was about 60 percent of the total) is 20.1 percent of Goldsmith's estimate of outstanding short-term consumer debt for 1929. But between 1935 and 1939, interest payments on just personal, nonbrokerage debt (estimated in *National Income: 1954 Edition*) averaged only 9.2 percent of Goldsmith's debt estimates. Using 1927 as the beginning of the late 1920s stock market boom, I estimate consumer interest payments to business as 9.25 percent of Goldsmith's outstanding short-term consumer debt for 1897–1926, 20.1 percent for 1929, and interpolate linearly for the intervening two years. The resulting estimate of consumer interest payments to business in 1929 equals the national product accounts estimate, $1,532 million.

For 1869–96, the estimates of consumer interest payments to business are based on the adjusted Kuznets-Kendrick estimates of expenditure for services. The average ratio of interest payments to the adjusted Kuznets-Kendrick estimates of services expenditure for 1898–1904, 1.3 percent, is used to extrapolate the interest payments series back to 1869.

As the final step, the annual estimates of consumer interest payments to business, 1869–1928, are subtracted from the adjusted Kuznets-Kendrick estimates of expenditure for services, yielding estimates of nominal expenditure for services that link to the national product accounts estimates at 1929 and are conceptually consistent with those estimates.

NOTE 6: DISPOSABLE PERSONAL INCOME

For 1929 on, annual estimates of disposable personal income (personal income less personal tax and nontax payments) are from U.S. Bureau of Economic Analysis, *National Income and Product Accounts, 1929–82* (and updates), table 2.1, line 25. For the years before 1929, annual estimates of disposable personal income are derived by estimating separately personal income, and personal tax and nontax payments.

To estimate personal income, I first needed estimates of gross national product. Kuznets's annual estimates of gross national product, 1869–1928, were revised by Kendrick to make them conceptually consistent with Department of Commerce estimates. Kendrick published decade averages of these revised estimates (the Kuznets-Kendrick estimates) for 1869–78 and 1879–88 and annual estimates for 1889–1929 in *Productivity Trends*, table A-IIb. The Kuznets-Kendrick estimate of gross national product for 1929 equals the *National Income: 1954 Edition* estimate, but due to subsequent statistical revisions and conceptual changes (consumer interest payments to business are now excluded from gross national product) it does not equal the current national product accounts estimate of gross national product for 1929.

To derive estimates of gross national product, 1869–1929, that are conceptually consistent with *National Income: 1954 Edition* but that incorporate the subsequent statistical revisions, the Kuznets-Kendrick estimates of gross national product, 1869–1929, are multiplied by 1.0095 (105,432/104,436). This extrapolates the sum of the national product accounts estimates of gross national product and consumer interest payments to business back to 1869.

To estimate personal income, 1897–1929, this adjusted gross national product series is multiplied by the annual ratios of Goldsmith's estimate of personal income to his estimate of gross national product (*Study of*

Saving, 3:table N-1). Consumer interest payments to business are not first subtracted from the adjusted gross national product series since Goldsmith's estimates of gross national product also include consumer interest payments to business. These personal income estimates are extrapolated to 1869 using the adjusted estimates of gross national product. To link these estimates of personal income to the national product accounts estimates at 1929, the estimates of personal income, 1869–1929, are multiplied by 0.9752 (84.3/86.442).

Kendrick provides annual estimates, 1889–1929, and decade averages, 1869–78 and 1879–88, of personal tax and nontax payments (*Productivity Trends*, table A-IIb). Within rounding error, his estimate for 1929 equals the current national product accounts estimate of personal tax and nontax payments for 1929. Kendrick's estimates of personal tax and nontax payments are subtracted from the adjusted estimates of personal income, yielding estimates of nominal disposable personal income, 1869–1928, that link directly to the national product accounts estimates at 1929.

NOTE 7: GROSS RENTAL VALUE OF CONSUMER DURABLE GOODS

To estimate gross rental value of consumer durable goods, the Department of Commerce procedures for accounting for the imputed rental value of owner-occupied housing was used as a framework. In the national product accounts, the gross rental value of owner-occupied housing equals the sum of depreciation, government subsidies, indirect business tax and nontax liability, net mortgage interest payments (total mortgage interest paid by persons less mortgage interest received by persons), and imputed rental income to persons. Net rental value, which equals net interest payments plus rental income, is included in personal income as well as in gross national product; the remaining three components of gross rental value are included in gross national product but not in personal income.[4]

To treat consumer durable goods the same way, only estimates of depreciation, interest payments, and rental income are necessary. To the best of my knowledge, there has never been a government program to subsidize purchases of durable goods, and thus this component of gross rental value is assumed to equal zero. Indirect business tax and nontax liability consists primarily of property, sales, and excise taxes. Absent data that could be used to estimate the burden of these taxes for durable goods only, I assume that these taxes are negligible for consumer durable goods. To the extent this assumption is invalid, the adjusted personal saving rates reported in chapter 2 are overstated; tax liabilities contribute to gross rental value (and thus to adjusted expenditure for services) but not to net rental value (and thus not to adjusted personal income).

Depreciation estimates are from table A.12. To estimate interest payments on loans used to purchase consumer durable goods, I first assume that no interest payments are made to other households; equivalently, that gross and net interest payments are equal. Interest payments are based on estimates of outstanding consumer debt for acquisition of durable goods. For 1919–74, the Federal Reserve Board's estimates of outstanding automobile paper, outstanding paper for other consumer goods, and outstanding repair and modernization loans are summed ("Consumer Credit," table 1, updated in the *Federal Reserve Bulletin*). Goldsmith's estimates of total outstanding short-term consumer debt are used to extrapolate these estimates to 1900 (*Study of Saving*, 1:table D-1).

The Federal Reserve Board revised the conceptual basis of their outstanding debt estimates in 1975, and the new series do not exactly correspond to the old. For 1975–86, estimates of outstanding automobile paper are from June issues of *Federal Reserve Bulletin*, table 1.55, line 3. For 1975–86, the sum of outstanding paper for other consumer goods and outstanding repair and modernization loans is extended forward from 1974 using the sum of outstanding consumer installment debt for mobile homes (line 19) and for other major nonrevolving credit (line 23) from June issues of *Federal Reserve Bulletin*, table 1.55.

Annual interest payments are estimated as the product of outstanding durable goods debt (as of December 31) and the interest rate on consumer loans. Using Juster's estimates of interest rates on consumer loans, the interest rate equals 6.0 for 1900–1906 and 15.0 for 1925–86 and is interpolated linearly for the intervening years (*Household Capital Formation and Financing*, notes to table B-2). Note: when gross rental value of durable goods is included with consumer expenditure for services, consumer interest payments to business (a component of consumer outlays) must be reduced by the value of interest payments on durable goods debt to avoid double counting.

To estimate rental income on durable goods, I followed the methodology suggested by Juster (notes to table B-2): rental income is estimated as a percentage of equity (existing net stock less outstanding debt) where the percentage reflects the rate of return earned on the assets. All durable goods debt is assumed to be for acquisition of major durable goods. The rate of return was chosen by assuming that households "operate at the margin" in the long run, earning a marginal rate of return on durable assets that equals the best alternative rate of return for assets of similar liquidity. For minor durable goods, this alternative rate of return is that earned on liquid assets. Scanning the estimates of U.S. government bond yields (U.S. Bureau of the Census, *Historical Statistics*, Series X474) led to estimates of the rate of return on liquid assets that equal 3.0 for 1900–1956, 3.5 for 1957 and 1958, 4.0 for 1959, 6.5 for 1971 on, and which are linearly interpolated for intervening years, 1960–70.[5]

Following Juster, I assume that households "require" a higher rate of return from major durable goods than from minor durable goods to compensate for the relative illiquidity of the major durables. The rate of return is assumed to be the rate charged on loans obtained to acquire durable goods (the rate used above to estimate interest payments).

Gross rental value was also calculated under five alternative rate of return assumptions, including that major and minor durable goods earn the same rate of return, the rate of liquid assets. Since rental income is a relatively small part of gross rental value, the adjusted personal saving rates of table 2.10 are essentially insensitive to any reasonable changes in rate of return.

Net rental value of durable goods (rental income plus net interest payments on durable goods debt) is included in personal income when household expenditure for durable goods is treated as investment rather than current consumption expenditure. Since consumer interest payments to business (which include interest payments on durable goods debt) are otherwise included in personal income, only rental income needs to be added to personal income to derive the estimates of adjusted personal income for table 2.10.

NOTE 8: NET WEALTH OF HOUSEHOLDS

Annual estimates of net wealth were developed for the regression analysis of chapter 3. Unless otherwise indicated, all estimates discussed in this note are end-of-year, current dollar values.

For 1900–1958, annual estimates of "private net worth" are given in Modigliani, "Life Cycle Hypothesis of Saving," appendix B. For 1945–58, Modigliani's estimates are from the annual balance sheet estimates in Goldsmith, Lipsey, and Mendelson, *Studies in the National Balance Sheet*. They equal the sum of equities of nonfarm households (table III-1) and equities of agriculture (table III-3). Note that equities of nonfarm households includes equities of nonprofit organizations.

These annual balance sheet estimates are extended to 1975 in Goldsmith, *National Balance Sheet*. However, the economy is broken down differently in this more recent volume; all households (farm and nonfarm) and all nonprofit organizations are contained in the sector "households" (*National Balance Sheet*, p. 30). Exact replication of the 1953–58 estimates of household net wealth given in Goldsmith, Lipsey, and Mendelson is not possible with the data given in Goldsmith, *National Balance Sheet*. The difference between the two sets of estimates is very minor, however (less than 2 percent). I presume that this difference is due to statistical revisions in the underlying data, but the supporting documentation in Goldsmith (1982) is too sparse to allow verification of this.

To obtain one continuous series of net household wealth, 1900–1983, I combined estimates from several sources. For 1900–1952, Modigliani's estimates of private net worth of households are used. For 1953–58, the estimates are the product of Goldsmith's estimates of household assets and his estimates of household equity as a percent of assets (Goldsmith, *National Balance Sheet*, tables 48 and 50, respectively). The difference between these estimates and Modigliani's is minor.

For 1959–75, the estimates equal the difference between Goldsmith's estimates of household assets (*National Balance Sheet*, table 48) and the Federal Reserve Board's estimates of household liabilities (*Flow of Funds Accounts*, "Households," pp. 5–6). These estimates of net wealth are slightly smaller than those implied by Goldsmith's estimates of household equity as a percent of household assets, but the difference is less than 1 percent.

To extend the estimates of net wealth to 1983 first required extending Goldsmith's annual estimates of household assets. Those estimates include the value of tangible assets (land, structures, durable and semidurable goods) and the value of financial assets (deposits, securities and bonds, corporate business equities, farm business equities, nonfarm noncorporate business equities, mortgages held by households, open market paper, insurance and pension fund reserves, common and individual trust funds, and other financial assets; see *National Balance Sheet*, table 12). Values for most of these assets can be obtained from published documents: values of net stocks of structures, noncorporate equipment, and of durable goods are in U.S. Bureau of Economic Analysis, *Fixed Reproducible Tangible Wealth, 1925–85* and updates; values of financial assets other than trust funds are in Federal Reserve Board, *Flow of Funds Accounts*. Combining these values forms a series that covers most but not all of the assets included in Goldsmith's estimates. This partial accounting of household assets (which excludes only the value of land held by households, farms, and nonfarm businesses and the value of trust funds) accounts for over 80 percent of Goldsmith's estimates of household assets between 1960 and 1975.

Final estimates of the value of household assets, 1976–83, are obtained by extrapolating Goldsmith's estimate for 1975 forward to 1983 with this partial accounting of household assets. Final estimates of household net wealth, 1976–83, equal the difference between these estimates of household assets and the estimates of household liabilities in Federal Reserve Board, *Flow of Funds Accounts*, "Households," pp. 5–6.

For 1900–1983, the constant dollar estimates of net wealth of households are computed by deflating the current dollar estimates by the implicit price deflator for all consumer goods and services (derived as discussed in the notes to table 2.5).

♦ APPENDIX C ♦

TECHNICAL NOTES:
ESTIMATING DEMAND

T his appendix contains technical notes regarding the empirical analysis of demand for durable goods and the statistical tests conducted for chapter 3, the sources and values of the independent variables, and the estimated regression equations themselves.

DERIVATION OF DEMAND EQUATION: GRADUAL STOCK-ADJUSTMENT MODEL

Total demand for consumer durable goods, Q, combines replacement demand, R, and net demand, N. Replacement demand maintains the existing stock of durable goods at its previous level by offsetting current depreciation. By assumption, replacement demand therefore equals current-period depreciation, D. Net demand alters the level of stock above or below its previous level. Each household gradually adjusts its actual stock of durable goods toward some desired level. Net demand is therefore some proportion, a, of the difference between the desired level of stock, S^*, and the actual level of stock, S. For each household i, total demand for durable goods during period t therefore equals

$$Q_{i,t} = R_{i,t} + N_{i,t} = D_{i,t} + a(S^*_{i,t} - S_{i,t-1}) \qquad (C.1)$$

Since replacement demand equals depreciation, net demand by each household therefore equals

$$N_{i,t} = a\,(S^*_{i,t} - S_{i,t-1}) \qquad (C.2)$$

As developed in chapter 3, for each household, desired stock, S^*, depends upon the household's disposable personal income, Y, and net wealth, W (together a proxy for the household's life-cycle income); and the relative price of durable goods, p (a proxy for the relative price of the good's services). Assuming a linear relationship and including a constant term, for each household the desired level of stock at the end of period t equals

$$S^*_{i,t} = b_0 + b_1 p_t + b_2 Y_{i,t} + b_3 W_{i,t} \qquad (C.3)$$

where the subscript i denotes each individual household and subscript t marks time. Net expenditure by each household therefore equals

$$N_{i,t} = a (b_0 + b_1 p_t + b_2 Y_{i,t} + b_3 W_{i,t} - S_{i,t-1}) \qquad (C.4)$$

Aggregating over all households in the economy, H, yields

$$N_t = Q_t - D_t = a (b_0 H_t + b_1 p_t H_t + b_2 Y_t + b_3 W_t - S_{t-1}) \quad (C.5)$$

where N_t is aggregate net expenditure during period t, Q_t is aggregate gross expenditure during period t, D_t is aggregate depreciation during period t, H_t is the number of households in the economy at the end of period t, p_t is the relative price of the durable good in period t, Y_t is aggregate disposable personal income during period t, W_t is aggregate net household wealth at the end of period t, and S_{t-1} is the aggregate value of the existing stock at the end of period t − 1. Deflating by the number of households yields

$$\frac{N_t}{H_t} = \frac{Q_t - D_t}{H_t} = a (b_0 + b_1 p_t + b_2 \frac{Y_t}{H_t} + b_3 \frac{W_t}{H_t} - \frac{S_{t-1}}{H_t}) \quad (C.6)$$

Newly formed households may have a different level of desired stock, S^*, but respond to changes in price, income, and wealth in the same manner as previously established households. Desired level of stock for newly formed households, j, is thus represented by

$$S^*_{j,t} = (b_0 + b_4) + b_1 p_t + b_2 Y_{j,t} + b_3 W_{j,t} \qquad (C.7)$$

where b_4 is the newly formed households' differential desire for stock. Since these households have no prior stock of durable goods ($S_{t-1} = 0$ for newly formed households), their net expenditure is

$$N_{j,t} = a [(b_0 + b_4) + b_1 p_t + b_2 Y_{j,t} + b_3 W_{j,t}] \qquad (C.8)$$

The total number of households in the economy at the end of period t is the sum of previously existing households, H_{t-1}, and newly formed households, ΔH_t, which equals $H_t - H_{t-1}$. Aggregating net expenditure across all households

$$N_t = \sum_{i=1}^{H_{t-1}} a \, [b_0 + b_1 p_t + b_2 Y_{i,t} + b_3 W_{i,t} - S_{i,t-1}]$$

$$+ \sum_{j=1}^{\Delta H_t} a \, [(b_0 + b_4) + b_1 p_t + b_2 Y_{j,t} + b_3 W_{j,t}] \qquad \text{(C.9)}$$

yields

$$N_t = a \, (b_0 H_t + b_4 \Delta H_t + b_1 p_t H_t + b_2 Y_t + b_3 W_t - S_{t-1}) \qquad \text{(C.10)}$$

Deflating by the number of households, H_t, yields

$$\frac{N_t}{H_t} = a \, (b_0 + b_1 p_t + b_2 \frac{Y_t}{H_t} + b_3 \frac{W_t}{H_t} + b_4 \frac{\Delta H_t}{H_t} - \frac{S_{t-1}}{H_t}) \qquad \text{(C.11)}$$

DERIVATION OF DEMAND EQUATION: HABIT-FORMATION MODEL

An alternative model of household demand for durable goods is an autoregressive or habit-formation model.[1] In this model, a household's net expenditure is determined by some slowly moving process that is best captured statistically by the level of stock in the previous period. Fluctuations in other variables may result in slight fluctuations in expenditure, but expenditure is largely a force of habit, determined statistically by an autoregressive process. That is, for each household i

$$S_{i,t} = (A) \, S_{i,t-1} + \mathbf{B} \cdot \mathbf{X}_{i,t} \qquad \text{(C.12)}$$

where $\mathbf{X}_{i,t}$ is a vector of all other variables that determine stock. Net expenditure equals the difference between current and previous-period stock. Equation C.12 is therefore equivalent to

$$N_{i,t} = S_{i,t} - S_{i,t-1} = (A-1) \, S_{i,t-1} + \mathbf{B} \cdot \mathbf{X}_{i,t} \qquad \text{(C.13)}$$

Assume the vector $\mathbf{X}_{i,t}$ contains the same variables that determine desired stock in the gradual stock-adjustment model. Assume further that newly formed households may again have a different desire for stock. Aggregating across all households and deflating by the number of households, we obtain

$$\frac{N_t}{H_t} = (A - 1)\frac{S_{t-1}}{H_t} + B_0 + B_1 p_t + B_2 \frac{Y_t}{H_t} + B_3 \frac{W_t}{H_t} + B_4 \frac{\Delta H_t}{H_t} \quad (C.14)$$

HABIT-FORMATION AND GRADUAL STOCK-ADJUSTMENT MODELS

To estimate the demand equation, we need not know in advance whether the habit-formation or gradual stock-adjustment model best describes household behavior; the estimable forms of the habit-formation and gradual stock-adjustment models are indistinguishable. In both cases, the estimable form of the regression equation is

$$\frac{N_t}{H_t} = A_0 + A_1 p_t + A_2 \frac{Y_t}{H_t} + A_3 \frac{W_t}{H_t} + A_4 \frac{\Delta H_t}{H_t} + A_5 \frac{S_{t-1}}{H_t} \quad (C.15)$$

Interpreting the coefficients—especially the lagged stock coefficient—does require knowing which model best applies, however.[2]

If all households purchasing durable goods exhibit gradual stock-adjustment behavior, then net expenditure for durable goods is described in the aggregate by equation C.11, and the estimated lagged stock coefficient will be negative and greater than − 1. If all households exhibit habit-formation behavior, then aggregate net expenditure is described by equation C.14. In this case if stock is increasing over time, the structural coefficient A is greater than 1, and the estimated lagged stock coefficient $(A_5 = A - 1)$ is positive. But if stock is decreasing over time, A is positive but less than 1, and the estimated lagged stock coefficient is negative but greater than − 1.

But what if there is a mix of households, with some exhibiting stock-adjustment behavior and others exhibiting habit-formation behavior? As ever more stock is owned by households exhibiting gradual stock-adjustment behavior, the lagged stock coefficient becomes increasingly negative. In general, the estimated lagged stock coefficient, A_5, is

$$A_5 = (A - 1)(PS_{HF}) - a(PS_{GSA}) \quad (C.16)$$

where A and a are the structural coefficients from equations C.14 and C.11 respectively, PS_{HF} is the percentage of stock owned by habit-formation households, and PS_{GSA} is the percentage of stock owned by stock-adjusting households ($PS_{HF} + PS_{GSA} = 1$).

We can interpret changes in the lagged stock coefficient over time as signifying which behavior, habit-formation or gradual stock-adjustment, is becoming more dominant among those households buying durables. If among those households buying durables there is a shift away from habit-formation and toward gradual stock-adjustment behavior, the lagged stock coefficient will be initially positive but then move negative. Equivalently if large numbers of households exhibiting gradual stock adjustment enter a market formerly dominated by households practicing (and continuing to practice) habit-formation behavior, over time the lagged stock coefficient will move from positive to negative as ever more goods are acquired by the stock-adjusting households. In the midst of this transition, the estimated lagged stock coefficient may not be significantly different from zero.

The remaining estimated coefficients can also reflect a mix of behavior among those households buying durables. The estimated constant, A_0, is

$$A_0 = ab_0 - PH_{HF}(ab_0 - B_0) \tag{C.17}$$

and the estimated relative price coefficient, A_1, is

$$A_1 = ab_1 - PH_{HF}(ab_1 - B_1) \tag{C.18}$$

where a, b_0, and b_1 are the structural coefficients from equation C.11, B_0 and B_1 are the structural coefficients from equation C.14, and PH_{HF} is the percentage of households exhibiting habit-formation behavior. The estimated income coefficient, A_2, is

$$A_2 = ab_2 - PY_{HF}(ab_2 - B_2) \tag{C.19}$$

where the structural coefficients are as above and PY_{HF} is the percentage of aggregate income earned by habit-formation households. The estimated wealth coefficient, A_3, is

$$A_3 = ab_3 - PW_{HF}(ab_3 - B_3) \tag{C.20}$$

where the structural coefficients are as above and PW_{HF} is the percentage of aggregate household net wealth owned by habit-formation households.

If most purchases and most of the income and wealth are in habit-formation households, then equations C.17 through C.20 indicate that the estimated coefficients will approximate the structural coefficients of the habit-formation model, B. As increasingly more households in the market exhibit gradual stock-adjustment behavior, and as greater shares of aggregate income and wealth accumulate to stock-adjusting households, the estimated coefficients will move toward the structural coefficients of the gradual stock-adjustment model, ab_i.

Households adjust stock gradually rather than immediately because selling a used durable good is costly; owning but underutilizing a durable good is also costly (in an opportunity sense); and saving up enough money for purchase can be time-consuming. It is reasonable to suppose that these three factors are much less prohibitive for wealthy and high-income households. Such households would have less cause to make a "distress sale" of a used durable good, could absorb the opportunity costs more readily, and might not need to save up at all. Upper-income and wealthy households would have much less reason to adjust stock gradually. They may practice gradual stock-adjustment behavior but have an adjustment coefficient near 1, or they may exhibit primarily habit-formation behavior.

As a product moves from a luxury good for the upper class to a mass-produced, mass-marketed product bought by hoards of new market initiates who are of middle-income and moderate- to low-wealth status, what happens to the aggregate demand for durables? Since the new buyers own no previous stock, the lagged stock coefficient is still dominated by habit-formation households. Unless wealth is distributed fairly evenly (an unlikely scenario), the estimated wealth coefficient will also remain dominated by habit-formation households. If the bulk of households buying the product are now these new stock-adjusting households, the constant term and relative price coefficient will be dominated by the behavior of the new households. Income tends to be distributed more evenly than wealth (though still far from perfectly evenly), and thus as a product enters mass-market status, the income coefficient will become dominated by gradual stock-adjustment behavior. The result? In the period when a product is first mass marketed and ceases to be primarily a product for just the wealthy, aggregate demand for durables can seem to respond slowly to any gap between actual and desired stock. Moreover, if habit-formation households primarily respond to last period's stock and hardly at all to changes in the other factors (that is, if their B coefficients are quite small), then during the initial mass-marketing stage the aggregate demand for durables will respond relatively strongly to changes in relative price and perhaps income, and weakly to changes in wealth. As the product moves fully into the mass-marketing stage and existing stock is distributed fairly evenly among purchasing households, the lagged stock coefficient will become more negative and the aggregate responsiveness to changes in relative price and income will increase. These patterns can help explain the otherwise puzzling regression results obtained for some commodity groups for the interwar period, as noted in chapter 3.

DATA SOURCES

Annual net expenditures per household evaluated in constant prices are analyzed by commodity group and for three aggregates. Demand is estimated for the aggregates total durable goods, major durable goods, and minor durable goods, and for each of the following commodity groups: automobiles and parts, transportation vehicles, furniture, household appliances, radios and musical instruments, china and tableware, house furnishings, jewelry and watches, orthopedic and ophthalmic products, books and maps, and miscellaneous other durable goods. For pre–World War I and interwar years, demand is also estimated for the two subgroups of radios and musical instruments: radios and phonographs, and pianos and other musical instruments. Absence of data prevents disaggregating radios and musical instruments in the post–World War II period.

Net expenditure equals gross expenditure less current depreciation. Estimates of gross expenditure are from table A.7. Estimates of depreciation are from table A.12. All estimates are in 1982 dollars.

The relative price variable, p_t of equation C.11, is the ratio of the implicit price deflator for the commodity group or aggregate of concern to the implicit price deflator for all consumer goods and services. Annual values of the implicit price deflators are from table A.8. Derivation of the implicit price deflator for all consumer goods and services is described in the notes to table 2.5.

The effect of life-cycle income on demand for durable goods can be captured by the combination of the effects of current-period income and net wealth.[3] The income variable, Y_t, is constant price disposable personal income, derived as discussed in the notes to table 2.9. Current price estimates of household net wealth are derived as discussed in appendix B, note 8. These estimates are deflated by the implicit price deflator for all consumer goods and services to obtain the constant price estimates of household net wealth, W_t, that are used in the regression analysis.

For 1900–1969, estimates of the number of households are from U.S. Bureau of the Census, *Historical Statistics*, Series A350.[4] For 1970–83, estimates are from U.S. Bureau of the Census, *Current Population Reports* (and updates), table 6. For each year, the household formation rate equals the number of households at the end of that year less the number of households at the end of the previous year, as a percent of the number of households in the current year.[5]

Estimates of stock of durable goods are from table A.13. After 1925, these estimates are from U.S. Bureau of Economic Analysis, *Fixed Reproducible Tangible Wealth, 1925–85*, table A17.

Annual estimates of real disposable personal income, real household net wealth, the household formation rate, and the number of households, 1900–1983, are given in table C.1.

INSTRUMENTAL VARIABLES

Equation C.11 is one equation of a simultaneous system of equations specifying both demand and supply. To estimate one equation from a simultaneous system, two stage least squares (instrumental variables) methods are used. In the first stage, a set of variables that influence supply but not demand—the instruments—are used to statistically purge those variables affecting both supply and demand, here, relative price. In the second stage, a resulting purged price variable is substituted for the original price variable in the demand equation, and the equation is then estimated.

The instruments used should ideally affect supply but not demand. In practice, the choice of instruments is limited by the availability of continuous series covering 1900–1983. The instruments used are measures of the actual and opportunity costs of capital (four- to six-month commercial

Table C.1. Independent Variables Used in Regression Analysis

Year	Disposable Income per Household (1982 $)	Net Wealth per Household (1982 $)	Number of Households (Thousands)	Household Formation Rate (Percent)
1900	11,182	59,241	15,992	1.78
1901	12,382	64,384	16,345	2.16
1902	12,074	65,106	16,716	2.22
1903	12,356	65,409	17,108	2.29
1904	12,155	64,285	17,521	2.36
1905	12,748	67,624	17,939	2.33
1906	14,230	69,956	18,394	2.47
1907	14,286	66,063	18,863	2.49
1908	12,471	67,979	19,294	2.23
1909	14,016	71,202	19,734	2.23
1910	13,421	71,093	20,183	2.22
1911	13,805	71,970	20,620	2.12
1912	14,164	71,650	21,075	2.16
1913	14,304	71,488	21,606	2.46
1914	12,781	70,720	22,110	2.28
1915	12,919	71,474	22,501	1.74
1916	14,006	70,424	22,926	1.85
1917	13,352	63,783	23,323	1.70
1918	15,112	63,158	23,519	0.83
1919	15,121	77,815	23,873	1.48
1920	15,037	68,957	24,467	2.43
1921	14,130	58,414	25,119	2.60
1922	14,277	73,696	25,687	2.21
1923	15,808	74,826	26,298	2.32
1924	16,118	78,025	26,941	2.39
1925	15,491	77,110	27,540	2.18
1926	16,154	79,624	28,101	2.00

Table C.1, continued

Year	Disposable Income per Household (1982 $)	Net Wealth per Household (1982 $)	Number of Households (Thousands)	Household Formation Rate (Percent)
1927	16,217	85,680	28,632	1.85
1928	15,800	91,127	29,124	1.69
1929	16,854	93,922	29,582	1.55
1930	15,309	94,180	29,997	1.38
1931	14,505	88,342	30,272	0.91
1932	12,491	80,855	30,439	0.55
1933	12,050	84,002	30,802	1.18
1934	12,512	78,058	31,306	1.61
1935	13,417	78,322	31,892	1.84
1936	14,769	82,351	32,454	1.73
1937	14,964	81,445	33,088	1.92
1938	13,733	76,318	33,683	1.77
1939	14,531	79,160	34,409	2.11
1940	15,110	78,192	35,153	2.12
1941	16,820	76,632	35,929	2.16
1942	19,037	76,655	36,445	1.42
1943	19,600	79,360	36,833	1.05
1944	20,208	82,315	37,115	0.76
1945	19,733	91,140	37,503	1.03
1946	18,859	89,288	38,370	2.26
1947	17,768	87,547	39,107	1.88
1948	18,097	84,291	40,532	3.52
1949	17,373	82,187	42,182	3.91
1950	18,179	86,986	43,554	3.15
1951	18,330	86,407	44,673	2.50
1952	18,543	85,606	45,538	1.90
1953	18,967	84,683	46,385	1.83

Table C.1, continued

Year	Disposable Income per Household (1982 $)	Net Wealth per Household (1982 $)	Number of Households (Thousands)	Household Formation Rate (Percent)
1954	19,031	91,354	46,962	1.23
1955	19,729	96,455	47,874	1.90
1956	20,229	98,695	48,902	2.10
1957	20,371	96,091	49,673	1.55
1958	20,384	104,277	50,474	1.59
1959	20,745	104,912	51,435	1.87
1960	20,662	102,808	52,799	2.58
1961	20,975	109,343	53,557	1.42
1962	21,370	105,039	54,764	2.20
1963	21,840	110,052	55,270	0.92
1964	22,993	111,570	56,149	1.57
1965	23,771	117,200	57,436	2.24
1966	24,506	114,019	58,406	1.66
1967	25,211	123,619	59,236	1.40
1968	25,506	129,377	60,813	2.59
1969	25,717	123,632	62,214	2.25
1970	26,313	120,903	63,401	1.87
1971	26,678	123,525	64,778	2.13
1972	26,958	127,530	66,676	2.85
1973	28,079	121,526	68,251	2.31
1974	27,146	111,396	69,859	2.30
1975	27,160	114,839	71,120	1.77
1976	27,459	119,003	72,867	2.40
1977	27,878	119,287	74,142	1.72
1978	28,507	121,619	76,030	2.48
1979	28,607	124,606	77,330	1.68
1980	27,415	124,509	80,776	4.27

Table C.1, continued

Year	Disposable Income per Household (1982 $)	Net Wealth per Household (1982 $)	Number of Households (Thousands)	Household Formation Rate (Percent)
1981	27,301	120,376	82,368	1.93
1982	27,075	119,293	83,527	1.39
1983	27,788	124,772	83,918	0.47

Sources: Constant (1982) dollar disposable income derived as for table 2.9 and divided by the number of households. Constant (1982) price household net wealth is equal to current price household net wealth (derived as discussed in appendix B, note 8) deflated by the implicit price deflator for all consumer goods and services (derived as for table 2.5) and divided by the number of households. Number of households, 1900-1969, U.S. Bureau of the Census, *Historical Statistics*, Ser. A350; 1970-83, U.S. Bureau of the Census, *Current Population Reports* and updates, table 6. Household formation rate is change in number of households since previous year, as a percent of current number of households.

paper rate, rate on municipal high-grade bonds, Standard and Poor's common stock index for industrials, Standard and Poor's total common stock index), shipping costs (railroad freight revenue per ton, railroad freight revenue per ton-mile), worker productivity (nonfarm output per worker-hour), labor costs (average annual earnings in manufacturing, average annual earnings in trade), other input costs (the wholesale price index for all commodities), and, when the Cochrane-Orcutt correction is used, the one-period lagged values of the dependent and independent variables. Their values are from U.S. Bureau of the Census, *Historical Statistics*, and various recent issues of U.S. *Statistical Abstract* as cited in the notes to table C.2.

DUMMY VARIABLES

As is common with time series data, the estimated equations have low Durbin-Watson statistics, indicating serious serial correlation of the error terms. A Cochrane-Orcutt procedure is therefore used when estimating the regression equations. The error terms are assumed to exhibit a one-period autoregressive pattern, that is,

$$e_t = (RHO)e_{t-1} + v_t \tag{C.21}$$

where by assumption v_t is distributed normally with mean zero and constant variance.

Implementation of this procedure requires continuous data series. Rather than omit the observations associated with World War I and World War II, dummy variables must therefore be introduced. In general the dummy variables take on the following values:

DUMWW1 = 1 for 1917–19
            0 for all other years

and

DUMWW2 = 1 for 1942–46
            0 for all other years

These values do a poor job of capturing World War I changes in expenditure for three groups: automobiles and parts, transportation vehicles, and orthopedic and ophthalmic products. For automobiles and parts and for transportation vehicles, the World War I dummy variable is:

AUTWW1 = 1 for 1917
          4 for 1918
          2 for 1919
          0 for all other years

For orthopedic and ophthalmic products, where expenditure is strongly affected by wartime injuries, the dummy variable is:

MEDWW1 = 1 for 1917
           4 for 1918
        −4 for 1919
           0 for all other years

The World War II dummy variable is the same for all commodity groups.

Table C.2. Instrumental Variables Used in Regression Analysis

Year	4- to 6-Month Commercial Paper Rate (Percent) (1)	Rate on Municipal High-grade Bonds (Percent) (2)	S&P Stock Index: Industrials (1941-43 =10) (3)	S&P Stock Index: Total (1941-43 =10) (4)	Railroad Freight Revenue Per Ton (Dollars) (5)	Railroad Freight Revenue Per Ton-Mile (Cents) (6)	Nonfarm Output Per Worker-Hour (1958 =100) (7)	Average Annual Earnings: Manufacturing (Dollars) (8)	Average Annual Earnings: Trade (Dollars) (9)	Wholesale Price Index: All Goods (1967 =100) (10)
1900	5.71	3.12	3.38	6.15	1.80	0.729	29.0	487	508	28.9
1901	5.40	3.13	4.00	7.84	1.92	0.750	31.6	511	510	28.5
1902	5.81	3.20	3.92	8.42	1.84	0.757	30.1	537	521	30.4
1903	6.16	3.38	3.20	7.21	1.87	0.763	30.6	548	537	30.7
1904	5.14	3.45	2.92	7.05	1.93	0.780	30.6	538	551	30.8
1905	5.18	3.40	4.11	8.99	1.85	0.766	31.3	561	561	31.0
1906	6.25	3.57	4.82	9.64	1.83	0.748	33.7	577	569	32.0
1907	6.66	3.86	3.84	7.84	1.87	0.759	33.9	598	580	33.6
1908	5.00	3.93	3.74	7.78	1.90	0.754	32.1	548	593	32.4
1909	4.67	3.78	4.99	9.71	1.90	0.763	35.0	599	609	34.9
1910	5.72	3.97	5.02	9.35	1.88	0.753	33.9	651	630	36.4
1911	4.75	3.98	4.82	9.24	1.92	0.757	35.3	632	666	33.5

Table C.2, continued

Year	4- to 6-Month Commercial Paper Rate (Percent) (1)	Rate on Municipal High-grade Bonds (Percent) (2)	S&P Stock Index: Industrials (1941-43 = 10) (3)	S&P Stock Index: Total (1941-43 = 10) (4)	Railroad Freight Revenue Per Ton (Dollars) (5)	Railroad Freight Revenue Per Ton-Mile (Cents) (6)	Nonfarm Output Per Worker-Hour (1958 = 100) (7)	Average Annual Earnings: Manufacturing (Dollars) (8)	Average Annual Earnings: Trade (Dollars) (9)	Wholesale Price Index: All Goods (1967 = 100) (10)
1912	5.41	4.02	5.18	9.53	1.91	0.744	34.8	651	666	35.6
1913	6.20	4.22	4.56	8.51	1.92	0.729	37.1	689	685	36.0
1914	5.47	4.12	4.50	8.08	1.88	0.737	33.9	696	706	35.2
1915	4.01	4.16	5.22	8.31	1.99	0.735	34.8	661	720	35.8
1916	3.84	3.94	6.62	9.47	1.98	0.719	38.6	751	760	44.1
1917	5.07	4.20	6.15	8.50	2.10	0.728	35.7	883	828	60.6
1918	6.02	4.50	5.57	7.54	2.56	0.862	40.1	1,107	941	67.6
1919	5.37	4.46	7.13	8.78	3.05	0.987	43.1	1,293	1,070	71.4
1920	7.50	4.98	6.50	7.98	3.24	1.069	43.0	1,532	1,270	79.6
1921	6.62	5.09	5.07	6.86	3.93	1.294	46.6	1,346	1,260	50.3
1922	4.52	4.23	6.35	8.41	3.67	1.194	45.4	1,283	1,261	49.9

Table C.2, continued

Year	4- to 6-Month Commercial Paper Rate (Percent) (1)	Rate on Municipal High-grade Bonds (Percent) (2)	S&P Stock Index: Industrials (1941-43 =10) (3)	S&P Stock Index: Total (1941-43 =10) (4)	Railroad Freight Revenue Per Ton (Dollars) (5)	Railroad Freight Revenue Per Ton-Mile (Cents) (6)	Nonfarm Output Per Worker-Hour (1958 =100) (7)	Average Annual Earnings: Manufacturing (Dollars) (8)	Average Annual Earnings: Trade (Dollars) (9)	Wholesale Price Index: All Goods (1967 =100) (10)
1923	5.07	4.25	6.54	8.57	3.40	1.132	47.5	1,403	1,272	51.9
1924	3.98	4.20	6.83	9.05	3.45	1.132	50.5	1,427	1,314	50.5
1925	4.02	4.09	8.69	11.15	3.44	1.114	50.1	1,450	1,359	53.3
1926	4.34	4.08	10.04	12.59	3.41	1.096	51.4	1,476	1,416	51.6
1927	4.11	3.98	12.53	15.34	3.45	1.095	51.6	1,502	1,480	49.3
1928	4.85	4.05	16.92	19.95	3.48	1.094	52.0	1,534	1,573	50.0
1929	5.85	4.27	21.35	26.02	3.45	1.088	54.1	1,543	1,594	49.1
1930	3.59	4.07	16.42	21.03	3.40	1.074	52.5	1,488	1,569	44.6
1931	2.64	4.01	10.51	13.66	3.50	1.062	53.3	1,369	1,495	37.6
1932	2.73	4.65	5.37	6.93	3.66	1.056	51.6	1,150	1,315	33.6
1933	1.73	4.71	7.61	8.96	3.45	1.009	50.4	1,086	1,183	34.0

Table C.2, continued

Year	4- to 6-Month Commercial Paper Rate (Percent) (1)	Rate on Municipal High-grade Bonds (Percent) (2)	S&P Stock Index: Industrials (1941-43 =10) (3)	S&P Stock Index: Total (1941-43 =10) (4)	Railroad Freight Revenue Per Ton (Dollars) (5)	Railroad Freight Revenue Per Ton-Mile (Cents) (6)	Nonfarm Output Per Worker-Hour (1958 =100) (7)	Average Annual Earnings: Manufacturing (Dollars) (8)	Average Annual Earnings: Trade (Dollars) (9)	Wholesale Price Index: All Goods (1967 =100) (10)
1934	1.02	4.03	9.00	9.84	3.33	0.989	55.9	1,153	1,228	38.6
1935	0.75	3.40	10.13	10.60	3.40	0.998	57.7	1,216	1,279	41.3
1936	0.75	3.07	14.69	15.47	3.32	0.984	60.2	1,287	1,295	41.7
1937	0.94	3.10	14.97	15.41	3.19	0.945	59.7	1,376	1,352	44.5
1938	0.81	2.91	11.39	11.49	3.54	0.994	61.4	1,296	1,352	40.5
1939	0.59	2.76	11.77	12.06	3.45	0.983	63.6	1,363	1,360	39.8
1940	0.56	2.50	10.69	11.02	3.35	0.955	66.1	1,432	1,382	40.5
1941	0.53	2.10	9.72	9.82	3.48	0.944	67.2	1,653	1,478	45.1
1942	0.66	2.36	8.78	8.67	4.02	0.940	66.7	2,023	1,608	50.9
1943	0.69	2.06	11.49	11.50	4.41	0.940	67.4	2,349	1,781	53.3
1944	0.73	1.86	12.34	12.47	4.53	0.957	72.7	2,517	1,946	53.6

306

Table C.2, continued

Year	4- to 6-Month Commercial Paper Rate (Percent) (1)	Rate on Municipal High-grade Bonds (Percent) (2)	S&P Stock Index: Industrials (1941-43 =10) (3)	S&P Stock Index: Total (1941-43 =10) (4)	Railroad Freight Revenue Per Ton (Dollars) (5)	Railroad Freight Revenue Per Ton-Mile (Cents) (6)	Nonfarm Output Per Worker-Hour (1958 =100) (7)	Average Annual Earnings: Manufacturing (Dollars) (8)	Average Annual Earnings: Trade (Dollars) (9)	Wholesale Price Index: All Goods (1967 =100) (10)
1945	0.75	1.67	14.72	15.16	4.43	0.967	76.8	2,517	2,114	54.6
1946	0.81	1.64	16.48	17.08	4.10	0.986	73.3	2,517	2,378	62.3
1947	1.03	2.01	14.85	15.17	4.43	1.085	72.8	2,793	2,632	76.5
1948	1.44	2.40	15.34	15.53	5.12	1.262	74.8	3,037	2,824	82.8
1949	1.49	2.21	15.00	15.23	5.57	1.352	78.4	3,107	2,899	78.7
1950	1.45	1.98	18.33	18.40	5.58	1.341	83.8	3,330	3,045	81.8
1951	2.16	2.00	22.68	22.34	5.66	1.348	85.1	3,652	3,178	91.1
1952	2.33	2.19	24.78	24.50	6.16	1.443	85.6	3,894	3,298	88.6
1953	2.52	2.72	24.84	24.73	6.27	1.491	88.8	4,133	3,470	87.4
1954	1.58	2.37	30.25	29.69	6.19	1.433	91.2	4,224	3,595	87.6
1955	2.18	2.53	42.40	40.49	5.94	1.382	95.9	4,481	3,755	87.8

Table C.2, continued

Year	4- to 6-Month Commercial Paper Rate (Percent) (1)	Rate on Municipal High-grade Bonds (Percent) (2)	S&P Stock Index: Industrials (1941-43 = 10) (3)	S&P Stock Index: Total (1941-43 = 10) (4)	Railroad Freight Revenue Per Ton (Dollars) (5)	Railroad Freight Revenue Per Ton-Mile (Cents) (6)	Nonfarm Output Per Worker-Hour (1958 = 100) (7)	Average Annual Earnings: Manufacturing (Dollars) (8)	Average Annual Earnings: Trade (Dollars) (9)	Wholesale Price Index: All Goods (1967 = 100) (10)
1956	3.31	2.93	49.80	46.62	5.97	1.396	95.6	4,739	3,936	90.7
1957	3.81	3.60	47.63	44.38	6.26	1.457	97.6	4,928	4,109	93.3
1958	2.46	3.56	49.36	46.24	6.57	1.477	100.0	5,148	4,246	94.6
1959	3.97	3.95	61.45	57.38	6.53	1.459	103.5	5,413	4,442	94.8
1960	3.85	3.73	59.43	55.85	6.26	1.417	104.7	5,545	4,597	94.9
1961	2.97	3.46	69.99	66.27	6.27	1.388	107.8	5,701	4,719	94.5
1962	3.26	3.18	65.54	62.38	6.27	1.362	113.0	5,916	4,894	94.8
1963	3.55	3.23	73.39	69.87	6.14	1.323	116.3	6,111	5,071	94.5
1964	3.97	3.22	86.19	81.37	6.04	1.295	120.3	6,417	5,261	94.7
1965	4.38	3.27	93.48	88.17	6.11	1.281	123.8	6,564	5,436	96.6
1966	5.55	3.82	91.09	85.26	6.15	1.271	127.1	6,801	5,636	99.8
1967	5.10	3.98	99.18	91.93	6.23	1.283	128.1	7,044	5,870	100.0

308

Table C.2, continued

Year	4- to 6-Month Commercial Paper Rate (Percent) (1)	Rate on Municipal High-grade Bonds (Percent) (2)	S&P Stock Index: Industrials (1941-43 =10) (3)	S&P Stock Index: Total (1941-43 =10) (4)	Railroad Freight Revenue Per Ton (Dollars) (5)	Railroad Freight Revenue Per Ton-Mile (Cents) (6)	Nonfarm Output Per Worker-Hour (1958 =100) (7)	Average Annual Earnings: Manufacturing (Dollars) (8)	Average Annual Earnings: Trade (Dollars) (9)	Wholesale Price Index: All Goods (1967 =100) (10)
1968	5.90	4.51	107.49	98.70	6.56	1.325	131.5	7,534	6,206	102.5
1969	7.83	5.81	107.13	97.84	6.77	1.362	130.9	7,970	6,540	106.5
1970	7.71	6.51	91.29	83.22	7.08	1.443	131.2	8,378	6,886	110.4
1971	5.11	5.70	108.35	98.29	8.15	1.608	135.2	8,883	7,243	114.0
1972	4.73	5.27	121.79	109.20	8.35	1.634	139.5	9,450	7,679	119.1
1973	8.15	5.18	120.44	107.43	8.67	1.632	142.0	10,027	8,080	134.7
1974	9.84	6.09	92.91	82.84	9.88	1.876	138.9	10,843	8,748	160.1
1975	6.32	6.89	96.56	87.17	10.63	2.060	141.4	11,899	9,381	174.9
1976	5.34	6.49	114.35	102.01	11.96	2.214	145.1	12,835	9,959	183.0
1977	5.61	5.56	108.40	98.20	12.66	2.306	147.3	13,859	10,518	194.2
1978	7.99	5.90	106.20	96.02	14.40	2.374	148.5	14,940	11,211	209.3
1979	10.91	6.39	114.80	103.01	15.49	2.608	146.1	16,252	12,143	235.6

Table C.2, continued

Year	4- to 6-Month Commercial Paper Rate (Percent) (1)	Rate on Municipal High-grade Bonds (Percent) (2)	S&P Stock Index: Industrials (1941-43 =10) (3)	S&P Stock Index: Total (1941-43 =10) (4)	Railroad Freight Revenue Per Ton (Dollars) (5)	Railroad Freight Revenue Per Ton-Mile (Cents) (6)	Nonfarm Output Per Worker-Hour (1958 =100) (7)	Average Annual Earnings: Manufacturing (Dollars) (8)	Average Annual Earnings: Trade (Dollars) (9)	Wholesale Price Index: All Goods (1967 =100) (10)
1980	12.29	8.51	134.50	118.78	17.42	2.869	145.5	17,954	13,274	268.8
1981	14.76	11.23	144.20	128.05	19.75	3.197	147.0	19,598	14,289	293.4
1982	11.89	11.57	133.60	119.71	20.03	3.231	146.1	21,044	15,108	299.3
1983	8.89	9.47	180.50	160.41	19.82	3.138	151.1	22,150	15,696	303.1

Sources: Column 1: Prime commercial paper, 4 to 6 months. 1900-1970, U.S. Bureau of the Census, *Historical Statistics,* Ser. X445; 1971-83, U.S. Office of the President, *Economic Report of the President 1986,* table B68, col. 9, p. 332.

Column 2: Municipal high-grade bonds. 1900-1970, U.S. Bureau of the Census, *Historical Statistics,* Ser. X475; 1971-83, U.S. Office of the President, *Economic Report of the President 1986,* table B68, col. 7, p. 332.

Column 3: Standard and Poor's index of common stocks: industrials. 1900-1970, U.S. Bureau of the Census, *Historical Statistics,* Ser. X496; 1971-73, U.S. Bureau of the Census, *Statistical Abstract 1974,* table 756, p. 465, line 5; 1974-83, U.S. Bureau of the Census, *Statistical Abstract 1985,* table 851, p. 506, line 6.

Column 4: Standard and Poor's index of common stocks: total. 1900-1970, U.S. Bureau of the Census, *Historical Statistics,* Ser. X495; 1971-83, U.S. Office of the President, *Economic Report of the President 1986,* (Washington 1987), table B91, col. 7, p. 358.

Column 5: Railroad freight revenue per ton. Total railroad freight revenue divided by revenue-tons originated. 1900-1970, U.S. Bureau of the Census, *Historical Statistics,* Ser. Q344; 1971-72, U.S. Bureau of the Census, *Statistical Abstract 1974,* table 953,

Table C.2, continued

pp. 33 and 34, line 568; 1973-74, U.S. Bureau of the Census, *Statistical Abstract 1976*, table 1012, p. 604, lines 35 and 36; 1975-78, U.S. Bureau of the Census, *Statistical Abstract 1980*, table 1140, p. 660, lines 35 and 36; 1979-80, U.S. Bureau of the Census, *Statistical Abstract 1982/83*, table 1088, p. 626, lines 36 and 37; 1981-83, 1980 estimate linked to estimates for Class I Railroads only in U.S. Bureau of the Census, *Statistical Abstract 1985*, table 1061, p. 608, line 39 divided by line 40.

Column 6: Railroad freight revenue per ton-mile. 1900-1970, U.S. Bureau of the Census, *Historical Statistics*, Ser. Q345; 1971, U.S. Bureau of the Census, *Statistical Abstract 1974*, table 953, p. 568, line 37; 1972-1974, U.S. Bureau of the Census, *Statistical Abstract 1977*, table 1083, p. 647, line 39; 1975-78, U.S. Bureau of the Census, *Statistical Abstract 1980*, table 1140, p. 660, line 39; 1979-80, U.S. Bureau of the Census, *Statistical Abstract 1982/83*, table 1088, p. 626, line 40; 1981-83, 1980 estimate linked to estimates for Class I Railroads only in U.S. Bureau of the Census, *Statistical Abstract 1985*, table 1061, p. 608, line 43.

Column 7: NBER Index of nonfarm output per worker-hour. 1900-1970, U.S. Bureau of the Census, *Historical Statistics*, Ser. D684; 1971-83, U.S. Office of the President, *Economic Report of the President 1986*, Table B43, col. 2, p. 302 divided by 0.679 to convert to 1958 base.

Column 8: Average annual earnings per full-time employee: manufacturing. 1900-1970, U.S. Bureau of the Census, *Historical Statistics*, Ser. D740; 1971-82, U.S. BEA, *National Income and Product Accounts, 1929-82*, table 6.8B, line 13, pp. 279-81; 1983, *Survey of Current Business* (July 1987) table 6.8B, line 13, p. 61.

Column 9: Average annual earnings per full-time employee: wholesale and retail trade. 1900-1970, U.S. Bureau of the Census, *Historical Statistics*, Ser. D753; 1971-82, values are annual wages and salaries in wholesale and retail trade, divided by annual full-time equivalent employees in wholesale and retail trade. Linked to *Historical Statistics* series at 1970. U.S. BEA, *National Income and Product Accounts, 1929-82*, table 6.5B, sum of lines 50 and 51, pp. 267-69 divided by table 6.7B, sum of lines 50 and 51, pp. 276-77; 1983, *Survey of Current Business* (July 1987) table 6.5B, sum of lines 50 and 51, p. 59, divided by table 6.7B, sum of lines 50 and 51, p. 60.

Column 10: Wholesale price index (Bureau of Labor Statistics--BLS): all commodities. 1900-1970, U.S. Bureau of the Census, *Historical Statistics*, Ser. E23; 1971-73, U.S. Bureau of the Census, *Statistical Abstract 1977*, table 763, p. 472, col. 1; 1974-83, U.S. Office of the President, *Economic Report of the President 1986*.

REGRESSION RESULTS

The estimated demand equation is:

$$\frac{N_t}{H_t} = A_0 + A_1 p_t + A_2 \frac{Y_t}{H_t} + A_3 \frac{W_t}{H_t} + A_4 \frac{\Delta H_t}{H_t} + A_5 \frac{S_{t-1}}{H_t}$$

$$+ A_6 DUMWW1 + A_7 DUMWW2 + e_t \qquad (C.22)$$

where $e_t = (RHO)e_{t-1} + v_t$ and, by assumption, v_t is a serially independent random variable distributed normally with mean zero and constant
variance. All regressions were run using MicroTSP, version 6.0. For each
commodity group, the equation is estimated for six periods: pre–World
War I (1902–19), interwar (1920–41), post–World War II (1947–83), combined post–World War I (1920–83), combined pre–World War II (1902–41),
and full sample periods (1902–83). The regression results are presented in
tables C.3 through C.18. Standard errors are in parentheses. Whether an
estimated coefficient is significantly different from zero is denoted in the
tables with asterisks (*). All regressions were run both with and without
the household formation rate variable. A weak standard was applied; the
reported results include this variable if its estimated coefficient is at least
as large as its standard error. For the borderline cases (those where the t-
statistic is in the neighborhood of 1), inclusion or exclusion of this variable does not alter the qualitative results.

F-TEST RESULTS

An F-test comparing the standard errors of the estimated regressions (SEE)
is used to test a hypothesis of stability of the entire demand relationship
between two periods. For comparisons of the pre–World War I and interwar
periods and of the pre–World War I and post–World War I periods, the F-
statistic is calculated as

$$F_{k,\,n-2k} =$$

$$\left(\frac{(SEE_{\text{periods 1 \& 2 combined}})^2 (n-k)}{(SEE_{\text{period 1}})^2 (n_1 - k) + (SEE_{\text{period 2}})^2 (n_2 - k)} - 1 \right) \frac{n-2k}{k}$$

$$(C.23)$$

where n_1 is the number of observations in subperiod 1, n_2 is the number of observations in subperiod 2, n (which equals $n_1 + n_2$) is the number of observations in periods 1 and 2 combined, and k is the number of regressors in each estimated equation.[6] The pre–World War I period was the base period for each of these two comparisons: if the household formation rate variable was included in the pre–World War I regression, it was also included in the regressions for the interwar and full pre–World War II periods, and only if the Cochrane-Orcutt correction procedure was needed for the pre–World War I regression was it used for the regressions for the other two periods.

For comparison of the interwar and post–World War II periods, a slightly weaker form of the F-test is used. Here, the F-statistic is

$$F_{n_2, n_1 - k} = \left(\frac{(\text{SEE}_{\text{combined periods}})^2 (n - k)}{(\text{SEE}_{\text{period 1}})^2 (n_1 - k)} - 1 \right) \frac{n_1 - k}{n_2}$$
(C.24)

where n_1 is the number of observations in subperiod 1, n_2 is the number of observations in *un*estimated subperiod 2, n (which equals $n_1 + n_2$) is the number of observations in periods 1 and 2 combined, and k is the number of regressors in each estimated equation. Here, the post–World War II period was designated the base period. If the household formation rate variable entered the post–World War II equation, it was also used for the post–World War I regression. Similarly, if the Cochrane-Orcutt procedure was needed for the post–World War II regression, it was also used for the post–World War I regression. The calculated F-statistics are in table C.19.

Table C.3. Estimated Coefficients: Automobiles and Parts (Standard Errors in Parentheses)

Independent Variable	1902-1919	1920-1941	1947-1983	1902-1941	1920-1983	1902-1983
Constant	66.9** (26.1)	-512.5 (364.9)	-1036.8* (553.2)	-464.0*** (154.2)	-530.6 (440.7)	-579.4*** (160.6)
Relative Price	0.001 (0.007)	0.19 (1.13)	0.43 (1.99)	-0.14* (0.08)	-0.32 (1.40)	-0.31*** (0.11)
Disposable Income	5.24** (1.92)	41.7*** (10.6)	102.9*** (30.0)	7.81 (12.4)	43.4*** (13.8)	36.7*** (10.3)
Net Wealth	-1.48*** (0.44)	0.89 (2.51)	1.85 (3.16)	3.20 (1.91)	3.19 (2.27)	4.73** (2.31)
Household Formation	-16.0 (9.0)			114.1** (52.1)		
Lagged Stock	0.44*** (0.03)	-0.15* (0.08)	-0.50*** (0.17)	-0.03 (0.05)	-0.22*** (0.05)	-0.20*** (0.04)
DUMWW1	-39.0*** (3.4)			28.9 (22.2)		-64.4** (26.7)
DUMWW2					-460.1*** (76.7)	-381.0*** (68.8)
RHO	-0.22 (0.35)	0.39 (0.35)	0.64*** (0.14)	0.49*** (0.18)	0.49*** (0.12)	0.55*** (0.10)
Adjusted R^2	0.98	0.79	0.61	0.66	0.73	0.71
SEE	4.74	37.36	61.06	37.63	65.83	65.61
Durbin-Watson	2.08	2.16	2.05	2.02	1.93	1.92
Mean Net Exp. per Household	26.5	55.8	198.8	42.6	127.8	105.6
Mean Gross Exp. per Household	44.0	262.6	798.7	164.3	555.6	443.3
Price Elasticity	0.01 (0.09)	0.13 (0.78)	0.07 (0.34)	-0.32* (0.17)	-0.09 (0.39)	-0.17*** (0.06)
Income Elasticity	1.61** (0.59)	2.35*** (0.60)	3.01*** (0.88)	0.68 (1.08)	1.57*** (0.50)	1.55*** (0.43)

*Statistically significant at the 90 percent level of confidence.
**Statistically significant at the 95 percent level of confidence.
***Statistically significant at the 99 percent level of confidence.

Table C.4. Estimated Coefficients: Transportation Vehicles (Standard Errors in Parentheses)

Independent Variable	1902-1919	1920-1941	1947-1983	1902-1941	1920-1983	1902-1983
Constant	-53.3 (65.8)	-562.5 (371.3)	-993.3 (605.9)	-660.5*** (200.7)	-68.0 (452.3)	-549.9*** (174.0)
Relative Price	0.13* (0.06)	0.22 (1.19)	-0.57 (2.45)	0.32 (0.43)	-2.28 (1.56)	-0.29 (0.38)
Disposable Income	10.1** (4.1)	43.8*** (10.7)	118.3*** (34.6)	15.3 (11.5)	43.3*** (14.6)	37.7*** (9.5)
Net Wealth	-2.34** (1.04)	1.06 (2.52)	-2.67 (3.92)	2.33 (1.80)	1.29 (2.56)	2.35 (1.81)
Household Formation	-32.4* (17.0)			110.8** (52.4)		15.6 (13.8)
Lagged Stock	0.68*** (0.09)	-0.14* (0.08)	-0.37*** (0.13)	0.03 (0.06)	-0.18*** (0.04)	-0.12*** (0.03)
DUMWW1	-53.2*** (8.5)			25.7 (23.2)		-16.7 (20.0)
DUMWW2					-471.7*** (84.5)	-312.5*** (57.0)
RHO	0.36 (0.34)	0.34 (0.35)	0.57*** (0.15)	0.66*** (0.18)	0.39*** (0.13)	0.58*** (0.10)
Adjusted R^2	0.90	0.78	0.55	0.64	0.70	0.77
SEE	9.86	38.04	79.38	39.36	81.96	68.73
Durbin-Watson	1.88	2.15	1.65	2.02	1.76	1.75
Mean Net Exp. per Household	21.5	56.0	234.3	40.5	148.3	120.5
Mean Gross Exp. per Household	74.5	273.1	907.4	183.7	622.7	502.3
Price Elasticity	0.38* (0.18)	0.15 (0.79)	-0.08 (0.37)	0.34 (0.46)	-0.56 (0.38)	-0.10 (0.13)
Income Elasticity	1.84** (0.74)	2.38*** (0.58)	3.05*** (0.89)	1.18 (0.90)	1.40*** (0.47)	1.40*** (0.35)

*Statistically significant at the 90 percent level of confidence.
**Statistically significant at the 95 percent level of confidence.
***Statistically significant at the 99 percent level of confidence.

Table C.5. Estimated Coefficients: Furniture (Standard Errors in Parentheses)

Independent Variable	1902-1919	1920-1941	1947-1983	1902-1941	1920-1983	1902-1983
Constant	-16.1	-152.5*	339.2**	-39.0	190.8*	172.4
	(123.4)	(71.8)	(148.7)	(93.9)	(106.7)	(105.7)
Relative Price	-2.39***	-1.34**	-1.78**	-1.56***	-1.08**	-1.06***
	(0.30)	(0.52)	(0.73)	(0.36)	(0.48)	(0.40)
Disposable Income	14.8***	20.0***	19.4***	13.7***	17.6***	15.3***
	(2.5)	(3.8)	(3.6)	(2.8)	(3.5)	(3.2)
Net Wealth	3.14***	-0.61	0.018	0.60	-0.31	0.36
	(0.80)	(0.70)	(0.396)	(0.52)	(0.45)	(0.47)
Household Formation	39.8***	34.0**		41.0***	5.03	4.23
	(8.6)	(13.3)		(10.1)	(3.46)	(3.71)
Lagged Stock	-0.17**	0.01	-0.36***	-0.07	-0.27***	-0.27***
	(0.07)	(0.03)	(0.07)	(0.04)	(0.06)	(0.05)
DUMWW1	4.41			5.56		-21.8
	(10.77)			(15.57)		(14.5)
DUMWW2					-38.5**	-34.8***
					(14.7)	(12.9)
RHO	0.73**	0.26	0.63***	0.71***	0.92***	0.95***
	(0.25)	(0.27)	(0.15)	(0.15)	(0.06)	(0.03)
Adjusted R^2	0.92	0.90	0.74	0.87	0.85	0.82
SEE	8.67	12.17	7.71	12.55	12.99	13.86
Durbin-Watson	1.27	1.83	1.72	1.57	1.64	1.97
Mean Net Exp. per Household	20.8	14.2	52.8	17.2	35.2	32.0
Mean Gross Exp. per Household	218.3	182.9	242.3	198.9	214.2	215.1
Price Elasticity	-0.99***	-0.87**	-0.93**	-0.82***	-0.63**	-0.58***
	(0.12)	(0.34)	(0.38)	(0.19)	(0.28)	(0.22)
Income Elasticity	0.92***	1.62***	1.87***	0.98***	1.65***	1.33***
	(0.16)	(0.31)	(0.35)	(0.20)	(0.33)	(0.28)

*Statistically significant at the 90 percent level of confidence.
**Statistically significant at the 95 percent level of confidence.
***Statistically significant at the 99 percent level of confidence.

Table C.6. Estimated Coefficients: Household Appliances (Standard Errors in Parentheses)

Independent Variable	1902- 1919	1920- 1941	1947- 1983	1902- 1941	1920- 1983	1902- 1983
Constant	46.2* (22.6)	41.8 (25.3)	-156.2 (126.4)	-22.4 (16.3)	21.3 (59.5)	95.9 (62.6)
Relative Price	-0.023 (0.049)	-0.27*** (0.04)	0.16 (0.28)	-0.20*** (0.04)	-0.32*** (0.11)	-0.47*** (0.14)
Disposable Income	2.00*** (0.50)	4.18*** (0.78)	14.4*** (2.3)	3.44*** (0.71)	7.78*** (2.32)	3.63 (2.41)
Net Wealth	0.26* (0.12)	0.14 (0.14)	-0.67 (0.58)	0.21* (0.13)	-0.11 (0.34)	0.30 (0.33)
Household Formation		4.00 (2.77)	4.37* (2.55)	5.53* (2.81)	9.69** (4.09)	5.34* (3.10)
Lagged Stock	-0.58*** (0.18)	-0.12* (0.06)	-0.13*** (0.04)	0.08* (0.05)	-0.15*** (0.03)	-0.14*** (0.04)
DUMWW1	11.09*** (2.70)			-2.05 (4.39)		-31.4*** (10.9)
DUMWW2					-63.6*** (12.8)	-39.3*** (10.8)
RHO	0.78*** (0.14)	0.57*** (0.14)	0.10 (0.15)	0.69*** (0.14)	0.50*** (0.13)	0.82*** (0.08)
Adjusted R^2	0.68	0.92	0.71	0.79	0.80	0.81
SEE	1.74	2.51	8.11	3.17	10.60	10.06
Durbin- Watson	2.18	1.78	1.38	1.85	2.07	2.02
Mean Net Exp. per Household	6.0	8.6	42.6	7.4	26.8	22.2
Mean Gross Exp. per Household	28.7	42.8	169.2	36.5	114.8	95.9
Price Elasticity	-0.21 (0.45)	-2.05*** (0.28)	0.16 (0.28)	-1.64*** (0.33)	-0.64*** (0.23)	-1.18*** (0.35)
Income Elasticity	0.94*** (0.24)	1.45*** (0.27)	1.99*** (0.32)	1.34*** (0.28)	1.36*** (0.41)	0.71 (0.47)

*Statistically significant at the 90 percent level of confidence.
**Statistically significant at the 95 percent level of confidence.
***Statistically significant at the 99 percent level of confidence.

Table C.7. Estimated Coefficients: Radios and Musical Instruments
(Standard Errors in Parentheses)

Independent Variable	1902-1919	1920-1941	1947-1983	1902-1941	1920-1983	1902-1983
Constant	-13.2 (8.4)	-50.4** (20.5)	-188.7* (107.4)	-25.8*** (7.4)	-62.5** (27.5)	-44.0* (22.5)
Relative Price	-0.008 (0.005)	-0.006 (0.004)	0.13 (0.13)	-0.006 (0.004)	0.01 (0.02)	0.006 (0.013)
Disposable Income	0.74*** (0.23)	2.03** (0.77)	4.24 (3.85)	1.53*** (0.38)	0.79 (1.68)	0.57 (1.33)
Net Wealth	0.16* (0.08)	0.16 (0.13)	0.58 (0.42)	0.13 (0.08)	0.50* (0.28)	0.38 (0.23)
Household Formation	2.60** (0.90)	3.63 (3.63)	-2.69 (1.75)	2.48 (1.81)		
Lagged Stock	-0.12 (0.17)	0.12 (0.22)	0.08** (0.04)	-0.07 (0.07)	0.07*** (0.02)	0.07*** (0.02)
DUMWW1	2.23* (1.21)			2.22 (2.28)		-5.70 (6.86)
DUMWW2					-11.1 (7.6)	-10.6* (6.1)
RHO	0.75*** (0.23)	0.39 (0.27)	0.85*** (0.13)	0.62*** (0.16)	0.78*** (0.10)	0.78*** (0.09)
Adjusted R^2	0.62	0.73	0.92	0.69	0.93	0.94
SEE	0.80	1.98	7.71	1.65	7.34	6.45
Durbin-Watson	1.89	2.43	1.17	2.01	1.41	1.40
Mean Net Exp. per Household	2.3	2.5	40.7	2.4	24.5	19.6
Mean Gross Exp. per Household	9.8	15.8	132.8	13.1	83.6	67.4
Price Elasticity	-0.70 (0.49)	-0.27 (0.18)	0.26 (0.26)	-0.34 (0.23)	0.06 (0.09)	0.05 (0.11)
Income Elasticity	1.02*** (0.32)	1.91** (0.72)	0.75 (0.68)	1.66*** (0.41)	0.19 (0.40)	0.16 (0.37)

*Statistically significant at the 90 percent level of confidence.
**Statistically significant at the 95 percent level of confidence.
***Statistically significant at the 99 percent level of confidence.

Table C.8. Estimated Coefficients: Radios and Phonographs (Standard Errors in Parentheses)

Independent Variable	1902-1919	1920-1941	1947-1983	1902-1941	1920-1983	1902-1983
Constant	-5.81** (2.39)	-35.9*** (7.4)		-25.5*** (5.4)		
Relative Price	-0.005 (0.003)	-0.004 (0.005)		-0.003 (0.004)		
Disposable Income	0.05 (0.11)	2.27*** (0.46)		1.46*** (0.33)		
Net Wealth	0.09* (0.05)	0.09 (0.10)		0.13 (0.09)		
Household Formation	1.22** (0.42)					
Lagged Stock	0.32** (0.14)	0.02 (0.11)		-0.03 (0.07)		
DUMWW1	0.44 (0.60)			1.83 (2.24)		
DUMWW2						
RHO	0.80*** (0.20)	0.28 (0.25)		0.51*** (0.16)		
Adjusted R^2	0.92	0.67		0.64		
SEE	0.35	1.95		1.68		
Durbin-Watson	1.64	2.06		1.95		
Mean Net Exp. per Household	1.2	3.0		2.2		
Mean Gross Exp. per Household	2.8	12.3		8.0		
Price Elasticity	-1.49 (0.94)	-0.22 (0.28)		-0.27 (0.45)		
Income Elasticity	0.25 (0.50)	2.73*** (0.55)		2.59*** (0.59)		

*Statistically significant at the 90 percent level of confidence.
**Statistically significant at the 95 percent level of confidence.
***Statistically significant at the 99 percent level of confidence.

Table C.9. Estimated Coefficients: Pianos and Other Musical Instruments (Standard Errors in Parentheses)

Independent Variable	1902-1919	1920-1941	1947-1983	1902-1941	1920-1983	1902-1983
Constant	2.82 (2.37)	-4.2 (3.4)		6.6* (3.9)		
Relative Price	-0.005** (0.002)	-0.004*** (0.001)		0.002 (0.001)		
Disposable Income	0.60*** (0.13)	0.58*** (0.16)		0.18 (0.22)		
Net Wealth	-0.008 (0.032)	-0.06 (0.04)		-0.11* (0.06)		
Household Formation	2.05*** (0.42)	0.72 (0.56)		0.90 (0.97)		
Lagged Stock	-0.30*** (0.06)	0.05 (0.04)		-0.13** (0.05)		
DUMWW1	0.19 (0.45)			1.37 (1.10)		
DUMWW2						
RHO	-0.05 (0.30)	-0.14 (0.28)		0.06 (0.23)		
Adjusted R^2	0.86	0.84		0.67		
SEE	0.35	0.48		0.77		
Durbin-Watson	2.21	2.11		1.96		
Mean Net Exp. per Household	1.1	-0.5		0.2		
Mean Gross Exp. per Household	7.0	3.5		5.1		
Price Elasticity	-0.58** (0.22)	-0.87*** (0.28)		0.33 (0.22)		
Income Elasticity	1.16*** (0.25)	2.49*** (0.67)		0.52 (0.62)		

*Statistically significant at the 90 percent level of confidence.
**Statistically significant at the 95 percent level of confidence.
***Statistically significant at the 99 percent level of confidence.

Table C.10. Estimated Coefficients: China and Tableware (Standard Errors in Parentheses)

Independent Variable	1902-1919	1920-1941	1947-1983	1902-1941	1920-1983	1902-1983
Constant	455.0**	337.8***	1.56	566.4***	385.3***	502.6***
	(196.7)	(109.3)	(72.54)	(108.4)	(61.6)	(67.2)
Relative Price	-3.42**	-2.96***	-1.37***	-3.73***	-3.10***	-3.81***
	(1.27)	(0.68)	(0.37)	(0.56)	(0.57)	(0.56)
Disposable Income	8.22*	3.77*	6.39***	1.02	4.36***	5.62***
	(3.81)	(2.13)	(1.67)	(2.80)	(1.40)	(1.60)
Net Wealth	-1.56	-0.05	0.12	-0.78	-0.32	-0.66
	(0.93)	(0.38)	(0.20)	(0.58)	(0.36)	(0.40)
Household Formation	36.1**		1.33	9.44	6.15*	7.70*
	(12.9)		(0.87)	(11.14)	(3.51)	(4.19)
Lagged Stock	-0.35**	-0.21***	-0.09	-0.33***	-0.26***	-0.34***
	(0.12)	(0.04)	(0.06)	(0.06)	(0.06)	(0.05)
DUMWW1	26.3			14.7		22.8
	(15.8)			(16.9)		(14.9)
DUMWW2					-16.8	-26.2**
					(10.5)	(12.0)
RHO	0.52	0.04	0.92***	0.56***	0.59***	0.63***
	(0.40)	(0.28)	(0.04)	(0.17)	(0.15)	(0.11)
Adjusted R^2	0.82	0.73	0.95	0.80	0.76	0.76
SEE	11.46	10.95	4.04	12.83	10.24	11.83
Durbin-Watson	1.56	1.92	1.18	1.83	1.90	1.82
Mean Net Exp. per Household	31.1	-1.2	14.2	13.3	8.9	13.8
Mean Gross Exp. per Household	175.8	122.0	133.2	146.2	128.2	138.7
Price Elasticity	-1.42**	-2.16***	-0.97***	-2.09***	-2.23***	-2.42***
	(0.52)	(0.50)	(0.26)	(0.32)	(0.41)	(0.36)
Income Elasticity	0.63*	0.46*	1.12***	0.10	0.68***	0.76***
	(0.29)	(0.26)	(0.29)	(0.27)	(0.22)	(0.22)

*Statistically significant at the 90 percent level of confidence.
**Statistically significant at the 95 percent level of confidence.
***Statistically significant at the 99 percent level of confidence.

Table C.11. Estimated Coefficients: Durable House Furnishings (Standard Errors in Parentheses)

Independent Variable	1902-1919	1920-1941	1947-1983	1902-1941	1920-1983	1902-1983
Constant	705.6 (421.1)	-114.1** (40.8)	49.7 (167.4)	193.7** (94.6)	299.5*** (73.7)	268.5*** (61.9)
Relative Price	-1.21 (0.75)	-0.30 (0.21)	-0.65 (0.80)	-1.39*** (0.26)	-1.74*** (0.35)	-1.67*** (0.32)
Disposable Income	9.52** (4.11)	15.7*** (1.0)	11.7*** (4.1)	10.8*** (1.9)	12.5*** (2.3)	12.4*** (2.1)
Net Wealth	-2.48* (1.30)	-0.25 (0.15)	-0.15 (0.51)	0.18 (0.35)	-0.07 (0.34)	-0.06 (0.33)
Household Formation	35.3*** (10.5)			11.6 (7.5)		5.05* (2.97)
Lagged Stock	-0.81* (0.40)	-0.07*** (0.03)	-0.21* (0.11)	-0.29*** (0.09)	-0.35*** (0.05)	-0.33*** (0.05)
DUMWW1	-15.9 (19.7)			-2.76 (11.23)		-14.1 (11.1)
DUMWW2					-28.1*** (10.5)	-29.7*** (10.0)
RHO	0.29 (0.50)	-0.51** (0.18)	0.83*** (0.15)	0.79*** (0.13)	0.82*** (0.09)	0.79*** (0.08)
Adjusted R^2	0.72	0.91	0.77	0.80	0.85	0.83
SEE	9.33	6.42	9.16	8.59	9.48	9.89
Durbin-Watson	1.31	1.88	1.17	1.73	1.42	1.62
Mean Net Exp. per Household	10.7	7.9	38.1	9.2	25.7	22.4
Mean Gross Exp. per Household	153.9	128.6	209.7	140.0	175.0	170.3
Price Elasticity	-0.85 (0.53)	-0.35 (0.25)	-0.42 (0.52)	-1.31*** (0.25)	-1.44*** (0.28)	-1.34*** (0.26)
Income Elasticity	0.84** (0.36)	1.81*** (0.11)	1.30*** (0.46)	1.10*** (0.20)	1.44*** (0.27)	1.36*** (0.23)

*Statistically significant at the 90 percent level of confidence.
**Statistically significant at the 95 percent level of confidence.
***Statistically significant at the 99 percent level of confidence.

Table C.12. Estimated Coefficients: Jewelry and Watches (Standard Errors in Parentheses)

Independent Variable	1902-1919	1920-1941	1947-1983	1902-1941	1920-1983	1902-1983
Constant	5.19 (55.79)	-43.5* (21.2)	71.3 (109.6)	-49.9 (59.0)	-33.8 (40.0)	-21.5 (56.0)
Relative Price	-0.43*** (0.13)	-0.18*** (0.05)	-1.14** (0.45)	-0.12 (0.11)	-0.26** (0.11)	-0.28 (0.18)
Disposable Income	6.61*** (1.41)	6.98*** (0.73)	6.38** (3.07)	3.20** (1.44)	4.80*** (1.65)	4.00** (1.71)
Net Wealth	0.74* (0.35)	-0.18 (0.12)	-0.13 (0.34)	0.62** (0.27)	0.29 (0.23)	0.47* (0.25)
Household Formation	21.7*** (4.3)			9.66 (5.77)		
Lagged Stock	-0.33*** (0.07)	-0.03 (0.02)	-0.07** (0.04)	-0.13 (0.16)	-0.07** (0.03)	-0.08** (0.04)
DUMWW1	4.06 (5.76)			7.40 (8.94)		-4.81 (6.71)
DUMWW2					1.06 (6.50)	1.67 (7.10)
RHO	0.35 (0.32)	-0.06 (0.24)	0.87*** (0.05)	0.90*** (0.15)	0.91*** (0.06)	0.92*** (0.05)
Adjusted R^2	0.91	0.87	0.91	0.75	0.93	0.89
SEE	4.27	4.12	6.64	6.98	6.51	7.43
Durbin-Watson	1.74	1.90	1.50	2.32	1.34	1.91
Mean Net Exp. per Household	10.8	-0.8	32.3	4.4	20.2	18.1
Mean Gross Exp. per Household	60.7	41.1	120.1	49.9	88.3	82.2
Price Elasticity	-1.37*** (0.43)	-0.97*** (0.28)	-1.34** (0.53)	-0.50 (0.47)	-0.52** (0.23)	-0.61 (0.39)
Income Elasticity	1.47*** (0.31)	2.52*** (0.26)	1.24** (0.60)	0.91** (0.41)	1.10*** (0.38)	0.91** (0.39)

*Statistically significant at the 90 percent level of confidence.
**Statistically significant at the 95 percent level of confidence.
***Statistically significant at the 99 percent level of confidence.

Table C.13. Estimated Coefficients: Orthopedic and Ophthalmic Products (Standard Errors in Parentheses)

Independent Variable	1902-1919	1920-1941	1947-1983	1902-1941	1920-1983	1902-1983
Constant	1.45 (14.16)	33.8 (30.1)	37.0 (26.7)	29.1** (14.0)	0.33 (9.05)	13.1 (11.8)
Relative Price	-0.001 (0.038)	-0.14*** (0.03)	-0.37 (0.22)	-0.13*** (0.04)	-0.07* (0.04)	-0.12** (0.05)
Disposable Income	0.20 (0.41)	0.52 (0.39)	2.69*** (0.77)	0.86** (0.41)	1.60*** (0.54)	1.79*** (0.55)
Net Wealth	0.01 (0.16)	-0.01 (0.06)	-0.14 (0.10)	-0.04 (0.09)	-0.05 (0.07)	-0.12 (0.08)
Household Formation	-2.83 (2.22)			-3.33*** (1.20)		
Lagged Stock	0.15 (0.09)	-0.17 (0.16)	-0.27** (0.10)	-0.14 (0.11)	-0.14*** (0.05)	-0.16*** (0.05)
DUMWW1	2.37** (0.60)			1.45*** (0.36)		1.23*** (0.44)
DUMWW2					-0.28 (1.95)	-0.27 (1.94)
RHO	0.55 (0.32)	0.97*** (0.14)	0.48** (0.19)	0.86*** (0.16)	0.63*** (0.12)	0.71*** (0.09)
Adjusted R^2	0.96	0.80	0.44	0.82	0.71	0.69
SEE	0.92	1.25	1.93	1.63	1.95	2.13
Durbin-Watson	1.52	1.70	2.08	1.65	2.03	1.86
Mean Net Exp. per Household	3.1	0.7	5.6	1.8	4.1	3.9
Mean Gross Exp. per Household	12.8	16.9	48.8	15.0	36.5	31.3
Price Elasticity	-0.02 (0.52)	-1.54*** (0.37)	-0.86 (0.52)	-1.59*** (0.52)	-0.26* (0.14)	-0.55** (0.24)
Income Elasticity	0.21 (0.44)	0.46 (0.34)	1.29*** (0.37)	0.81** (0.39)	0.88*** (0.30)	1.07*** (0.33)

*Statistically significant at the 90 percent level of confidence.
**Statistically significant at the 95 percent level of confidence.
***Statistically significant at the 99 percent level of confidence.

Table C.14. Estimated Coefficients: Books and Maps (Standard Errors in Parentheses)

Independent Variable	1902-1919	1920-1941	1947-1983	1902-1941	1920-1983	1902-1983
Constant	-10.7 (43.2)	0.6 (29.5)	42.0 (57.1)	-8.2 (35.7)	42.1* (22.9)	35.2* (19.5)
Relative Price	-0.23 (0.19)	-0.47** (0.22)	-0.19 (0.46)	-0.41** (0.18)	-0.36* (0.20)	-0.33 (0.20)
Disposable Income	-0.64 (1.18)	3.10*** (1.01)	5.55*** (1.44)	2.02** (0.83)	2.93** (1.12)	2.60*** (0.94)
Net Wealth	0.33 (0.32)	0.16 (0.16)	-0.38 (0.23)	0.36** (0.17)	-0.12 (0.17)	-0.02 (0.17)
Household Formation			-1.15 (1.04)	3.61 (3.48)		
Lagged Stock	0.07 (0.09)	-0.03 (0.05)	-0.29** (0.13)	-0.05 (0.06)	-0.15** (0.07)	-0.15** (0.06)
DUMWW1	-0.38 (3.55)			-4.98 (5.40)		-5.20 (4.94)
DUMWW2					3.62 (4.49)	2.55 (4.07)
RHO			0.86*** (0.16)	0.28 (0.17)	0.76*** (0.13)	0.74*** (0.12)
Adjusted R^2	0.18	0.75	0.64	0.60	0.74	0.74
SEE	3.18	3.67	4.35	3.70	4.59	4.38
Durbin-Watson	2.08	1.96	1.58	2.05	1.62	1.83
Mean Net Exp. per Household	2.5	3.0	10.1	2.8	8.7	7.4
Mean Gross Exp. per Household	55.6	48.6	80.3	51.8	68.7	65.8
Price Elasticity	-0.34 (0.28)	-1.00** (0.47)	-0.22 (0.54)	-0.75** (0.32)	-0.51* (0.28)	-0.46 (0.28)
Income Elasticity	-0.16 (0.29)	0.95*** (0.31)	1.62*** (0.42)	0.56** (0.23)	0.86** (0.33)	0.74*** (0.27)

*Statistically significant at the 90 percent level of confidence.
**Statistically significant at the 95 percent level of confidence.
***Statistically significant at the 99 percent level of confidence.

Table C.15. Estimated Coefficients: Miscellaneous Other Durables
(Standard Errors in Parentheses)

Independent Variable	1902-1919	1920-1941	1947-1983	1902-1941	1920-1983	1902-1983
Constant	52.1*** (14.0)	0.36 (12.65)	-580.2*** (209.5)	18.0 (13.7)	-43.7 (62.3)	-33.7 (51.1)
Relative Price	-0.15*** (0.03)	-0.05* (0.03)	2.05** (0.98)	-0.09*** (0.03)	-0.12 (0.18)	-0.07 (0.13)
Disposable Income	0.48 (0.60)	2.20*** (0.30)	17.1*** (4.0)	0.82 (0.55)	4.06** (2.01)	2.95* (1.71)
Net Wealth	-0.19 (0.13)	-0.13* (0.07)	-0.63 (0.52)	-0.03 (0.09)	0.16 (0.35)	0.14 (0.32)
Household Formation	8.85*** (2.13)			5.23** (2.18)		
Lagged Stock	-0.30*** (0.09)	-0.08 (0.10)	0.02 (0.05)	-0.17 (0.10)	-0.03 (0.03)	-0.01 (0.03)
DUMWW1	4.39* (2.38)			3.70 (2.54)		-6.95 (7.76)
DUMWW2					-11.9 (8.3)	-7.55 (7.11)
RHO	0.17 (0.30)	0.92*** (0.16)	0.53*** (0.16)	0.65*** (0.20)	0.79*** (0.11)	0.80*** (0.10)
Adjusted R^2	0.83	0.93	0.83	0.73	0.89	0.89
SEE	1.66	1.15	9.79	2.16	8.45	7.87
Durbin-Watson	2.27	1.89	1.75	1.77	1.49	1.62
Mean Net Exp. per Household	1.4	2.2	37.1	1.8	23.0	18.3
Mean Gross Exp. per Household	16.1	18.3	134.1	17.3	86.3	70.9
Price Elasticity	-2.53*** (0.46)	-0.58* (0.31)	2.08** (0.99)	-1.30*** (0.43)	-0.23 (0.35)	-0.18 (0.36)
Income Elasticity	0.40 (0.50)	1.78*** (0.24)	2.98*** (0.69)	0.67 (0.45)	0.95** (0.47)	0.78* (0.45)

*Statistically significant at the 90 percent level of confidence.
**Statistically significant at the 95 percent level of confidence.
***Statistically significant at the 99 percent level of confidence.

Table C.16. Estimated Coefficients: Major Durable Goods (Standard Errors in Parentheses)

Independent Variable	1902-1919	1920-1941	1947-1983	1902-1941	1920-1983	1902-1983
Constant	853.7*** (234.5)	-863.2** (301.1)	-187.5 (1030.4)	-825.1*** (196.4)	-576.9 (523.2)	-794.1*** (246.8)
Relative Price	-1.20*** (0.25)	1.15 (1.23)	-3.58 (4.06)	-0.07 (0.65)	-1.03 (2.17)	-0.74 (1.10)
Disposable Income	20.0** (6.5)	76.1*** (9.2)	134.9*** (35.2)	39.0*** (8.9)	83.3*** (14.4)	70.2*** (15.0)
Net Wealth	5.2** (1.8)	-0.34 (2.25)	-5.50 (4.42)	1.35 (1.68)	0.23 (2.82)	3.15 (3.07)
Household Formation	51.9** (18.4)			125.9*** (43.0)		44.3 (36.5)
Lagged Stock	-0.73*** (0.13)	-0.14** (0.06)	-0.25*** (0.08)	-0.002 (0.069)	-0.15*** (0.03)	-0.14*** (0.03)
DUMWW1	127.8*** (21.6)			76.3 (64.0)		-214.9** (105.4)
DUMWW2					-667.3*** (92.8)	-551.6*** (106.2)
RHO	0.25 (0.37)	0.35 (0.27)	0.49*** (0.16)	0.63*** (0.19)	0.38*** (0.13)	0.45*** (0.13)
Adjusted R^2	0.79	0.91	0.59	0.84	0.81	0.80
SEE	18.00	36.58	92.14	38.28	92.00	91.44
Durbin-Watson	1.86	1.84	1.55	1.66	1.78	1.84
Mean Net Exp. per Household	50.5	81.3	370.4	67.4	234.9	194.4
Mean Gross Exp. per Household	331.3	514.6	1451.8	432.1	1035.3	880.8
Price Elasticity	-0.57*** (0.12)	0.42 (0.45)	-0.36 (0.41)	-0.03 (0.26)	-0.16 (0.34)	-0.14 (0.20)
Income Elasticity	0.81** (0.27)	2.19*** (0.26)	2.17*** (0.57)	1.29*** (0.29)	1.62*** (0.28)	1.49*** (0.32)

*Statistically significant at the 90 percent level of confidence.
**Statistically significant at the 95 percent level of confidence.
***Statistically significant at the 99 percent level of confidence.

Table C.17. Estimated Coefficients: Minor Durable Goods (Standard Errors in Parentheses)

Independent Variable	1902-1919	1920-1941	1947-1983	1902-1941	1920-1983	1902-1983
Constant	719.5** (253.3)	133.7 (134.2)	-41.9 (555.6)	427.7** (186.8)	747.1*** (185.7)	749.1*** (175.2)
Relative Price	-4.72*** (1.22)	-3.33*** (0.70)	-4.27 (3.04)	-4.65*** (0.66)	-6.44*** (1.04)	-6.67*** (1.17)
Disposable Income	35.7*** (6.6)	40.0*** (3.1)	44.8*** (8.9)	24.0*** (5.0)	26.3*** (5.9)	28.8*** (5.6)
Net Wealth	-0.54 (1.40)	-0.62 (0.54)	-0.10 (1.05)	1.16 (0.90)	0.97 (0.90)	0.89 (0.92)
Household Formation	83.3*** (17.7)			53.8*** (19.3)		11.8 (8.5)
Lagged Stock	-0.36*** (0.08)	-0.11*** (0.02)	-0.14** (0.05)	-0.18*** (0.05)	-0.18*** (0.03)	-0.20*** (0.03)
DUMWW1	41.9 (24.7)			13.8 (27.2)		-21.6 (30.4)
DUMWW2					-4.57 (25.91)	-41.5 (27.7)
RHO	0.36 (0.38)	0.09 (0.27)	0.92*** (0.06)	0.65*** (0.14)	0.86*** (0.07)	0.82*** (0.07)
Adjusted R^2	0.89	0.91	0.92	0.86	0.92	0.88
SEE	16.88	16.97	20.43	21.93	25.35	28.51
Durbin-Watson	1.54	1.81	1.46	1.89	1.26	1.84
Mean Net Exp. per Household	59.6	11.8	137.5	33.3	90.5	83.8
Mean Gross Exp. per Household	474.9	375.4	726.3	420.2	582.9	559.2
Price Elasticity	-1.09*** (0.28)	-1.22*** (0.26)	-0.71 (0.50)	-1.38*** (0.20)	-1.42*** (0.23)	-1.48*** (0.26)
Income Elasticity	1.02*** (0.19)	1.58*** (0.12)	1.44*** (0.29)	0.81*** (0.17)	0.91*** (0.20)	0.96*** (0.19)

*Statistically significant at the 90 percent level of confidence.
**Statistically significant at the 95 percent level of confidence.
***Statistically significant at the 99 percent level of confidence.

Table C.18. Estimated Coefficients: Total Durable Goods (Standard Errors in Parentheses)

Independent Variable	1902-1919	1920-1941	1947-1983	1902-1941	1920-1983	1902-1983
Constant	3066.6** (1088.4)	-913.6** (399.0)	1404.6 (1544.8)	-1018.9** (437.9)	-395.8 (757.5)	-276.1 (321.2)
Relative Price	-2.20 (2.46)	-1.33 (2.06)	-11.3 (7.1)	-2.75** (1.12)	-2.93 (3.60)	-4.71** (1.99)
Disposable Income	38.8*** (9.9)	117.1*** (10.8)	153.9*** (41.2)	58.3*** (11.8)	103.3*** (20.9)	92.1*** (19.0)
Net Wealth	0.001 (4.154)	-2.29 (2.35)	-8.63 (5.71)	4.36* (2.19)	0.55 (3.89)	3.43 (3.90)
Household Formation	144.4*** (43.6)			198.5*** (58.0)		63.8 (41.1)
Lagged Stock	-0.84*** (0.24)	-0.07 (0.05)	-0.23*** (0.07)	-0.004 (0.088)	-0.13*** (0.04)	-0.14*** (0.03)
DUMWW1	97.7** (43.0)			50.5 (77.5)		-267.6** (130.5)
DUMWW2					-696.9*** (132.4)	-575.0*** (130.6)
RHO	0.87*** (0.10)	0.19 (0.28)	0.48*** (0.16)	0.58*** (0.19)	0.53*** (0.13)	0.53*** (0.13)
Adjusted R^2	0.73	0.91	0.68	0.84	0.84	0.83
SEE	34.99	50.19	113.88	53.25	114.45	112.54
Durbin-Watson	1.78	1.71	1.48	1.75	1.79	1.95
Mean Net Exp. per Household	110.1	93.1	507.9	100.7	325.4	278.1
Mean Gross Exp. per Household	806.2	890.1	2178.0	852.3	1618.2	1439.9
Price Elasticity	-0.35 (0.39)	-0.25 (0.38)	-0.71 (0.45)	-0.48** (0.20)	-0.27 (0.33)	-0.47** (0.20)
Income Elasticity	0.65*** (0.17)	1.95*** (0.18)	1.65*** (0.44)	0.97*** (0.20)	1.28*** (0.26)	1.20*** (0.25)

*Statistically significant at the 90 percent level of confidence.
**Statistically significant at the 95 percent level of confidence.
***Statistically significant at the 99 percent level of confidence.

Table C.19. Value of F-Statistic Testing Stability of Demand Relationship

Commodity Group	Interwar versus Post-WWII Period[a]	Pre-WWI versus Post-WWI Period[b]	Pre-WWI versus Interwar Period[b]
TRA	$F_{27,30} = 1.14$	$F_{9,64} = -0.36$	$F_{8,24} = 3.31^*$
AUT	$F_{27,30} = 1.34$	$F_{9,64} = 2.69^*$	$F_{8,24} = 3.07^*$
FUR	$F_{27,30} = 4.58^{**}$	$F_{9,64} = 2.90^{**}$	$F_{8,24} = 2.35$
APP	$F_{27,29} = 2.46^{**}$	$F_{8,66} = 1.36$	$F_{7,26} = 7.77^{**}$
MUS	$F_{27,29} = 0.81$	$F_{9,64} = 0.15$	$F_{8,24} = 1.29$
RAD			$F_{8,24} = 1.89$
PIA			$F_{8,24} = 9.67^{**}$
CHI	$F_{27,29} = 12.24^{**}$	$F_{9,64} = 3.36^{**}$	$F_{8,24} = 2.09$
HSF	$F_{27,30} = 1.15$	$F_{9,64} = 1.64$	$F_{8,24} = 1.78$
JWL	$F_{27,30} = 0.92$	$F_{9,64} = 4.47^{**}$	$F_{8,24} = 7.87^{**}$
MED	$F_{27,30} = 1.05$	$F_{9,64} = 3.57^{**}$	$F_{8,24} = 4.98^{**}$
BKS	$F_{27,29} = 1.28$	$F_{7,68} = 2.86^*$	$F_{6,28} = 2.70^*$
MIS	$F_{27,30} = 0.46$	$F_{9,64} = 2.73^{**}$	$F_{8,24} = 6.47^{**}$
MJR	$F_{27,30} = 0.99$	$F_{9,64} = 2.34^*$	$F_{8,24} = 3.32^*$
MNR	$F_{27,30} = 2.14^*$	$F_{9,64} = 4.08^{**}$	$F_{8,24} = 3.51^{**}$
TOT	$F_{27,30} = 1.02$	$F_{9,64} = 2.17^*$	$F_{8,24} = 3.06^{**}$

Source: F-statistics calculated from residual sums of squares using equations C.23 and C.24.

Notes: Three-letter commodity group abbreviations as follows: TRA, transportation vehicles; AUT, automobiles and parts; FUR, furniture; APP, household appliances; MUS, musical instruments, radios, and phonographs; RAD, radios and phonographs; PIA, pianos and other musical instruments; CHI, china and tableware; HSF, house furnishings; JWL, jewelry and watches; MED, orthopedic and ophthalmic products; BKS, books and maps; MIS, miscellaneous other durable goods; MJR, major durable goods; MNR, minor durable goods; TOT, total durable goods.

[a]Base period for comparison is the post-World War II period.
[b]Base period for comparison is the pre-World War I period.
*Reject null hypothesis of stability at 95 percent level of confidence.
**Reject null hypothesis of stability at 99 percent level of confidence.

♦ APPENDIX D ♦

ANALYSIS OF
PRINT ADVERTISEMENTS

his appendix documents development of the annual series of advertisements, 1901–41. Due to the size of the data base, not all of the raw
data can be reprinted here. Readers who wish a copy of the data base for
their own scholarly work should contact the author.

DATA GATHERED

From October issues of *Ladies Home Journal*, annual series measuring the
number and pages of print advertisements were constructed for 1901 to
1941. Every advertisement was counted, measured, and classified. The
series are disaggregated by general product type.

For durable goods, additional information was gathered regarding
whether a picture or drawing of the product was included, whether availability of credit financing was mentioned, and whether price information
(explicit or implicit) was included. Early attempts at further analysis of the
copy of durable goods advertisements to determine, for instance, whether
persuasive or informative copy dominated were abandoned due to lack of
sufficient personnel and other resources necessary to conduct a proper
content analysis.[1]

Ladies Home Journal was chosen for this study because it was a leading
women's magazine throughout the early twentieth century. Furthermore,
it did not undergo any significant editorial, stylistic, or other changes
during the forty-year period.

October was chosen as the month to survey primarily because it is not a holiday month. Only one influence of Halloween on October advertisements appeared; in a few issues, the Dennison Paper Company advertisement featured crepe paper for Halloween party decorations.[2] An equally important reason for choosing October was that hard copies of the October issues of *Ladies Home Journal* were available locally for every year of the study, eliminating the need to rely on microfilm.

MEASURING SIZE OF ADVERTISEMENTS

Every advertisement was physically measured in order to determine its size. Size was measured not in square inches but in "full-page equivalent" units, which eliminates problems that otherwise enter when the size of a page changes. Small variations in the amount of white border space are also therefore ignored.

Ladies Home Journal always had four columns to a page; thus the width of an advertisement was one-fourth, one-half, three-fourths, or one, depending upon the number of columns it covered. Specially constructed rulers that measure length in fractions of one page were used to measure length. An advertisement that occupies one-fourth of a column has length one-fourth, for example. The size of an advertisement is then the product of width and length, both measured in fractions. Fractions were converted to decimals when tabulating the results.

CLASSIFICATION SCHEMES

Each advertisement was placed into a product category as determined by the featured product. For nondurable goods, the categories are food, clothing, personal care, housing, home care, and other nondurable goods or services.

The vast majority of items were easily classified. Placement of a few advertisements was less obvious. In all cases, decisions about where to place any particular good were guided by the classification decisions indicated in U.S. Bureau of Economic Analysis, *National Income and Product Accounts, 1929–82*; Kuznets, *Commodity Flow and Capital Formation*;

and Shaw, *Value of Commodity Output.* Table D.1 lists the products included in each nondurable category.

In addition to size, the following information for each advertisement for a durable good was also recorded: the page on which the advertisement appears; whether or not a picture, drawing, or other visual depiction of the product is included; whether or not credit availability is mentioned; and whether or not price is mentioned. If the advertisement mentions credit, more specific information was also noted: where credit is mentioned (headline with no special typeface, headline using bold print, bold print within text, within text but no special typeface, or footnote—defined as smaller typeface at the end of the advertisement), the terms available (maturity or contract length, interest rate or rate of finance charge, dollar amount or percentage down payment), and any additional comments regarding credit that are in the advertisement. If the advertisement mentions price, the following details were also recorded: where price is mentioned (same choices as above); the specific price or range of prices stated; whether the reference to price is only a general reference, such as "low prices" or "why pay more?," with no dollar figures quoted; and any additional comments regarding product price that are contained in the advertisement.

Advertisements for durable goods were classified using the same set of categories as in appendix A: automobiles and parts (AUT), horse-drawn vehicles (HDV), furniture (FUR), household appliances (APP), pianos and other musical instruments (PIA), radios and phonographs and records (RAD), china and tableware (CHI), house furnishings (HSF), jewelry and watches (JWL), orthopedic and ophthalmic products (MED), books and maps (BKS), miscellaneous other durable goods (MIS), and tombstones (TMB). Again, decisions regarding where to place any particular advertisement were guided by the sources noted above. Only a few categories warrant special comment. "China and tableware" includes china, silverware, glassware, nonelectric cookware, and small kitchen appliances. "Durable house furnishings" includes floor coverings, pillows, art products, lamps, clocks, typewriters, hand tools, garden tools, and power tools. Table D.2 notes more fully what products are in each durable good category.

Table D.1. Classification of Products: Nondurable Goods and Services

Food
baking ingredients
beverages
cooking ingredients
food

Clothing
batting
buttons
cloth
clothing
luggage
other leather accessories
other sewing accessories
pocketbooks
sewing patterns
shoes and boots
thread

Personal Care
hair brushes and combs
hot water bottles
medicines
toiletries
wigs

Housing
fencing
house plans
paint
plumbing fixtures
wall enamel
wallpaper

Home Care
baby bottles
blankets, cotton
cleaning brushes
cleaning supplies
comforters and quilts
flashlight batteries
household oil
lace doilies
leather for upholstering
linens (sheets, towels)
other household supplies
shades, curtains, and drapes
varnish

Other Nondurable Goods and Services
banking services
cameras
candles
dog food
dolls and accessories
education and travel services
fountain pens
other paper products
other services
reprints of works of art
rubber products
stationery
tobacco

SUMMARY TABLES

Table D.3 contains the number and total pages of advertisements by general product type. Table D.4 contains the same information for durable goods only.

Because over 1,800 different advertisements for durable goods appeared in the forty-year period, it is clearly infeasible to reprint here all the credit and price information gathered for each advertisement. That information is available from the author on floppy disk, formatted for a popular spread-

Table D.2. Classification of Products: Durable Goods

Automobiles and Parts
- car heaters
- car radios
- cars
- snow chains
- tires

Horse-drawn Vehicles
- horse carriages

Furniture
- baby carriages
- baby cribs
- baby high chairs
- baby jumpers
- baby swings
- baby walkers
- beds
- bookcases
- buffets
- chairs
- chests
- couches
- furniture items
- kitchen cabinets
- mattresses
- service wagons
- sideboards
- sofa beds
- tables
- trunks
- wall shelving
- wrought-iron ware

Household Appliances
- boilers
- carpet sweepers
- chimney stoves
- cooking ranges
- curling irons
- dishwashers
- electric coffee makers
- electric light bulbs
- electric lights
- electric motors
- enamel for appliances
- fire extinguishers
- fireless cookers
- fireplace inserts
- floor polishers
- food mixers
- furnaces
- heaters
- heating stoves
- irons and ironers
- knitting machines
- laundry tubs and wringers
- radiators
- refrigerators
- sewing machines
- tabletop cooking stoves
- thermometers
- toasters
- vacuum cleaners
- waffle irons
- washers
- water heaters
- wringers

Pianos, Musical Instruments
- books about pianos
- cornets
- harmonicas
- pianos
- player pianos
- saxophones

Radios and Phonographs
phonographs
radios
radio speakers
records

China and Tableware
bread makers
cake makers
china and glassware
chromeware
coffee pots
coffee service
cookers
cooking gadgets
cookware
cut glass
cutlery
dishes
dutch ovens
enamelware
food thermometers
glassware
jars
kettles
kitchenware
mop wringer
onyx ware
ovenware
pots and pans
pottery (food service)
pressure cookers
Pyrex products
roasters
silverware
skillet
spoons
sterling silver products
tableware
teapots
thermos
utensils
vases
wafer irons
waffle irons

House Furnishings
air moistener
ash sifter
baskets
bathroom scales
bed coverings
blankets, wool or woven
bolster rolls
bookends
candlesticks
carpets
chamber pots
clocks
floor coverings
garbage cans
gas mantles
lamps
linoleum
picture frames
pillows
pottery (pieces of art)
rugs
scissors
slip covers
tapestries
typewriters
wall hangings

Jewelry and Watches
brooches
chains and fobs
diamonds and other gems
jewelry
sterling silver pins
thimble, silver
watches

Orthopedic, Ophthalmic Products
eyeglasses
eyeglass holder
hearing aids
wheelchairs

Table D.2, continued

Books and Maps
  books
  encyclopedias
  leather book cover

Tombstones
  gravestone
  grave vault

Miscellaneous Other Durable Goods
  bicycle chains
  billiard tables
  go-carts
  guns
  pocket knives
  skates
  sleighs
  toys
  toy wagons
  tricycle

sheet package. Reprinted here are the summary statistics. Table D.5 reports the number of advertisements and number of pages of advertisements that contain a picture or other visual depiction of the product. Table D.6 reports the same information for advertisements that mention credit. Table D.7 does so for advertisements that mention price.

Table D.3A. Number of Advertisements, 1901-1941

Year	Food	Clothing	Personal Care	Housing	Home Care	Other Nondurable Goods and Services	Major Durables	Minor Durables	Total
1901	20	62	15	6	14	25	27	20	189
1902	24	92	15	7	20	34	27	28	247
1903	34	101	23	5	24	41	33	35	296
1904	28	116	15	4	25	41	35	30	294
1905	33	91	32	5	31	39	26	36	293
1906	34	109	22	6	29	60	39	45	344
1907	21	103	24	8	28	37	41	36	298
1908	26	124	28	8	24	48	36	27	321
1909	28	113	20	10	39	30	34	25	299
1910	34	57	20	12	26	27	29	22	227
1911	38	107	21	5	40	20	26	27	284
1912	46	93	23	7	37	36	28	20	290
1913	35	100	24	7	29	24	27	30	276
1914	33	66	27	6	23	31	19	25	230

Table D.3A, continued

Year	Food	Clothing	Personal Care	Housing	Home Care	Other Nondurable Goods and Services	Major Durables	Minor Durables	Total
1915	30	74	23	6	26	31	15	21	226
1916	36	70	33	5	22	33	20	24	243
1917	32	72	33	6	24	35	25	18	245
1918	33	71	23	2	18	31	14	15	207
1919	48	78	32	8	14	27	24	19	250
1920	43	50	26	4	11	20	29	21	204
1921	30	64	24	5	20	40	15	18	216
1922	44	63	34	10	24	42	32	31	280
1923	45	72	46	7	32	38	47	33	320
1924	42	56	32	4	28	42	30	24	258
1925	47	51	39	6	28	47	37	28	283
1926	54	55	48	4	33	48	33	25	300
1927	50	41	43	5	29	42	33	19	262
1928	59	42	47	2	33	43	29	19	274

339

Table D.3A, continued

Year	Food	Clothing	Personal Care	Housing	Home Care	Other Nondurable Goods and Services	Major Durables	Minor Durables	Total
1929	59	39	43	2	29	41	32	24	269
1930	43	26	55	5	26	31	18	17	221
1931	44	14	49	3	25	37	19	12	203
1932	29	16	29	5	17	20	9	7	132
1933	38	15	38	2	23	17	7	10	150
1934	41	27	40	1	20	31	8	12	180
1935	35	26	34	4	22	26	5	10	162
1936	32	30	39	5	21	35	5	13	180
1937	30	25	41	2	19	24	6	12	159
1938	33	24	39	2	19	32	3	9	161
1939	30	29	31	3	22	34	8	12	169
1940	34	36	37	3	17	33	11	18	189
1941	50	37	66	4	22	38	14	20	251

Table D.3B. Pages of Advertisements, 1901-1941

Year	Food	Clothing	Personal Care	Housing	Home Care	Other Nondurable Goods and Services	Major Durables	Minor Durables	Total
1901	2.37	5.04	3.24	0.27	1.17	0.85	1.75	2.82	17.50
1902	3.56	8.74	3.16	0.45	1.49	1.78	1.80	2.04	23.03
1903	5.80	7.79	4.20	0.31	1.58	1.90	2.89	3.06	27.52
1904	3.88	8.85	0.78	0.15	1.76	1.95	2.94	3.15	23.46
1905	5.68	10.22	4.92	0.14	2.49	1.97	5.10	3.73	34.25
1906	7.19	11.88	3.99	0.71	4.13	4.23	7.17	3.80	43.10
1907	7.47	15.53	3.63	0.84	3.33	2.13	7.73	5.40	46.06
1908	8.81	18.25	3.86	0.75	3.36	3.83	5.33	2.21	46.41
1909	8.50	19.96	3.22	1.03	6.51	2.75	7.18	2.02	51.19
1910	11.11	11.67	2.46	2.12	4.50	2.38	5.10	3.20	42.54
1911	12.62	20.55	3.53	0.78	4.66	0.66	4.99	3.73	51.52
1912	14.14	17.95	4.30	1.27	5.53	2.93	4.16	3.49	53.78
1913	10.76	20.48	4.82	1.06	6.48	2.92	3.85	5.27	55.64
1914	10.12	16.22	5.48	0.91	5.50	4.08	3.64	5.31	51.24

341

Table D.3B, continued

Year	Food	Clothing	Personal Care	Housing	Home Care	Other Nondurable Goods and Services	Major Durables	Minor Durables	Total
1915	10.16	16.30	5.29	0.76	6.85	6.04	5.87	3.81	55.08
1916	14.32	18.89	7.27	1.04	6.37	1.91	6.29	7.36	63.46
1917	16.94	21.72	11.47	1.18	7.80	3.51	11.32	6.19	80.13
1918	22.15	24.87	11.66	0.23	9.29	4.42	6.41	6.13	85.16
1919	31.60	34.18	18.43	2.51	8.35	4.16	12.75	9.83	121.81
1920	29.90	25.46	21.13	2.25	7.50	7.23	24.29	12.25	130.00
1921	19.61	28.09	18.25	0.65	12.71	6.74	7.20	7.78	101.03
1922	27.85	29.76	20.80	2.61	15.48	4.37	16.49	11.28	128.64
1923	23.36	30.86	23.50	2.38	17.85	6.39	21.96	13.45	139.75
1924	28.25	24.23	19.72	2.50	16.50	5.33	18.21	12.53	127.27
1925	34.63	26.44	23.22	3.08	16.82	7.43	25.29	16.81	153.73
1926	41.26	28.66	28.22	1.09	19.04	9.46	21.55	12.93	162.20
1927	37.68	15.88	28.81	1.98	15.48	9.46	22.39	12.87	144.55
1928	42.16	19.19	31.75	0.75	19.95	10.26	24.16	10.90	159.12

Table D.3B, continued

Year	Food	Clothing	Personal Care	Housing	Home Care	Other Nondurable Goods and Services	Major Durables	Minor Durables	Total
1929	41.42	19.63	29.24	0.75	16.46	9.94	26.63	15.75	159.83
1930	32.62	15.42	35.01	2.38	13.53	4.64	13.58	10.59	127.78
1931	34.93	8.10	36.91	1.57	13.21	7.49	14.10	6.20	122.53
1932	17.83	6.69	21.25	3.13	7.36	2.86	5.26	5.61	69.99
1933	25.25	5.47	28.91	0.75	8.53	3.59	6.00	6.35	84.86
1934	27.47	9.73	25.40	0.50	7.46	4.70	4.58	7.13	86.97
1935	23.03	7.15	19.46	0.85	9.40	5.33	2.67	5.14	73.03
1936	21.34	10.65	20.86	1.56	8.47	5.45	2.11	7.84	78.27
1937	21.91	10.23	20.94	0.66	6.98	1.26	3.88	7.03	72.88
1938	19.54	10.78	17.77	0.63	5.33	4.50	2.13	3.24	63.92
1939	17.96	10.40	12.17	0.93	4.90	3.78	5.00	4.84	59.98
1940	18.92	13.52	19.59	1.13	5.62	3.55	5.63	6.47	74.42
1941	26.73	10.20	29.78	2.02	7.01	4.71	8.13	10.29	98.86

343

Table D.4A. Number of Advertisements for Durable Goods, 1901-1941

Year	AUT	HDV	OMV	FUR	APP	PIA	RAD	CHI	HSF	JWL	MED	BKS	MIS	TMB
1901	0	0	0	13	11	3	0	7	4	4	0	2	3	0
1902	0	1	0	10	7	9	0	11	4	7	2	1	3	0
1903	1	0	0	12	9	11	0	12	10	6	2	3	2	0
1904	0	0	0	18	6	9	2	10	9	6	2	1	2	0
1905	0	0	0	13	7	6	0	16	12	5	2	0	1	0
1906	0	0	0	16	13	8	2	18	13	7	1	3	3	0
1907	0	0	0	14	16	10	1	15	9	6	3	0	3	0
1908	0	0	0	17	12	6	1	9	12	2	1	2	1	0
1909	1	0	0	18	8	6	1	10	7	3	1	3	1	0
1910	1	0	0	11	13	4	0	9	10	2	0	1	0	0
1911	1	0	0	11	10	3	1	12	6	8	1	0	0	0
1912	1	0	0	8	13	5	1	9	7	3	1	2	0	0
1913	0	0	0	10	13	3	1	14	8	3	0	3	0	0
1914	0	0	0	6	9	3	1	13	7	4	0	1	0	0
1915	2	0	0	1	9	2	1	8	4	4	1	4	0	0
1916	2	0	0	7	7	3	1	9	6	6	0	2	1	0

Table D.4A, continued

Year	AUT	HDV	OMV	FUR	APP	PIA	RAD	CHI	HSF	JWL	MED	BKS	MIS	TMB
1917	2	0	0	10	8	2	3	6	7	2	0	3	0	0
1918	1	0	0	4	7	0	2	4	8	0	0	3	0	0
1919	2	0	0	7	11	0	4	10	3	3	0	2	1	0
1920	3	0	0	5	14	1	6	10	5	3	0	2	1	0
1921	0	0	0	7	6	0	2	7	9	1	0	1	0	0
1922	3	0	0	12	14	1	2	15	11	2	0	3	0	0
1923	6	0	0	16	21	3	1	15	10	4	0	3	1	0
1924	3	0	0	9	15	0	3	11	10	2	0	0	0	1
1925	6	0	0	13	14	1	3	14	13	0	0	1	0	0
1926	8	0	0	9	12	1	3	12	11	0	0	2	0	0
1927	6	0	0	8	12	2	5	8	9	0	0	1	0	1
1928	6	0	0	7	10	4	2	6	9	1	0	3	0	0
1929	5	0	0	6	16	1	4	10	11	1	0	2	0	0
1930	6	0	0	2	10	0	0	7	9	0	0	0	1	0
1931	5	0	0	1	12	0	1	2	9	0	0	1	0	0
1932	1	0	0	1	6	0	1	3	4	0	0	0	0	0

Table D.4A, continued

Year	AUT	HDV	OMV	FUR	APP	PIA	RAD	CHI	HSF	JWL	MED	BKS	MIS	TMB
1933	2	0	0	2	3	0	0	3	7	0	0	0	0	0
1934	1	0	0	2	5	0	0	4	8	0	0	0	0	0
1935	0	0	0	1	4	0	0	3	7	0	0	0	0	0
1936	0	0	0	0	4	0	1	4	9	0	0	0	0	0
1937	0	0	0	2	3	0	1	6	6	0	0	0	0	0
1938	0	0	0	1	2	0	0	5	4	0	0	0	0	0
1939	0	0	0	2	6	0	0	7	4	1	0	0	0	0
1940	1	0	0	1	8	0	1	12	6	0	0	0	0	0
1941	0	0	0	6	7	0	1	10	8	1	0	1	0	0

Table D.4B. Pages of Advertisements for Durable Goods, 1901-1941

Year	AUT	HDV	OMV	FUR	APP	PIA	RAD	CHI	HSF	JWL	MED	BKS	MIS	TMB
1901	0	0	0	0.77	0.75	0.23	0	0.73	0.18	0.50	0	1.05	0.36	0
1902	0	0.07	0	0.74	0.35	0.64	0	0.87	0.18	0.59	0.06	0.02	0.32	0
1903	0.07	0	0	0.95	0.83	1.03	0	1.20	0.48	0.65	0.08	0.63	0.02	0
1904	0	0	0	1.35	0.58	0.83	0.19	1.70	0.77	0.52	0.04	0.07	0.04	0
1905	0	0	0	2.46	2.00	0.64	0	1.79	1.16	0.65	0.10	0	0.02	0
1906	0	0	0	2.77	3.18	0.71	0.50	2.01	0.81	0.66	0.04	0.21	0.07	0
1907	0	0	0	2.68	2.76	1.29	1.00	3.94	0.78	0.47	0.12	0	0.09	0
1908	0	0	0	2.50	1.74	0.84	0.25	1.38	0.58	0.06	0.04	0.14	0.03	0
1909	0.25	0	0	4.59	1.09	1.00	0.25	1.44	0.33	0.09	0.03	0.10	0.02	0
1910	0.25	0	0	2.41	1.73	0.71	0	2.49	0.57	0.14	0	0.01	0	0
1911	0.25	0	0	2.15	1.16	0.43	1.00	2.24	0.26	1.19	0.04	0	0	0
1912	0.25	0	0	0.89	1.50	0.52	1.00	1.51	0.77	1.13	0.08	0	0	0
1913	0	0	0	0.76	1.18	0.91	1.00	3.58	0.60	0.52	0	0.57	0	0
1914	0	0	0	0.81	1.18	0.65	1.00	3.65	0.64	1.02	0	0.01	0	0
1915	2.25	0	0	0.04	2.18	0.40	1.00	2.53	0.36	0.68	0.04	0.20	0	0
1916	2.25	0	0	1.74	0.82	0.48	1.00	3.42	2.32	1.54	0	0.06	0.02	0

Table D.4B, continued

Year	AUT	HDV	OMV	FUR	APP	PIA	RAD	CHI	HSF	JWL	MED	BKS	MIS	TMB
1917	3.00	0	0	2.79	2.15	0.38	3.00	3.84	1.70	0.38	0	0.27	0	0
1918	1.00	0	0	0.20	3.21	0	2.00	1.18	4.37	0	0	0.58	0	0
1919	2.00	0	0	2.69	4.56	0	3.50	6.93	1.09	0.46	0	0.35	1.00	0
1920	3.00	0	0	2.79	11.00	1.00	6.50	5.75	3.50	0.75	0	1.25	1.00	0
1921	0	0	0	3.30	1.90	0	2.00	2.63	4.82	0.18	0	0.15	0	0
1922	2.00	0	0	5.44	6.93	0.13	2.00	6.13	4.95	0.16	0	0.04	0	0
1923	6.00	0	0	6.23	8.16	0.57	1.00	7.50	4.26	0.98	0	0.57	0.13	0
1924	3.00	0	0	4.78	7.43	0	3.00	5.74	5.80	0.75	0	0	0	0.25
1925	6.00	0	0	8.23	7.80	0.25	3.00	8.04	8.71	0	0	0.06	0	0
1926	8.00	0	0	5.10	5.70	0.25	2.50	8.17	4.49	0	0	0.27	0	0
1927	6.00	0	0	5.34	8.02	0.40	2.63	6.75	5.37	0	0	0.50	0	0.25
1928	6.00	0	0	6.58	6.57	2.00	3.00	3.77	4.88	1.00	0	1.25	0	0
1929	6.25	0	0	5.52	9.85	1.00	4.00	8.04	5.96	1.00	0	0.75	0	0
1930	4.75	0	0	1.25	7.58	0	0	5.54	4.80	0	0	0	0	0.25
1931	5.00	0	0	1.00	7.60	0	0.50	0.75	4.95	0	0	0.50	0	0
1932	0.04	0	0	1.00	3.21	0	1.00	3.25	2.36	0	0	0	0	0

Table D.4B, continued

Year	AUT	HDV	OMV	FUR	APP	PIA	RAD	CHI	HSF	JWL	MED	BKS	MIS	TMB
1933	2.00	0	0	2.00	2.00	0	0	1.75	4.60	0	0	0	0	0
1934	1.00	0	0	1.06	2.52	0	0	2.03	5.10	0	0	0	0	0
1935	0	0	0	1.00	1.67	0	0	1.50	3.64	0	0	0	0	0
1936	0	0	0	0	2.00	0	0.11	2.09	5.75	0	0	0	0	0
1937	0	0	0	2.00	1.63	0	0.25	3.03	4.00	0	0	0	0	0
1938	0	0	0	1.00	1.13	0	0	1.74	1.50	0	0	0	0	0
1939	0	0	0	2.00	3.00	0	0	1.46	2.38	1.00	0	0	0	0
1940	0.50	0	0	1.00	3.88	0	0.25	3.34	3.13	0	0	0	0	0
1941	0	0	0	3.88	4.00	0	0.25	3.70	5.08	1.00	0	0.50	0	0

Notes: Three-letter commodity group abbreviations defined as follows: AUT, automobiles and parts; HDV, horse-drawn vehicles; OMV, other motor vehicles; FUR, furniture; APP, household appliances; PIA, pianos and other musical instruments; RAD, radios and phonographs; CHI, china and tableware; HSF, house furnishings; JWL, jewelry and watches; MED, orthopedic and ophthalmic products; BKS, books and maps; MIS, miscellaneous other durable goods; and TMB, grave stones and vaults.

349

Table D.5A. Number of Advertisements for Durable Goods Including Picture of Product, 1901-1941

Year	AUT	HDV	OMV	FUR	APP	PIA	RAD	CHI	HSF	JWL	MED	BKS	MIS	TMB
1901	0	0	0	10	9	2	0	7	1	3	0	0	3	0
1902	0	1	0	7	5	5	0	9	2	5	1	0	3	0
1903	1	0	0	11	7	7	0	9	5	5	2	2	0	0
1904	0	0	0	15	4	4	1	10	8	5	1	0	2	0
1905	0	0	0	12	7	5	0	14	8	3	1	0	1	0
1906	0	0	0	16	13	5	2	16	8	4	1	1	3	0
1907	0	0	0	10	14	8	0	13	5	5	3	0	5	0
1908	0	0	0	17	11	3	0	8	10	2	0	1	1	0
1909	1	0	0	18	8	6	1	10	5	3	1	1	1	0
1910	1	0	0	11	13	3	0	8	8	2	0	0	0	0
1911	1	0	0	11	9	2	0	11	3	7	1	0	0	0
1912	1	0	0	7	10	3	0	8	5	2	1	0	0	0
1913	0	0	0	10	12	3	0	13	5	3	0	2	0	0
1914	0	0	0	6	9	3	1	12	4	4	0	0	0	0
1915	2	0	0	1	8	2	1	8	4	4	0	0	0	0
1916	2	0	0	7	7	3	1	8	5	6	0	0	1	0

Table D.5A, continued

Year	AUT	HDV	OMV	FUR	APP	PIA	RAD	CHI	HSF	JWL	MED	BKS	MIS	TMB
1917	2	0	0	9	8	2	2	6	7	2	0	0	0	0
1918	1	0	0	4	7	0	2	4	6	0	0	0	0	0
1919	2	0	0	7	11	0	4	10	3	3	0	1	1	0
1920	3	0	0	5	14	1	6	10	5	3	0	1	1	0
1921	0	0	0	7	6	0	2	7	9	1	0	1	0	0
1922	1	0	0	12	13	1	1	15	11	1	0	0	0	0
1923	3	0	0	14	19	3	1	14	10	4	0	3	1	0
1924	2	0	0	9	14	0	3	10	10	2	0	0	0	1
1925	4	0	0	13	13	1	2	14	13	0	0	1	0	0
1926	8	0	0	9	11	1	3	12	10	0	0	1	0	0
1927	6	0	0	8	11	2	5	8	8	0	0	0	0	1
1928	6	0	0	6	8	4	2	5	9	1	0	2	0	0
1929	5	0	0	6	14	1	3	10	11	1	0	0	0	0
1930	4	0	0	2	8	0	0	7	9	0	0	0	0	1
1931	4	0	0	1	12	0	1	2	9	0	0	1	0	0
1932	1	0	0	1	4	0	1	3	4	0	0	0	0	0

Table D.5A, continued

Year	AUT	HDV	OMV	FUR	APP	PIA	RAD	CHI	HSF	JWL	MED	BKS	MIS	TMB
1933	1	0	0	2	2	0	0	3	7	0	0	0	0	0
1934	1	0	0	2	4	0	0	4	8	0	0	0	0	0
1935	0	0	0	1	4	0	0	3	6	0	0	0	0	0
1936	0	0	0	0	3	0	1	4	8	0	0	0	0	0
1937	0	0	0	2	2	0	1	5	5	0	0	0	0	0
1938	0	0	0	1	2	0	0	5	4	0	0	0	0	0
1939	0	0	0	2	5	0	0	7	4	1	0	0	0	0
1940	0	0	0	1	7	0	1	12	6	0	0	0	0	0
1941	0	0	0	5	7	0	0	10	8	0	0	0	0	0

Table D.5B. Pages of Advertisements for Durable Goods Including Picture of Product, 1901-1941

Year	AUT	HDV	OMV	FUR	APP	PIA	RAD	CHI	HSF	JWL	MED	BKS	MIS	TMB
1901	0	0	0	0.46	0.57	0.18	0	0.73	0.04	0.40	0	0	0.36	0
1902	0	0.07	0	0.56	0.31	0.42	0	0.75	0.07	0.49	0.05	0	0.32	0
1903	0.07	0	0	0.89	0.68	0.75	0	0.75	0.17	0.53	0.08	0.56	0	0
1904	0	0	0	1.08	0.37	0.53	0.13	1.70	0.77	0.49	0.04	0	0.04	0
1905	0	0	0	2.39	2.00	0.51	0	1.66	0.79	0.40	0.09	0	0.02	0
1906	0	0	0	2.77	3.18	0.45	0.50	1.70	0.76	0.34	0.04	0.05	0.07	0
1907	0	0	0	2.42	2.64	1.01	0	3.44	0.59	0.43	0.12	0	0.18	0
1908	0	0	0	2.50	1.67	0.30	0	1.27	0.54	0.06	0	0.07	0.03	0
1909	0.25	0	0	4.59	1.09	1.00	0.25	1.44	0.23	0.09	0.03	0.05	0.02	0
1910	0.25	0	0	2.41	1.73	0.68	0	2.24	0.55	0.14	0	0		0
1911	0.25	0	0	2.15	0.91	0.38	0	1.99	0.15	1.17	0.04	0	0	0
1912	0.25	0	0	0.85	0.94	0.48	0	1.39	0.51	1.10	0.08	0	0	0
1913	0	0	0	0.81	1.07	0.91	0	3.54	0.47	0.52	0	0.27	0	0
1914	0	0	0	0.81	1.18	0.65	1.00	3.59	0.58	1.02	0	0	0	0
1915	2.25	0	0	0.04	2.07	0.40	1.00	2.53	0.36	0.68	0	0	0	0
1916	2.25	0	0	1.74	0.82	0.48	1.00	3.32	2.31	1.54	0	0	0.02	0

Table D.5B, continued

Year	AUT	HDV	OMV	FUR	APP	PIA	RAD	CHI	HSF	JWL	MED	BKS	MIS	TMB
1917	3.00	0	0	2.66	2.15	0.38	2.00	3.84	1.70	0.38	0	0	0	0
1918	1.00	0	0	0.20	3.21	0	2.00	1.18	3.12	0	0	0	0	0
1919	2.00	0	0	2.69	4.56	0	3.50	6.93	1.09	0.46	0	0.14	1.00	0
1920	3.00	0	0	2.79	11.00	1.00	6.50	5.75	3.50	0.75	0	1.00	1.00	0
1921	0	0	0	3.30	1.90	0	2.00	2.63	4.82	0.18	0	0.15	0	0
1922	1.00	0	0	5.44	5.93	0.13	1.00	6.13	4.95	0.13	0	0	0	0
1923	3.00	0	0	4.98	7.86	0.57	1.00	7.47	4.26	0.98	0	0.57	0.13	0
1924	2.00	0	0	4.78	6.43	0	3.00	5.72	5.80	0.75	0	0	0	0.25
1925	4.00	0	0	8.23	6.80	0.25	2.00	8.04	8.71	0	0	0.06	0	0
1926	8.00	0	0	5.10	4.70	0.25	2.50	8.17	4.45	0	0	0.25	0	0
1927	6.00	0	0	5.34	7.73	0.40	2.63	6.75	5.12	0	0	0	0	0.25
1928	6.00	0	0	6.50	5.50	2.00	3.00	3.75	4.88	1.00	0	1.00	0	0
1929	6.25	0	0	5.52	8.35	1.00	3.00	8.04	5.96	1.00	0	0	0	0
1930	3.50	0	0	1.25	6.08	0	0	5.54	4.80	0	0	0	0	0.25
1931	4.00	0	0	1.00	7.60	0	0.50	0.75	4.95	0	0	0.50	0	0
1932	0.04	0	0	1.00	2.92	0	1.00	3.25	2.36	0	0	0	0	0

Table D.5B, continued

Year	AUT	HDV	OMV	FUR	APP	PIA	RAD	CHI	HSF	JWL	MED	BKS	MIS	TMB
1933	1.00	0	0	2.00	1.50	0	0	1.75	4.60	0	0	0	0	0
1934	1.00	0	0	1.06	2.02	0	0	2.03	5.10	0	0	0	0	0
1935	0	0	0	1.00	1.67	0	0	1.50	3.51	0	0	0	0	0
1936	0	0	0	0	1.50	0	0.11	2.09	5.63	0	0	0	0	0
1937	0	0	0	2.00	0.63	0	0.25	2.03	3.75	0	0	0	0	0
1938	0	0	0	1.00	1.13	0	0	1.74	1.50	0	0	0	0	0
1939	0	0	0	2.00	2.50	0	0	1.46	2.38	1.00	0	0	0	0
1940	0	0	0	1.00	3.38	0	0.25	3.34	3.13	0	0	0	0	0
1941	0	0	0	3.63	4.00	0	0	3.70	5.08	0	0	0	0	0

Note: Three-letter commodity group abbreviations as for table D.4.

Table D.6A. Number of Advertisements for Durable Goods Mentioning Credit Availability, 1901-1941

Year	AUT	HDV	OMV	FUR	APP	PIA	RAD	CHI	HSF	JWL	MED	BKS	MIS	TMB
1901	0	0	0	0	0	2	0	0	0	0	0	0	0	0
1902	0	0	0	0	0	3	0	0	0	0	0	0	0	0
1903	0	0	0	0	0	6	0	0	0	1	0	2	0	0
1904	0	0	0	0	0	5	0	0	0	0	0	0	0	0
1905	0	0	0	1	0	5	0	0	0	0	0	0	0	0
1906	0	0	0	0	0	4	0	0	0	0	0	0	0	0
1907	0	0	0	0	2	4	0	0	0	0	0	0	0	0
1908	0	0	0	0	1	2	0	0	1	0	0	0	0	0
1909	0	0	0	1	0	3	0	0	0	0	0	0	0	0
1910	0	0	0	1	0	2	0	0	0	0	0	0	0	0
1911	0	0	0	1	0	2	0	0	0	0	0	0	0	0
1912	0	0	0	1	1	2	0	0	0	0	0	0	0	0
1913	0	0	0	0	2	2	0	0	0	0	0	0	0	0
1914	0	0	0	0	2	1	0	0	0	0	0	0	0	0
1915	0	0	0	1	2	1	0	0	0	0	0	0	0	0
1916	0	0	0	1	2	3	0	0	0	0	0	0	0	0

Table D.6A, continued

Year	AUT	HDV	OMV	FUR	APP	PIA	RAD	CHI	HSF	JWL	MED	BKS	MIS	TMB
1917	0	0	0	3	2	2	0	0	0	0	0	0	0	0
1918	0	0	0	0	0	0	0	0	0	0	0	0	0	0
1919	0	0	0	0	4	0	0	0	0	0	0	0	0	0
1920	0	0	0	1	3	0	0	0	0	0	0	0	0	0
1921	0	0	0	0	1	0	0	0	0	0	0	0	0	0
1922	0	0	0	1	2	0	0	0	0	0	0	0	0	0
1923	0	0	0	2	5	1	0	0	1	0	0	0	0	0
1924	0	0	0	1	3	0	1	1	0	0	0	0	0	0
1925	1	0	0	2	2	0	0	1	0	0	0	0	0	0
1926	0	0	0	1	4	0	1	1	0	0	0	0	0	0
1927	1	0	0	0	1	0	1	0	0	0	0	0	0	0
1928	0	0	0	0	1	2	0	0	0	0	0	1	0	0
1929	1	0	0	0	2	1	1	0	0	0	0	1	0	0
1930	0	0	0	0	2	0	0	0	1	0	0	0	0	0
1931	1	0	0	0	4	0	0	0	0	0	0	0	0	0
1932	0	0	0	0	1	0	0	0	0	0	0	0	0	0

357

Table D.6A, continued

Year	AUT	HDV	OMV	FUR	APP	PIA	RAD	CHI	HSF	JWL	MED	BKS	MIS	TMB
1933	0	0	0	0	0	0	0	0	0	0	0	0	0	0
1934	0	0	0	1	0	0	0	0	1	0	0	0	0	0
1935	0	0	0	1	0	0	0	0	0	0	0	0	0	0
1936	0	0	0	0	0	0	0	0	0	0	0	0	0	0
1937	0	0	0	0	0	0	0	0	0	0	0	0	0	0
1938	0	0	0	0	1	0	0	1	0	0	0	0	0	0
1939	0	0	0	1	0	0	0	0	0	1	0	0	0	0
1940	0	0	0	1	0	0	0	0	0	0	0	0	0	0
1941	0	0	0	0	0	0	0	2	1	0	0	0	0	0

Table D.6B. Pages of Advertisements for Durable Goods Mentioning Credit Availability, 1901-1941

Year	AUT	HDV	OMV	FUR	APP	PIA	RAD	CHI	HSF	JWL	MED	BKS	MIS	TMB
1901	0	0	0	0	0	0.18	0	0	0	0	0	0	0	0
1902	0	0	0	0	0	0.23	0	0	0	0	0	0	0	0
1903	0	0	0	0	0	0.67	0	0	0	0.14	0	0.56	0	0
1904	0	0	0	0	0	0.46	0	0	0	0	0	0	0	0
1905	0	0	0	0.13	0	0.51	0	0	0	0	0	0	0	0
1906	0	0	0	0	0	0.34	0	0	0	0	0	0	0	0
1907	0	0	0	0	0.27	0.34	0	0	0	0	0	0	0	0
1908	0	0	0	0	0.25	0.16	0	0	0.03	0	0	0	0	0
1909	0	0	0	1.00	0	0.48	0	0	0	0	0	0	0	0
1910	0	0	0	0.35	0	0.43	0	0	0	0	0	0	0	0
1911	0	0	0	0.50	0	0.18	0	0	0	0	0	0	0	0
1912	0	0	0	0.28	0.25	0.15	0	0	0	0	0	0	0	0
1913	0	0	0	0	0.18	0.63	0	0	0	0	0	0	0	0
1914	0	0	0	0	0.25	0.12	0	0	0	0	0	0	0	0
1915	0	0	0	0.04	0.15	0.12	0	0	0	0	0	0	0	0
1916	0	0	0	0.04	0.25	0.48	0	0	0	0	0	0	0	0

Table D.6B, continued

Year	AUT	HDV	OMV	FUR	APP	PIA	RAD	CHI	HSF	JWL	MED	BKS	MIS	TMB
1917	0	0	0	1.16	1.06	0.38	0	0	0	0	0	0	0	0
1918	0	0	0	0	0	0	0	0	0	0	0	0	0	0
1919	0	0	0	0	1.67	0	0	0	0	0	0	0	0	0
1920	0	0	0	1.00	3.00	0	0	0	0	0	0	0	0	0
1921	0	0	0	0	0.50	0	0	0	0	0	0	0	0	0
1922	0	0	0	1.00	0.50	0	0	0	0	0	0	0	0	0
1923	0	0	0	2.00	1.79	0.07	0	0	0.25	0	0	0	0	0
1924	0	0	0	1.00	2.25	0	1.00	0	0	0	0	0	0	0
1925	1.00	0	0	2.04	2.00	0	0	1.00	0	0	0	0	0	0
1926	0	0	0	1.00	1.60	0	0.50	0.50	0	0	0	0	0	0
1927	1.00	0	0	0	1.00	0	1.00	0	0	0	0	0	0	0
1928	0	0	0	0	0.07	1.25	0	0	0	0	0	0.25	0	0
1929	2.00	0	0	0	1.25	1.00	1.00	0	0	0	0	0.25	0	0
1930	0	0	0	0	2.00	1.00	0	0	1.00	0	0	0	0	0
1931	1.00	0	0	0	3.25	0	0	0	0	0	0	0	0	0
1932	0	0	0	0	0.25	0	0	0	0	0	0	0	0	0

Table D.6B, continued

Year	AUT	HDV	OMV	FUR	APP	PIA	RAD	CHI	HSF	JWL	MED	BKS	MIS	TMB
1933	0	0	0	0	0	0	0	0	0	0	0	0	0	0
1934	0	0	0	1.00	0	0	0	0	0.50	0	0	0	0	0
1935	0	0	0	1.00	0	0	0	0	0	0	0	0	0	0
1936	0	0	0	0	0	0	0	0	0	0	0	0	0	0
1937	0	0	0	0	0	0	0	0	0	0	0	0	0	0
1938	0	0	0	0	1.00	0	0	0.50	0	0	0	0	0	0
1939	0	0	0	1.00	0	0	0	0	0	1.00	0	0	0	0
1940	0	0	0	1.00	0	0	0	0	0	0	0	0	0	0
1941	0	0	0	0	0	0	0	1.00	0	1.00	0	0	0	0

Note: Three-letter commodity group abbreviations as for table D.4.

Table D.7A. Number of Advertisements for Durable Goods Mentioning Price, 1901-1941

Year	AUT	HDV	OMV	FUR	APP	PIA	RAD	CHI	HSF	JWL	MED	BKS	MIS	TMB
1901	0	0	0	7	3	1	0	2	0	2	0	1	2	0
1902	0	1	0	3	3	0	0	4	1	1	0	0	3	0
1903	1	0	0	3	2	3	0	3	4	2	0	3	0	0
1904	0	0	0	11	2	1	2	3	4	3	0	1	1	0
1905	0	0	0	3	2	2	0	7	6	5	0	0	0	0
1906	0	0	0	3	2	2	0	6	5	5	0	2	1	0
1907	0	0	0	3	2	2	1	5	4	4	1	0	0	0
1908	0	0	0	7	2	0	0	4	3	1	0	0	0	0
1909	1	0	0	11	2	2	1	2	3	2	0	2	0	0
1910	0	0	0	5	2	2	0	2	5	1	0	1	0	0
1911	0	0	0	6	3	2	1	5	2	1	0	0	0	0
1912	1	0	0	3	2	1	0	1	2	2	0	0	0	0
1913	0	0	0	5	5	1	1	4	4	2	0	3	0	0
1914	0	0	0	3	3	0	1	5	4	3	0	0	0	0
1915	2	0	0	0	4	1	1	4	4	3	0	2	0	0
1916	2	0	0	1	4	2	1	4	4	5	0	1	0	0

Table D.7A, continued

Year	AUT	HDV	OMV	FUR	APP	PIA	RAD	CHI	HSF	JWL	MED	BKS	MIS	TMB
1917	1	0	0	3	4	1	2	3	5	2	0	1	0	0
1918	1	0	0	1	2	0	2	1	1	0	0	2	0	0
1919	0	0	0	1	0	0	3	3	0	3	0	2	1	0
1920	0	0	0	0	1	0	3	2	3	3	0	2	1	0
1921	0	0	0	2	1	0	2	4	6	1	0	1	0	0
1922	1	0	0	1	2	1	2	3	8	1	0	3	0	0
1923	2	0	0	3	6	0	1	8	3	3	0	2	1	0
1924	0	0	0	3	4	1	2	5	3	2	0	0	0	0
1925	2	0	0	3	8	0	1	7	3	0	0	0	0	0
1926	5	0	0	1	7	0	3	6	3	0	0	1	0	0
1927	3	0	0	4	3	0	5	4	2	0	0	0	0	0
1928	3	0	0	3	0	2	1	6	3	1	0	0	0	0
1929	2	0	0	5	3	1	3	6	4	1	0	0	0	0
1930	4	0	0	1	6	0	0	6	3	0	0	0	0	0
1931	4	0	0	1	5	0	1	2	5	0	0	0	0	0
1932	1	0	0	1	2	0	1	3	3	0	0	0	0	0

Table D.7A, continued

Year	AUT	HDV	OMV	FUR	APP	PIA	RAD	CHI	HSF	JWL	MED	BKS	MIS	TMB
1933	1	0	0	1	0	0	0	2	1	0	0	0	0	0
1934	0	0	0	1	1	0	0	2	3	0	0	0	0	0
1935	0	0	0	1	2	0	0	2	3	0	0	0	0	0
1936	0	0	0	0	2	0	1	3	1	0	0	0	0	0
1937	0	0	0	1	0	0	1	4	1	0	0	0	0	0
1938	0	0	0	1	0	0	0	3	0	0	0	0	0	0
1939	0	0	0	1	3	0	0	5	1	1	0	0	0	0
1940	0	0	0	1	7	0	0	10	1	0	0	0	0	0
1941	0	0	0	2	3	0	1	5	2	1	0	0	0	0

Table D.7B. Pages of Advertisements for Durable Goods Mentioning Price, 1901-1941

Year	AUT	HDV	OMV	FUR	APP	PIA	RAD	CHI	HSF	JWL	MED	BKS	MIS	TMB
1901	0	0	0	0.53	0.28	0.13	0	0.17	0	0.27	0	0.05	0.32	0
1902	0	0.07	0	0.26	0.14	0	0	0.33	0.03	0.04	0	0	0.32	0
1903	0.07	0	0	0.33	0.15	0.49	0	0.27	0.24	0.07	0	0.63	0	0
1904	0	0	0	0.94	0.19	0.21	0.19	0.22	0.47	0.08	0	0.07	0.02	0
1905	0	0	0	1.31	0.20	0.16	0	0.63	0.60	0.65	0	0	0	0
1906	0	0	0	1.18	0.32	0.19	0	0.42	0.29	0.64	0	0.18	0.02	0
1907	0	0	0	0.42	0.19	0.34	1.00	1.47	0.45	0.33	0.07	0	0	0
1908	0	0	0	0.99	0.58	0	0	0.40	0.18	0.04	0	0	0	0
1909	0.25	0	0	3.27	0.42	0.38	0.25	0.30	0.10	0.07	0	0.09	0	0
1910	0	0	0	1.16	0.33	0.56	0	1.10	0.29	0.02	0	0.01	0	0
1911	0	0	0	1.02	0.59	0.30	1.00	1.10	0.08	0.02	0	0	0	0
1912	0.25	0	0	0.22	0.33	0.02	0	0.50	0.29	1.02	0	0	0	0
1913	0	0	0	0.44	0.62	0.50	1.00	0.96	0.40	0.27	0	0.30	0	0
1914	0	0	0	0.40	0.28	0	1.00	1.61	0.58	0.77	0	0	0	0
1915	2.25	0	0	0	0.33	0.28	1.00	1.40	0.36	0.43	0	0.05	0	0
1916	2.25	0	0	0.25	0.55	0.35	1.00	1.64	2.06	1.48	0	0.04	0	0

Table D.7B, continued

Year	AUT	HDV	OMV	FUR	APP	PIA	RAD	CHI	HSF	JWL	MED	BKS	MIS	TMB
1917	2.00	0	0	0.79	0.96	0.25	2.00	1.59	0.65	0.38	0	0.14	0	0
1918	1.00	0	0	0.05	1.50	0	2.00	0.50	1.00	0	0	0.55	0	0
1919	0	0	0	1.00	0	0	2.50	3.00	0	0.46	0	0.35	1.00	0
1920	0	0	0	0	0.25	0	3.00	1.50	1.50	0.75	0	1.25	1.00	0
1921	0	0	0	0.27	0.50	0	2.00	1.75	3.26	0.18	0	0.15	0	0
1922	0.50	0	0	0.50	0.40	0	2.00	2.00	3.20	0.13	0	0.04	0	0
1923	2.00	0	0	1.00	1.70	0.25	1.00	4.03	1.39	0.48	0	0.32	0.13	0
1924	0	0	0	2.25	1.15	0	2.00	3.11	2.16	0.75	0	0	0	0
1925	2.00	0	0	2.04	4.27	0.25	1.00	5.04	2.25	0	0	0	0	0
1926	5.00	0	0	0.04	2.49	0	2.50	4.50	1.75	0	0	0.02	0	0
1927	3.00	0	0	2.14	3.00	0	2.63	4.00	1.50	0	0	0	0	0
1928	3.00	0	0	1.58	0	1.25	1.00	3.77	1.25	1.00	0	0	0	0
1929	3.00	0	0	5.50	1.00	1.00	3.00	4.88	2.38	1.00	0	0	0	0
1930	2.75	0	0	1.00	4.58	0	0	5.50	1.38	0	0	0	0	0
1931	4.00	0	0	1.00	2.25	0	0.50	0.75	2.35	0	0	0	0	0
1932	0.04	0	0	1.00	0.46	0	1.00	3.25	2.25	0	0	0	0	0

Table D.7B, continued

Year	AUT	HDV	OMV	FUR	APP	PIA	RAD	CHI	HSF	JWL	MED	BKS	MIS	TMB
1933	1.00	0	0	1.00	0	0	0	1.50	1.00	0	0	0	0	0
1934	0	0	0	1.00	0.02	0	0	1.00	2.50	0	0	0	0	0
1935	0	0	0	1.00	1.04	0	0	1.00	2.15	0	0	0	0	0
1936	0	0	0	0	0.50	0	0.11	1.09	0.25	0	0	0	0	0
1937	0	0	0	1.00	0	0	0.25	1.42	1.00	0	0	0	0	0
1938	0	0	0	1.00	0	0	0	1.19	0	0	0	0	0	0
1939	0	0	0	1.00	1.75	0	0	1.21	1.00	1.00	0	0	0	0
1940	0	0	0	1.00	3.38	0	0	2.34	0.13	0	0	0	0	0
1941	0	0	0	2.00	1.25	0	0.25	2.03	1.25	1.00	0	0	0	0

Note: Three-letter commodity group abbreviations as for table D.4.

◆ NOTES ◆

CHAPTER I

Chapter 1 has no notes.

CHAPTER 2

1. The definition was first formulated by Simon Kuznets and is found in Kuznets, *National Income and Capital Formation*, p. 36.

2. Oshima, "Consumer Asset Formation," p. 20. His category major durable goods is equivalent to the sum of the three Department of Commerce categories furniture, household appliances, and automobiles, plus televisions. Oshima explicitly excluded radios from major durable goods.

3. The definition is in Juster, *Household Capital Formation and Financing*, p. 14. The commodity group designations are given in his notes to table A-1, cols. 4 and 5, pp. 102–3. The commodity groups are from Goldsmith, *Study of Saving*, 1:table Q-5, p. 680, and related tables. Goldsmith's Department of Commerce source was U.S. Office of Business Economics, *National Income: 1954 Edition*.

4. See appendix A for details on development of estimates of expenditure for horse-drawn vehicles.

5. Twentieth-century estimates of spending are in general from the Department of Commerce publication *Fixed Reproducible Tangible Wealth, 1925–85*. Sources and methodology used to extend their estimates back to 1869 are discussed in appendix A, to which the interested reader is referred. Estimates of spending for durable goods per household begin in 1880; Census Bureau estimates of the number of households have been extrapolated from 1900 back to 1880 using estimates of population.

6. The definitions are from Kuznets, *National Income and Capital Formation*, p. 36. Following Kuznets, semidurable goods are shoes, clothing (including military issue), semidurable house furnishings, nondurable toys and sports equipment, and one-half the difference between expenditure abroad by United States residents and personal remittances in kind to foreigners. Kuznets, *Capital in the American Economy*, notes to table R-3, cols. 1–3, p. 489.

7. Kuznets published the numbers this way because of excessive volatility and unreliability of the annual estimates themselves.

8. Christina Romer, in "New Estimates of Prewar Gross National Product and Unemployment," has pointed out problems with Kuznets's early estimates. These problems are due to an implicit assumption of an absence of cyclical movement of distribution costs, an assumption invoked in moving from Shaw's estimates of output which are valued at producer prices, to Kuznets's estimates of output which are valued at final (consumer) prices. Romer argues that for cyclical analysis, Kuznets's numbers are too

volatile because distribution costs probably moved countercyclically, tempering the volatility of production and wide swings in wholesale costs. Romer's point regarding distribution costs applies to the estimates of expenditure for durable goods developed in appendix A and reported here. Although valid, Romer's concerns are less relevant to the current exercise, however. Here we are looking at long-term secular patterns, not short-run cyclical ones. Following Kuznets, long-run intertemporal comparisons have been facilitated by computing averages and thus smoothing out any excess volatility in the annual estimates. Even if distribution costs did move countercyclically rather than remain constant over the business cycle, so long as each industry's movements in distribution costs are the same, the inter-industry comparisons made here remain valid despite Romer's objections.

9. The decline in expenditure for new automobiles during World War II is particularly striking. From expenditure for new automobiles of $2,552 million in 1941, spending fell to $127 million in 1942, $136 million in 1943, $50 million in 1944, $37 million in 1945, and then jumped back to $2,024 million in 1946 and $4,027 million in 1947. Data from U.S. Bureau of Economic Analysis (BEA), *National Income and Product Accounts, 1929–76*, table 2.4, pp. 89–90. Expenditure estimates are rounded to the nearest tenth of a billion dollars in the most recent edition of the national accounts (U.S. BEA, *National Income and Product Accounts, 1929–82*, table 2.4) but are otherwise consistent with these more detailed estimates.

10. The estimates in table 2.6 cannot be derived directly from those in table 2.1, nor can those in the upcoming table 2.7 be derived directly from the estimates in table 2.2. The estimates in tables 2.6 and 2.7 are averages of annual estimates of the percentage share of expenditure for each commodity group in total consumer durable goods expenditure; they are *not* the percentage share of the average expenditure for each commodity group in average total consumer durable goods expenditure. Only in the latter case could the figures be derived from those in tables 2.1 and 2.2. The difference between averaging percentage shares and computing percentage shares of averages are generally small (on the order of one-tenth of a percentage point) and do not alter the substantive conclusions in the least.

11. Bicycles and motorcycles are not included in transportation vehicles but are instead part of miscellaneous other durable goods. Between 1889 and 1929 expenditure for bicycles and motorcycles (primarily bicycles) accounted for anywhere from 10 to 50 percent of total expenditure for miscellaneous other durable goods.

12. See U.S. BEA, *National Income and Product Accounts, 1929–82*, table A, pp. xvi–xvii. The Department of Commerce's current definition of personal outlays is different from what they used in the 1950s and 1960s when Goldsmith, Juster, Kuznets, and others were developing estimates to link with Department of Commerce estimates. Through the 1960s, personal outlays and personal consumption expenditure were identical; consumer interest payments to business and net personal transfer payments to foreigners were both components of consumer services. These two items are now excluded from gross national product and from consumer expenditure, reflecting the assumption that neither contribute directly to the nation's output.

13. This theoretical treatment of consumer durable goods is consistent with that in the life-cycle hypothesis of saving associated with Franco Modigliani. See Modigliani and Brumberg, "The Consumption Function," pp. 392–93.

14. We could also make this distinction for some semidurable goods since their expected service lives are in some cases greater than one year.

15. What of the placement of acquisition of consumer durable goods in the national expenditure accounts? The Department of Commerce places consumer durables with total consumption expenditure not for theoretical but for practical empirical reasons: absence of reliable estimates of the value of services produced by durable goods. They do, however, treat purchases of consumer durables as investment in capital assets in U.S. BEA, *Fixed Reproducible Tangible Wealth, 1925–85*. A number of economists argue that consumer durable goods should be counted as investment in the national income and product accounts as well. Ruggles, "United States National Income Accounts," provides a review of the positions of economists on this issue.

16. If in one year a household with disposable income of $60,000 purchases $40,000 in goods and services and uses the remaining $20,000 as down payment on a $100,000 newly constructed house, the household will have total consumption expenditure of $40,000 and saving of $20,000. The money spent on the house is not included in total consumption expenditure.

17. See U.S. BEA, *National Income and Product Accounts, 1929–82*, p. xi.

18. The average value of the conventionally defined saving rate for 1900–1916 is the same as the average for 1898–1916, so the decline between 1900–1916 and the 1920s is also about one-third.

CHAPTER 3

1. An aside to the nonspecialist. While efforts were made to keep this chapter as accessible as possible, it would be folly to argue that it is completely accessible to all readers alike. Algebraic derivations are confined to appendix C, as are some of the more technical comments regarding the econometric analysis. Equations, regressions, and statistical tests cannot be passed over altogether, though, as they are the only method available for sorting out the economist's dilemma over the Consumer Durables Revolution.

2. Oshima, "Consumer Asset Formation." The exchange is found in Vatter and Thompson, "Consumer Asset Formation and Economic Growth"; Juster and Lipsey, "Note on Consumer Asset Formation"; Vatter, "Consumer-Asset Formation in the United States: A Rejoinder"; and Vatter, "Has There Been a Twentieth-Century Consumer Durables Revolution?"

3. Oshima, "Consumer Asset Formation," pp. 20–22. Oshima distinguishes between the "mass of households" and upper-income and professional households. Businesses and upper-income and professional households provide the bulk of savings that are channeled through capital markets to the "mass of households" (self-employed, clerical, sales, skilled, semiskilled, unskilled, and service workers) for credit-financed purchases of major durable goods.

4. Vatter and Thompson, "Consumer Asset Formation and Economic Growth," p. 314.

5. Ibid., p. 319 n. 3.

6. Juster and Lipsey, "Note on Consumer Asset Formation," p. 840. Juster and Lipsey

used Raymond Goldsmith's estimates of consumer durables expenditure by commodity group to measure major and minor durable goods. Goldsmith, *Study of Saving*, 1:tables P-13 and P-16, pp. 892, 898. Unfortunately, Goldsmith's estimates contain a serious bias; due to his treatment of passenger automobiles purchased by consumers for business use, Goldsmith's estimates of consumer automobile expenditure are some 30 percent higher than Department of Commerce estimates.

7. Vatter, "Has There Been a Twentieth-Century Consumer Durables Revolution?" It is here that Professor Vatter advances the phrase "Consumer Durables Revolution." However, Vatter argued against, not for, the existence of such a revolution. His title seems to have stuck with more tenacity than his conclusion.

8. Vatter, "Has There Been a Twentieth-Century Consumer Durables Revolution?" In another article, Vatter did allow that an "automobile revolution" occurred since expenditure for automobiles relative to total consumption expenditure and to gross national product have increased substantially over the twentieth century. Vatter, "Consumer-Asset Formation in the United States: A Rejoinder," p. 855.

9. The estimates reported in chapter 2 are based on a newly developed data set. Many of these estimates, especially those for the years before 1929, could not have been computed twenty years ago with the then-available data.

10. Vatter, "Has There Been a Twentieth-Century Consumer Durables Revolution?," pp. 4–5.

11. Briefly, an elasticity measures the responsiveness of household demand for some product to changes in income, price, or other determining factors. See also the discussion below regarding elasticity.

12. Stone and Rowe, "Demand for Durable Goods." Stone and Rowe's model is used as the theoretical framework for the vast majority of empirical studies of demand for durable goods. Many of the studies that do not rely upon this gradual stock-adjustment framework are based explicitly upon a microeconomic model in which consumers maximize some form of an intertemporal utility function. An example of this latter type of model is Weber, "Interest Rates, Inflation, and Consumer Expenditures." The analysis of durable goods demand reported below is presented in abbreviated form in Olney, "Demand for Durable Goods."

13. At any point in time, the value of the services that remain embodied in a durable good is part of a household's total stock of assets. This value, the "net stock" of the durable good, is equal to the difference between the good's original price and the cumulative value of depreciation of the good.

14. Depreciation is an estimate of the value of a good's services that, in the current period, are consumed, lost through accidental damage or destruction, or foregone due to obsolescence or other reason.

15. The model is sometimes referred to as one of partial rather than gradual stock adjustment. Either way, actual stock is partially adjusted toward desired stock in each period; over time, actual stock gradually adjusts toward desired stock. Gradual adjustment of actual capital stock to a desired level is also characteristic of some models of business investment expenditure.

Stone and Rowe, in "Demand for Durable Goods," p. 425, refer to the desired stock of a durable good as "equilibrium stock." Their terminology can be misleading since absence of immediate adjustment is not due to an inadequate supply of the goods but is itself an equilibrium condition.

16. Net stock equals gross stock less the cumulative value of depreciation, where gross stock is simply the good's original purchase price. A contemporary and familiar example illustrates the concepts. The original purchase price of your car is its gross stock value each and every year of that car's life. The blue book value (its current fair market value) is an estimate of your car's net stock value. This value changes over time as your car depreciates.

17. "Net stock" is an awkward phrase. Unless otherwise noted, henceforth "stock" will be used in place of "net stock." Note also that end-of-period stock, $S_{i,t}$, equals the sum of previous end-of-period stock and this period's net investment expenditure.

18. It might also be argued that demand for some semidurable goods is best modeled as a process of gradual rather than immediate adjustment. Demand for some semidurable goods is indeed modeled this way in Houthakker and Taylor, *Consumer Demand in the United States.*

19. Akerlof, "Market for 'Lemons.'" This point is developed in Mishkin, "Illiquidity, Consumer Durable Expenditure, and Monetary Policy." The household's subjective probability of "making a distress sale" is an explicit part of Mishkin's model of demand for durable goods. Mishkin applies his model to an analysis of demand for durable goods during the Great Depression in Mishkin, "Household Balance Sheet and the Great Depression."

20. A decrease in the minimum down payment on a consumer loan also increases the adjustment factor by decreasing the time needed to accumulate the amount of the down payment. This effect may not be observable with annual data. Grieves, "Demand for Consumer Durables," explicitly introduces credit availability into a model of demand for durable goods as a determinant of desired stock. In addition, Grieves assumes desired stock is inversely related to a household's perceived risk of future income loss and uses the national unemployment rate as a proxy for each household's perception of that risk.

In addition to lumpiness, illiquidity, and relatively high prices of durable goods, the relative infrequency of purchase of any particular durable good may also slow the adjustment process. Households purchase many nondurable goods and services frequently, so the marginal cost of acquiring information regarding price, quality, and other product characteristics is negligible. But information about durable goods is gathered only infrequently, and thus the marginal costs, either pecuniary (purchase of consumer literature) or nonpecuniary (time spent gathering the information), may not be negligible. Within the context of an intertemporal utility maximization model, Richard W. Parks examines the effect of transactions costs associated with gathering product information on individual demand for durable goods. The nonpecuniary (time) cost is modeled separately from the pecuniary costs to allow for a role for consumer income. Parks, "Demand and Supply of Durable Goods," especially pp. 41, 46.

21. Modigliani and Brumberg, "The Consumption Function," pp. 391–93, and Modigliani, "Life Cycle Hypothesis of Saving," pp. 162, 177–78.

22. For example, Chow, "Statistical Demand Functions for Automobiles"; Darby, "Allocation of Transitory Income"; Grieves, "Demand for Consumer Durables"; Juster and Wachtel, "Models of Durable Goods Demand"; and Levedahl, "Household Automobile Expenditures." One argument is that permanent income influences desired stock through its effect on desired services, while transitory income affects the adjustment coefficient. Increased transitory income may speed accumulation of financial resources and lead to earlier realization of planned expenditures, for instance. Houthakker and

Taylor use total consumption expenditure as a proxy for a long-run income variable, arguing that an appropriately specified long-run income variable would be correlated with total consumption expenditure. Houthakker and Taylor, *Consumer Demand in the United States*, p. 33.

23. Modigliani, "Life Cycle Hypothesis of Saving," p. 184.

24. Including only one relative price variable reflects an implicit assumption that households face only two commodities: the product of concern and an aggregate of all other goods and services. Conceptualizing such a two-commodity world and then using a relative price variable that has a price index for all consumer goods and services as the denominator is not entirely consistent, however. Using the price index of *all* consumer goods and services rather than that of *all other* goods and services introduces double-counting; the price of the product is included in both numerator and denominator of relative price. This formulation of relative price does allow an empirical study of demand to be incorporated into a larger econometric model, however. Since the statistical effect is generally minor, the convention found in the literature is followed here.

25. Once a durable good is produced, both the good's life span and the quantity of services produced by the good in each period are, by assumption, predetermined and therefore cannot change with economic conditions. Households can vary their rate of consumption of these services only by foregoing some of the services available to them in that period. If households could instead respond to economic conditions by altering the rate at which a durable good's services are produced, the value of services produced in a period and the good's life span would be affected. Decreased production of a good's services in one period should increase its expected longevity, for instance. Incorporating these possibilities into the presentation introduces unnecessary complications, however, and does not significantly alter the gist of the argument.

26. This equation is presented in discrete rather than continuous time primarily for ease of presentation. Although the equations would change if continuous compounding of interest were assumed, the argument would not.

27. Changes in the quality of durable goods introduce further complications into the use of the good's price as a proxy for the price of the good's services. As the quality of durable goods increases, measured price increases will overstate "true" quality-adjusted price increases, and therefore measured price elasticities will understate "true" price elasticities. One solution to this problem is use of hedonic prices, which take product quality into account. For a project of this magnitude, such a solution is impractical. Some scholars have developed hedonic price indexes for automobiles for limited time periods. See, for example, Court, "Hedonic Price Indexes." Robert Gordon's new and impressive work on prices of durable goods, *Measurement of Durable Goods Prices*, covers a great many durable goods and the entire post–World War II period; it also took fifteen years to complete. Extending the effort throughout the twentieth century would be an impressive project in its own right.

28. This possibility is taken into account in Hendricks, Youmans, and Keller, *Consumer Durables and Installment Debt*; Lippitt, *Demand for House Furnishings and Equipment*; and Levedahl, "Household Automobile Expenditures."

29. Statistical insignificance of relative price in estimates of demand for durable goods groups is not unusual. Houthakker and Taylor estimated no price coefficient for motor vehicles, furniture, or radios and television receivers. They used annual observations and estimated demand for 1929–61, excluding 1942–45 as the years of World War II.

Houthakker and Taylor, *Consumer Demand in the United States*, pp. 30–36, 81–82, 112–13, 130–31.

30. The habit-formation model of demand is discussed in detail in appendix C, where the complications that arise when at least some households buying or owning durable goods practice habit-formation behavior are also considered.

31. Johnston, *Econometric Methods*, p. 160.

32. The dependent variable in equation 3.7 can be expressed as a function of present and one-period lagged values of the independent and dependent variables, allowing the lagged stock variable to be dropped from the estimation. Nerlove, "Market Demand for Durable Goods." This transformation is unnecessary here since we have annual estimates of depreciation and stock.

33. Vatter, "Has There Been a Twentieth-Century Consumer Durables Revolution?," pp. 1–2.

34. The formulas for the F-test, given in appendix C, are taken from Maddala, *Econometrics*, pp. 197–200. The test was originally presented in Chow, "Tests of Equality."

35. Income elasticity is calculated for each period by multiplying the income coefficient by the ratio of the average value of gross expenditure to the average value of income over that period. Similarly, own-price elasticity is the product of the relative price coefficient and the ratio of the average value of gross expenditure to the average value of the relative price over that time period.

36. Changes in the discount rate can be ruled out as the culprit; if changes in the discount rate had made the good's relative price a poor proxy for the variable of concern, the relative price of the good's services, it would be a poor proxy for *all* commodity groups and not just these few.

37. Other empirical studies of demand for durable goods include Suits and Sparks, "Consumption Regressions"; Juster and Wachtel, "Models of Durable Goods Demand"; Mishkin, "Illiquidity, Consumer Durable Expenditure, and Monetary Policy"; and Grieves, "Demand for Consumer Durables."

38. Studies estimating or citing elasticities include Burstein, "Demand for Household Refrigeration"; Houthakker and Taylor, *Consumer Demand in the United States*; and Mishkin, "Illiquidity, Consumer Durable Expenditure, and Monetary Policy."

39. The test results also underscore the dangers of relying on heavily aggregated statistics for this sort of analysis. Comparing pre–World War I and interwar periods, the aggregate major durable goods shows solid evidence of changing demand, but only one of its component product groups, household appliances, shows clear evidence of shifting until the test's stringency is relaxed. Similarly, comparing interwar and post–World War II periods, all minor durable goods but china and tableware show no evidence of shifting, yet we obtain mixed results for the aggregate minor durable goods. Combining pianos and other musical instruments and radios and phonographs into one commodity group, radios and musical instruments, may be misleading as well; demand for pianos and other musical instruments shows the strongest evidence of shift according to the F-test, but demand for radios and phonographs and for the combined group, radios and musical instruments, shows the opposite.

40. See also the discussion in appendix C of the statistical artifacts of a mix of habit-formation and gradual stock-adjustment behaviors in the economy. Positive lagged stock coefficients for these products before World War I are consistent with the proposition that most of these goods were owned by well-to-do households whose purchases were

largely undertaken out of habit rather than in response to changes in relative prices or life-cycle income.

41. The sign of the wealth coefficient indicates whether households viewed durable goods primarily as assets or as consumables. The coefficient is interpreted only for the pre–World War I and interwar periods, those periods in which correlation between wealth and lagged stock is relatively weak.

CHAPTER 4

1. Tracking outstanding debt-to-income ratios over time provides a useful measure of trends in aggregate indebtedness. But when outstanding debt is long-term rather than short-term, with say fifteen or thirty years maturity, then comparing the total of outstanding debt with annual income vastly overstates the burden of debt. In such a case, a more accurate measure of the burden would use, for instance, the annual repayment requirements of total outstanding debt.

2. These deflated estimates are not included in table 4.2 primarily because they should be consulted only for their broad outlines as summarized in the text. The interested reader can easily compute the estimates by using the nominal debt estimates of table 4.2 and the price index numbers from table A.8.

3. Goldsmith, *Study of Saving*, 1:892, assumes instead that only 10 percent of all vehicle sales were to business. Goldsmith's assumption may indeed be more accurate for the 1920s; the National Association of Sales Finance Companies (NASFC) notes that before 1927, only "some small percentage" of total vehicle financing was for business customers. NASFC, "Composite Experience . . . , 1937." If we follow Goldsmith and assume that 90 rather than 70 percent of total vehicle sales were to households, each estimate is increased by about 30 percent. In 1919, 6.3 percent of households would have bought a car on installments; 19.5 percent would have done so in 1929. In 1929, 31 percent of households would have bought a car through some means.

4. Seligman, *Economics of Instalment Selling*, 1:100–108.

5. Ibid.

6. Charles Holt estimates that in the 1920s the lower 95 percent of the nonfarm population received on average only 95 percent of the economy-wide average annual income. Holt, "Who Benefited from the Prosperity of the Twenties?" But Gene Smiley notes that Holt's estimates for 1920–24 are probably an overstatement since the tax returns that served as his data source are believed to under-report income of wealthy individuals in those years. Smiley, "Did Incomes for Most of the Population Fall from 1923 through 1929?"

7. The calculations assume real interest rates are zero; that is, the interest income that the household would earn on savings would be exactly offset by increases in the car's price. If interest accumulated more quickly than the car's price increased, the number of months needed to save up enough money would have decreased slightly.

8. The point is made in William H. Grimes, *Story of Commercial Credit*, pp. 4, 16.

9. Such tactics of furniture dealers are recounted in Rau, "Home Furnishings' Stake in Consumer Credit Expansion," pp. 26–27.

10. NAFC notes, however, that under the Uniform Commercial Sales Act, goods re-

possessed after 50 percent or more of the purchase price has been paid had to be resold, and any amount received in excess of the remaining balance due plus costs of "resale, retaking, keeping and storing" the good must be returned to the buyer. They do not note whether there were restrictions on the level of such costs. NAFC, *NAFC News* 36 (December 1930): 2–3. Elsewhere NAFC reports that the figures of one "well managed" sales finance company showed, however, that almost 70 percent of repossessions occur before the fourth payment is made. NAFC, "Memo to Members: Repossession and Other Experience with Retail Automobile Paper."

11. In the late 1920s, about one-third of used car contracts were purchased without recourse. NAFC, "Composite Experience for 1931 and Prior Years." Analogous estimates for new car financing are not given. As of 1932, no-recourse contracts were not written for any goods other than automobiles. NAFC, "Diversified Financing Methods," p. 3. Sloan discusses the reasons General Motors Acceptance Corporation (GMAC) switched from the full-recourse plan to the repurchase plan in Sloan, *My Years with General Motors*, pp. 358–60.

12. The National Housing Act of 1934 provided federal guarantees for repair and modernization loans. Robbins includes these insured loans with "all other lenders" regardless of the type of financial institution. Robbins, *Consumer Instalment Loans*, tables 3 and 4, pp. 17, 19.

13. These practices are reported in a number of institutional histories including William A. Grimes, *Financing Automobile Sales*, p. 48, and Seligman, *Economics of Instalment Selling*, 1:289.

14. The standards are reported in NAFC, "Resolution Adopted at the General Meeting, December 1924."

15. Holdbacks were a common practice in the early 1920s, but by the late 1920s most sales finance companies held back nothing on new auto contracts and 5 to 10 percent on used cars. The extent of the holdback depended upon the finance company's assessment of the likelihood of bad contracts written by a particular dealer and sometimes varied between dealers of one product line. Ayres, "Diversification and the Future of Financing." NAFC urged its member companies not to forego the holdback since it increased finance company profit without adding to retail buyers' financing costs. NAFC, "Diversified Financing Methods," p. 2.

16. The contract is the only sample filed in *NAFC Miscellaneous Publications* (Baker Library, Harvard University). It was provided by the association as an example of a typical sales financing contract.

17. Precise estimates vary. Seligman, *Economics of Instalment Selling*, 1:48–49, estimates there were about 1,000 sales finance companies in 1922 but between 1,600 and 1,700 in 1925. In a 1934 memo to its members, NAFC noted that in response to surveys, it had found there were 1,297 sales finance companies operating on July 1, 1928, and only 1,099 companies as of January 1, 1934, the decline reflecting mergers or absorptions of small companies but not outright failures. NAFC, "Memo to Members: Few Finance Company Failures." In its monthly newsletter in October 1931, NAFC cited the same July 1, 1928, survey and also noted that there were 1,134 companies as of December 31, 1930, but only 1,007 as of August 1, 1931. William A. Grimes, *Financing Automobile Sales*, p. 80, guessed in 1926 that there had been approximately 1,400 sales finance companies as of December 1924 but only 850 remaining by mid-1926. His numbers are repeated by Hanch, "Benefits of Installment Selling," in a 1928 article distributed by

NAFC to its members. Ayres, "Installment Selling and Industrial Recession," provides the 1920 estimate.

18. According to the NAFC, banks suffered only five losses from underwriting auto sales finance companies in the five years preceding 1935. Each loss was "very small." By way of contrast, the association notes that between 1929 and 1934, "thousands of banks have lost millions of dollars through direct loans to automobile dealers and other installment merchants." NASFC, *Directory*, p. 5. (NAFC amended its name by inserting "Sales" in 1935 so as to clearly distinguish its member companies from more general types of finance companies.)

19. NASFC, *Directory*, p. 3. Only 9 of the 103 companies that offered diversified financing did not also offer motor vehicles financing.

20. The 1935 population estimate is the geometric interpolation of the 1930 and 1940 population estimates by state that are given in U.S. Bureau of the Census, *Historical Statistics*, Ser. A195, pp. 24–37. The dependent variable of the regression is the percentage of sales finance company offices by state; the independent variable is the percentage of total population by state. The coefficient on the independent variable is 1.026 with standard error of 0.046. The constant term is −0.052.

21. This is stated in its extreme form primarily but not entirely for expository purposes. Clearly both the supply of and demand for credit can shift simultaneously. The relative sizes of these shifts determine whether the relative price of credit falls (if supply shifts dominate) or rises (if demand shifts dominate). Regardless of the relative sizes of the changes in supply and in demand, however, an increase in the supply of consumer credit can be seen as a cause of the Consumer Durables Revolution, and an increase in demand for credit can be seen as an effect of the Consumer Durables Revolution. The burgeoning credit economy can thus be both cause and effect of the Consumer Durables Revolution simultaneously.

22. For an installment contract with finance charges assessed on the amount financed, lengthening the payback period of the contract just decreases monthly payments without any offsetting effect on total charges paid.

23. Economists have used any one of these three variables to measure the costs of credit. Lippitt, *Demand for House Furnishings and Equipment*, uses average maturity of loans, as do Juster and Wachtel, "Models of Durable Goods Demand." Grieves, "Demand for Consumer Durables," constructs a variable measuring credit availability using an index drawn from bankers' replies to a Federal Reserve Board survey concerning their willingness to extend consumer loans. Additional theoretical complications arise when deciding the proper price index to use to determine the *relative* price of credit. Do households compare the price of credit with prices of all other goods and services? With rates of return on financial assets? And do lending institutions use an identical measure of the relative price of credit? Luckily, resolving these issues is unnecessary for the present discussion.

24. NAFC, "Resolution Adopted at the General Meeting, December 1924."

25. This point is claimed in Board of Governors of the Federal Reserve System, *Consumer Instalment Credit*, vol. 1, pt. 1, p. 27.

26. The down payment and contract maturity figures are from Seligman, *Economics of Installment Selling*, 1:100–101.

27. The standards are given in NASFC, *Directory*, p. 7.

28. The survey is reported in NAFC, "Diversified Financing Methods."

29. Phelps, *Financing the Instalment Purchases of the American Family*, p. 41.

30. Seligman, *Economics of Installment Selling*, 1:100–101. Seligman did not clearly state whether these were discount or effective interest rates. If his evidence is consistent with that from other studies, however, they must be discount rates.

31. Clark, *Financing the Consumer*, p. 134.

32. Reid, *Consumers and the Market*, pp. 264–65. Included in her underlying calculation of the effective interest rates are costs of insurance and any charges or fees. This accounts for part of the difference between Reid's and Clark's findings.

33. The table is in NAFC, "Diversified Financing Methods."

34. This section of chapter 4 is drawn heavily from Olney, "Credit as a Production-Smoothing Device."

35. Precise estimates vary. See Ralph C. Epstein, *Automobile Industry*, p. 164, and Katz, *Decline of Competition in the Automobile Industry*, pp. 15–18.

36. Many of these details are now well known. Two of the best contemporary studies of the auto industry which provided background information for much of the detail reported here are Ralph C. Epstein, *Automobile Industry*, especially pp. 39, 137–39, and Seltzer, *Financial History of the American Automobile Industry*, especially p. 53.

37. A recent analysis is Marx, "Development of the Franchise Distribution System." See also Ralph C. Epstein, *Automobile Industry*, pp. 132–36.

38. This change is noted in William A. Grimes, *Financing Automobile Sales*, pp. 21–22, and Seltzer, *Financial History of the American Automobile Industry*, p. 99.

39. Ford's policy is discussed in Nevins, *Ford: The Times, the Man, the Company*, pp. 344, 403. That dealers were often men with useful technical knowledge is noted in Ralph C. Epstein, *Automobile Industry*, p. 140. The existence of such "good-faith" deposits is pointed out in Hewitt, *Automobile Franchise Agreements*, p. 16.

40. Franchise contracts are discussed in Marx, "Development of the Franchise Distribution System," p. 466, and Katz, *Decline of Competition in the Automobile Industry*, p. 79. The cancellation clause is discussed in Macaulay, *Law and the Balance of Power*, pp. 11–12. See also Hewitt, *Automobile Franchise Agreements*, pp. 24–25.

41. Estimates of monthly variation in sales are in Chandler, *Giant Enterprise*, p. 133; Prescott, "Twenty-Five Years of Growth," pp. 94–95; and, for General Motors, NAFC, *NAFC News* 18 (June 1929): 1. See also Moran, "Automobiles—Big Business by Small Business Men," p. 61.

42. William A. Grimes, *Financing Automobile Sales*, p. 20, argues the point regarding depreciation of idle equipment. Concerns over labor problems are recounted in Chandler, *Giant Enterprise*, p. 134. In light of these arguments made by the auto industry at the time, it seems surprising that manufacturers soon abandoned their efforts to smooth production by allowing inventory fluctuations. As total production increased, however, and winter inventory buildups became almost obscenely large, manufacturers switched gears and designed strategies to control both unnecessary seasonal swings in production and excessive inventory buildups. See Kuhn, *GM Passes Ford, 1918–1938*, pp. 206, 212.

43. Following large inventory buildups in the 1924 recession, inventory and production control measures were instituted by General Motors. The change in policy is discussed in Sloan, *My Years with General Motors*, pp. 153–59, and is seen clearly in figure 4.4. After 1925, production moved more nearly with sales and thus exhibited much more seasonal variation than in the early 1920s.

44. William A. Grimes, *Financing Automobile Sales*, p. 21. In 1923, one analyst esti-

mated it would tie up $50 million of Ford cash if the company were to carry winter inventories on its books. Prentiss, *Ford Products and Their Sale*, pp. 424–25. NAFC estimated that about 75,000 General Motors cars and trucks were in dealers' stocks before the spring 1923 buying season commenced. NAFC, *NAFC News* 18 (June 1929): 1.

45. The claim is made by Creekmur, "Floor Plan Problems."

46. Seltzer, *Financial History of the American Automobile Industry*, pp. 53–54, notes the need for financing.

47. It was no secret that bankers refused to lend. See Sloan, *My Years with General Motors*, pp. 354–55, and Moran, "Automobiles—Big Business by Small Business Men," p. 60. Burying it in a footnote, Nevins and Hill note without comment that for many years, the Ford Motor Company quietly pursued a policy of depositing large sums of money in banks around the country with the understanding that the bankers would therefore make financing available to Ford dealers. Nevins and Hill, *Ford: Expansion and Challenge*, p. 662 n. 11.

48. The history of the efforts of auto dealers along these lines is recounted in NADA, *Back to Selling*, p. 8.

49. One selling manual offering such advice is Nystrom, *Automobile Selling*, pp. 33–34.

50. Macaulay, *Law and the Balance of Power*, p. 11, and Hewitt, *Automobile Franchise Agreements*, p. 25, link dealership demand and the resulting power of manufacturers as exercised through the franchise agreement.

51. The speeches are excerpted in NADA, *Back to Selling*, pp. 54–56.

52. The point is also made in Seligman, *Economics of Instalment Selling*, 1:29–30; Seidman, *Accounts Receivable and Inventory Financing*, p. 15; and NADA, *Sell Cars—Not Terms*, p. 16.

53. William H. Grimes, *Story of Commercial Credit*, p. 1.

54. Phelps, *Role of the Sales Finance Companies*, p. 52, makes this claim.

55. William H. Grimes, *Story of Commercial Credit*, pp. 58–60. William A. Grimes, *Financing Automobile Sales*, p. 108, notes that CCC offered a "special time sales price" for all Chryslers. Although dealers were free to sell retail contracts to any sales finance company, they were "forbidden" from writing retail contracts at any higher price than that offered by CCC. CCC's low price was possible because Chrysler agreed that every new car sold would be insured with an insurance company associated with CCC.

56. William H. Grimes, *Story of Commercial Credit*, p. 4.

57. Phelps, *Role of the Sales Finance Companies*, p. 52.

58. Seligman, *Economics of Instalment Selling*, 1:43, makes this claim. Others have repeated it, and to my knowledge none have disputed that this San Franciscan was the first to establish such a company.

59. William H. Grimes, *Story of Commercial Credit*, p. 24.

60. Ibid., p. 30.

61. Ibid., pp. 58–60.

62. Ayres, "Evolution in the Financing and Selling of Motor Vehicles," p. 3, cited in Phelps, *Role of the Sales Finance Companies*, p. 56. A letter from William C. Durant to J. Amory Haskell, GMAC's first president, makes the same point. The letter is quoted in Sloan, *My Years With General Motors*, pp. 354–55.

63. The 1919 annual report is reprinted in Chandler, *Giant Enterprise*, p. 67.

64. Ford's policies in general were much less accommodative of dealers than were General Motors's. In his comparative study, Arthur Kuhn characterizes Ford as viewing dealers as "parasites" sucking profit out of the company, while GM viewed dealers as "partners" in the enterprise. Kuhn, *GM Passes Ford: 1918–1938*, p. 270.

65. This practice is noted in Nevins and Hill, *Ford: Expansion and Challenge*, p. 662 n. 11. They comment that the practice was begun by Hawkins, who had joined the company in 1907, and was continued when William Ryan replaced Hawkins at the end of 1918.

66. The clause is pointed out in Hewitt, *Automobile Franchise Agreements*, p. 64 n. 30.

67. Descriptions of the plan are in William A. Grimes, *Financing Automobile Sales*, p. 35, and Nevins and Hill, *Ford: Expansion and Challenge*, pp. 267–68.

68. Nevins and Hill, *Ford: Expansion and Challenge*, p. 465. In addition to the factory-tied companies noted above, finance companies were also established by the manufacturers of Pierce-Arrow autos and Packard autos, and the independently established Industrial Finance Corporation received a Studebaker contract.

69. In 1955 Ford Motor Company again established a subsidiary credit company, Ford Motor Credit Company. Ford executives today privately recount that the company apparently wished to establish the credit company some years earlier but first awaited resolution of a federal antitrust case involving General Motors and GMAC. Sloan discusses the lawsuit and its eventual resolution in Sloan, *My Years with General Motors*, pp. 361–62.

70. Seligman, *Economics of Instalment Selling*, 1:48.

71. Ayres, "Instalment Selling through the Depression," asserts this point.

72. That independent sales finance companies pursued such a strategy is noted in Creekmur, "Floor Plan Problems"; Ayres, "Instalment Selling through the Depression"; William A. Grimes, *Financing Automobile Sales*, p. 31; and NAFC, *NAFC News* 38 (February 1931): 2.

73. The claim is made in Chandler, *Giant Enterprise*, p. 168. There are no other nationally operating sales finance companies listed among the American companies in *Moody's Manual of Investments: American and Foreign* for 1928.

74. The estimate is from Seligman, *Economics of Instalment Selling*, 1:49.

75. The figures are all from *Moody's Manual of Investments: American and Foreign*, 1928.

76. Manufacturers readily admitted this difference. See Floyd A. Allen, "Trends and Policies in Modern Business"; William H. Grimes, *Story of Commercial Credit*, p. 60; Hewitt, *Automobile Franchise Agreements*, p. 98; and William A. Grimes, *Financing Automobile Sales*, p. 108.

77. These advantages are pointed out in Floyd A. Allen, "Trends and Policies in Modern Business"; William A. Grimes, *Financing Automobile Sales*, p. 80; and Sims, "Local Company and the National Association."

78. NADA, *Sell Cars—Not Terms*, pp. 18–19. Sloan notes, however, that GMAC eventually "added a nonrecourse plan to its service . . . because of competitive pressure." He does not date this change, unfortunately. Sloan, *My Years with General Motors*, p. 360.

79. The subsidy is noted in Ayres, *Installment Selling and Its Financing*, p. 43, and

Seligman, *Economics of Instalment Selling*, 1:83. In addition, several manufacturers guaranteed that an insurance company affiliated with the sales finance company would be used to insure all autos financed through the factory-tied finance company. William A. Grimes, *Financing Automobile Sales*, p. 108; Sloan, *My Years with General Motors*, p. 359.

80. The claim is made in Brown, "Operating a Successful Independent Finance Company," and William A. Grimes, *Financing Automobile Sales*, pp. 67–73. It is supported by the evidence cited below from *Moody's Manual of Investments*.

81. The ratios are from William A. Grimes, *Financing Automobile Sales*, p. 66, and Brown, "Operating a Successful Independent Finance Company." NAFC notes that its member finance companies usually borrow two to three times their capital-plus-surplus. NASFC, *Directory*, p. 5.

82. The figures are given in NAFC, "Collateral Trust Agreements," p. 14.

83. NAFC, "Collateral Trust Agreements"; Brown, "Operating a Successful Independent Finance Company." In 1922 borrowers paid 6 to 8.5 percent on collateral trust notes but 10 to 11 percent for bank loans. Merrick, *Modern Credit Company*, pp. 15–16.

84. The connection between rates and Federal Reserve policy is made in Lewis, "Tight Money and Time Sales," pp. 38–39ff. Brown, "Financing under Depression Conditions," urges NAFC members to continue lobbying the Fed for a change in its discount policy.

85. *Ladies Home Journal* 24 (October 1907): 13.

86. Ayres, *Installment Selling and Its Financing*, p. 13.

87. Phelps, *Role of the Sales Finance Companies*, pp. 39–40.

88. Hardy, *Consumer Credit and Its Uses*, p. 127.

89. Ibid., p. 129.

90. Frederick Lewis Allen, *Only Yesterday*, pp. 139–40.

91. Nugent, *Consumer Credit and Economic Stability*, p. 96.

92. Reid, *Consumers and the Market*, p. 247.

93. Robinson and Nugent, *Regulation of the Small Loan Business*, table 3, pp. 57–58.

94. Ibid., pp. 113–17; Michelman, *Consumer Finance*, pp. 141–42. See Gallert, Hilborn, and May, *Small Loan Legislation*, for a thorough discussion of the early twentieth-century history of small loan legislation.

95. The maximum is cited in National Consumer Finance Association, *Consumer Finance Industry*, p. 5.

96. Ibid., p. 6.

97. Robinson and Nugent, *Regulation of the Small Loan Business*, p. 164.

98. Phelps, *Financing the Instalment Purchases of the American Family*, p. 89.

99. The motivation for control versus disclosure of terms of credit is noted in Curran, *Consumer Credit Legislation*, p. 2.

CHAPTER 5

1. The assertion is made by Hardy, *Consumer Credit and Its Uses*, pp. 136–37.

2. Pope, *Making of Modern Advertising*, p. 294.

3. Ibid., p. 143.

4. Ibid., p. 22–25. Here Pope discusses in detail the apparent development of and

problems with the *Printers' Ink* estimates. Neil Borden also comments on but then uses the *Printers' Ink* estimates to develop his own estimates of total advertising volume. Acknowledging the peculiarity of the annual estimates, Borden rounds his estimates to the nearest $100 million. Otherwise, Borden's estimates are essentially the same as those from *Printers' Ink*. Borden, *Economic Effects of Advertising*, table 3, pp. 56–57.

5. The estimates are in Peterson, *Magazines in the Twentieth Century*, p. 78. Daniel Starch's estimates of the dominance of the Curtis publications are somewhat lower, but it is not clear if Starch and Peterson were measuring the same thing. Writing in 1923, Starch claimed the three Curtis publications "carried about 33 percent of all magazine advertising space" in 1920. Starch, *Principles of Advertising*, p. 751. It seems unlikely, however, that Starch measured the physical space of all magazine advertising for 1920, so this is most likely also a comparison of advertising revenue.

6. Schmalensee discusses the creation of his measure of "real advertising" in an appendix. See, particularly, Schmalensee, *Economics of Advertising*, p. 245.

7. The alternative size measure is square inches. The size of an issue of *Ladies Home Journal* changed in the 1930s, decreasing from 9.5 by 14.25 inches to 9.5 by 12.25 inches. Measuring size in full-page equivalent units eliminates problems otherwise introduced by this change in size. A full-page ad is a 1.0 page ad, whether it occupies 135 square inches or 116 square inches.

8. Pollay notes the stability of the editorial policies of the *Ladies Home Journal* in Pollay, "Distorted Mirror," p. 26. Stability of readership is noted in Dornbusch and Hickman, "Other-Directedness in Consumer-Goods Advertising," p. 100.

9. The circulation estimate is from Peterson, *Magazines in the Twentieth Century*, p. 14. The population estimate is from U.S. Bureau of the Census, *Historical Statistics*, Ser. A119–A134, p. 15.

10. The rankings are given in Pollay, "Subsiding Sizzle," fig. 1, p. 27.

11. Starch, *Principles of Advertising*, pp. 183–89. My interpretation of these estimates follows the text of Starch's book. But his estimates of the percentage of women who read each magazine sum to 100, which would be surprising if the numbers indeed report what share of the 700 women surveyed read each of the several women's magazines. This implies the percentage of women who read *Ladies Home Journal* could be higher if many women read more than one magazine, or lower than one-third if many women read no magazine at all. Either way, *Ladies Home Journal* was the most popular magazine among these women.

12. Julian Simon cites the study in discussing the cyclical behavior of advertising expenditure in Simon, *Issues in the Economics of Advertising*, p. 67.

13. Poffenberger, *Psychology in Advertising*, p. 181.

14. Starch, *Principles of Advertising*, p. 539.

15. Pollay, "Subsiding Sizzle," p. 28.

16. Ibid.

17. Starch, *Principles of Advertising*, p. 542.

18. Strong, "Effect of Size of Advertisements and Frequency of Their Presentation," p. 152.

19. Representative texts are Lucas and Benson, *Psychology for Advertisers*, p. 148; Lucas and Britt, *Advertising Psychology and Research*, p. 245; and Poffenberger, *Psychology in Advertising*, pp. 174–76. In their 1950 edition (*Advertising Psychology and Research*), Lucas and Britt note that the full-page advertisement had become the most

popular size ad. Surprisingly, size is not mentioned at all in the 1963 version (*Measuring Advertising Effectiveness*), perhaps signaling the complete absence of any remaining controversy over the value of size.

20. Presbrey, *History and Development of Advertising*, p. 567.

21. Pollay, "Twentieth-Century Magazine Advertising," p. 73.

22. This can be seen from the estimates in table 2.3.

23. Margaret Reid obtained similar results when she estimated the 1935 distribution of advertisements for two women's magazines. She found that food accounted for 30 percent, personal cleaners and cosmetics for 20 percent, household cleaners for approximately 10 percent, household equipment for less than 8 percent, and clothing for less than 6 percent of total advertisements in 1935. Assorted other product groups accounted for the remainder of the advertisements. Reid, *Consumers and the Market*, p. 287.

24. *Ladies Home Journal* 32 (October 1915): 79.

25. The distribution of products advertised are given by decade in Pollay, "Subsiding Sizzle," p. 28. Pollay's product groups are nearly identical to those used in this analysis of *Ladies Home Journal*. His groupings are given in an appendix in "Subsiding Sizzle"; those for the *Ladies Home Journal* study reported here are noted below in appendix D.

26. Ford's advertising history is discussed in the most detail in Nevins and Hill, *Ford: Expansion and Challenge*, pp. 262–64. Others also note Ford's reliance on free publicity rather than paid advertising. See, for example, Vaile, "Use of Advertising during Depression," p. 330.

27. Pope, *Making of Modern Advertising*, p. 42.

28. Hotchkiss, *Milestones of Marketing*, p. 244.

29. This swing is noted in Marchand, *Advertising the American Dream*, pp. 7, 156–57. Indeed, Ford sedans were advertised in the 1925, 1928, 1929, and 1930 October issues of *Ladies Home Journal*.

30. Presbrey, *History and Development of Advertising*, p. 560.

31. Vaile, *Economics of Advertising*, p. 40.

32. The characterization of the post-World War I market as a replacement market is from Thomas, *Growth of the Automobile Industry*. Thomas makes this claim regarding advertising, a claim that is a natural outgrowth of his characterization of the changing nature of the industry. Thomas, *Growth of the Automobile Industry*, p. 235. Presbrey, *History and Development of Advertising*, p. 560, also notes the change in the content of auto advertisements.

33. The survey and resulting advertising campaign are discussed in Sloan, *My Years at General Motors*, p. 119.

34. Presbrey, *History and Development of Advertising*, p. 556.

35. Ibid., p. 562.

36. Vaile, *Economics of Advertising*, pp. 105–6.

37. Before 1924, refrigerator advertising was almost entirely local advertising. Borden, *Economic Effects of Advertising*, pp. 403–21. In *Ladies Home Journal*, refrigerators were first advertised in 1923. From then until 1935 (but excluding 1933), at least one refrigerator advertisement appeared per issue. There were two and sometimes three refrigerator ads per issue between 1927 and 1931 but none from 1936 to 1940.

38. Borden, *Economic Effects of Advertising*, pp. 500–501.

39. The advertisement is reprinted in Roberts, *Any Color So Long As It's Black*, p. 111.

40. The advertisement is quoted in Marchand, *Advertising the American Dream*, p. 157. Marchand located a copy of the advertisement in the *Chicago Tribune*.

41. Those who prepared the advertisements were well aware of the effectiveness of headlines and bold print. Advertising texts often included full chapters on typeface, size of print, and use of bold print, as well as effective design of headlines. Starch reminded his readers that the headline is the "guidepost" to an advertisement, particularly since 90 percent of readers never look at more than the headline. Starch, *Principles of Advertising*, p. 485. Lucas and Benson make a similar point, referring to the headline as the "heart" of the advertisement. Lucas and Benson, *Psychology for Advertisers*, p. 153.

42. Pope, *Making of Modern Advertising*, pp. 74–75.

43. It is important to note that there are so few advertisements for any durable goods in the 1930s that little meaning should be attached to the year-to-year differences in the percentage figures in table 5.6.

44. Starch, *Principles of Advertising*, pp. 440–41.

45. The figures are given in Pollay, "Twentieth-Century Magazine Advertising," table 2, p. 67.

46. For example, in his history of the N. W. Ayer and Son advertising agency, Ralph Hower comments that agency copywriters increasingly stressed price rather than product quality during the 1930s. Hower, *History of an Advertising Agency*, p. 147.

47. Pollay, "Twentieth-Century Magazine Advertising," table 3, p. 68.

48. While implying this interpretation, Pollay attaches little import to it. An analysis of variance of the information content of the 2,000 advertisements he studied shows that little of the variance in information content is explained by the product advertised, size of advertisement, or other such factors. Pollay concludes therefore that differences in content occur because "copywriters and creative teams choose" to write advertisements with different amounts of information. Pollay, "Twentieth-Century Magazine Advertising," p. 73. In a less rigorous analysis, Starch also notes that advertisements for durable goods contain more information in general; he argues that this is because the goods are purchased so infrequently that buyers must rely on advertisements for much of their product information. Starch, *Principles of Advertising*, p. 370.

49. Pope implies an explanation for this difference. He argues that manufacturers with large-scale production and high fixed costs advertised to avoid demand fluctuations and price competition. Pope, *Making of Modern Advertising*, p. 61. We would hardly expect such companies to then encourage price competition by featuring prices in their advertisements. If high fixed cost production is more characteristic of major than minor durable goods, Pope's argument implies that price would be featured less often in advertisements for major than for minor durables.

50. These changes in Ayer's business are noted in Hower, *History of an Advertising Agency*, pp. 207–8.

51. That advertisers offered this argument is noted in Pope, *Making of Modern Advertising*, pp. 74–75, and Durstine, *This Advertising Business*, pp. 34–35. In his history of the interwar advertising industry and its efforts to regulate itself, Otis Pease reports that the most common argument for advertising offered by advertising agencies and found in "countless places" in advertising trade journals of the 1920s and 1930s was that "national advertising was the most efficient device for obtaining a mass market and a mass market would save a manufacturer more than it cost him to advertise for it; that, in

short, it almost invariably paid to advertise." Pease, *Responsibilities of American Advertising*, pp. 16–17.

52. Not until Neil Borden's careful analysis of the economics of advertising, published in 1942, was there widely accepted dissent. Borden notes that advertising allows large-scale production that can lower costs, but that large firms do not necessarily have lower production costs than smaller firms, and furthermore not all industries are characterized by decreasing costs. Economies of scale can be exploited in some but certainly not all industries, he concludes. Borden, *Economic Effects of Advertising*, pp. 172, 489–524.

53. The claim is made in Hotchkiss, "Economic Defence of Advertising," p. 21. Others argued or simply presumed that advertising would ultimately lower production costs. Presbrey argues for advertising's role in decreasing automobile production costs. Presbrey, *History and Development of Advertising*, p. 562. Although he explicitly disputes the claim that automobile advertising should receive credit for decreasing auto production costs, Roland Vaile earlier discusses how advertising can decrease production costs in general. Vaile, *Economics of Advertising*, pp. 13, 60–96. Without mentioning production costs per se, Lucas and Benson also comment on the dependence of mass production on advertising. Lucas and Benson, *Psychology for Advertisers*, pp. 4–5.

54. Pope, *Making of Modern Advertising*, pp. 32–34. Pope further notes, however, that the ability of advertising to allow economies of scale to be exploited was characteristic of the years 1900–1920, when capital-intensive production methods were being adopted. After about 1920 increased efficiency in production came not so much from the adoption of wholly new technologies or methods as from reorganization of the work process within the same technological environment. Pope, *Making of Modern Advertising*, pp. 259–60.

55. The argument is repeated several times in Vaile, *Economics of Advertising*, pp. 61, 97, 102–5.

56. Presbrey, *History and Development of Advertising*, pp. 621–22. The full text of President Coolidge's speech is reprinted there, pp. 619–25.

57. Burns and Mitchell, *Measuring Business Cycles*, p. 78. The Federal Reserve Board Index of Production for all manufactures shows similar timing but a more protracted downturn. The index next achieved its January 1920 level in November 1922. *Federal Reserve Bulletin*, February and March 1927.

58. Presbrey, *History and Development of Advertising*, pp. 568–69, makes the claim.

59. Chandler, *Visible Hand*, pp. 456, 460. Frank Rowsome also links the increase in advertising with the 1920–21 business cycle. Rowsome, *They Laughed When I Sat Down*, p. 165.

60. Schmalensee, who refers to the "percentage of sales rule," is characteristic of present-day economists in the emphasis on sales determining advertising rather than vice versa. Schmalensee, *Economics of Advertising*, pp. 9ff. Jacobson and Nicosia, "Advertising and Public Policy," review and critique much of the literature. Their critique focuses on the common use of multiple regression analysis in empirical studies, which by its nature implies that the investigator has presumed a direction of causality between sales and advertising.

61. Peterson comments that before 1920 advertisers "accepted the efficacy of advertising largely on faith. They had seen the success of companies that spent large sums on advertising and they concluded that advertising must be effective." Peterson, *Magazines in the Twentieth Century*, p. 28.

62. Vaile, "Use of Advertising during Depression," p. 326. There is conspicuous absence of the contention that firms that experienced financial success through the 1920–21 recession continued their advertising efforts in proportion to sales while firms that survived but suffered through the episode cut their advertising expense as sales revenue fell.

63. Borden, *Economic Effects of Advertising*, p. 125. Those who argue that businesses increasingly recognized advertising as a means to build or sustain demand include Frederick Lewis Allen, *Only Yesterday*, p. 140; Wandersee, *Women's Work and Family Values*, p. 16; and Borden, *Economic Effects of Advertising*, p. 49. For Borden, this is just one of a list of reasons he gives for postbellum growth of advertising. He also credits an increasing gap between producers and consumers, variety of new products, need to create distinctions between products, competition, transportation developments that increased market size, and promotion of advertising by advertisers. Borden, *Economic Effects of Advertising*, pp. 49–51. Kuhn comments that GM believed advertising was effective in avoiding short-term fluctuations in demand for their product. Kuhn, *GM Passes Ford, 1918–1938*, p. 210.

64. Using assorted language, a number of authors connect increased advertising in the 1920s and development of underconsumption tendencies then. Hower, *History of an Advertising Agency*, p. 126, and Pease, *Responsibilities of American Advertising*, pp. 22–26, link advertising with the consumers' failure to buy all the products available in the 1920s. Marchand, *Advertising the American Dream*, pp. 1–2, points to "the dangers of over-production" and the resulting need for advertising. David Potter calls it "economic abundance," claiming that abundance (when the potential supply of goods exceeds aggregate demand) created the institution of national advertising. Potter, *People of Plenty*, pp. 77, 167–73.

65. The claim was made in a 1927 article in *Printers' Ink* that is cited and quoted more fully in Presbrey, *History and Development of Advertising*, pp. 604–6.

66. Pease, *Responsibilities of American Advertising*, p. 17. Presbrey, *History and Development of Advertising*, p. 565, notes the Red Cross effort. The role of advertising in the Liberty and Victory Bond campaigns is also discussed in Hotchkiss, *Milestones of Marketing*, p. 233; Hower, *History of an Advertising Agency*, pp. 107–8; and Frank W. Fox, *Madison Avenue Goes to War*, p. 3.

67. Presbrey, *History and Development of Advertising*, p. 566.

68. Quoted from Hower, *History of an Advertising Agency*, p. 110.

69. The reaction of bankers is noted in Pease, *Responsibilities of American Advertising*, p. 11.

70. Quoted from Pease, *Responsibilities of American Advertising*, p. 17. The same point is made in Stephen Fox, *Mirror Makers*, p. 76. A general discussion of the industry's efforts to become recognized as a "profession" are in Pope, *Making of Modern Advertising*, pp. 174–76, and Pease, *Responsibilities of American Advertising*, pp. 9–11. The most complete analysis of the effort to professionalize is Schultze, " 'An Honorable Place.' "

71. The tax rates are given in Studenski and Krooss, *Financial History of the United States*, pp. 285–86, 295–98. The bills are also outlined in Gilbert, *American Financing of World War I*, pp. 96, 111.

72. The effect of this surtax on advertising expenditure is discussed in a number of texts, including Presbrey, *History and Development of Advertising*, p. 567; Hower, *His-*

tory of an Advertising Agency, p. 109; Frank W. Fox, *Madison Avenue Goes to War*, pp. 11–12; Pope, *Making of Modern Advertising*, p. 158; and Stephen Fox, *Mirror Makers*, pp. 76–77.

73. Presbrey links the excess profits tax and the beginning of the "permanent revision upward" in the size of print advertisements. Presbrey, *History and Development of Advertising*, p. 567. An emphasis on the switch from product to good will advertising is in Frank W. Fox, *Madison Avenue Goes to War*, pp. 11–12, and Stephen Fox, *Mirror Makers*, p. 74.

74. Frank W. Fox, *Madison Avenue Goes to War*, p. 12, notes the switch in emphasis.

75. Allen, *Only Yesterday*, pp. 140, 142. These differences in tone are also noted in Pease, *Responsibilities of American Advertising*, pp. 33–41.

76. Pollay, "Subsiding Sizzle," table 4, p. 30. Frank W. Fox, *Madison Avenue Goes to War*, p. 95, notes the same switch toward increased emphasis on benefits of use and decreased emphasis on the product itself.

77. Marchand, *Advertising the American Dream*, pp. 206–34. More generally, Pease notes that two of the most common themes in 1920s advertisements are the American family at home and the importance of romantic love. Pease, *Responsibilities of American Advertising*, pp. 38–39.

78. Dornbusch and Hickman, "Other-Directedness in Consumer-Goods Advertising," p. 102.

79. Schultze, " 'An Honorable Place' "; Pope, *Making of Modern Advertising*, pp. 173–75.

80. Schultze notes the event and claims it signals the beginning of professional cooperation between the two fields. Schultze, " 'An Honorable Place,' " pp. 17–18. David Kuna reports that psychologists first studied advertising as early as 1896. Kuna, "Early History of Advertising Psychology," p. 347.

81. Kuna, "Early History of Advertising Psychology," p. 353. Lucas and Benson note that advertisers' acceptance of psychologists' offerings dates from about 1909. Lucas and Benson, *Psychology for Advertisers*, p. 276.

82. Cochran, *American Business in the Twentieth Century*, pp. 65–66; Rowsome, *They Laughed When I Sat Down*, pp. 162–63.

83. Pope, *Making of Modern Advertising*, p. 14.

84. Quoted from Pollay, "Subsiding Sizzle," p. 25.

85. A few illustrative examples are Strong, *Psychology of Selling and Advertising*; Poffenberger, *Psychology in Advertising*; and Lucas and Benson, *Psychology for Advertisers*.

86. Strong, *Psychology of Selling and Advertising*, p. vii.

87. Lucas and Benson, *Psychology for Advertisers*, pp. 9–13.

88. Starch, *Principles of Advertising*, pp. 272–73. There was little variance to the wants included in each text. See also Lucas and Benson, *Psychology for Advertisers*, pp. 51–67, and Poffenberger, *Psychology in Advertising*, pp. 45–81.

89. The study was conducted by Stuart Chase. The results are reported in Vaile, *Economics of Advertising*, p. 165, but the original source is not cited.

90. The conflict is widely noted but variously described. Historian T. J. Jackson Lears uses the descriptions above, as does Stephen Fox. Lears, "Rise of American Advertising," pp. 157–59; Stephen Fox, *Mirror Makers*, pp. 70–74. Marchand refers to reason-why and

human-interest approaches. Marchand, *Advertising the American Dream*, pp. 9–10. Lucas and Benson call them reason-why and suggestive copy, as does Starch. Lucas and Benson, *Psychology for Advertisers*, pp. 137–42; Starch, *Principles of Advertising*, pp. 384–405. Kuna calls reason-why the "rationalist" approach and contrasts it with an "impressionist" approach. Kuna, "Early History of Advertising Psychology," p. 348. Reason-why advertising was far from "rational" in its appeals, however. Noting this, Pope nevertheless refers to the alternative as the "nonrationalist" view. Pope, *Making of Modern Advertising*, pp. 238–42.

91. Lears, "Rise of American Advertising," p. 158.

92. Ibid., p. 157.

93. One copy of the advertisement is found in *Ladies Home Journal* 26 (October 1909): back cover. Starch reports that Colgate received 60,000 letters in response. That contemporaries were surprised by the positive reception of the suggestive ad is apparent from Starch's phrasing of his conclusion: "Hence the latter [the suggestive one] apparently stands in as high favor with the consumer as the former." Starch, *Principles of Advertising*, p. 390.

94. Stephen Fox, *Mirror Makers*, p. 74. Lears comments that by the 1920s, reason-why and atmosphere advertising had converged; amidst persuasive atmosphere, the reader was given the "reasons why" the advertised product should be bought. Lears, "Rise of American Advertising," p. 159.

95. Starch, *Principles of Advertising*, p. 370. This argument is consistent with Pollay's findings of greater information content in durable goods advertisements than in other advertisements. Pollay, "Twentieth-Century Magazine Advertising," p. 67.

96. Lucas and Benson, *Psychology for Advertisers*, pp. 142–43. The same point is also made in Pope, *Making of Modern Advertising*, pp. 238–42, and Borden, *Economic Effects of Advertising*, pp. 665–68. Lucas and Benson's emphasis upon male buyers is surprising. As is discussed further below, women were typically viewed as the audience of advertising.

97. Lears, "Rise of American Advertising," p. 159.

98. Pope, *Making of Modern Advertising*, p. 61.

99. Starch, *Principles of Advertising*, p. 105.

100. Hotchkiss, *Milestones of Marketing*, p. 214.

101. Lears, "Rise of American Advertising," p. 160.

102. Marchand, *Advertising the American Dream*, pp. 33–38, 66–69.

103. Durstine, *This Advertising Business*, pp. 27, 40. The same point is made by Starch, *Principles of Advertising*, p. 338. Presbrey explains the rapid 1920s expansion of advertising for toiletries as a result of wartime employment of women, which gave them economic independence and permanently altered the buying habits of the general public. Presbrey, *History and Development of Advertising*, p. 568. Pease notes, as does Thomas, that by the late 1920s automobile advertisements were "increasingly directed at middle-class women." Pease, *Responsibilities of American Advertising*, p. 36; Thomas, *Growth of the Automobile Industry*, p. 236.

104. Vaile, "Use of Advertising during Depression," pp. 328–29.

105. Wandersee, *Women's Work and Family Values*, p. 16.

106. The headline is quoted in Lucas and Benson, *Psychology for Advertisers*, p. 154.

107. Cowan, " 'Industrial Revolution' in the Home," p. 21. In contrast, Hotchkiss

comments not that appliances allowed one to "fire the maid" but that the rapid disappearance of domestic servants meant that "labor-saving household appliances were required to take their places." Hotchkiss, *Milestones of Marketing*, p. 243.

108. Cowan, " 'Industrial Revolution' in the Home," pp. 16, 21. See also Cowan, *More Work for Mother.*

109. Reid, *Consumers and the Market*, p. 278. Public opposition to advertising practices had begun before World War I. Fox argues that the efforts did not coalesce until the 1930s, when a growing consumer movement, which despite its growth never had much clout, rallied against dishonest and offensive advertising. Frank W. Fox, *Madison Avenue Goes to War*, p. 17.

110. Among authors noting the effectiveness or importance of advertising for new products or inventions are Borden, *Economic Effects of Advertising*, pp. 610–13, who notes specifically the speed of adoption of automobiles, electrical appliances, and phonographs; Simon, *Issues in the Economics of Advertising*, pp. 62–66; Vaile, *Economics of Advertising*, p. 60; Hotchkiss, *Milestones of Marketing*, p. 210; Hower, *History of an Advertising Agency*, p. 127; and Holder, "The Family Magazine and the American People," p. 276.

111. Borden, *Economic Effects of Advertising*, pp. 436–37.

112. Griliches, "Hybrid Corn," especially pp. 503–6.

113. Coolidge's proclamation is in Presbrey, *History and Development of Advertising*, p. 620.

114. Schudson notes that advertising is typically a small part of a business's budget. Schudson, *Advertising, The Uneasy Persuasion*, p. 10. Sloan barely mentions advertising in discussing the General Motors marketing strategy. Sloan, *My Years with General Motors*, p. 119. In his comparative analysis of General Motors and Ford Motor Company, Arthur Kuhn discusses but deemphasizes differences in advertising policies as accounting for the companies' relative successes. Kuhn, *GM Passes Ford, 1918–1938*, pp. 210–21, 301–3.

115. A classic study demonstrating this is Schmalensee, *Economics of Advertising.*

116. Julian Simon refutes the claim that advertising can increase consumption by noting that in Modigliani's life-cycle hypothesis, consumption depends upon life-cycle income and is impervious to short-term influences. Simon, *Issues in the Economics of Advertising*, p. 195. What Simon overlooks is Modigliani's careful definition of how one measures life-cycle consumption. Consumption excludes purchases of consumer durable goods and includes instead the annual provision of services of the stock of durable goods, as explained in Modigliani and Brumberg, "The Consumption Function," pp. 392–93. Changing merely the form in which consumers purchase such services does not change consumption expenditure as defined by Modigliani. It does, however, change total consumption expenditure as defined and measured by the U.S. Department of Commerce for the national product accounts.

CHAPTER 6

1. Consumerism, the development of a social ethos that holds material purchases and possessions as a worthy goal, is seen as having a profound impact on society, families,

relationships, and more. See, for example, Horowitz, *Morality of Spending*. Carole Shammas provides a useful overview of recent literature on consumerism and the development of a consumer culture in the United States in Shammas, "Explaining Past Changes." This book contributes to that literature by documenting shifts in demand for the most expensive material items, durable goods, and by analyzing the changes in installment credit and advertising, but otherwise the book is only tangentially related to these important efforts to study consumerism. One question raised by this work, however, is the nature of the relationship between consumerism and the Consumer Durables Revolution: To what extent did the rise of a consumer culture contribute to shifting demand for durables, and to what extent did shifting demand for durables contribute to the development of a consumer culture?

2. Carole Shammas, in comments on an earlier paper that demonstrates the results in chapter 3, notes that while I and other economic historians studying such issues continually talk of "households" and their economic behavior, these were in fact *people* making decisions to buy more durable goods. Shammas, "Explaining Past Changes," pp. 64–65. Shammas's point is well taken. By using the term "household," I am drawing a distinction between individual and collective decision making; for the economist, the alternative "economic decision-making unit" is the individual consumer, clearly the wrong choice when studying spending for durable goods. By no means did I intend to imply that decisions to purchase durable goods were undertaken by some amorphous economic bodies. Indeed, I strove to avoid calling them "families" because some households that function as one economic unit are composed of individuals not necessarily related by blood or marriage but who consider themselves one family, not, as the Census Bureau would have it, two families. As Shammas points out, however, the possibility of conflict within households is not part of this analysis.

3. The identity is derived as follows. In equilibrium, output equals aggregate demand, that is, Y = AD. Aggregate demand is the sum of consumption (C), investment (I), government (G), and export (X) spending, less spending on imports (M). Recall that saving (S) is the difference between disposable income (YD) and consumption (C), and that disposable income (YD) is the sum of income (Y) and government transfer payments (TR) less government tax receipts (TA). We then have

$$
\begin{aligned}
Y &= AD \\
Y &= C + I + G + X - M \\
Y &= (YD - S) + I + G + X - M \\
Y &= (Y + TR - TA - S) + I + G + X - M \\
S + (M - X) &= I + (G + TR - TA) \\
S + TD &= I + BD
\end{aligned}
$$

where TD is the international trade deficit and BD is the government's budget deficit.

4. David and Scadding, "Private Savings," pp. 234–37. See also Denison, "Private Saving."

5. Temin, *Did Monetary Forces Cause the Great Depression?*, pp. 62–83. Drawing from estimates in U.S. BEA, *National Income and Product Accounts, 1929–76*, table 1.2, pp. 6–10 (and using this version because the estimates are more detailed but otherwise consistent with the more recent edition of the national product accounts), we see that consumption constituted over two-thirds of gross national product in 1929. About 10 percent of consumer expenditure was for durable goods, about 45 percent was for

perishable and semidurable goods, and about 45 percent was for services. Between 1929 and 1930, as total durable goods expenditure fell by over 20 percent, total consumption expenditure fell by just over 7 percent, and gross national product fell by 9.5 percent. The change in consumption accounted for 52 percent of the change in gross national product between 1929 and 1930, 35 percent between 1930 and 1931, 49 percent between 1931 and 1932, and 68 percent between 1932 and 1933. By contrast, the change in consumption was only 29 percent of the change in gross national product between fourth quarter of 1973 and fourth quarter of 1974 and less than 3 percent of the change in gross national product between third quarter of 1957 and second quarter of 1958. Part of the argument in this section of chapter 6 was previously presented in Olney, "Consumer Durables in the Interwar Years."

6. See Mayer, "Consumption in the Great Depression," and Olney, "Consumer Durables in the Interwar Years." The quote is from Temin, *Did Monetary Forces Cause the Great Depression?*, p. 83.

7. Mishkin, "Illiquidity, Consumer Durable Expenditure, and Monetary Policy," and "Household Balance Sheet and the Great Depression."

8. Mishkin, "Household Balance Sheet and the Great Depression," p. 928.

9. Romer, "Great Crash and the Onset of the Great Depression."

10. Ayres, "Installment Selling and Industrial Recession."

11. Ibid.

12. U.S. Bureau of the Census, *Sixteenth Census: 1940 . . . Retail Trade: 1939, Part I,* p. 798.

13. By contrast with the argument being developed here, J. Bradford DeLong and Lawrence H. Summers argue that credit *stabilizes* consumption in the face of declining income. DeLong and Summers, "Changing Cyclical Variability of Economic Activity in the United States." The difference between their conclusion of the stabilizing influence of credit and mine of a destabilizing influence may be explained in part by differences in the expected extent or duration of the disruption to income. If workers are out of work for only a week or two, taking on new debt may enable them to maintain consumption despite the temporary drop in income. But if workers expect their income stream to be disrupted for several months or longer, taking on new installment debt will only put at risk the products being purchased, and those households already in debt will find their tangible wealth increasingly at risk of repossession. In addition, whether credit is a stabilizing or destabilizing influence in a declining economy will depend upon the consequences of default, as discussed in the text. Workers buying groceries on credit will not expect the food to be "repossessed" if they are late making payments to the grocer. Not so with durable goods bought on installment contracts.

APPENDIX A

1. Shaw, *Value of Commodity Output*, tables I-1 and I-2, pp. 30–69; Kuznets, *Commodity Flow and Capital Formation*, table II-5, pp. 146–48; Goldsmith, *Study of Saving*, 1:table Q-5, pp. 678, 680, 1:table A-24, pp. 780, 784, and 1:table Q-16, p. 696; U.S. BEA, *National Income and Product Accounts, 1929–82* (and updates), tables 2.4 and 2.5, pp. 106–18; U.S. BEA, *Fixed Reproducible Tangible Wealth, 1925–85* (and, for stock data,

updates), tables A17 and A18 for stock data, pp. 267–68, and tables B10 and B11 for expenditure data, pp. 361–62.

2. U.S. BEA, *Fixed Reproducible Tangible Wealth, 1925–85*, p. xix. These are revisions of the 1972 base estimates presented in U.S. BEA, *Fixed Reproducible Tangible Wealth, 1925–1979*. Both sets of BEA-Wealth estimates were developed by John Musgrave of the Bureau of Economic Analysis. In 1984 telephone conversations with John Musgrave, I was told there is no supporting documentation available other than that given in Musgrave, "Durable Goods Owned by Consumers." More recently, Musgrave sent a reprint of pages i–xxvi of the 1987 release, *Fixed Reproducible Tangible Wealth, 1925–85*. Earlier versions of this appendix were sent to Musgrave with a letter calling attention to some of the more surprising aspects of the BEA's apparent methodology (particularly some errors made in their estimation of net stock). Musgrave voiced no objection to its publication.

3. Goldsmith discusses his methodology in Goldsmith, *Study of Saving*, 2:Chapter 10, pp. 412–24. Much additional documentation is contained in the notes to each table in that publication.

4. Both Goldsmith's and the BEA's estimates of nominal expenditure use Shaw's estimates of "Value of Finished Commodities Destined for Domestic Consumption," in *Value of Commodity Output*, tables I-1 and I-2, pp. 30–69.

5. Goldsmith, *Study of Saving*, 2:415. The original source is Kuznets, *Commodity Flow and Capital Formation*, table V-6, p. 307.

6. Goldsmith, *Study of Saving*, 1:notes to table Q-5, p. 678.

7. Ibid., 2:415. Christina Romer highlights the problems introduced with such smooth markup assumptions in her critique of the pre–World War II GNP estimates. Romer, "New Estimates of Prewar Gross National Product and Unemployment." No doubt Goldsmith and Kuznets used essentially the same estimates of markup; Goldsmith notes that his estimates are from an (unnamed) National Bureau of Economic Research study (Goldsmith, *Study of Saving*, 1:686). Unfortunately we do not yet have better annual estimates of retail markup; no one has taken up Romer's call for more accurate annual (or even quarterly) estimates.

8. Barger, *Distribution's Place in the American Economy*, table 26, p. 92.

9. Kuznets, *Commodity Flow and Capital Formation*, table II-5, pp. 146–48. See also Shaw, *Value of Commodity Output*, pp. 104–5.

10. The national product accounts estimates for 1929 on are given in U.S. BEA, *National Income and Product Accounts, 1929–76* (1981 edition), and U.S. BEA, *National Income and Product Accounts, 1929–82* (1986 edition). The 1986 edition rounds expenditure values to the nearest $100 million; the 1981 edition rounds to the nearest $1 million. Where the two estimates are otherwise the same, those from the 1981 edition are used. Both sets of estimates result from a comprehensive revision of the national income and product accounts completed in 1980 and described in U.S. BEA, "National Income and Product Accounts: Introduction to the Revised Estimates." In general, the BEA-Wealth estimates of expenditure exceed those given in the national product accounts. The increases are introduced to give special treatment to used durable goods, particularly for the estimation of existing stock, and are relatively small—never more than 1.0 percent and generally between 0 and 0.5 percent. For discussion, see the section "Treatment of Used Goods" in the text below.

11. Goldsmith discusses his exclusion of tires and tubes in Goldsmith, *Study of Sav-*

ing, 2:412. Luggage is now included with "clothing and accessories except shoes" in the national product accounts. See U.S. BEA, *National Income and Product Accounts, 1929–82,* table 2.4 n. 2, p. 112.

12. "Net expenditure" has a different meaning here than in chapter 3. In chapter 3, net expenditure was total expenditure for durable goods less the value of depreciation (an estimate of replacement expenditure). Here, net expenditure refers to the difference between consumer purchases and consumer sales of used cars.

13. U.S. BEA, *Fixed Reproducible Tangible Wealth, 1925–85,* pp. xxiii–xxiv. The Polk Company data are reprinted in *Automobile Facts and Figures,* an annual publication of the Automobile Manufacturers Association, first published in 1919.

14. In addition, the totals for automobiles and parts are split back out into two components, expenditure for automobiles (new and used) and expenditure for automobile parts (tires and other accessories). These estimates are not included herein but are available from the author upon request.

15. Here and below, the series number in parentheses—such as (#20a)—is the number Shaw assigned in *Value of Commodity Output,* tables I-1 and I-2, pp. 30–69.

16. Goldsmith's estimates of consumers' net expenditure for used automobiles are from Goldsmith, *Study of Saving,* 1:table P-16, sum of cols. 2 and 4, pp. 898–99. Goldsmith discusses his methodology in the notes to table P-13, col. 1, p. 892, and the notes to table P-16, col. 3, p. 898.

17. The ratio of the BEA-Wealth estimates to the derived estimates of nominal expenditure for automobiles and parts jumps all around between 1918 and 1929, as seen below.

Year	BEA-Wealth Estimate to Olney Estimate	Year	BEA-Wealth Estimate to Olney Estimate
1918	0.51	1924	0.87
1919	0.76	1925	0.77
1920	0.59	1926	0.81
1921	1.14	1927	0.85
1922	0.79	1928	0.86
1923	0.87	1929	0.92

The adjustment factor of 0.84 is from the 1919–29 and 1922–29 averages of these ratios. This means the estimates do not exactly link up at 1918—the BEA-Wealth estimate for 1918 is $676 million, and the final adjusted derived estimate is $1,109 million. This gap does not affect the empirical analysis of chapter 3 since 1918 falls in the midst of the World War I period which is "dummied out" of each regression equation. It may, however, help explain why it was necessary to devise a special World War I dummy variable just for automobiles and parts.

18. Shaw, *Value of Commodity Output,* footnote to table 3, p. 13. See also Kuznets, *Commodity Flow and Capital Formation,* table I-4, minor group 34, pp. 92–93.

19. Kuznets, *Commodity Flow and Capital Formation,* table I-4, pp. 92–93.

20. The estimates of total output, before adjustment for net exports, are: Shaw, consumer wagons, $27,230 thousand; business wagons, $42,413 thousand; total wagons, $69,643 thousand; Kuznets, consumer wagons, $60,474 thousand; business wagons, $8,418 thousand; total wagons, $68,892 thousand. Shaw's estimates are from Shaw,

Value of Commodity Output, table II-1, pp. 123, 130. Kuznets's estimates are from Kuznets, *Commodity Flow and Capital Formation*, table I-4, pp. 92–93.

21. Goldsmith estimated a constant 24 percent markup for business horse-drawn vehicles. Goldsmith, *Study of Saving*, 1:774. The level of the retail markup is immaterial; only the temporal pattern affects the final estimates of expenditure. Use of the 43 percent markup that Goldsmith applies to purchases of farm equipment or the 45 percent markup applied to new automobiles would not affect the final results since in all cases the markup is held constant over the full period, 1869–1929. No further consumer allocation factor was necessary since an adjustment for consumer versus nonconsumer purchases was made before estimating output of horse-drawn vehicles *for consumers* as a share of total farm equipment. For those readers planning to use the extended series of consumer durable stocks and flows developed here in conjunction with the remainder of the capital stock and investment series provided in U.S. BEA, *Fixed Reproducible Tangible Wealth, 1925–85*, note that their expenditure series for "Agricultural Machinery," tables B2 and B3, col. 5, pp. 321–22, 327–38, and their stock series for "Agricultural Machinery," table A4, p. 129, must be adjusted downward to reflect allocation of consumer horse-drawn vehicles to the consumer durables category. At present, horse-drawn vehicles, both business and nonbusiness usage, are included in "Agricultural Machinery." Failure to adjust this category would result in double counting of horse-drawn vehicles for nonbusiness usage when the estimates presented here are used.

22. Goldsmith's estimates of nominal consumer expenditure for other durable house furnishings is the sum of the estimates in Goldsmith, *Study of Saving*, 1:table Q-5, col. 4, pp. 678, 680, and 1:table A-24, col. 4, pp. 780, 784.

23. U.S. Office of Business Economics, "National Income and Product, 1929–50," table 30, pp. 196–97. For 1942 only, the estimates are from U.S. Office of Business Economics, "National Income: 1947 Edition," table 30, pp. 41–44.

24. Shaw, *Value of Commodity Output*, table II-1, p. 117.

25. Kuznets, *Commodity Flow and Capital Formation*, table I-4, p. 85.

26. The annual estimates are in Kuznets, "Annual Estimates, 1869–1953," table T-6, variant III, col. 7, p. T-11. Professor Kuznets granted me permission to use these unpublished data in this work with the understanding that the annual estimates would remain unpublished. The five-year moving averages computed from these data are in Kuznets, *Capital in the American Economy*, tables R-27 and R-28, pp. 565–71. Kuznets's method of interpolation between Shaw's census year estimates is described in Kuznets, *National Product since 1869*, table II-3, col. 1, p. 95.

27. The ratios of my estimates to Kuznets's estimates of total nominal expenditure for consumer durables are: 0.916 for 1869; 0.934 for 1879; and 0.904 for 1889. The equations used to estimate total expenditure for consumer durables for the intervening years are:

1870–78: (Olney total) = −57.677 + 1.0471(Kuznets total)
1880–88: (Olney total) =   38.563 + 0.8591(Kuznets total)

28. The estimates of expenditure for consumer durable goods that are published in U.S. BEA, *Fixed Reproducible Tangible Wealth, 1925–85*, end with 1985. Updates of the stock estimates are published annually in August issues of the *Survey of Current Business*. Reflecting revisions to the national product accounts expenditure estimates, the BEA revised its stock estimates for 1983 on after publication of *Fixed Reproducible*

Tangible Wealth, 1925–85. This implies that the expenditure estimates for 1983–85 in the published volume have also been revised, but unfortunately the BEA only publishes updated values for gross and net stock. The expenditure estimates for 1983–86 presented in this appendix have therefore been derived by extrapolating the BEA-Wealth 1983 value of expenditure forward with the national product accounts expenditure estimates.

29. Goldsmith's methodology is described in Goldsmith, *Study of Saving,* 1:notes to table Q-16, pp. 696–97.

30. A weighted harmonic mean of two variables, P_1 and P_2, with weights w_1 and w_2, is equal to

$$\frac{w_1 + w_2}{\dfrac{w_1}{P_1} + \dfrac{w_2}{P_2}}$$

31. When Shaw provides two estimates of output for 1919, the two series are first spliced at 1919 before deriving the weights for computing the harmonic mean.

32. Goldsmith, *Study of Saving,* 1:notes to table P-17, p. 898.

33. Shaw, *Value of Commodity Output,* pp. 292–93.

34. U.S. BEA, *National Income and Product Accounts, 1929–82,* table 7.10, p. 346.

35. Use of the automobile accessories retail markup factors follows the procedure used to develop the estimates of nominal expenditure for tires.

36. The expenditure estimates are from the 1947 edition of the national product accounts, the last edition in which accessories and tires are listed separately.

37. The Commerce Department did not publish price estimates for farm equipment in the most recent version of the national product accounts. The price deflators for 1929–33 were therefore derived as the ratios of current to constant (1982) price estimates of expenditure for agricultural machinery, except tractors. Current price estimates of expenditure are from U.S. BEA, *National Income and Product Accounts, 1929–76,* table 5.6, line 7, p. 212 (rounded to the nearest tenth of a billion dollars in the revised edition of the national product accounts, but otherwise consistent). Constant price estimates of expenditure are from U.S. BEA, *National Income and Product Accounts, 1929–82,* table 5.7, line 24, p. 234.

38. Goldsmith, *Study of Saving,* 1:table Q-16, notes to col. 3, p. 696.

39. Ibid., notes to col. 7.

40. Ibid., notes to col. 6.

41. Ibid., notes to col. 10.

42. Shaw, *Value of Commodity Output,* table IV-1, pp. 292–95.

43. Kuznets, "Annual Estimates, 1869–1953," table T-7, variant III, col. 7, p. T-3. The equations used to estimate total real expenditure for consumer durable goods for the years between 1869, 1879, and 1889 are:

1870–78: (Olney total) = − 185.87 + 5.13(Kuznets total)
1880–88: (Olney total) =   872.55 + 4.15(Kuznets total)

44. The consumer durable stock estimates are given in tables A17 and A18 of U.S. BEA, *Fixed Reproducible Tangible Wealth, 1925–85,* pp. 267–78. For other assets, the BEA also estimates "historical-cost" stock estimates, derived directly from their estimates of nominal expenditure.

45. U.S. BEA, *Fixed Reproducible Tangible Wealth, 1925–85*, pp. viii, xxvi. Net stock is the difference between cumulative investment (total purchases of consumer durable goods) and cumulative depreciation. Gross stock is the difference between cumulative investment and cumulative discards. In turn, the annual value of discards is the sum of the original acquisition prices of those goods that reach the end of their service lives in that year. Alternatively, discards can be defined as the value of depreciation when depreciation is calculated according to the "one-horse shay" method, under which depreciation is zero during the life of the good and equals the good's full original value in the period the good ceases to exist. Net stock and gross stock are equal when this "one-horse shay" method is used. For a discussion of the "one-horse shay" method, see Tice, "Depreciation, Obsolescence, and Measurement of the Aggregate Capital Stock," pp. 121–23.

46. The depreciation and stock estimates are sensitive to the BEA's assumptions. However, while altering their assumptions does affect the levels of both depreciation and net stock, the effect is relatively stable over time. The conclusions drawn from the short-run analysis of chapter 3 are therefore relatively insensitive to the BEA's methodological assumptions. Assumptions to which the depreciation and stock estimates are particularly sensitive are noted below. Whether or not these are the "best" assumptions is irrelevant; the goal here is replicating and extending the BEA-Wealth estimates, not deriving a "best" set of stock estimates.

47. U.S. BEA, *Fixed Reproducible Tangible Wealth, 1925–85*, p. viii. For a theoretical discussion of the impact of alternative methods of determining depreciation on estimates of stock, see Tice, "Depreciation, Obsolescence, and Measurement of the Aggregate Capital Stock," pp. 119–54.

48. The average life lengths used by the BEA are in U.S. BEA, *Fixed Reproducible Tangible Wealth, 1925–85*, table B, p. xxii. Justification for distributing these averages about some mean is discussed on pp. xxi–xxiii. The modified distribution is in table C, p. xxiv. This is a modification of the survivor curve, type L-2, published in Winfrey, *Industrial Property Retirements*, table 21, p. 103. From a study of 176 survivor curves representing a wide variety of industrial property, Winfrey derived eighteen "typical survivor curves" and their mathematical equations. These eighteen survivor curves are of three general types: left-modal, right-modal, and symmetrical curves. The L-2 curve used by the BEA for the study of consumer durable goods is a left-modal curve, representing a distribution where the mode is less than the mean. Winfrey's curves and distributions describe the percent of goods surviving at each age, where age is given as a percent of the average life length. To develop these survivor curves, Winfrey did not examine consumer durable but rather producer durable goods and structures. The list of property examined is given in Winfrey, *Industrial Property Retirements*, table 27, pp. 142–49.

49. In the process of modifying Winfrey's original L-2 survivor curve, the BEA introduced an approximation error. In condensing the distribution and thereby altering the "percent surviving" associated with each age, the BEA increased the mean of the distribution from 1 to 1.001. This approximation error is not in itself a serious problem.

50. Although this interpretation of table A.10 is consistent with that given in the BEA-Wealth study, it is a misinterpretation of Winfrey. Winfrey's L-2 type curve relates age and "percent surviving" at that age, with age measured as a percent of the average service life for the particular type of good(s). "Percent surviving" is a stock concept;

"percent discarded" is a flow concept. To move from the stock of survivors at a point in time to the flow of discards during a period of time requires a method of interpolating between two stock estimates. Winfrey suggested the use of linear interpolation between stock benchmarks. Winfrey, *Industrial Property Retirements*, p. 13. Winfrey's original survivor distributions have a mean of 1 when linear interpolation is used. In the current case, correctly interpreting Winfrey would decrease each of the "percent of average service life" entries in table A.10 by 5 percentage points, implying that 1.5 percent of total expenditures is for goods with an expected service life that is 20 (not 25) percent of the average service life, and so on. This "recalibration" of table A.10 yields a distribution with a mean of 1.001; the distribution given in table A.10 has a mean of 1.051.

51. It is not necessary to round the expected service lives to their nearest integer value in order to use the straight-line method of depreciation; annual depreciation rates can be determined even when the expected life length is not an integer value, though these rates will not be merely the inverse of the expected life length. Taken together with the misinterpretation of Winfrey's survivor curves, this approximation results in mean service lives that are, in general, greater than the average service lives used as an input to the process of deriving the distribution of expected service lives. Only when the average life length is ten years does the rounding error fully offset the "misinterpretation error." The effect of first misinterpreting Winfrey and then rounding the expected service lives to their nearest integer values on the resulting mean service life associated with each commodity group is as follows:

Average Life Length in Years (input)	Commodity Group(s)	Mean Life Length in Years (output)
3	Automobile Accessories	3.165
6	Ophthalmic Products and Orthopedic Appliances	6.205
7.5	Radios, TVs, Phonographs (subgroup)	7.884
8	Other Motor Vehicles; Horse-Drawn Vehicles	8.405
9	Radios, TVs, Pianos, etc. (full group)	9.494
10	China; House Furnishings; Books; Wheel Goods, Durable Toys, etc.	10.010
11	Household Appliances; Jewelry	11.526
14	Furniture	14.612
16	Pianos, Musical Instruments (subgroup)	16.812

52. This assumption was not explicit in the BEA-Wealth study but is implied by the analysis. When the expected service lives are integer values and the analysis is conducted on an annual basis, an equivalent assumption is that all expenditures in each year occur at the midpoint of that year.

53. Equation A.1 is correct only for service lives that are integer values. It is a special case of a more general formulation that allows the expected service life to take any value of one year or more.

54. In the BEA-Wealth study, it is stated that "net stock . . . is the value of the gross stock less cumulative depreciation on the items in the gross stock," where "gross stock equals cumulative gross investment less cumulative discards." U.S. BEA, *Fixed Reproducible Tangible Wealth, 1925–85*, p. xxvi. A literal interpretation implies that net stock should be calculated by aggregating past and current-year expenditures, subtracting past and current-year discards (yielding the gross stock), and then subtracting the aggregate of past and current-year depreciation on those items that remained in the gross stock at the beginning of the current year. However, since the straight-line method of depreciation fully depreciates each purchase by the end of that good's lifetime, it can be shown that this method of calculating the net stock is equivalent to computing the difference between cumulative investment and cumulative depreciation, where both investment and depreciation are cumulated since 1869. That is, use of equation A.4 for estimating end-of-year stock is equivalent to the method indicated by literal interpretation of the BEA's definitions.

55. The quotation (edited to correct obvious typographical errors) is from the earlier edition of the BEA-Wealth study, U.S. BEA, *Fixed Reproducible Tangible Wealth, 1925–1979*, p. T-10. In the 1987 edition, they simply state, "The NIPA series were modified in some instances, primarily to revalue transfers of used assets between types of owners. . . ." U.S. BEA, *Fixed Reproducible Tangible Wealth, 1925–85*, p. xi.

56. U.S. BEA, *Fixed Reproducible Tangible Wealth, 1925–85*, pp. xxiii–xxiv.

57. This is from the earlier version, U.S. BEA, *Fixed Reproducible Tangible Wealth, 1925–1979*, p. T-13. In the recent release, U.S. BEA, *Fixed Reproducible Tangible Wealth, 1925–85*, discussion of the BEA's use of the Polk Company data omits mention of how depreciation or net stock were determined from these data.

58. This step uses the separate estimates of real expenditure for automobiles and for automobile parts that were developed as outlined in this appendix and that are available from the author.

59. According to the 1982 release of the BEA-Wealth study, the BEA used a constant ten-year life-length assumption to determine the annual depreciation amount *per* automobile. But the age distribution of automobiles in use that is used to determine *total* annual depreciation of automobiles does not reflect a constant ten-year life. Since the distribution of table A.10 is used by the BEA in the derivation of depreciation estimates for all other commodity groups, it is applied to automobiles as well and used here to extend the BEA-Wealth estimates back of 1925.

60. In general the adjustment factor is the inverse of 1 minus the 1925 percentage estimation error, where that error is the BEA-Wealth 1925 stock estimate less my initial 1925 estimate, as a percentage of the BEA-Wealth estimate. For automobiles and for other motor vehicles, however, the adjustment factor is the average of the values of the adjustment factor for 1925–83, following the development of nominal expenditure estimates. For 1925–83, my initial estimates of stock exceed the BEA-Wealth estimates by an average of 2.32 percent. For 1925 only, the difference is 3.43 percent.

61. U.S. BEA, *Fixed Reproducible Tangible Wealth, 1925–85*, p. xxii. This is a decrease from its earlier assumption of seventeen years as the average life length for agricultural

machinery except tractors. U.S. BEA, *Fixed Reproducible Tangible Wealth, 1925–1979*, p. T-17.

62. Goldsmith, *Study of Saving*, 1:notes to table A-16, col. 3, p. 772. Goldsmith used an average life length of fifteen years for "farm equipment and machinery" (p. 772).

63. The BEA's documentation is far from clear on this point. When discussing its table B, "Service Life Assumptions by Type of Asset," the BEA mentions automobiles as the only consumer asset for which the service life given in the table is *not* an average (p. xxiii), suggesting that automobiles are the only special case and that stock estimates of other motor vehicles are therefore derived with equations A.2 and A.4. Further, the BEA's discussion of the use of the Polk Company data is addressed entirely to automobiles, again suggesting that this group is the only special case. However, several other factors indicate that the BEA used Polk Company data in the derivation of stock and depreciation estimates for other motor vehicles. First, the BEA-Wealth estimates of real expenditure for other motor vehicles begin in 1922. With the assumed eight-year average life length, the stock estimates derived from the BEA's published estimates of real expenditure would therefore not be available for years prior to 1939, yet the BEA-Wealth estimates of stock of other motor vehicles begin in 1925. Second, the BEA-Wealth stock estimates cannot be replicated with equation A.2 and A.4 using its real expenditure estimates, an average life length of eight years, and the distribution of table A.11. Third, annual estimates of the number and age distribution of motor trucks and buses are tabulated by the Polk Company and are published in Automobile Manufacturers Association, *Automobile Facts and Figures*, with the corresponding estimates for automobiles. A definition of other motor vehicles was not located, but presumably motor trucks and buses constitute at least part of the commodity group. The BEA could thus use this second set of Polk Company data in its estimation of the stock of other motor vehicles.

64. This assumption is based on the BEA's own estimate of the average life length of other motor vehicles. U.S. BEA, *Fixed Reproducible Tangible Wealth, 1925–85*, p. xxii. Note that this is the same average life length used to derive the estimates of depreciation and net stock for horse-drawn vehicles.

65. Goldsmith, *Study of Saving*, 1:table Q-12, pp. 688–89.

66. Lenore A. Epstein, "Consumers' Tangible Assets," p. 442.

APPENDIX B

1. Since 1954, the Office of Business Economics in the Department of Commerce has also undergone an identity change: it is now the Bureau of Economic Analysis.

2. This value is taken from U.S. BEA, *National Income and Product Accounts, 1929–76*, table 2.4, p. 89. It is rounded to $27.3 billion in the current version of the national product accounts, U.S. BEA, *National Income and Product Accounts, 1929–82*. In most cases below, the benchmark values are taken from the earlier version of the national product accounts since those estimates provide greater detail.

3. These estimates were computed using data from U.S. Office of Business Economics, *National Income: 1954 Edition*, and U.S. BEA, *National Income and Product Accounts, 1929–76*.

4. See U.S. BEA, *National Income and Product Accounts, 1929–82*, tables A and 8.9, pp. xvi–xvii, 394–99.

5. Juster used a rate of return of 3.0 percent for 1900–1962. Juster, *Household Capital Formation and Financing*, notes to table B-2, col. 3, p. 140.

APPENDIX C

1. The model is described as a "habit-formation" or "inertia" model in Houthakker and Taylor, *Consumer Demand in the United States*, p. 9. For a general discussion of consumption as an autoregressive process, see Hall, "Stochastic Implications of the Life Cycle–Permanent Income Hypothesis."

2. Responsiveness of expenditure to changes in price or income does not depend upon which type of behavior—gradual stock adjustment or habit formation—dominates, so we can estimate elasticities without knowing which model is most appropriate. To calculate the estimated elasticities, we multiply the estimated coefficient by the ratio of the means of that variable (for example, relative price) to gross expenditure.

3. Modigliani, "Life Cycle Hypothesis of Saving," p. 184.

4. The Census Bureau does not consider "household" and "family" synonymous. A "household" consists of all persons occupying a single housing unit, be that unit a house, apartment, or single room used as separate living quarters. If the residents of one household are not related by blood or marriage, the household is composed of more than one "family." For 1910 and 1920, the definitions of household used by the Census Bureau included "quasi-households" or group quarters, households such as prisons or dormitories that contain five or more persons unrelated to the person in charge. U.S. Bureau of the Census, *Historical Statistics*, notes to Ser. A288–A319, p. 6.

5. This may seem an odd construction of the household formation rate variable. Usually a percentage change is computed as a percentage of the previous year's value. But here, since the form of the household formation rate variable is dictated by equation C.11, we compute the change as a percentage of the current year's value.

6. Equations C.23 and C.24 are taken from Maddala, *Econometrics*, pp. 197–200.

APPENDIX D

1. Readers seeking an analysis of the content of print advertisements should refer to Marchand, *Advertising the American Dream*, for the interwar period. For decade-by-decade comparisons covering 1900–1980, see Pollay, "Twentieth-Century Magazine Advertising," "Subsiding Sizzle," and "Distorted Mirror."

2. In the early 1920s, Daniel Starch studied seasonal patterns in quantity of print advertising. He found that although the pattern changed slightly over the first twenty years of this century, there was relative stability in the seasonal pattern, and, furthermore, October was consistently a month with proportionately more advertisements than most other months. Starch, *Principles of Advertising*, pp. 744–45. Other studies demonstrate that despite notable variation in the quantity of advertising from month to month, the ratio of advertising to total pages nevertheless remains stable. Lucas and Britt, *Advertising Psychology and Research*, p. 229.

◆ REFERENCES ◆

Akerlof, George A. "The Market for 'Lemons': Qualitative Uncertainty and the Market Mechanism." *Quarterly Journal of Economics* 84 (August 1970): 488–500.

Allen, Floyd A. "Trends and Policies in Modern Business." Address before the sixth annual meeting of the National Association of Finance Companies, November 1929. *National Association of Finance Companies Addresses* (Baker Library, Harvard University).

Allen, Frederick Lewis. *Only Yesterday: An Informal History of the 1920's*. New York: Harper and Row, 1931.

Automobile Manufacturers Association. *Automobile Facts and Figures*. Various issues.

Ayres, Milan V. "Diversification and the Future of Financing." Address before the fifth annual conference of the National Association of Finance Companies, New York City, November 20–21, 1928. *National Association of Finance Companies Addresses* (Baker Library, Harvard University).

_____. "Evolution in the Financing and Selling of Motor Vehicles." *Time Sales Financing* 4 (July 1939).

_____. "Installment Selling and Industrial Recession." *The Journal of Commerce and Commercial* (April 21, 1930). Reprinted by the National Association of Finance Companies for distribution to its members. *National Association of Finance Companies Miscellaneous Publications* (Baker Library, Harvard University).

_____. *Installment Selling and Its Financing: A Report by the Economic Policy Commission to the Executive Council and a Report to the Economic Policy Commission*. N.p.: American Bankers Association, May 1926.

_____. "Instalment Selling through the Depression." *American Bankers Association Journal* 24 (March 1931): 742, 743, 783, 784, 790.

Barger, Harold. *Distribution's Place in the American Economy since 1869*. Princeton: Princeton University Press, 1955.

Board of Governors of the Federal Reserve System. *Consumer Instalment Credit*. 3 vols. Washington, D.C.: Board of Governors, 1957.

_____. *Flow of Funds Accounts, Assets and Liabilities Outstanding, 1959–82*. Washington, D.C.: Board of Governors, 1983.

_____. Supplement to *Banking and Monetary Statistics*. Section 16 (New): Consumer Credit. Washington, D.C.: Board of Governors, September 1965.

Borden, Neil H. *The Economic Effects of Advertising*. Chicago: Richard D. Irwin, 1942.

Brown, Victor L. "Financing under Depression Conditions." Address before the eighth annual meeting of the National Association of Finance Companies, Chicago, November 17, 1931. *National Association of Finance Companies Addresses* (Baker Library, Harvard University).

_____. "Operating a Successful Independent Finance Company." Address before the sixth annual meeting of the National Association of Finance Companies, New York City, November 1929. *National Association of Finance Companies Addresses* (Baker Library, Harvard University).

Burns, Arthur F., and Wesley C. Mitchell. *Measuring Business Cycles*. New York: National Bureau of Economic Research, 1946.

Burstein, M. L. "The Demand for Household Refrigeration in the United States." In *The Demand for Durable Goods*, edited by Arnold C. Harberger, pp. 99–145. Chicago: University of Chicago Press, 1960.

Chandler, Alfred D., Jr. *The Visible Hand: The Managerial Revolution in American Business*. Cambridge, Mass: Harvard University Press, 1977.

————, ed. *Giant Enterprise: Ford, General Motors, and the Automobile Industry: Sources and Readings*. New York: Harcourt, Brace and World, 1964.

Chow, Gregory C. "Statistical Demand Functions for Automobiles and Their Use for Forecasting." In *The Demand for Durable Goods*, edited by Arnold C. Harberger, pp. 149–78. Chicago: University of Chicago Press, 1960.

————. "Tests of Equality between Sets of Coefficients in Two Linear Regressions." *Econometrica* 28 (July 1960): 591–605.

Christensen, Laurits R., and Dale W. Jorgenson. "The Measurement of U.S. Real Capital Input, 1929–1967." *Review of Income and Wealth* 15 (December 1969): 293–320.

————. "U.S. Income, Saving, and Wealth, 1929–1969." *Review of Income and Wealth* 19 (December 1973): 329–62.

Clark, Evans. *Financing the Consumer*. New York: Harper and Brothers, 1931.

Cochran, Thomas C. *American Business in the Twentieth Century*. Cambridge, Mass: Harvard University Press, 1972.

Comanor, William S., and Thomas A. Wilson. "The Effect of Advertising on Consumption: A Survey." *Journal of Economic Literature* 17 (June 1979): 453–76.

Court, A. T. "Hedonic Price Indexes: With Automotive Examples." In *The Dynamics of Automobile Demand*, pp. 99–119. Papers presented at a joint meeting of the American Statistical Association and the Econometric Society. New York: General Motors Corporation, 1939.

Cowan, Ruth Schwartz. "The 'Industrial Revolution' in the Home: Household Technology and Social Change in the 20th Century." *Technology and Culture* 17 (January 1976): 1–23.

————. *More Work for Mother*. New York: Basic Books, 1983.

Cox, Reavis, and Ralph F. Breyer. *Consumer Plant and Equipment*. Washington, D.C.: Retail Credit Institute of America, 1945.

Creekmur, John W. "Floor Plan Problems." Address before the eighth annual meeting of the National Association of Finance Companies, Chicago, November 17, 1931. *National Association of Finance Companies Addresses* (Baker Library, Harvard University).

Curran, Barbara A. *Trends in Consumer Credit Legislation*. Chicago: University of Chicago Press, 1965.

Darby, Michael R. "The Allocation of Transitory Income among Consumers' Assets." *American Economic Review* 62 (December 1972): 928–41.

Dauten, Carl A. *Financing the American Consumer*. Consumer Credit Monograph no. 1. St. Louis: American Investment Company of Illinois, 1956.

David, Paul A., and John L. Scadding. "Private Savings: Ultrarationality, Aggregation, and 'Denison's Law.'" *Journal of Political Economy* 82 (March/April 1974): 225–49.

DeLong, J. Bradford, and Lawrence H. Summers. "The Changing Cyclical Variability of Economic Activity in the United States." In *The American Business Cycle: Continu-*

ity and Change, edited by Robert J. Gordon, pp. 679–734. Chicago: University of Chicago Press, 1986.

Denison, Edward F. "A Note on Private Saving." *Review of Economics and Statistics* 40 (August 1958): 261–67.

Dornbusch, Sanford M., and Lauren C. Hickman. "Other-Directedness in Consumer-Goods Advertising: A Test of Riesman's Historical Theory." *Social Forces* 38 (December 1959): 99–102.

Duesenberry, James S., Gary Fromm, Lawrence R. Klein, and Edwin Kuh, eds. *The Brookings Quarterly Econometric Model of the United States.* Chicago: Rand McNally, 1965.

Durand, David. *Risk Elements in Consumer Instalment Financing (Technical Edition).* National Bureau of Economic Research, Studies in Consumer Instalment Financing, no. 8. New York: National Bureau of Economic Research, 1941.

Durstine, Roy S. *This Advertising Business.* New York: Scribner's Sons, 1928.

Epstein, Lenore A. "Consumers' Tangible Assets." In vol. 12 of *Studies in Income and Wealth*, National Bureau of Economic Research Conference on Research in Income and Wealth, pp. 409–60. New York: National Bureau of Economic Research, 1950.

Epstein, Ralph C. *The Automobile Industry: Its Economic and Commercial Development.* Chicago: A. W. Shaw, 1928. Reprint. New York: Arno Press, 1972.

Foss, Murray F., ed. *The U.S. National Income and Product Accounts: Selected Topics.* Vol. 47 of *Studies in Income and Wealth*, National Bureau of Economic Research Conference on Research in Income and Wealth. Chicago: University of Chicago Press, 1983.

Fox, Frank W. *Madison Avenue Goes to War: The Strange Military Career of American Advertising, 1941–45.* Charles E. Merrill Monograph Series in the Humanities and Social Sciences. Provo, Utah: Brigham Young University Press, 1975.

Fox, Stephen. *The Mirror Makers: A History of American Advertising and Its Creators.* New York: Morrow, 1984. Reprint. New York: Vintage Books, 1985.

Gallert, David J., Walter S. Hilborn, and Geoffrey May. *Small Loan Legislation: A History of the Regulation of the Business of Lending Small Sums.* New York: Russell Sage Foundation, 1932.

Gilbert, Charles. *American Financing of World War I.* Contributions in Economics and Economic History, no. 1. Westport, Conn.: Greenwood, 1970.

Goldsmith, Raymond W. *The National Balance Sheet of the United States, 1953–1980.* Chicago: University of Chicago Press, 1982.

———. *A Study of Saving in the United States.* 3 vols. Princeton: Princeton University Press, 1955.

Goldsmith, Raymond W., Robert E. Lipsey, and Morris Mendelson. *Studies in the National Balance Sheet of the United States.* 2 vols. Princeton: Princeton University Press, 1963.

Gordon, Robert Aaron. *Economic Instability and Growth: The American Record.* New York: Harper and Row, 1974.

Gordon, Robert J. *The Measurement of Durable Goods Prices.* Chicago: University of Chicago Press, 1990.

Grieves, Robin. "The Demand for Consumer Durables." *Journal of Money, Credit and Banking* 15 (August 1983): 316–26.

Griliches, Zvi. "Hybrid Corn: An Exploration in the Economics of Technological

Change." *Econometrica* 25 (October 1957): 501–22.

Grimes, William A. *Financing Automobile Sales by the Time-Payment Plan*. Chicago: A. W. Shaw, 1926.

Grimes, William H. *The Story of Commercial Credit Company, 1912–1945*. Baltimore, Md.: Commercial Credit Company, 1946.

Hall, Robert E. "Stochastic Implications of the Life Cycle–Permanent Income Hypothesis: Theory and Evidence." *Journal of Political Economy* 86 (December 1978): 971–87.

Hamburger, Michael J., and Burton Zwick. "Installment Credit Controls, Consumer Expenditures and the Allocation of Real Resources." *Journal of Finance* 32 (December 1977): 1557–69.

Hanch, C. C. "Benefits of Installment Selling." *American Bankers Association Journal* (March 1928). Reprinted by National Association of Finance Companies for distribution to its members. *National Association of Finance Companies Miscellaneous Publications* (Baker Library, Harvard University).

Harberger, Arnold C., ed. *The Demand for Durable Goods*. Chicago: University of Chicago Press, 1960.

Hardy, Charles O., ed. *Consumer Credit and Its Uses*. New York: Prentice-Hall, 1938.

Hendricks, Gary, Kenwood C. Youmans, and Janet Keller. *Consumer Durables and Installment Debt: A Study of American Households*. Ann Arbor: Institute for Social Research, University of Michigan, 1973.

Hewitt, Charles Mason, Jr. *Automobile Franchise Agreements*. Indiana University School of Business, Bureau of Business Research, study no. 39. Homewood, Ill.: Richard D. Irwin, 1956.

Holder, Stephen C. "The Family Magazine and the American People." *Journal of Popular Culture* 7 (Fall 1973): 264–79.

Holt, Charles F. "Who Benefited from the Prosperity of the Twenties?" *Explorations in Economic History* 14 (July 1977): 277–89.

Horowitz, Daniel. *The Morality of Spending: Attitudes toward the Consumer Society in America, 1875–1940*. Baltimore, Md.: Johns Hopkins University Press, 1985.

Hotchkiss, George Burton. "An Economic Defence of Advertising." *American Economic Review* 15 Supplement (March 1925): 14–22.

———. *Milestones of Marketing: A Brief History of the Evolution of Market Distribution*. New York: Macmillan, 1938.

Houthakker, H. S., and Lester D. Taylor. *Consumer Demand in the United States, 1929–1970: Analyses and Projections*. Cambridge, Mass: Harvard University Press, 1966.

Hower, Ralph M. *The History of an Advertising Agency: N. W. Ayer and Son at Work, 1869–1949*. Rev. ed. Cambridge, Mass: Harvard University Press, 1949.

Jacobson, Robert, and Nicosia, Franco M. "Advertising and Public Policy: The Macroeconomic Effects of Advertising." *Journal of Marketing Research* 18 (February 1981): 29–38.

Johnston, J. *Econometric Methods*. 2d ed. New York: McGraw-Hill, 1972.

Juster, F. Thomas. *Household Capital Formation and Financing: 1897–1962*. New York: National Bureau of Economic Research, 1966.

Juster, F. Thomas, and Robert E. Lipsey. "A Note on Consumer Asset Formation in the United States." *Economic Journal* 77 (December 1967): 834–47.

Juster, F. Thomas, and Paul Wachtel. "Anticipatory and Objective Models of Durable

Goods Demand." *American Economic Review* 62 (September 1972): 564–79.

Katz, Harold. *The Decline of Competition in the Automobile Industry, 1920–1940.* Ph.D. dissertation, Columbia University, 1970. Reprint. New York: Arno Press, 1977.

Kendrick, John W. *Productivity Trends in the United States.* Princeton, N.J.: Princeton University Press for the National Bureau of Economic Research, 1961.

Kessler-Harris, Alice. *Out to Work: A History of Wage-Earning Women in the United States.* Oxford: Oxford University Press, 1982.

Kuhn, Arthur J. *GM Passes Ford, 1918–1938: Designing the General Motors Performance-Control System.* University Park: Pennsylvania State University Press, 1986.

Kuna, David P. "The Concept of Suggestion in the Early History of Advertising Psychology." *Journal of the History of the Behavioral Sciences* 12 (October 1976): 347–53.

Kuznets, Simon. "Annual Estimates, 1869–1953: Technical Tables Underlying Series in *Supplement to Summary Volume on Capital Formation and Financing.*" Manuscript. n.d.

_____. *Capital in the American Economy: Its Formation and Financing.* New York: National Bureau of Economic Research, 1961.

_____. *Commodity Flow and Capital Formation.* New York: National Bureau of Economic Research, 1938.

_____. *National Income and Capital Formation, 1919–1935.* New York: National Bureau of Economic Research, 1937.

_____. *National Product since 1869.* New York: National Bureau of Economic Research, 1946.

Lears, T. J. Jackson. "The Rise of American Advertising." *Wilson Quarterly* 7 (Winter 1983): 156–67.

Levedahl, J. William. "The Impact of Permanent and Transitory Income on Household Automobile Expenditures." *Journal of Consumer Research* 7 (June 1980): 55–66.

Lewis, H. Bertram. "Tight Money and Time Sales: High Interest Rates Will Not Affect Car Sales As Long As We Stick to Sound Terms." *Automobile Trade Journal and Motor Age* (February 1929): 38ff.

Lippitt, Vernon G. *Determinants of Consumer Demand for House Furnishings and Equipment.* Cambridge, Mass.: Harvard University Press, 1959.

Lucas, Darrell Blaine, and C. E. Benson. *Psychology for Advertisers.* New York: Harper and Brothers, 1930. Reprint. New York: Garland, 1985.

Lucas, Darrell Blaine, and Steuart Henderson Britt. *Advertising Psychology and Research: An Introductory Book.* New York: McGraw-Hill, 1950.

_____. *Measuring Advertising Effectiveness.* New York: McGraw-Hill, 1963.

Macaulay, Stewart. *Law and the Balance of Power: The Automobile Manufacturers and Their Dealers.* New York: Russell Sage Foundation, 1966.

Maddala, G. S. *Econometrics.* New York: McGraw-Hill, 1977.

Marchand, Roland. *Advertising the American Dream: Making Way for Modernity, 1920–1940.* Berkeley: University of California Press, 1985.

Marx, Thomas G. "The Development of the Franchise Distribution System in the U.S. Automobile Industry." *Business History Review* 59 (Autumn 1985): 465–74.

Mayer, Thomas. "Consumption in the Great Depression." *Journal of Political Economy* 86 (February 1978): 139–45.

Merrick, Robert G. *The Modern Credit Company: Its Place in Business Financing.* Baltimore, Md.: Norman, Remington, 1922.

Michelman, Irving S. *Consumer Finance: A Case History in American Business*. Preface by Leon Henderson. New York: Frederick Fell, 1966.

Mishkin, Frederic S. "The Household Balance Sheet and the Great Depression." *Journal of Economic History* 38 (December 1978): 918–37.

———. "Illiquidity, Consumer Durable Expenditure, and Monetary Policy." *American Economic Review* 66 (September 1976): 642–54.

Modigliani, Franco. "The Life Cycle Hypothesis of Saving, the Demand for Wealth and the Supply of Capital." *Social Research* 33 (Summer 1966): 160–217.

Modigliani, Franco, and Richard Brumberg. "Utility Analysis and the Consumption Function: An Interpretation of Cross-Section Data." In *Post-Keynesian Economics*, edited by Kenneth K. Kurihara, pp. 388–436. New Brunswick, N.J.: Rutgers University Press, 1954.

Moody's Manual of Investments, American and Foreign. Banks—Insurance Companies—Investment Trusts—Real Estate—Finance and Credit Companies. New York: Moody's Investors Services, 1928.

Moran, Lee. "Automobiles—Big Business by Small Business Men." In *Proceedings: Consumer-Instalment Credit Conference*, edited by American Bankers Association, pp. 56–65. New York: American Bankers Association, Commission on Consumer Credit, 1947.

Musgrave, John C. "Durable Goods Owned by Consumers in the United States, 1925–77." *Survey of Current Business* 59 (March 1979): 17–25.

National Association of Finance Companies. "Collateral Trust Agreements." Proceedings of the group meeting of the eleventh annual meeting, Chicago, October 4–5, 1934. *National Association of Finance Companies Addresses* (Baker Library, Harvard University).

———. "Composite Experience of Sales Finance Companies and Automobile Dealers for 1931 and Prior Years." April 27, 1932. *National Association of Finance Companies Composite Experience* (Baker Library, Harvard University).

———. "Diversified Financing Methods." Bulletin distributed by the Association, May 1932. *National Association of Finance Companies Miscellaneous Publications* (Baker Library, Harvard University).

———. "Memo to Members: Few Finance Company Failures." April 5, 1934. *National Association of Finance Companies Miscellaneous Publications* (Baker Library, Harvard University).

———. "Memo to Members: Repossession and Other Experience with Retail Automobile Paper." March 21, 1928. *National Association of Finance Companies Miscellaneous Publications* (Baker Library, Harvard University).

———. *NAFC News*. Various issues.

———. "Resolution Adopted at the General Meeting, December 1924, 'Supplementing the Fundamental Principles for Financing the Sale of Passenger Automobiles Payable in Monthly Installments.'" 1924. *National Association of Finance Companies Miscellaneous Publications* (Baker Library, Harvard University).

National Association of Sales Finance Companies. "Composite Experience of Sales Finance Companies and Automobile Dealers, 1937: Revised Issue." 1938. *National As-*

sociation of Finance Companies Composite Experience (Baker Library, Harvard University).

_____. "Composite Experience of Sales Finance Companies and Automobile Dealers— 1939." 1940. *National Association of Finance Companies Composite Experience* (Baker Library, Harvard University).

_____. *Directory of Accredited Sales Finance Companies*. Chicago: National Association of Sales Finance Companies, 1935.

National Automobile Dealers Association. *Back to Selling: 1921 Yearbook*. Proceedings of the fourth annual convention, January 31–February 1, 1921. St. Louis, Mo.: National Automobile Dealers Association, 1921.

_____. *Sell Cars—Not Terms: 1926 Yearbook*. Proceedings of the ninth annual convention. St. Louis, Mo.: National Automobile Dealers Association, 1926.

National Consumer Finance Association. *The Consumer Finance Industry*. Englewood Cliffs, N.J.: Prentice-Hall, 1962.

Nerlove, Marc. "The Market Demand for Durable Goods: A Comment." *Econometrica* 28 (January 1960): 132–42.

Nevins, Allan. *Ford: The Times, the Man, the Company*. New York: Scribner's Sons, 1954.

Nevins, Allan, and Frank Ernest Hill. *Ford: Expansion and Challenge, 1915–1933*. New York: Scribner's Sons, 1957.

Nugent, Rolf. *Consumer Credit and Economic Stability*. New York: Russell Sage Foundation, 1939.

Nystrom, Paul H. *Automobile Selling: A Manual for Dealers*. New York: *Motor, the National Magazine of Motoring*, 1919.

Olney, Martha L. "Advertising, Consumer Credit, and the 'Consumer Durables Revolution' of the 1920s." Ph.D. dissertation, University of California, Berkeley, 1985.

_____. "Consumer Durables in the Interwar Years: New Estimates, New Patterns." *Research in Economic History* 12 (1989): 119–50.

_____. "Credit as a Production-Smoothing Device: The Case of Automobiles, 1913–1938." *Journal of Economic History* 49 (June 1989): 377–91.

_____. "Demand for Consumer Durable Goods in 20th Century America." *Explorations in Economic History* 27 (July 1990): 322–49.

Oshima, Harry T. "Consumer Asset Formation and the Future of Capitalism." *Economic Journal* 71 (March 1961): 20–35.

Parks, Richard W. "The Demand and Supply of Durable Goods and Durability." *American Economic Review* 64 (March 1974): 37–55.

Pease, Otis. *The Responsibilities of American Advertising: Private Control and Public Influence, 1920–1940*. New Haven, Conn.: Yale University Press, 1958.

Peterson, Theodore. *Magazines in the Twentieth Century*. Urbana: University of Illinois Press, 1956.

Phelps, Clyde William. *Financing the Instalment Purchases of the American Family: The Major Function of the Sales Finance Company*. Baltimore, Md.: Commercial Credit Company, 1954.

_____. *The Role of the Sales Finance Companies in the American Economy*. Baltimore, Md.: Commercial Credit Company, 1952.

Poffenberger, Albert T. *Psychology in Advertising*. Chicago: A. W. Shaw, 1925.

Pollay, Richard W. "The Distorted Mirror: Reflections on the Unintended Consequences of Advertising." *Journal of Marketing* 50 (April 1986): 18–36.

———. "The Subsiding Sizzle: A Descriptive History of Print Advertising, 1900–1980."
Journal of Marketing 49 (Summer 1985): 24–37.

———. "Twentieth-Century Magazine Advertising: Determinants of Informativeness."
Written Communication 1 (January 1984): 56–77.

Pope, Daniel. *The Making of Modern Advertising*. New York: Basic Books, 1983.

Potter, David M. *People of Plenty: Economic Abundance and the American Character*.
Chicago: University of Chicago Press, 1954.

Prentiss, Don C. *Ford Products and Their Sale: A Manual for Ford Salesman and Dealers in Six Books*. Detroit: Franklin Press, 1923.

Presbrey, Frank. *The History and Development of Advertising*. Ca. 1929. Reprint. New
York: Greenwood Press, 1968.

Prescott, R. B. "Twenty-Five Years of Growth." *Automobile Trade Journal* (December 1,
1924).

Printers' Ink. Advertisers' Annual: 1955. New York: Reinhold, 1954.

Rau, Roscoe R. "Home Furnishings' Stake in Consumer Credit Expansion." In *Proceedings: Consumer-Instalment Credit Conference*, edited by American Bankers Association, pp. 24–29. New York: American Bankers Association, Commission on Consumer Credit, 1947.

Reid, Margaret G. *Consumers and the Market*. New York: F. S. Crofts, 1938.

Robbins, W. David. *Consumer Instalment Loans: An Analysis of Loan by Principal
Types of Lending Institutions and by Types of Borrowers*. Columbus: Bureau of Business Research, Ohio State University, 1955.

Roberts, Peter. *Any Color So Long As It's Black . . . : The First Fifty Years of Automobile Advertising*. New York: William Morrow, 1976.

Robinson, Louis N., and Rolf Nugent. *Regulation of the Small Loan Business*. New
York: Russell Sage Foundation, 1935.

Romer, Christina D. "The Great Crash and the Onset of the Great Depression." *Quarterly Journal of Economics* 105 (August 1990): 597–624.

———. "New Estimates of Prewar Gross National Product and Unemployment." *Journal of Economic History* 46 (June 1986): 341–52.

Rowsome, Frank, Jr. *They Laughed When I Sat Down: An Informal History of Advertising in Words and Pictures*. New York: McGraw-Hill, 1959.

Ruffin, Marilyn Doss, and Katherine S. Tippett. "Service-Life Expectancy of Household
Appliances: New Estimates from the USDA." *Home Economics Research Journal* 3
(March 1975): 159–70

Ruggles, Richard. "The United States National Income Accounts, 1947–1977: Their
Conceptual Basis and Evolution." In *The U.S. National Income and Product Accounts: Selected Topics*, edited by Murray F. Foss, pp. 15–106. Vol. 47 of National Bureau of Economic Research Conference on Research in Income and Wealth. *Studies in
Income and Wealth*. Chicago: University of Chicago Press, 1983.

Schmalensee, Richard. *The Economics of Advertising*. Amsterdam: North-Holland,
1972.

Schudson, Michael. *Advertising, The Uneasy Persuasion: Its Dubious Impact on American Society*. New York: Basic Books, 1984.

Schultze, Quentin J. " 'An Honorable Place': The Quest for Professional Advertising Education, 1900–1917." *Business History Review* 56 (Spring 1982): 16–32.

Seidman, Walter S. *Accounts Receivable and Inventory Financing*. Ann Arbor, Mich.: Masterco Press, 1957.

Seligman, Edwin R. A. *The Economics of Instalment Selling: A Study in Consumers' Credit with Special Reference to the Automobile*. 2 vols. New York: Harper and Brothers, 1927.

Seltzer, Lawrence H. *A Financial History of the American Automobile Industry*. Boston: Houghton Mifflin, 1928.

Shammas, Carole. "Explaining Past Changes in Consumption and Consumer Behavior." *Historical Methods* 22 (Spring 1989): 61–67.

Shaw, William H. *Value of Commodity Output since 1869*. New York: National Bureau of Economic Research, 1947.

Simon, Julian L. *Issues in the Economics of Advertising*. Urbana: University of Illinois Press, 1970.

Sims, Lee G. "The Local Company and the National Association." Address before the eleventh annual meeting of the National Association of Finance Companies, Chicago, October 4–5, 1934. *National Association of Finance Companies Addresses* (Baker Library, Harvard University).

Sloan, Alfred P., Jr. *My Years with General Motors*. New York: Doubleday, 1963. Reprint. Garden City, N.Y.: Anchor Books, 1972.

Smiley, Gene. "Did Incomes for Most of the Population Fall from 1923 through 1929?" *Journal of Economic History* 43 (March 1983): 209–16.

Starch, Daniel. *Principles of Advertising*. Chicago: A. W. Shaw, 1923.

Stone, Richard, and D. A. Rowe. "The Market Demand for Durable Goods." *Econometrica* 25 (July 1957): 423–43.

Strong, Edward K., Jr. "The Effect of Size of Advertisements and Frequency of Their Presentation." *Psychological Review* 21 (March 1914): 136–52.

———. *The Psychology of Selling and Advertising*. New York: McGraw-Hill, 1925.

Studenski, Paul, and Herman E. Krooss. *Financial History of the United States*. 2d ed. New York: McGraw-Hill, 1963.

Suits, Daniel B., and Gordon R. Sparks. "Consumption Regressions with Quarterly Data." In *The Brookings Quarterly Econometric Model of the United States*, edited by James S. Duesenberry et al., pp. 203–26. Chicago: Rand McNally, 1965.

Temin, Peter. *Did Monetary Forces Cause the Great Depression?* New York: Norton, 1976.

Thomas, Robert Paul. *An Analysis of the Pattern of Growth of the Automobile Industry, 1895–1929*. Ph.D. dissertation, Northwestern University, 1965. Reprint. New York: Arno Press, 1977.

Tice, Helen Stone. "Depreciation, Obsolescence, and the Measurement of the Aggregate Capital Stock of the United States, 1900–1962." *Review of Income and Wealth* 13 (June 1967): 119–54.

U.S. Bureau of Economic Analysis. *Fixed Reproducible Tangible Wealth in the United*

States, 1925–1979. Washington, D.C.: Government Printing Office, March 1982.

———. *Fixed Reproducible Tangible Wealth in the United States, 1925–85*. Washington, D.C.: Government Printing Office, June 1987.

———. "The National Income and Product Accounts of the United States: An Introduction to the Revised Estimates for 1929–1980." *Survey of Current Business* 60 (December 1980): 1–36.

———. *The National Income and Product Accounts of the United States, 1929–76: Statistical Tables*. Washington, D.C.: Government Printing Office, September 1981.

———. *The National Income and Product Accounts of the United States, 1929–82: Statistical Tables*. Washington, D.C.: Government Printing Office, September 1986.

U.S. Bureau of the Census. *Census of Bankruptcies among Consumers, 1931*. Washington, D.C.: Government Printing Office, 1934.

———. *Current Population Reports: Population Characteristics*. Ser. P-20, no. 391. Washington, D.C.: Government Printing Office, August 1984.

———. *Fifteenth Census of the United States: 1930. Distribution, Volume I. Retail Distribution: Part I*. Washington, D.C.: Government Printing Office, 1933.

———. *Historical Statistics of the United States: Colonial Times to 1970*. 2 vols. Washington, D.C.: Government Printing Office, 1975.

———. *Sixteenth Census of the United States: 1940. Census of Business, Volume I. Retail Trade: 1939, Part I*. Washington, D.C.: Government Printing Office, 1943.

U.S. Office of Business Economics. "National Income and Product Statistics of the United States, 1929–46." Supplement to the *Survey of Current Business*. Washington, D.C.: Government Printing Office, July 1947.

———. "National Income and Product of the United States, 1929–50." Supplement to the *Survey of Current Business*. Washington, D.C.: Government Printing Office, July 1951.

———. *National Income: 1954 Edition*. Supplement to the *Survey of Current Business*. Washington, D.C.: Government Printing Office, 1954.

Vaile, Roland S. *Economics of Advertising*. New York: Ronald Press, 1927.

———. "The Use of Advertising during Depression." *Harvard Business Review* 5 (April 1927): 323–30.

Vatter, Harold G. "Consumer-Asset Formation in the United States: A Rejoinder." *Economic Journal* 77 (December 1967): 848–55.

———. "Has There Been a Twentieth-Century Consumer Durables Revolution?" *Journal of Economic History* 27 (March 1967): 1–16.

Vatter, Harold G., and Robert L. Thompson. "Consumer Asset Formation and Economic Growth—The United States Case." *Economic Journal* 76 (June 1966): 312–27.

Wandersee, Winifred D. *Women's Work and Family Values, 1920–1940*. Cambridge, Mass.: Harvard University Press, 1981.

Weber, Warren E. "Interest Rates, Inflation, and Consumer Expenditures." *American Economic Review* 65 (December 1975): 843–58.

Winfrey, Robley. *Statistical Analyses of Industrial Property Retirements*. Iowa Engineering Experiment Station bulletin 125. Ames: Iowa State College, 1935.

◆ INDEX ◆

Jones, Arthur H., 126
Juster, F. Thomas, 7, 59, 286, 287, 369
(n. 3), 370 (n. 12), 371 (n. 2), 371–72
(n. 6), 373–74 (n. 22), 375 (n. 37), 378
(n. 23), 401 (n. 5)

Katz, Harold, 379 (nn. 35, 40)
Keller, Janet, 374 (n. 28)
Kendrick, John, 23, 278–79, 281, 284–85
Kickbacks: to sales finance companies,
129
Krooss, Herman, 387 (n. 71)
Kuhn, Arthur, 379 (n. 42), 381 (n. 64), 387
(n. 63), 390 (n. 114)
Kuna, David, 174, 388 (nn. 80, 81), 389
(n. 90)
Kuznets, Simon, 23, 191, 193, 205–6, 208,
211, 212, 227, 278–79, 281, 284, 332,
369 (nn. 1, 6, 7), 369–70 (n. 8), 370
(n. 12), 392 (n. 1), 393 (nn. 5, 7, 9), 394
(nn. 18, 19), 394–95 (n. 20), 395 (nn. 25,
26, 27), 396 (n. 43); criticism of estimates by, 369–70 (n. 8)
Kuznets-Kendrick estimates of consumption expenditure, 278–79, 281–85

Ladies Home Journal: advertising series,
4, 139–44, 331; advertising revenue of,
138–39; circulation, 140; editorial policies, 140; readership, 140; size of issue,
140; use of full-page advertisements in,
142; stability of advertising in, 152; size
of page in, 383 (n. 7)
Lagged stock coefficient: in demand model, 73; interpretation of, 84–85, 293–96
Lears, T. J. Jackson, 176, 177, 388 (n. 90),
389 (nn. 91, 92, 94, 97, 101)
Legislative reform of credit industry, 131–
32
Levedahl, J. William, 373–74 (n. 22), 374
(n. 28)
Lewis, H. Bertram, 382 (n. 84)
Liberty Bond campaign: and advertising,
4, 171–72, 173
Life-cycle hypothesis of saving, 66
Life-cycle income, 67
Life length of durable good: by com-

modity group, 236, 245, 398 (n. 51); and
price, 374 (n. 25); Winfrey distribution
of, 397 (n. 48)
Lippitt, Vernon G., 374 (n. 28), 378 (n. 23)
Lipsey, Robert, 59, 288, 371 (n. 2), 371–72
(n. 6)
Liquidity preference theory, 187
Little, John L., 126
Lucas, Darrell, 175, 176, 178, 383–84
(n. 19), 385 (n. 41), 386 (n. 53), 388
(nn. 81, 85, 87, 88), 389 (n. 90, 96, 106),
401 (n. 2)

Macaulay, Stewart, 379 (n. 40), 380 (n. 50)
Maddala, G. S., 375 (n. 34), 401 (n. 6)
Magazine advertising. See Advertisements; Advertising series
Major durable goods: defined, 7, 8, 58, 369
(n. 2); expenditure for, 9, 22, 23–24, 40,
56; and total consumption expenditure,
23–24, 26, 28–29; relative prices of, 26,
28–29, 30–31, 56; and disposable income, 47; and saving, 56; demand for,
81–83; elasticity of demand for, 81–83;
advertising for, 144, 148, 164, 168; rate
of return on, 287. See also individual
durable goods
Marchand, Roland, 174, 177, 384 (n. 29),
385 (n. 40), 387 (n. 64), 388 (n. 77), 388–
89 (n. 90), 389 (n. 102), 401 (n. 1)
Marketing: credit as a device for, 3, 4, 5,
118, 183
Marx, Thomas G., 379 (nn. 37, 40)
Mass markets: and demand, 133–34, 295;
and advertising, 385–86 (n. 51)
Mass production: and advertising, 169–70
Maturity of installment contracts, 112–13
May, Geoffrey, 382 (n. 94)
Mayer, Thomas, 392 (n. 6)
Medical products. See Orthopedic and
ophthalmic products
Mendelson, Morris, 288
Merrick, Robert G., 382 (n. 83)
Methods of the economist, 61–62
Michelman, Irving S., 382 (n. 94)
Minor durable goods: defined, 7, 8; expen-
diture for, 9, 22, 23–24, 40, 56; and total